The Brief Wadsworth Handbook

Laurie G. Kirszner | Stephen R. Mandell

CENGAGE
Learning·

Australia • Brazil • Japan • Korea • Mexico • Singapore • Spain • United Kingdom • United States

The Brief Wadsworth Handbook

The Brief Wadsworth Handbook, Seventh Edition
Laurie G. Kirszner | Stephen R. Mandell
© 2013, 2010, 2007 Wadsworth, Cengage Learning. All rights reserved.

Executive Editors:
Maureen Staudt
Michael Stranz

Senior Project Development Manager:
Linda deStefano

Marketing Specialist:
Courtney Sheldon

Senior Production/
Manufacturing Manager:
Donna M. Brown

Production Editorial Manager:
Kim Fry

Sr. Rights Acquisition
Account Manager:
Todd Osborne

For product information and technology assistance, contact us at
Cengage Learning Customer & Sales Support, 1-800-354-9706

For permission to use material from this text or product,
submit all requests online at **cengage.com/permissions**
Further permissions questions can be emailed to
permissionrequest@cengage.com

This book contains select works from existing Cengage Learning resources and was produced by Cengage Learning Custom Solutions for collegiate use. As such, those adopting and/or contributing to this work are responsible for editorial content accuracy, continuity and completeness.

Compilation © 2012. Cengage Learning.

ISBN-13: 978-1-285-03230-6

ISBN-10: 1-285-03230-6

Cengage Learning
5191 Natorp Boulevard
Mason, Ohio 45040
USA

Cengage Learning is a leading provider of customized learning solutions with office locations around the globe, including Singapore, the United Kingdom, Australia, Mexico, Brazil, and Japan. Locate your local office at:
international.cengage.com/region.

Cengage Learning products are represented in Canada by Nelson Education, Ltd.

For your lifelong learning solutions, visit **www.cengage.com/custom.**
Visit our corporate website at **www.cengage.com.**

Printed in the United States
of America

How to Use This Book

We would like to introduce you to the seventh edition of *The Brief Wadsworth Handbook*, a compact, easy-to-use reference guide for college students that comes out of our years of experience as full-time teachers of writing. This handbook offers concise yet complete coverage of the writing process, critical thinking, argumentation, common sentence errors, grammar and style, word choice, punctuation and mechanics, English for speakers of other languages, and college survival skills. In addition, it includes the most up-to-date information on writing in a digital environment; MLA, APA, Chicago, and CSE documentation styles; writing in the disciplines; and document design.

Throughout, we balance what is new with practical advice from our years in the classroom. For this reason, despite its compact size, *The Brief Wadsworth Handbook* is more than just a quick reference; it is a comprehensive guide for writing in college and beyond. Most of all, it is a book that writers can depend on not only for sound, sensible advice about grammar and usage but also for up-to-date information about writing in an electronic environment.

What's New in the Seventh Edition?

In this new edition, we kept what students and instructors told us worked well, and we fine-tuned what we thought could work better. In addition, we expanded our coverage to include the material students need to function in today's classrooms—and in today's world.

- **New collaborative writing icons** appear alongside features that emphasize peer review and other collaborative work.
- **New coverage of reading electronic texts and writing critical responses** in Chapter 2, "Reading Texts," offers key critical reading and analysis strategies.
- **Two new student papers**, "*Wikipedia*: Friend or Foe?" and "The Great Debate: *Wikipedia* and College-Level Research," now illustrate the writing process in Chapters 4–6 and the research process in Chapter 15. Additionally, updated and expanded coverage of **MLA, APA, Chicago, and CSE documentation styles** in Chapters 21–24 includes numerous model citations that help students correctly apply the latest documentation guidelines when writing in various disciplines.
- **Expanded coverage of field research** in Chapter 17, "Finding and Evaluating Library Sources," and **a new field research report** in Chapter 13,

"Writing in the Social Sciences," emphasize the importance of practical research outside the library.

- **New coverage of avoiding intentional and unintentional plagiarism** in Chapter 20, "Avoiding Plagiarism," offers students strategies for managing their time and producing original work.
- **A new Chapter 57, "Adjusting to the US Classroom,"** offers bilingual and ESL writers practical advice on the writing process and English language basics.

Features of *The Brief Wadsworth Handbook*

Throughout the seventh edition of *The Brief Wadsworth Handbook*, we have focused on making the text clear, inviting, and easy to navigate. The book's many innovative pedagogical features, listed below, have helped us achieve these goals.

- **Frequently Asked Questions (FAQs)** appear at the beginning of each part, on the back of the tabbed dividers. Corresponding marginal FAQ icons appear in the chapters beside each answer.
- **Grammar checker boxes** illustrating sample errors show the advantages and limitations of using a grammar checker.
- **Numerous checklists** summarize key information.
- **Close-up boxes** provide an in-depth look at some of the more challenging writing-related issues students will encounter.
- **Parts 5–6** include the most up-to-date documentation and format guidelines from the Modern Language Association, the American Psychological Association, the University of Chicago Press, and the Coucil of Science Editors. Specially designed documentation directories make it easy to locate models for various kinds of sources, including those found in online databases such as *Academic Search Premier* and *LexisNexis*. In addition, annotated diagrams of sample works-cited entries clearly illustrate the elements of proper citations.
- **Marginal cross-references** throughout the book enable students to flip directly to other sections that treat topics in more detail.
- **Marginal ESL cross-references** throughout the book direct students to appropriate sections of Part 14, "Resources for Bilingual and ESL Writers," where concepts are presented as they apply specifically to second-language writers.
- **ESL tips** woven throughout the text explain concepts in relation to the unique experiences of bilingual students.

Acknowledgments

We would like to take this opportunity to thank Vici Casana for her thorough revisions to the Chicago documentation material; Douglas Eyman, George Mason University, for his expert technology advice; and Mary McMullen-Light, Metropolitan Community College, Longview, for her knowledgeable writing-across-the-curriculum advice. We would also like to thank the following students for allowing us to reprint their work: Emma Sawin, Sara Taggart, and Alice H. Thatcher for their field research report and Leeann Tan for her film review.

We also wish to thank the following reviewers for their advice, which helped us develop the seventh edition:

James Allen, *College of DuPage*
Allan Carter, *College of DuPage*
Katrina Cooper, *Bethany College*
Jennifer Cornette, *Christopher Newport University*
James Crooks, *Shasta College*
Christopher Ervin, *Western Kentucky University*
Karen Feldman, *Seminole State College of Florida*
Jean Filetti, *Christopher Newport University*
Mary Healy, *Christopher Newport University*
Catherine Hodges, *Porterville College*
Jeffrey Ihlenfeldt, *Harrisburg Area Community College*
Anna Maheshwari, *Schoolcraft College*
Jim McKeown, *McLennan Community College*
Miranda Miller, *Gillette College*
Bryan Moore, *Arkansas State University*
Billy Reynolds, *Abraham Baldwin Agricultural College*
Renie Stewart, *Mayland Community College*
Cynthia VanSickle, *McHenry County College*
Mary Wright, *Christopher Newport University*

At Wadsworth, we are grateful to Lyn Uhl, Senior Publisher; Kate Derrick, Acquiring Sponsoring Editor; Leslie Taggart, Senior Development Editor; Cat Salerno, Assistant Editor; and Abbie Rickard, Editorial Assistant, for keeping the project moving along, and to Corinna Dibble, Content Project Manager, for her careful attention to detail. Our biggest thanks go to Karen Mauk, our wonderful Development Editor; as always, it has been a pleasure to work with her.

The staff of Nesbitt Graphics did its usual stellar job, led by our talented Project Manager and Copyeditor Susan McIntyre. Carie Keller's exciting new interior design and Wing Ngan's cover design is the icing on the cake.

We would also like to thank our families for being there when we needed them. And, finally, we each thank the person on the other side of the ampersand for making our collaboration work one more time.

Laurie Kirszner
Steve Mandell
January 2012

Teaching and Learning Resources

Online College Workbook
ISBN: 1-1332-3286-8
This collection of grammar and composition exercises offers students reinforcement of basic skills.

Online Instructor's Resource Manual and Answer Key
ISBN: 978-1-133-11366-9
Designed to give instructors maximum flexibility in planning and customizing their courses, the **Online Instructor's Resource Manual and Answer Key** is now available online. It contains an abundance of instructor materials, including sample syllabi and activities; "Questions for Teachers," which provides a variety of pedagogical questions with solutions for instructors to consider as they teach with the handbook; an ESL insert aimed at helping instructors teach writing effectively to ESL students; and an insert on disability issues as they relate to teaching first-year composition.

English CourseMate
Printed Access Card (**ISBN:** 978-1-133-43583-9)
Instant Access Code (**ISBN:** 978-1-4282-7680-2)
The Brief Wadsworth Handbook includes English CourseMate, a complement to your textbook. English CourseMate includes:

- an interactive eBook
- interactive teaching and learning tools including:

  - Quizzes
  - Flashcards
  - Videos
  - and more

- Engagement Tracker, a first-of-its-kind tool that monitors student engagement in the course

Go to www.cengagebrain.com to access these resources, and look for this icon 🖥 which denotes a resource available within CourseMate.

WebTutor™ for Blackboard® and WebCT®
WebTutor™ for Blackboard® Printed Access Card (**ISBN:** 978-1-133-43586-0)
WebTutor™ for Blackboard® Instant Access Code (**ISBN:** 978-1-133-43579-2)
WebTutor™ for WebCT® Printed Access Card (**ISBN:** 978-1-133-43587-7)
WebTutor™ for WebCT® Instant Access Code (**ISBN:** 978-1-133-43580-8)

WebTutor™ for Blackboard® and WebCT® provides access to all the content of this text's English CourseMate from within an instructor's course management system. Extensive communication tools—such as a course calendar, asynchronous discussion, real-time chat, a whiteboard, and an integrated email system—make it easy to stay connected to the course.

Enhanced InSite™ for The Brief Wadsworth Handbook
Printed Access Card (1 semester) (ISBN: 978-1-133-43376-7)
Instant Access Code (1 semester) (ISBN: 978-1-133-43370-5)
Printed Access Card (2 semester) (ISBN: 978-1-133-43375-0)
Instant Access Code (2 semester) (ISBN: 978-1-133-43359-0)
From a single, easy-to-navigate site, instructors and students can manage the flow of papers online, check for originality, and conduct peer reviews. Students can access the multimedia eBook for a text-specific workbook, private tutoring options, and resources for writers that include anti-plagiarism tutorials and downloadable grammar podcasts. **Enhanced InSite™** provides the tools and resources instructors and students need plus the training and support they want. Learn more at **www.cengage.com/insite.** (*Access card/code is required.*)

InfoTrac® College Edition with InfoMarks™
ISBN: 0-534-55853-4   **ISBN-13:** 978-0-534-55853-6
InfoTrac® College Edition, an online research and learning center, offers over 20 million full-text articles from nearly 6,000 scholarly and popular periodicals. The articles cover a broad spectrum of disciplines and topics—ideal for every type of researcher.

Turnitin®
Printed Access Card 1-Semester User Guide 978-1-4130-3018-1
Printed Access Card 2-Semester User Guide 978-1-4130-3019-8
Turnitin is proven plagiarism-prevention software that helps students improve their writing and research skills and allows instructors to confirm originality before reading and grading student papers. Take a tour at academic.cengage.com/turnitin to see how **Turnitin** makes checking originality against billions of pages of Internet content, millions of published works, and millions of student papers fast and easy.

Personal Tutor
Printed Access Card (ISBN: 978-1-133-43378-1)
Instant Access Code (ISBN: 978-1-133-43374-3)
Access to **Personal Tutor's** private tutoring resources provides students with additional assistance and review as they write their papers. With this valuable resource, students will gain access to multiple sessions to be used as either tutoring services or paper submissions—whichever they need most.

Merriam Webster Dictionaries

MERRIAM-WEBSTER'S COLLEGIATE® DICTIONARY, 11/E

1,664 pages | Casebound | **ISBN:** 0-87779-809-5 **ISBN-13:** 978-0-87779-809-5
Available only when packaged with a Wadsworth text, the new 11/e of
America's bestselling hardcover dictionary merges print, CD-ROM, and
Internet-based formats to deliver unprecedented accessibility and flexibility
at one affordable price.

THE MERRIAM-WEBSTER DICTIONARY

960 pages | Paperbound | **ISBN:** 0-87779-930-X **ISBN-13:** 978-0-87779-930-6
Available only when packaged with a Wadsworth text, this high-quality,
economical language reference covers the core vocabulary of everyday life
with over 70,000 definitions.

MERRIAM-WEBSTER'S DICTIONARY AND THESAURUS

1,248 pages | Paperbound | **ISBN:** 0-87779-851-6 **ISBN-13:** 978-0-87779-851-4
Available only when packaged with a Wadsworth text, this dictionary
and thesaurus are two essential language references in one handy volume.
Included are nearly 60,000 alphabetical dictionary entries integrated with
more than 13,000 thesaurus entries including extensive synonym lists,
as well as abundant example phrases that provide clear and concise word
guidance.

CONTENTS

CHAPTER

Introduction

What is in this guide?

This booklet is designed to help students avoid the pitfalls of plagiarism. Chapters cover the correct way to credit sources, quote, cite, paraphrase, summarize, create a list of references, and more. Knowledge checks are provided at the end of each section for review.

Why is this guide important to you as a student?

What do you want from college? You probably want to succeed in your classes. The last thing you want is to fail a class for cheating or plagiarizing by mistake. If you are unfamiliar with the practices and rules of incorporating work from other sources, then you will find this guide a useful resource.

You can use the knowledge checks in each chapter or the quiz at the end of the booklet to practice all the skills necessary to use resources correctly. We've tried to make it as clear and simple as possible. Citing correctly can be confusing. Most colleges have very specific requirements about giving references, depending on the subject or instructor. Citing correctly is more involved than inserting footnotes or listing references at the end of a paper. This guide provides information and samples of the kinds of citations that are necessary to correctly reference different types of academic work.

What is plagiarism?

Plagiarism is using someone else's work and passing it off as one's own. The term comes from the Latin word *plagiarius*, which means *kidnapper*.

This means that if a student uses another writer's work without giving credit, it may be considered deceptive even if it is an honest mistake. Knowing the definition of plagiarism and when to cite sources is the best way to avoid problems.

When should you credit another author's work?

Because many things such as information, pictures, and music are now so easy to copy from the Internet, it's more tempting than ever to find and use those materials for free. How can you tell when it is appropriate to use something without a citation and when it isn't?

Generally any time you use someone else's work as a source of ideas or inspiration, credit is required. There are a few exceptions, such as when the information is common knowledge. An example of common knowledge is the fact that Christopher Columbus crossed the Atlantic Ocean in 1492. To be safe, if you consult a source and that source's ideas become part of your work, then you need to cite that source. If you use a direct quotation, then you need to reproduce it accurately and to cite it correctly. These practices will prevent inadvertent plagiarizing, and this guide will provide the basics to get you started.

> ***Tip***
> **When you consult a source,**
> **cite it correctly!**

There are also limitations to how much of someone else's work can be used as part of an assignment. Exclusively, excessively, or inappropriately using another author's work by copying, paraphrasing, summarizing, or directly quoting is plagiarizing. It is important to use your own words and ideas in a paper. One suggested rule of thumb for acceptable use of content in a submitted assignment is up to 10 percent, provided it is properly cited (Zaharoff). Make sure to check your instructor's preferences.

Many students worry that their own words do not sound as professional as those used by the original author. But that fear ignores the point of using a source in the first place. Instructors do not give assignments so students can give them back another author's work. Instructors do not expect the same quality of work from a novice as from an expert. College is a place of learning. If instructors wanted to read only the professional author's words and ideas, they could go directly to the original source and skip the student's work.

The whole point of having you use sources is to enable you to learn from those sources and to develop your own writing and analytical skills. It's important for you to work with ideas and to express them in writing so you can develop your own writing style, perspective, and voice. This is a big investment of time and effort. Often when students risk plagiarizing, they haven't allowed themselves sufficient time to complete an assignment. These types of miscalculations can lead to trouble.

Know the rules.

Because academic honesty and the validity of a college degree are vitally important to institutions of higher learning, schools create codes or policies governing instances of

> ***Tip***
> **Know the rules about plagiarism;**
> **ignorance is no excuse.**

dishonesty. Many of these policies are listed as Academic Integrity, Academic Honesty, Honor Code, Cheating, Student Conduct Code, or Plagiarism. The codes may consist of a list of rules, definitions, specific behaviors, procedures, and consequences of academic dishonesty. It is your responsibility to know the rules of your institution and to follow them. Rules are usually published in school catalogs and considered a part of the enrollment agreement for the college. If you have any questions about academic policies, then check with your instructor or the dean's office to get the facts.

When instructors suspect plagiarism, they will follow steps prescribed by the institution to address the problem. These steps include contacting the student and forwarding a report to the dean or a disciplinary committee, which will probably conduct a hearing.

Consequences to the student can include failing the assignment or the course, as well as being given community service or some other restitution to the campus community. Some students have been unhappily surprised to learn that the consequences for a first-time offense of plagiarism can be as severe as expulsion from the institution. Being caught as a plagiarizer is humiliating, can directly affect a student's progress toward a degree, is costly, and is entirely avoidable.

Knowledge Check: True or False?

1. Most students who plagiarize do so inadvertently.
2. Students cannot be accused of plagiarizing if they don't know the citation style expected by the instructor.
3. Using sources for educational purposes means that those sources are exempt from citation rules.

Answers

1. (True) Don't be one of them. This can be a costly mistake!
2. (False) It is your job to find out.
3. (False) All sources should be cited.

CHAPTER 2

How to Avoid Plagiarism

12 Tips to Avoid Plagiarizing

1. Do your own work, and use your own words.
2. Allow yourself enough time to research the assignment.
3. Keep careful track of your sources.
4. Take careful notes.
5. Assemble your thoughts, and make clear who is speaking.
6. If you use an idea, a quotation, paraphrase, or summary, then credit the source.
7. Learn how to cite sources correctly both in the body of your paper and in your List of Works Cited.
8. Quote accurately and sparingly.
9. Paraphrase carefully.
10. Do not patchwrite.
11. Summarize, don't auto-summarize.
12. Do not rework another student's paper or buy paper-mill papers.

Do your own work, and use your own words.

College gives you the opportunity to be exposed to new ideas, to formulate ideas of your own, and to develop skills to communicate your ideas. Strengthening your writing skills requires hard work and practice, but you will learn thinking and communicating skills that will benefit both your studies in college and your career.

Expressing a thought in your own words may seem overwhelming. The difficulty may stem from not understanding the language, not understanding the research material, or a lack of confidence in expressing ideas and concepts. Don't be discouraged that your paper may not sound as professional as you would like. By creating and practicing your own personal style, you will improve your ability to state ideas clearly and support arguments, and your vocabulary will increase.

These skills are not built by using another researcher's or student's words or by paying a service to write a paper for your class. Attempting to cheat on your paper cheats you the most because you are depriving yourself of the thinking, learning, and writing practice that would have benefited all of your classwork and beyond. But cheating also creates the risk of humiliation and punishment. Most professors are so familiar with the work in their field that they can spot a fake quickly. New plagiarism detection methods are also making it easier for professors to catch cheaters electronically. And as discussed in Chapter 1, all institutions will punish students who plagiarize. Doing honest work is the way to avoid the humiliation of being accused of cheating.

Allow yourself enough time to research the assignment.

Often students who are caught plagiarizing claim that they didn't have time to do the work. This excuse rarely works. Allow sufficient time to do all the steps necessary in an assignment. The best way is to plan for each part: selecting the topic, doing the research, then writing and refining your ideas. Minimizing the time it will take to do the work, or procrastinating because you feel that you do better work when you are anxious, will easily create trouble.

The most productive strategy is to begin the assignment as soon as it is given and try to complete it early. This allows you to adjust the schedule if you encounter any research difficulties, provides time for questions or clarification, and offsets other events that can interfere or cut into study time. If you are unsure about how to plot out your time for each step, then ask your instructor to help you plan your schedule.

Keep careful track of your sources.

As you look through books, articles, and electronic materials, you will be able to identify which content is relevant to your paper. The sources that you decide to take notes from are the ones you will need to keep careful records of.

Create a master list of all your sources that contains detailed bibliographic information for each item. (You will need to record the author; title of article or book; publisher, periodical title, electronic medium, or URL; date, and page number. See Chapter 6 for a detailed list of the information you will need and the format you will need to provide it in.) As you conduct your research, you will likely add or delete sources from this list, but keeping it current and complete will make your work much easier when it comes time to format the list into your formal List of Works Cited (for MLA papers) or Reference List (for APA papers). This list of references will enable the readers of your paper to locate the exact content you discuss in your paper-as well as to assist you to find it again, should you need to.

Take careful notes.

Some students find they take more complete notes (and can easily refer back to their sources) if they make photocopies of the relevant pages from their sources. If you decide to use this method, for print sources, such as articles and books, copy the copyright page and relevant content pages of each source. Make sure the page numbers or other identifiers are visible on each page. For electronic sources, such as the websites, databases, CDs, or even web logs, print out the home or copyright page and the relevant content pages, making sure that identifiers such as the URL and the date, or page numbers, are visible.

If you take notes on note cards or in computer files, then make sure to keep a detailed record of where each note came from and take down the information carefully and accurately.

Next scrutinize your resources, thinking about the ideas expressed, noting and recording the relevant points, and adding to the notes your reactions, questions, and thoughts. If you find a particular phrasing that you want to quote, then highlight it to separate it from the regular notes.

Assemble your thoughts, and make clear who is speaking.

As you write the first draft of your paper, make sure you are expressing your thoughts and ideas in your own voice. Use the thoughts or words of others only to support your own thoughts, *not to make your point for you.* Your writing should make clear at all times who is speaking.

Decide from your notes whether you need to quote, summarize, or paraphrase the source. (See Chapters 3, 4, and 5 for a discussion of each method.) Then make sure to introduce the guest voice (the source) and explain why the source's information is relevant to your topic.

If you use an idea, a quotation, paraphrase, or summary, then credit the source.

When you draft your paper, if you are stating another person's thought, then make clear where that thought came from. Identify the source of all borrowed content in your paper, even if it's from a blog on the Internet. Your readers need to know where to find the original source if they want to explore the idea further.

Identify your source by inserting a brief parenthetical citation in the paper where the source's content appears, and then list the complete source information at the end of the paper. Follow the documentation style directed by your instructor (usually MLA or APA; see Chapter 6 for examples.)

Cite sources correctly, both in the body of your paper and in your list of Works Cited.

A **citation**—that is, stating the source of an idea, a conclusion, or a specific collection of information—of another person's work is the highest form of respect that a serious writer can make. It is also the single best way to avoid accusations of plagiarism and cheating. Properly citing sources involves acknowledging them both in the body of your work (when and where your writing borrows from a given source) and in a list of all the sources at the end of your paper.

Citation styles differ by subject or discipline. There are styles for English, the Social Sciences, the Humanities, and the Sciences. Check with your instructor or writing center for the proper format style of your writing project.

See Chapter 3, Quotations; Chapter 4, Paraphrases; Chapter 5, Summaries; and Chapter 6, Citations, for basic models of citations. Guidebooks such as MLA, APA, and Chicago, which are available in most bookstores, provide models for all common types of sources. Online citation generators (see Chapter 8) can also help you with listing references in the correct format.

Quote accurately and sparingly.

Quotations should be used *only to emphasize your own point,* which you have already stated in your own words. A good quotation from an original source can underscore a theme and introduce thoughts or direction, but quotations should be relevant, necessary, accurate, and limited.

Using too many direct quotations (more than ten percent) is a sign both that you have not developed your own idea enough and that you are relying on others to make your point for you. Over-quoting is also an opportunity for plagiarism to creep in. If you are using several sources, then limit how much those sources contribute, and give correct citation and credit every time you use them.

Paraphrase carefully.

The practice of taking another writer's sentence and then looking up words and replacing them with synonyms is a common way for students to think they are paraphrasing from a source. (See Chapter 4.) Merely changing some of another writer's words, or reversing the order of the clauses in the sentences, is still copying. This is another way students can inadvertently plagiarize. Use paraphrase to state in your own words what another writer believes or argues.

Do not patchwrite.

Patchwriting consists of mixing several references together and arranging paraphrases and quotations to constitute much of a paper. In essence, the student has assembled others' works with a bit of embroidery here and there but with very little original thinking or expression. Turning in work that has been woven into a quilt with patches arranged together constitutes plagiarism. Instead, work on developing a position and bringing in sources to support the viewpoint or argument that you are presenting.

A way to avoid patchwriting is good preparation. Read the material several times to make sure you understand what the source is saying; then put it aside and think about it. Analyze the readings and what they mean, and then try to organize the main points. Create an outline of what you want to say, and then go back and pull in the supporting information from the sources. Good writers think of the reader as listening to what is being said; this process will help you create and organize your own, original work.

Summarize, don't auto-summarize.

Most word processors have an automatic summarize function that can take fifty pages and turn them into ten. The problem with this feature is that it condenses material by selecting key sentences. Therefore a summarized version is still in the exact words of the original source, only shorter and not necessarily making the same point as the original. The auto-summary feature is intended for writers to summarize their *own* work, *not* the work of others. If a student uses any portion of the auto-summary from another writer's work, then it is plagiarism.

If you wish to summarize another writer's work, then describe briefly in your own words the writer's idea (identifying who that writer is and providing a citation to the work) and state how it relates to your own ideas. (See Chapter 5.)

Do not rework another student's paper or buy papermill papers.

Don't cross the line from looking at someone else's paper as an example of how to do the assignment, to the action of using it as original work. Reworking someone else's paper is plagiarism. It also shows that the student is unwilling to think for him- or herself.

Similarly, buying papers from paper mills, or paying for someone else to write a paper, is obviously dishonest and is a clear example of plagiarizing and cheating. Databases of written papers are often kept by colleges and by plagiarism detection services, so instructors who have a question about the authenticity of a student's paper can easily verify its source.

Knowledge Check: True or False?

1. One way to avoid plagiarizing is to give yourself enough time to do a good job on the assignment.
2. As long as you put everything in quotation marks, you are not plagiarizing.
3. Getting a paper from a friend or the Internet is a good way to get a head start on your assignment.

Answers

1. (True) Most people who plagiarize use poor time management and even worse judgment.
2. (False) If you quote more than 10 percent of your paper, you may be graded down for over-quoting.
3. (False) Using a friend's paper or an Internet paper is plagiarizing and considered to be academic cheating.

CHAPTER 3

Using Quotations

Using quotations is an effective way to support your arguments and add credibility to your research paper. Quotations are most useful when they highlight or help to refine a point you are making. Inserting too many quotations in your paper distracts your readers from the argument you are trying to construct, and makes your paper sound as if you are letting others speak for you, so use quotations selectively and sparingly.

You can use a **direct quotation** (a word-for-word repetition from another source) or an **indirect quotation** (a recasting in your own words of the ideas of another person-see Chapters 4 and 5). Each time you insert a direct or indirect quotation into your paper, you must add a citation to the source at the quotation. This in-text citation follows an abbreviated, parenthetical format that points your reader to the full citation in a Works Cited or References list at the end of your paper (see Chapter 6).

Quotations can be used in various ways within a research paper. This chapter will cover some of those uses and the proper citation styles needed for each.

Follow these basic rules for using quotations:

- Use quotations sparingly.
- Make sure the quotation exactly fits the idea of your paragraph.
- Make sure direct quotations stay identical to the original passage. Do not change the wording, the spelling, or the punctuation of the original passage.
- Cite the source! Include a parenthetical citation for all quotations.
- If a direct quotation is longer than four lines, use a block quotation.

Using direct quotations

A direct quotation is an exact copy of the original author's work. Make your point first, and then enclose the quote in quotation marks (or if it is long set it apart as a block quotation) and provide a parenthetical citation directly after.

Example: parenthetical citation, MLA

The MLA style of citing a quotation includes the author's last name followed by the page number directly after the quotation. Note that no comma separates the name from the page number.

> Personal growth is a painful process, and part of that process is taking personal responsibility for your actions. This includes remembering that "you can't talk your way out of problems you behaved yourself into" (Covey 186).

Example: parenthetical citation, APA

The APA style of citing the same quotation includes the publication year as well as the author's last name and page number. Note that no comma separates the name from the date, but that a comma does follow the date and that the abbreviation *p.* precedes the page number.

> Personal growth is a painful process, and part of that process is taking personal responsibility for your actions. This includes remembering that "you can't talk your way out of problems you behaved yourself into" (Covey 1989, p. 186).

Notice that in both cases the citation is included in the sentence, with the period after the citation.

Example: author's name in text, MLA

You can introduce the name of the author in the text and then cite the page number for reference.

> Noted author Stephen Covey suggests that to be effective, one must "begin with the end in mind" (97).

Example: author's name in text, APA

Note that the APA style includes the year of publication directly after the author's name and the page number at the end for easy reference.

> Weeks (1994) believes that "we need to celebrate diversity, not fear it or perceive it as a threat" (33).

Quoting a secondary source

When using research sources it is common to find that the original author has quoted a **secondary source**, another author, in his or her work. The following example shows such a quotation and the proper citation for it.

Example: secondary source, MLA

The addition of *qtd. in* (for "quoted in") shows that this quote by Jung was found in a secondary resource, written by Byrne.

> Psychology has had its masters of theory and quite a bit of humor as well. C. G. Jung, a noted psychologist, once claimed, "Show me a sane man and I will cure him for you" (qtd. in Byrne 453).

Using ellipses to show omissions and brackets to show insertions

An **ellipsis** (shown by three evenly spaced periods: ...) is a break or omission of words within a direct quote. Using only part of a quotation is common practice, especially if the entire quotation is too long or cumbersome. But make sure to use ellipses cautiously so you don't present the author's words out of intended context.

Example: ellipses to show omitted words from the middle of a quote

> We can now plainly and painfully see that "components of human interaction ... often lead to conflict" (Weeks 33).

Example: bracketed insertion to make a sentence correct

Sometimes a quote will be worded in a way that could read awkwardly or make an incomplete sentence when inserted in a paper. If you need to add a word or phrase within a quotation to make your sentence grammatically correct or clearer, then put brackets around your insertion.

There are many examples of how "components of human interaction... [can] often lead to conflict" (Weeks 33).

In this instance the word *can* was added to clarify the thought for the reader.

Block quotations

A quotation from poetry, plays, or any text longer than four lines should be set apart in a block quotation format. A block quotation is indented about one inch (ten spaces) from the left margin and double-spaced. A block quotation needs no quotation marks and is introduced by a complete sentence. Often a colon, rather than a period, follows the introductory words.

> ***Tip***
> **Block quotations do not require quotation marks.**

Example: block quotation, MLA

The block quotation is introduced by a sentence that contains the author's name, ends with a colon, and uses ellipsis to show that it is not complete. Note that the page number is in parentheses after the period.

> As Jess Tavares explains, older students face different challenges when returning to school:
>
> As an older student, returning to the academic world was quite a shock. I hadn't seen a classroom in
>
> twenty-five years. But with a new backpack, pens, and a bill from the bookstore that equaled my rent,
>
> I sat in my very first college class, ... scared to death I could not pass the tests I had just set for myself. (2)

Knowledge Check: True or False?

1. Quotations must be used in original form.
2. Quotation marks are required for all direct quotations.
3. Brackets indicate that a word has been added that is not in the original text.

Answers

1. (True) Quotations should be identical to the original passage.
2. (False) Block quotations do not require quotation marks.
3. (True) Brackets show that text was added to the original passage.

CHAPTER 4

Paraphrasing

What is a paraphrase?

A **paraphrase** is a restatement of an author's writing by using your own words and accurately conveying the original information. You would paraphrase an author when you want to explain the content of his or her passage while maintaining your own voice and rhythm. You might also paraphrase after you have introduced a source earlier in your paper and wish to continue to discuss that source's ideas without needing to quote the source verbatim.

The length of a paraphrase should be about equal to the length of the original work. (By contrast, a summary - as explained in Chapter 5 - describes in just a few words the ideas or points made in another author's long passage or large work.)

It is vital that the paraphrase not alter the original meaning of the source. Adding words that distort the intention of the author or leaving out significant parts of what the author was intending misstates that author.

A paraphrase, because it's an indirect quotation, always requires a parenthetical citation. See the MLA and APA examples below.

To restate an author's ideas accurately but in your own words and writing style can be difficult. You might be tempted to shift some words around from the original, but doing so would be plagiarizing because those words and the idea still belong to the author. Remember that improving your writing skills is part of the goal of using others' works. Instructors want you to learn to write and think, not just to hand back what someone else has created.

Tips

DO
1. Use your own words.
2. Present the author's ideas without changing, adding to, or deleting from the original meaning.
3. Make the paraphrase about equal in length to the original.
4. Give credit to the source.

DON'T
1. Keep the author's sentences and just replace the words with synonyms.
2. Flip-flop clause and leave the words the same.
3. Lose track of original sources.

Accuracy is vital.

One way to develop paraphrasing skills is to read the material several times to make sure that you understand completely what the writer is saying. Next, put aside the author's work and try to explain the passage in your own words. This will help you to develop a personal voice and style. Compare the explanation with the original and decide whether it is accurate and conveys the original ideas. Consider whether something is missing that a person who didn't read the first passage would need to know in order to understand it. Make sure to explain for your reader how the paraphrased content relates to your idea. Once you have worked the paraphrase into your draft, be sure to cite the original.

Always give credit to the source of an idea.

It may be confusing when and how to add a citation to the original source. A good practice to follow is if a sentence or idea came from an outside source, then it should be acknowledged with a parenthetical citation.

Sample paraphrases

Example 1: paraphrase with citation, MLA

Original work

Poll after poll indicates that one of the primary concerns of contemporary U.S. citizens is violence. Terrorism is obviously one part of this concern, but there is also considerable concern about nonterrorist forms of violence. Violence among the nation's youth is especially troubling and difficult to explain. This difficulty is frequently the reason that social psychologists are often asked to make sense of seemingly senseless acts of violence. Why are there so many shootings in the U.S. high schools? Why are there so many gangs, and why are they growing at such alarming rates? (Potter 1999)

Incorrect paraphrase

<u>Survey</u> after <u>survey show</u> that one of the <u>big things</u> that <u>people</u> in the **U.S.** <u>worry</u> about <u>today</u> is **violence. Terrorism is** <u>clearly</u> a <u>reason</u> **but there is also** <u>a lot of worry</u> about <u>other</u> **forms of violence. Violence** <u>from the young people in this country</u> **is** <u>very confusing</u> **and** <u>hard to understand</u>. **This** <u>problem</u> **is** <u>often</u> **the** <u>issue</u> **that** <u>researchers</u> **are** <u>frequently required</u> to <u>explain incomprehensible violent crimes. What is the reason for the number of gun related crimes in schools in America? Is it because the number of</u> **gangs** <u>are going up</u>?

In the above example the writing style of the original piece was copied. It was plagiarized, not paraphrased. Sentence by sentence, the information is exactly restated using different words. The substituted words in exact sequence are <u>underlined</u>. The sequence of each idea and structure of each sentence is the same, and words have been replaced with synonyms. In some cases original phrases have been kept in order (shown in **bold**). This patchwork paraphrasing merely uses a thesaurus to find synonyms for words in the original text, but everything is essentially identical. Finally, there was no indication of the source of this paraphrase.

Correct paraphrase

Many recent **polls** have suggested that people in the United States are very concerned about **terrorism** and other acts of **violence**. Increasing violence, including **shootings**, among **high-school**-aged children is one of these concerns. People in the community want to understand why this is happening. **Social psychologists** have been asked to explain this troubling trend. It is difficult to understand why young people may be joining **gangs** and committing acts of violence in greater numbers. (Potter 306)

This example maintains the ideas of the original piece, but the style of writing is different. Instead of following an identical sequence to the original work, the correctly paraphrased paragraph conveys the information but does not pull out words and substitute them with synonyms. It uses some of the words from the original to accurately present the author's ideas and is complete in presenting the original author's ideas, but it uses the student's own original sentences. It also cites the author of the original work.

Example 2: paraphrase with citation, MLA

Original work

At first glance, there appears to be little justification for telling the story of California's early Indian wars. Aside from the brief Modoc conflict of 1873, and possibly the Mariposa war of 1851, few people are aware that California had any Indian troubles during the Gold Rush days of the 1850's. Certainly the Far West never had a Custer's Last Stand or a grand retreat such as that made by Chief Joseph of the Nez Perce. Here were no Sitting Bull or Geronimo, no spectacular uprisings, like Adobe Walls or Beecher's Islands. On the contrary, many California tribes were generally peaceful by nature, few having even a war club or a tomahawk as part of their culture. Yet in California, the bloodiest drama in the settlement of the West took place, a brutal disruption and destruction so devastating that by the 1870's many native groups were extinct. (Secrest xi)

Incorrect paraphrase

Unless you know about the events, you would think there isn't much reason to write about what happened in the **Indian wars** in **early California**. There were two conflicts, one in **1873** with the **Modoc** and another in **Mariposa in 1851**. But most people don't know anything about California having trouble with Indians during the **1850's Gold Rush**. The **Far West** didn't have any famous Indian conflicts like **Custer's Last Stand** or any other Indians that were well known like **Chief Joseph of the Nez Perce, Sitting Bull, or Geronimo**. It didn't have Indian revolts like **Adobe Walls or Beecher's Islands**. In California the Indians were peaceful and didn't carry weapons. But California had the **bloodiest** wars in the **West**. It was harsh and destructive and annihilated the Indians to the point where by the 1870's many of the groups were dead and gone.

This paragraph is plagiarized. Notice that the writing style of the original piece was copied. Sentence by sentence the information is restated using different words, and the sequence of each idea and sentence is the same. In most cases, words have been substituted for synonyms (see underlined). In some cases words have been kept (see **bold**). This is another example of patchwork paraphrasing. In addition, no indication of the source of this paraphrase is provided in the text.

Correct paraphrase

If history books are to be believed, there is little to say about the California Indian conflicts. Indeed it would seem that all of the great battles such as Custer's Last Stand and the great chiefs took place far away. While history shows us the Gold Rush and its effect on California, it also leaves us with the false impression that California Indians were peaceful, with no weapons or conflicts with the intruding whites. This type of historical omission negates the devastation and annihilation that the California Indians suffered; annihilation so complete "that by the 1870's many native groups were extinct". (Secrest, xi)

In this example the ideas of the original piece are maintained, but the style of writing is different and belongs to the writer of the paper. Instead of following an identical sequence to the original work, the correctly paraphrased paragraph conveys the information but does not pull out words and substitute them with synonyms. It still uses some of the phrasing from the original, but this instance is identified by quotation marks and is used to accurately convey and emphasize the ideas of the original author. It also cites the author of the original work.

To avoid the errors of adding information that wasn't in the original work or omitting something important to the original meaning, carefully track your sources and acknowledge them in your writing. You need to correctly present the meaning, and you need to cite the source accurately. Sometimes it is difficult to try to work with many different ideas, but remember that your professor is very familiar with many of the ideas and sources you'll use and can help you work out how best to present them.

Style of citation for paraphrases

Like direct quotations, the only difference between APA and MLA styles is the citation at the end.

Example: parenthetical citation, MLA

MLA style includes the name of the author and the page number. This example shows a block quotation.

> ...Yet in California, the bloodiest drama in the settlement of the West took place, a brutal disruption and destruction so devastating that by the 1870's many native groups were extinct. (Secrest xi)

Example: parenthetical citation, APA

APA style includes the name of the author and the date of publication. This example shows a block quotation.

> ...Yet in California, the bloodiest drama in the settlement of the West took place, a brutal disruption and destruction so devastating that by the 1870's many native groups were extinct. (Secrest, 2003)

Provide the complete information in your Works Cited or References list at the conclusion of your paper.

Knowledge Check: True or False?

1. Keeping the writing style of the original passage when you paraphrase is appropriate as long as you change most of the words.
2. Correct paraphrasing includes a citation for the original source after the paraphrased passage.
3. A paraphrase should be roughly the same length as the original.

Answers

1. (False) This is a common mistake students make because they don't know the rules and they lack confidence in their own writing ability. You should restate the writer's idea in your own words.
2. (True) Always acknowledge when you've used ideas from someone else, no matter whether it's a clause, sentence, or paragraph.
3. (True) The paraphrase restates another person's idea in your own words.

CHAPTER 5

Summarizing

What is a summary?

A **summary** condenses the idea of the original author while retaining the message of the original passage. A summary enables you to comment briefly on another writer's ideas and to express how they relate to your own ideas. Summarizing shortens the length of the original passage, whereas paraphrasing nearly matches the original in length.

Tips

DO
1. Be accurate to the original meaning.
2. Cite the original source.
3. Make your summary significantly shorter than the original.
4. Use your own words and explain how the writer's ideas relates to yours.

DON'T
1. Copy the original writing style; use your own.
2. Replace the original words with synonyms.
3. Change the meaning of a passage.

To summarize another writer's passage, read it several times-taking notes if necessary-to make sure you understand what the writer is saying. It might help to read the passage aloud so you can hear the words. Then say to yourself, "In other words, ..." and complete the thought. If you find that you are using almost as many words to explain or express the thought, then you need to revise it and make it simpler and briefer. Reduce the original passage to its basic idea. And make sure to explain for your reader how the writer's idea relates to the point you are making in your paper.

Sample summary

Original work

Polls show that large majorities of Americans believe that anyone who works hard can succeed, and even higher percentages of Americans say they admire people who get rich by their own efforts. Those who fall behind, meanwhile, are often blamed for their misery. In a typical recent survey finding, three quarters of Americans agreed with the statement that if a person is poor, their own "lack of effort" is to blame. In other words, Americans tend to make moral judgments about people based upon their level of economic success. Everybody loves a winner, the saying goes, and nowhere is that more true than in America. Winners are seen as virtuous, as people to admire and emulate. Losers get the opposite treatment for their own good, mind you. As Marvin Olasky, ... has said: "An emphasis on freedom should also include a willingness to step away for a time and let those who have dug their own hole 'suffer the consequences of their misconduct.'" The prevalence of a sink-or-swim mentality in the United States is unique among Western democracies, as is the belief that individuals have so much control over their destiny. Elsewhere people are more apt to believe that success or failure is determined by circumstances beyond individual control. Scholars attribute the difference in outlook to the "exceptionalism" of American and, especially to the American Dream ethos that dominates U.S. culture - an ethos at once intensely optimistic and brutally unforgiving. (Callahan 124-25)

Incorrect Summary

Polls show that large majorities of Americans believe that anyone who works hard can succeed, and even higher percentages of Americans say they admire people who get rich by their own efforts. Winners are seen as virtuous, as people to admire and emulate. Elsewhere people are more apt to believe that success or failure is determined by circumstances beyond individual control.

The above summary was created using the autosummarize feature of Word set for 25 percent. It selects key sentences from the original document and puts those sentences together to form an abbreviated copy. (Note that the auto-summarize feature is intended for writers to provide summaries of their *own* work, not the work of others.) This is *not* an acceptable summary because it is entirely copied, word for word. It is plagiarism. It does not change the writing style of the original author, nor does it give credit with a correct citation to indicate the source. Additional problems with this method of summary may be the altering of the original meaning of the piece. Note that the original piece was about the difference between how Americans view winners and losers, but the summary does not mention how losers are viewed. That thesis has not been mentioned in the summary. It is important to connect a summary to the point you fire making in your paper and the reason why you referred to the source you are summarizing.

Correct summary

According to Callahan, American culture, unlike other Western democracies, takes the moral perspective that success is the result of individual effort. According to polls, a person's success is considered to be a product of his or her labor and thus deserved. Conversely, a person's poverty or failure is viewed as the outcome of his or her lack of sufficient effort and therefore also deserved. (124-25)

In the correct summary, the ideas of the original passage are maintained, but the style of writing is different from the original passage. The summary is shorter than the original. The summary conveys the main points of the original, but it does not copy full sentences or pull out words and substitute them with synonyms. It still uses some of the words from the original to accurately present the author's ideas. When you use a summary is a paper, make sure it clearly addresses your thesis or argument and that you cite it correctly.

Knowledge Check: True or False?

1. You can keep the writing style of the original passage when you summarize as long as you significantly shorten the length and leave out some of the original.
2. Correct summarizing includes a citation for the original source next to the summarized passage.
3. A summary should convey the same meaning as the original.

Answers

1. (False) A summary should be in your own words and writing style but convey the message of the original. Do not use auto-summarize for someone else's work because it is just an abridged copy.
2. (True) Always acknowledge when you've used ideas from someone else, no matter whether it's a clause, sentence or paragraph, paraphrase or summary.
3. (True) Do not alter the meaning, just express it concisely and in your own words.

CHAPTER 6

Listing the Works Cited

As you draft your paper and decide how to use your final sources, you will assemble a complete list of the references that you use in your paper (as discussed in Chapters 3-5), and you will need to format that list of Works Cited and present that list at the end of your paper. This chapter presents the basics of how to format your reference list items in the MLA and APA styles, which your general coursework will likely require. You can find more detailed examples in your textbook, from your school's library or writing center, and from electronic resources such as those listed in Chapter 8.

> ***Tip***
> **Always check with your instructor for the documentation style that he or she requires.**

Content of citations

While the information presented in all styles is the same, the order of the information and how it is shown can be quite different. The basic information contained by all citation styles includes the following:

- Author name
- Title of article, essay, book, or Web site
- Publisher information
- Year of publication
- Place or form of publication

Basic format of citations

All documentation styles place the list of references at the end of the paper. Follow these basic formatting rules for all citation styles:

- Arrange all citations in alphabetical order by the author's last name.
- Arrange authors' names in a multiple-author work exactly as they appear in the source.
- Reverse the first author's name so that the last name appears first.
- Double-space your list of references, the way you double-space your paper.
- Indent the second and subsequent lines of a citation by 1/2 inch or 5 spaces, so the author's name always appears by itself at the left margin.
- Include in your list of references only the works that your paper refers to.

Always check with your course instructor for the preferred citation style. (See Chapter 8 for sources of citation styles for specific subject areas such as mathematics, biology, physics, and so on.) This guide does not discuss footnotes, as parenthetical citations are emphasized.

MLA citations: Books

The basic MLA style of citation for a book is as follows:

- Author last name first, first name followed by a period.
- <u>Book Title</u> underlined, followed by a period.
- City of publication followed by a colon.
- Publisher's name followed by a comma. Use only the first name of the publisher, and abbreviate University Press to UP.
- Year of publication followed by a period.

Example: single-author book

Maguire, Gregory. <u>Wicked: The Life and Times of the Wicked Witch of the West</u>. New York: Harper, 1995.

Examples: multiple authors of a book

When you are citing a book that has two or three authors, list them in the order that they appear on the title page. Invert the first author's name but not the names of the second or third author. Separate all the authors by commas.

For a book by four or more authors, MLA allows the listing to include all authors listed in order *or* just the first author followed by the Latin words **et al.** (which is short for *et alii*, meaning "and others"). Check with your instructor about the form that he or she prefers.

A book by two authors

Norman, Michael, and Beth Scott. <u>Historic Haunted America</u>. New York: Tor, 1995.

A book by four or more authors

Kauffman, James, Mark Mostert, Stanley Trent, and Daniel Hallahan. <u>Managing Classroom Behavior</u>. Boston: Allyn, 2002.

or

Kauffman, James, et al. <u>Managing Classroom Behavior</u>. Boston: Allyn, 2002.

MLA citations: Articles or essays

You might use an article from a periodical or an essay from an anthology. While the basic structure of citations for articles is the same as for books, there are some significant differences. You need to list both the title of the article or essay and the journal or book that it was published in.

Example: essay in an anthology

The information in a citation of a source from an anthology follows this order:

- Author of the article or essay (last name first) followed by a period.
- "Title of the article or essay" in quotation marks, followed by a period.
- <u>Title of the Book</u> underlined, followed by a period.
- Comp. (for Compiled by) or Ed. (for Edited by).
- Author of the book (first name first), followed by a period.
- City followed by a colon.
- Publisher followed by a comma.
- Year followed by a period.
- Page range (hyphenated) followed by a period.

Anson, Chris. "Taking Off." <u>Finding Our Way: A Writing Teacher's Sourcebook</u>. Ed. Wendy Bishop and Deborah Coxwell Teague. Boston: Houghton, 2005. 44-51.

For citations from an anthology or magazine, always include the page numbers.

Example: article from a magazine

Magazine or journal articles include the month of publication in the citation. Note the abbreviated month and the colon following the year.

Myers, Michaela. "Pole Results." <u>Horse Illustrated</u> Feb. 2005: 68-74.

Example: article from a journal

Note the volume number following the journal title, the year in parentheses, the colon following the year, and the inclusive page numbers.

Paulos, Lyn. "Sexuality in Women: Feminism in Conflict." <u>Women's Studies Weekly</u> 1 (2000): 15-20.

APA citations: Books

The APA style contains the same information as MLA, but it formats the content differently, putting more emphasis on the date of publication. The basic APA style of citation for a book is as follows:

- Author, last name first, then first initial, followed by a period. For a work by more than one author, invert all names, use initials instead of first names, and insert an ampersand (&) before the last author.
- Year of publication in parentheses, followed by a period.
- Book title *italicized* (capitalize the first word of the title, the first word of the subtitle, and any proper nouns), followed by a period.
- City and full publisher's name, separated by a colon and followed by a period.

Example: book

Maguire, G. (1995). *Wicked: The life and times of the Wicked Witch of the West.* New York: HarperCollins.

APA citations: Articles

The basic APA style of citation for a journal article by a single author is as follows:

- Author last name, and first initial followed by a period. For a work by more than one author, invert all names, use initials instead of first names, and insert an ampersand (&) before the last author.
- Year (in parentheses) with a period.
- Title of article (capitalize only first word and first word after a colon, no quotation marks), followed by a period.
- *Title of journal in italics* followed by a comma.
- *Volume number in italics* followed by a comma.
- Full page range of article, followed by a period.

Example: journal article by a single author

Paulos, L. (2000). Sexuality in women: Feminism in conflict. *Women's Studies Weekly, 1,* 15-20.

Example: journal article by two to five authors

Paulos, L., & Walker. K. (2005). Understanding twin rivalry: A case study. *Sibling Circular, 10,* 70-72.

Menager, R., Herch, S., Lewis, G., & Walker, K. (2005). Friends and family. *Relations, 5,* 21-24.

MLA and APA citations: Online sources

Provide the following information for online sources:

- Author (if available).
- Title of Web page.
- Title of full work (if available).
- Date of work (if available).
- File number (if available).
- Date that you accessed it.
- URL or Web address.

Example: MLA online citation

The MLA citation shows the author's full name and the date after the title. Note that the year of publication is followed by a period, that the date of access is inverted and abbreviated and that no punctuation follows it, that the URL is put in angle brackets, that the line break of the URL falls after a slash, and that a period follows the URL.

Warlick, David. "Landmarks Citation Machine: The Landmark Project. 2000. 19 Mar. 2005 <http:// www.landmarkproject.com/citationmachineindex.php>.

Example: APA online citation, no print source

APA electronic citations likewise follow the rules of normal APA style of formatting such as capitalization, first initial, year placement, and italics. Note that the retrieval date is spelled out, that a comma follows it, and that no punctuation follows the URL. If the URL extends to more than one line, then break it only after a slash or a period.

Lee. I. (1998). *A research guide for students: Research, writing, and style guides.* Retrieved March 19, 2005, from http://www.aresearchguide.com/styleguides.html

Example: APA online citation, print source

McCabe, D. L., Trevino, L. K., & Butterfield, K. D. (1999). Academic integrity in honor code and non-honor code environments: A qualitative investigation. *Journal of Higher Education, 70,* 211-234. Retrieved May 19, 2003, from http://www.questia.com/SM.qst

> ***Tip***
> **Always include the date of access, because Web sites often change.**

Example: online citation, no author, MLA style

If the Web site does not have an author or organization listed, then list the title of the Web site. Include the date of publication if available and the date of access.

Some Web sites are sponsored or maintained by universities or companies and do not list authors for their Web materials. If that is the case, list the university or company name in the author space of the citation.

<u>DSPS Policies and Procedures</u>. 2003. Santa Barbara City College. 3 Jan. 2004
   <http://www.sbcc.edu/dsps/>.

Example: online citation, no author, APA style

DSPS policies and procedures. (2003). Santa Barbara City College. Retrieved January 3, 2004, from
   http://www.sbcc.edu/dsps/

List of cited works

At the end of your paper, make sure to provide the complete list of works that you have cited
in the body of the paper.

Example: MLA Works Cited

Works Cited

Anson, Chris. "Taking Off." <u>Finding Our Way: A Writing Teacher's Sourcebook</u>. Ed. Wendy Bishop and
   Deborah Coxwell Teague. Boston: Houghton, 2005. 44-51.

<u>DSPS Policies and Procedures</u>. 2003. Santa Barbara City College. 3 Jan. 2004
   <http://www.sbcc.edu/dspsl>.

Kauffman, James, Mark Mostert, Stanley Trent, and Daniel Hallahan. <u>Managing Classroom Behavior</u>.
   Boston: Allyn, 2002.

Maguire, Gregory. <u>Wicked: The Life and Times of the Wicked Witch of the West.</u> New York:
   Harper, 1995.

Myers, Michaela. "Pole Results." <u>Horse Illustrated</u> Feb. 2005: 68-74.

Norman, Michael, and Beth Scott. <u>Historic Haunted America</u>. New York: Tor, 1995.

Paulos, Lyn. "Sexuality in Women: Feminism in Conflict." <u>Women's Studies Weekly</u> 1 (2000): 15-20.

Warlick, David. "Landmarks Citation Machine." <u>The Landmark Project</u>. 2000. 19 Mar. 2005
   <http:" www.landmarkproject.comlcitationmachine/index.php> .

Example: APA References

References

DSPS policies and procedures. (2003). Santa Barbara City College. Retrieved January 3, 2004, from
   http://www.sbcc.edu/dsps/

Lee, I. (1998). *A research guide for students: Research, writing, and style guides.* Retrieved March 19,
   2005, from http://www.aresearchguide.comlstyleguides.html

Maguire, G. (1995). *Wicked: The life and times of the Wicked Witch of the West.* New York: HarperCollins.

McCabe, D. L., Trevino, L. K., & Butterfield, K. D. (1999). Academic integrity in honor code and non-
   honor code environments: A qualitative investigation. *Journal of Higher Education, 70,* 211-
   234. Retrieved May 19, 2003, from http://www.questia.comISM.qst

Menager, R., Herch, S., Lewis, G., & Walker, K. (2005). Friends and family. *Relations, 5,* 21-24.

Paulos, L. (2000). Sexuality in women: Feminism in conflict. *Women's Studies Weekly, 1,* 15-20.

Paulos, L., & Walker. K. (2005). Understanding twin rivalry: A case study. *Sibling Circular, 10,* 70-72.

Knowledge Check: True or False?

1. Works Cited or References should be single-spaced.
2. Only works actually cited in the body of the paper should be listed in the Works Cited or Reference pages.
3. References or Works Cited should be listed in alphabetical order by author's last name.
4. Each reference item can be provided in any style (MLA, APA, etc.) as long as it's complete.

Answers

1. (False) All references should be double-spaced.
2. (True)
3. (True)
4. (False) All of the references should follow the style used in the body of the paper. The choice of style is determined by the academic subject (unless instructed otherwise by your professor).

CHAPTER 7

Practice Quiz

1. Cheating may include
a. plagiarizing or copying without attribution.
b. using an essay or paper from someone who has previously taken the course.
c. using answers to an exam from someone who has previously taken the course.
d. all of the above.

2. Plagiarism is
a. quoting someone else's work and giving credit to them.
b. using someone else's ideas, work, sentences, research, or information and presenting it as your own.
c. using original ideas in your written work.
d. using Web sources.

3. Citation of sources is required
a. whenever paraphrasing or summarizing another author's idea.
b. only in the works cited section of your paper.
c. when using your own ideas in an original paragraph.
d. a and b.

4. The word *paraphrase* means
a. to replace original words with synonyms.
b. to maintain the writing style of the original author.
c. to give an exact idea of the original author's meaning in your own writing style.
d. to give a general, but not exact, idea of the original author's meaning.

5. A paragraph is not properly paraphrased when
a. only a few words are different.
b. you express in your own words the general idea of what the author is saying.
c. the sentences have been rearranged but not changed much.
d. a and b.
e. a and c.

6. Correct summarizing includes
a. a copy of the original writing style.
b. replacing the original work with synonyms.
c. the accurate meaning of the original work but significantly shorter than the original.
d. using the autosummarize feature of your word processing program.

7. Citation of sources is required
a. when quoting a source in your paper that you use word for word.
b. when browsing the internet.
c. when describing another writer's idea in your paper.
d. a and c.

8. Over-quoting in your work
a. shows you have not synthesized or analyzed the material from your resources.
b. is acceptable because it shows the amount of work and research you have done.
c. means using too many direct quotes from your sources.
d. a and c.
e. a and b.

9. John's paper is based on several different sources,
including a research paper from a friend who took the same class last summer. Seeing that his friend's research closely matches his own, does John need to cite his friend in his final draft?
a. No, he just needs to cite the other sources.
b. Yes, anything John consults and incorporates needs to be cited.

10. Look at the original and choose which paraphrase is correct.

Original

> Because there are many ways to cheat, and there is temptation to do so, students may assume that this is something that everyone is doing. Surveys of college students show that cheating is a common occurrence, and some students consider it an accomplishment to get away with this type of behavior. These kinds of attitudes and behaviors are unethical and have consequences. (Menager-Beeley 2003)

a. Students can be tempted to cheat by the many resources available to them that make it easy. They may believe that a majority of students cheat in some form or another. Surveys done in colleges suggest that cheating is more rampant than once thought and that students see it as a triumph to cheat and not get caught. This shows a serious lack of ethics in behavior and can lead to repercussions from the academic institution. (Menager-Beeley, 2003)

b. Because there are so many different ways to cheat, and temptations for students are great, a lot of students think everyone is doing it. Students surveyed say that cheating is a common occurrence and it is an accomplishment to get away with it. This kind of attitude is unethical and can have some consequences.

Answers:

1. d   2. b   3. a   4. c   5. e   6. c   7. d   8. d   9. b   10. a

CHAPTER 8

Additional Sources of Information

The following links are subject to change. They were accessed March 25-26, 2005.

Web site with information on documentation styles, general

University of California, Berkeley
<http://www.lib.berkeley.edu/TeachingLib/Guides/Internet/Style.html>

Web sites with information on documentation styles, by discipline

Anthropology
<http://www.aaanet.org/pubs/style_guide.htm>

Biology
<http://www.wisc.edu/writing/Handbook/DocCBE.html>

Chemistry
<http://pubs.acs.org/books/references.shtml>

Legal
<http://www.law.cornell.edu/citation/>

Math
<http://www.longwood.edu/mathematics/stylesheet.html>

Physics
<http://www.aip.org/pubservs/style.html>

Sociology
<http://www.calstatela.edu/library/bi/rsalina/asa.styleguide.html>

Free Citation Generators

Landmark's Citation Machine
<http://www.citationmachine.net/>

Style Wizard
<http://www.stylewizard.com/>

Reference Tracking, Subscriptions, and Free Trials

Easy Bib
<http://easybib.com/>

RefWorks
<http://www.refworks.com>

Links for Articles on Plagiarism

Center for Academic Integrity
<http://www.academicintegrity.org/links.asp>

Plagiarism.org
<http://www.plagiarism.org/articles.html>

Samford University Library
<http://library.samford.edu/topics/plagiarism.html>

University of Indiana
<http://www.indiana.edu/~istd/definition.html>

Print Resources, Style Guides

American Psychological Association. *Concise Rules of APA Style.* Washington: APA, 2005. <http://www.apa.org/books/>.

Gibaldi, Joseph. *The MLA Style Guide for Writers of Research Papers.* 6th ed. New York: MLA, 2003. <http://www.mla.org/store/>.

Huth, Edward J. *Scientific Style and Format: The CBE Manual for Authors, Editors and Publishers.* 6th ed. New York: Cambridge UP, 1994. http://www.councilscienceeditors.org/publications/style.cfm>.

University of Chicago Press Staff. *The Chicago Manual of Style.* 15th ed. Chicago: U of Chicago P, 2003. <http://www.chicagomanualofstyle.org/about.html>.

CHAPTER 9

Works Cited

Byrne, Robert. *The 2,548 Best Things Anybody Ever Said.* New York: Galahad, 1996.
Sec. 453.

Covey, Stephen. *The Seven Habits of Highly Effective People.* New York: Simon, 1989. 97,
186.

Melville, Herman. Quotation 4797 in *Cole's Quotables.* 30 Mar. 2005
<http://www.quotationspage.com/ quotes/Herman _Melville/>.

Potter, W. James. "Is Media Violence Harmful to Children?" *Taking Sides: Clashing on
Controversial Psychological Issue.* 13th ed. Ed. Brent Slife. New York: McGraw,
2004. 306.

Secrest, William B. *When the Great Spirit Died: Destruction of the California Indians, 1850-
1860.* Sanger: Word Dancer, 2003.

Tavares, Jess. "Returning Students." Scholarship essay. May 2002.

Weeks, Dudley. *The Eight Essential Steps to Conflict Resolution.* 2002. New York: Tarcher-
Penguin, 1994.33.

Zaharoff, Howard. "A Writer's Guide to Fair Use in Copyright Law." *Writers Digest* Jan.
2001. 3 Mar. 2005
<http://www.writersdigest.com/articles/zaharoff_fair_copyright_law .asp>.

PART 1

Writing Essays

P A R T **1**

Writing Essays

? Frequently Asked Questions

CHAPTER 1

Understanding Purpose and Audience

Everyone who sets out to write confronts a series of choices. In the academic, public, and private writing you do in school, on the job, and in your personal life, your understanding of purpose and audience is essential, influencing the choices you make about content, emphasis, organization, style, and tone.

Note: Like written texts, **visual texts**—fine art, charts and graphs, photographs, maps, advertisements, and so on—are also created with specific purposes and audiences in mind.

See Ch. 3

1a   Determining Your Purpose

Your **purpose** for writing is what you want to accomplish. For instance, your purpose may be to **reflect,** to express private feelings, as in the introspective or meditative writing that appears in personal journals, diaries, and memoirs. Sometimes your purpose may be to **inform,** to convey factual information as accurately and as logically as possible, as in the informational or expository writing that appears in reports, news articles, and textbooks. At other times, your purpose may be to **persuade,** to convince your readers, as in advertising, proposals, editorials, and some business communications. Finally, your purpose may be to **evaluate,** to make a judgment about something, as in a book or film review, a recommendation report, or a comparative analysis.

1   Writing to Reflect

In diaries and journals, writers explore ideas and feelings to make sense of their experiences; in autobiographical memoirs, personal blog posts, and online course sites, they communicate their emotions and reactions to others.

> At the age of five, six, well past the time when most other children no longer easily notice the difference between sounds uttered at home and words spoken in public, I had a different experience. I lived in a world magically compounded of sounds. I remained a child longer than most; I lingered too long, poised at the edge of language—often frightened by the sounds of *los*

gringos, delighted by the sounds of Spanish at home. I shared with my family a language that was startlingly different from that used in the great city around us. (Richard Rodriguez, *Aria: Memoir of a Bilingual Childhood*)

2 Writing to Inform

In newspaper articles, writers report information, communicating factual details to readers; in reference books, instruction manuals, textbooks, and Web sites sponsored by nonprofit and government agencies, writers provide definitions and explain concepts or processes, trying to help readers see relationships and understand ideas.

> Most tarantulas live in the tropics, but several species occur in the temperate zone and a few are common in the southern U.S. Some varieties are large and have powerful fangs with which they can inflict a deep wound. These formidable-looking spiders do not, however, attack man; you can hold one in your hand, if you are gentle, without being bitten. Their bite is dangerous only to insects and small mammals such as mice; for man it is no worse than a hornet's sting. (Alexander Petrunkevitch, "The Spider and the Wasp")

Note: In your personal writing, you may write informally to convey information in *Facebook* updates, tweets, instant messages, and texts.

3 Writing to Persuade

In proposals and editorials, as well as in political blogs and in advertising, writers try to convince readers to accept their positions on various issues.

> America must make sure the melting pot continues to melt: immigrants must become Americans. Seymour Martin Lipset, professor of political science and sociology at the Hoover Institution, Stanford University, observes: "The history of bilingual and bicultural societies that do not assimilate are histories of turmoil, tension and tragedy. Canada, Belgium, Malaysia, Lebanon— all face crises of national existence in which minorities press for autonomy, if not independence. Pakistan and Cyprus have divided. Nigeria suppressed an ethnic rebellion. France faces difficulties with its Basques, Bretons and Corsicans." (Richard D. Lamm, "English Comes First")

Richard D. Lamm, "English Comes First," The New York Times, July 1, 1986.

4 Writing to Evaluate

In reviews of books, films, or performances and in reports, critiques, and program evaluations, writers assess the validity, accuracy, and quality of information, ideas, techniques, products, procedures, or services, perhaps assessing the relative merits of two or more things.

★☆☆☆☆ **Drivel,** February 28, 2008

By **AUGUSTINE J. FREDRICH "READER"** (Little Rock, AR, United States)—See all my reviews

   Pure unadulterated drivel. Grisham should be ashamed of himself. This book reads like something produced by a neophyte for a writer's workshop. Not only is the story one-dimensional, the characters are, without exception, stereotypes, and the plot is one only a conspiracy theorist with a liberal bent could love. Every action of every character is so predictable (and the writing so sophomoric) that one wonders what lowest-common-denominator reader Grisham had in mind when he sent this dog of a manuscript to the publisher. If, as some say, fiction is "chewing gum for the mind," this is a single Chiclet! I won't be reading any more of his "legal thrillers." (Amazon.com customer review of John Grisham's *The Appeal*)

Although writers write to reflect, to inform, to persuade, and to evaluate, these purposes are not mutually exclusive, and writers may have other purposes as well.

CHECKLIST
Determining Your Purpose

Before you begin to write, you need to determine why you are writing. Your purposes can include any of the following:

❏ to reflect	❏ to draw comparisons	❏ to take a stand
❏ to inform	❏ to make an analogy	❏ to identify problems
❏ to persuade	❏ to define	❏ to suggest solutions
❏ to evaluate	❏ to criticize	❏ to identify causes
❏ to explain	❏ to motivate	❏ to predict effects
❏ to amuse or entertain	❏ to satirize	❏ to interpret
❏ to discover	❏ to speculate	❏ to instruct
❏ to analyze	❏ to warn	❏ to inspire
❏ to debunk	❏ to reassure	

1b Identifying Your Audience

When you are in the early stages of a writing project, staring at a blank computer screen (or a blank sheet of paper), it is easy to forget that what you write will have an audience. But except for diaries and private journals, you always write for an **audience,** a particular reader or group of readers.

1 Writing for an Audience

At different times, in different roles, you address a variety of audiences.

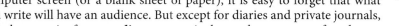

- **In your personal life,** you may send notes, emails, or text messages to friends and family members.

See
Ch. 30

- **In your public life,** as a citizen, a consumer, or a member of a community, civic, political, or religious group, you may respond to pressing social, economic, or political issues by writing letters or emails to newspapers, public officials, or representatives of special interest groups. You may also be called on to write media releases, brochures, flyers, or newsletters.

- **As an employee,** you may write emails, memos, proposals, and reports to your superiors, to staff members you supervise, or to coworkers; you may also be called on to address customers or critics, board members or stockholders, funding agencies or the general public.

See
Pt. 3

- **As a student,** you write reflective statements and response papers as well as essays, reports, exams, and research papers for your instructors in various academic **disciplines.** You may also participate in **peer review,** writing evaluations of classmates' essays and writing responses to their comments about your own work.

As you write, you shape your writing according to what you believe your audience needs and expects. Your assessment of your readers' interests, educational level, biases, and expectations determines not only the information you include but also what you emphasize and how you arrange your material.

2 The College Writer's Audience

Writing for Your Instructor As a student, you usually write for an audience of one: the instructor who assigns the paper. Instructors want to know what you know about your subject and whether you can express your ideas clearly and accurately. They assign written work to encourage you to

See
Ch. 8

think critically, so the way you organize and express your ideas can be as important as the ideas themselves.

As a group, instructors have certain expectations. Because they are trained as careful readers and critics, your instructors expect accurate information, standard grammar and correct spelling, logically presented ideas, and a reasonable degree of stylistic fluency. They also expect you to define your terms and to support your generalizations with specific examples. Finally, every instructor expects you to draw your own conclusions and to provide full and

See
Pts.
5–6

accurate **documentation** for ideas that are not your own.

If you are writing in an instructor's academic field, you can omit long overviews and basic definitions. Remember, however, that outside their areas of expertise, most instructors are simply general readers. If you think you may know more about a subject than your instructor does, be sure to provide background and to supply the definitions, examples, and analogies that will make your ideas clear.

All academic fields of study—or **disciplines**—share certain values. All disciplines value accuracy of information, careful selection and documentation of sources, and clear, correct writing. However, instructors in different disciplines are likely to emphasize different aspects of writing and use different formats, conventions, and citation systems. Often, their requirements will be different from those you will learn in composition classes. **Part 3** of this text highlights the key features of writing in other disciplines and includes examples of assignments from disciplines in the humanities, the social sciences, and the natural and applied sciences.

ESL TIP
If you did not attend school in the US, you may have trouble understanding your instructor's expectations or difficulty determining how much your instructor knows about your cultural background, native language, or home country. In these situations, it is usually a good idea to ask your instructor for advice.

Writing for Other Students   Before you submit a paper to an instructor, you may have an opportunity to participate in <u>peer review</u>, sharing your work with your fellow students and responding in writing to their work. Before you begin, you need to see your classmates as an audience whose needs you must take into account.

See 6c2

- **Writing Drafts** If you know that other students will read a draft of your paper, you need to consider how they might react to your ideas. For example, are they likely to disagree with you? To be shocked or offended by your paper's language or content? To be confused, or even mystified, by any of your references? Even if your readers are your own age, you cannot assume they share your values, political opinions, or cultural frame of reference. It is therefore very important that you maintain a neutral tone and use moderate language in your paper and that you be prepared to explain any historical, geographical, or cultural references that might be unfamiliar to your audience.

- **Writing Comments** When you respond in writing to another student's paper, you need to take into account how your reader will react to your comments. Here, too, your tone is important: you want to be as encouraging (and as polite) as possible. In addition, keep in mind that your purpose is not to show how clever you are but to offer constructive comments that can help your classmate write a stronger essay.

CHECKLIST
Writing for an Academic Audience

Before you respond to an assignment in your college courses, you need to identify the audience you are writing for. The following questions can help you understand what your audience expects:

- ❑ What discipline are you writing for?
- ❑ What kinds of assignments are typical of this discipline?
- ❑ What expectations do instructors in this discipline have?
- ❑ What style considerations are important in this discipline?
- ❑ What writing conventions are used in this discipline?
- ❑ What formats are used in this discipline?
- ❑ What research sources are used in this discipline?
- ❑ What documentation style is used in this discipline?

CHECKLIST
Audience Concerns for Peer-Review Participants

To get the most out of a peer-review session, keep the following guidelines in mind:

❏ **Know the material.** To be sure you understand what the student writer needs and expects from your comments, read the paper several times before you begin writing your response.

❏ **Focus on the big picture.** Try not to get bogged down in minor problems with punctuation or mechanics or become distracted by a paper's proofreading errors.

❏ **Look for a positive feature.** Try to zero in on what you think is the paper's greatest strength.

❏ **Be positive throughout.** Try to avoid words like *weak, poor,* and *bad;* instead, try using a compliment before delivering the "bad news": "Paragraph 2 is very well developed; can you add this kind of support in paragraph 4?"

❏ **Show respect.** It is perfectly acceptable to tell a student that something is confusing or inaccurate, but don't go on the attack.

❏ **Be specific.** Avoid generalizations like "needs more examples" or "could be more interesting"; instead, try to offer helpful, focused suggestions: "You could add an example after the second sentence in paragraph 2"; "Explaining how this process operates would make your discussion more interesting."

❏ **Don't give orders.** Ask questions, and make suggestions.

❏ **Include a few words of encouragement.** In your summary, try to emphasize the paper's strong points.

CHAPTER 2

Reading Texts

Central to developing effective reading skills is learning the techniques of **active reading.** Being an active reader means being actively involved with the text: reading with pen in hand and physically marking the text in order to identify parallels, question ambiguities, distinguish important points from not-so-important ones, and connect causes with effects and generalizations with specific examples. The understanding you gain from active reading prepares you to think (and write) critically about a text.

2a Previewing a Text

Before you actually begin reading a text, you should **preview** it—that is, skim it to get a sense of the writer's subject and emphasis.

When you preview a **periodical article,** skim the introductory and concluding paragraphs for summaries of the writer's main points. (Journal articles in the sciences and social sciences often begin with summaries called **abstracts.**) Thesis statements, topic sentences, repeated key terms, transitional words and phrases, and transitional paragraphs can also help you to identify the key points a writer is making. In addition, look for the **visual cues**—such as <u>headings and lists</u>—that writers use to emphasize ideas.

See
26b–c

When you preview a **book,** start by looking at its table of contents; then, turn to its index. A quick glance at the index will reveal the amount of coverage the book gives to subjects that may be important to you. As you leaf through the chapters, look at pictures, graphs, or tables and the captions that appear with them.

> **ESL TIP**
> When you read a text for the first time, don't worry about understanding every word. Instead, just try to get a general idea of what the text is about and how it is organized. Later on, you can use a dictionary to look up any unfamiliar words.

Close-Up VISUAL CUES

When you preview a text, don't forget to note the use of color and of various typographical elements—typeface and type size, boldface and italics—to emphasize ideas.

CHECKLIST
Previewing a Text

When you preview a text, try to answer these questions:

❑ What is the text's general subject?

❑ What are the writer's main points?

❑ How much space does the writer devote to topics relevant to your interests or research?

continued

Previewing a Text *(continued)*

❑ What other topics are covered?

❑ Who is the author of the text? What do you know about this writer?

❑ Is the text current?

❑ Does the text strike you as interesting, accessible, and useful?

2b Highlighting a Text

When you have finished previewing a work, photocopy relevant sections of books and articles, and print out useful material from online sources. Then, **highlight** the pages, using a system of graphic symbols and underlining to identify the writer's key points and their relationships to one another.

CHECKLIST
Using Highlighting Symbols

When you read a text, use strategies like the following to help you understand the material:

❑ Underline to indicate information you should read again.

❑ Box or circle key words or important phrases.

❑ Put question marks next to confusing passages, unclear points, or words you need to look up.

❑ Draw lines or arrows to show connections between ideas.

❑ Number points that are discussed in sequence.

❑ Draw a vertical line in the margin to set off an important section.

❑ Star especially important ideas.

2c Annotating a Text

After you have read through your material once, read it again—this time, more critically. At this stage, you should **annotate** the pages, recording your responses to what you read. This process of recording notes in the margins or between the lines will help you to better understand the writer's ideas and your own reactions to those ideas.

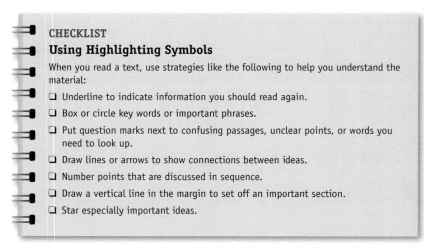

ESL TIP

You may find it useful to use your native language when you annotate a text.

Some of your annotations may convey information. For example, you may define new words, identify unfamiliar references, or jot down brief summaries. Other annotations may convey your reactions: you may identify a parallel between your own experience and one described in the reading selection, or you may note your opinion of the writer's position.

As you start to **think critically** about a text, your annotations may identify points that confirm (or dispute) your own ideas, question the appropriateness or accuracy of the writer's support, uncover the writer's biases, or even question (or challenge) the writer's conclusion.

See Ch. 8

The following passage illustrates a student's highlighting and annotations of a passage from Michael Pollan's book *The Omnivore's Dilemma*.

In the early years of the nineteenth century, Americans began drinking more than they ever had before or since, embarking on a collective bender that confronted the young republic with its first major public health crisis—the obesity epidemic of its day. Corn whiskey, suddenly superabundant and cheap, became the drink of choice, and in 1820 the typical American was putting away half a pint of the stuff every day. That comes to more than five gallons of spirits a year for every man, woman, and child in America. The figure today is less than one.

We drank as much as they do today

As the historian W. J. Rorabaugh tells the story in *The Alcoholic Republic*, we drank the hard stuff at breakfast, lunch, and dinner, before work and after and very often during. Employers were expected to supply spirits over the course of the workday; in fact, the modern coffee break began as a late-morning whiskey break called "the elevenses." (Just to pronounce it makes you sound tipsy.) Except for a brief respite Sunday morning in church, Americans simply did not gather—whether for a barn raising or quilting bee, corn husking or political rally—without passing the whiskey jug. Visitors from Europe—hardly models of sobriety themselves—marveled at the free flow of American spirits. "Come on then, if you love toping," the journalist William Cobbett wrote his fellow Englishmen in a dispatch from America. "For here you may drink yourself blind at the price of sixpence."

!! ? *

The results of all this toping were entirely predictable: a rising tide of public drunkenness, violence, and family abandonment, and a spike in alcohol-related diseases. Several of the Founding Fathers—including George Washington, Thomas Jefferson, and John Adams—denounced the excesses of "the Alcoholic Republic," inaugurating an American quarrel over drinking that would culminate a century later in Prohibition.

the take on?

Why?

But the outcome of our national drinking binge is not nearly as relevant to our own situation as its underlying cause. Which, put simply, was this: American farmers were producing far too much corn. This was particularly true in the newly settled regions west of the Appalachians, where fertile, virgin soils yielded one bumper crop after another. A

*

Examples from contemporary US farming?

?

This is his point

mountain of surplus corn piled up in the Ohio River Valley. <u>Much as today, the astounding productivity of American farmers proved to be their own worst enemy, as well as a threat to public health</u>. For when yields rise, the market is flooded with grain, and its price collapses. What happens next? The excess (biomass) works like a vacuum in reverse: <u>Sooner or later, clever marketers will figure out a way to induce the human omnivore to consume the surfeit of cheap calories.</u>

2d   Reading Electronic Texts

Even when electronic documents physically resemble print documents (as they do in online newspaper articles), the way they present information can be very different. Print documents are **linear;** that is, readers move in a straight line from the beginning of a document to the end. Print documents are also self-contained, including all the background information, explanations, supporting details, and visuals necessary to make their point.

Electronic documents, however, are usually not linear. They often include advertising, marginal commentary, and graphics, and they also include sound and video. In addition, links embedded in the text encourage readers to go to other sites for facts, statistical data, visuals, or additional articles that supplement the discussion. For example, readers of the electronic discussion of gun control pictured in Figure 2.1 could link to FBI data about the

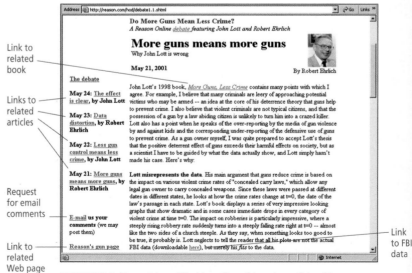

FIGURE 2.1 Excerpt from "Do More Guns Mean Less Crime?" A *Reason Online* Debate. Reprinted by permission of Reason.

connection between "concealed carry laws" and violent crime. Once they access this material, they can choose to read it carefully, skim it, or ignore it.

The format of electronic texts presents challenges to readers. First, because links to other material interrupt the document's flow, it may be hard for readers to focus on a writer's main idea and key points or to follow an argument's logic. In addition, pages may be very busy, crowded with distracting marginalia, visuals, and advertisements. For these reasons, it makes sense to use a slightly different process when you apply active reading strategies to an electronic text.

Previewing   During the previewing stage, you will probably want to skim the text online, doing your best to ignore visuals, marginal commentary, advertising, and links. If the text looks like something you will want to read more closely, you should print it out (taking care to print the "printer-friendly" version, which will usually omit the distracting material and enable you to focus on the text's content).

Highlighting and Annotating   Once you have hard copy of an electronic text, you can proceed to highlight and annotate it just as you would a print text. Reading on hard copy will enable you to follow the writer's main idea instead of clicking on every link. However, you should be sure to circle any links that look promising so you can explore them later on.

Note: You can also highlight and annotate Web-based texts by using a program like *Diigo*, which makes it possible for you to highlight and write self-stick notes on electronic documents.

2e   Writing a Critical Response

Once you have previewed, highlighted, and annotated a text, you should have the understanding (and the material) you need to write a **critical response** that *summarizes, analyzes,* and *interprets* the text's key ideas and perhaps *evaluates* them as well. It can also *synthesize* the ideas in the text with ideas in other texts.

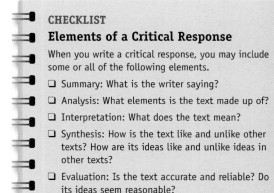

CHECKLIST

Elements of a Critical Response

When you write a critical response, you may include some or all of the following elements.

❑ Summary: What is the writer saying?

❑ Analysis: What elements is the text made up of?

❑ Interpretation: What does the text mean?

❑ Synthesis: How is the text like and unlike other texts? How are its ideas like and unlike ideas in other texts?

❑ Evaluation: Is the text accurate and reliable? Do its ideas seem reasonable?

The following is a student's critical response to the passage from *The Omnivore's Dilemma* on pages 11–12.

Author
and title
identified

Summary

Analysis
and inter-
pretation

Evaluation

In an excerpt from his book *The Omnivore's Dilemma*, Michael Pollan discusses the drinking habits of nineteenth-century Americans and makes a connection between the cause of this "national drinking binge" and the factors behind our twenty-first-century unhealthy diets. In both cases, he blames the overproduction of grain by American farmers. He links nineteenth-century overproduction of corn with "a rising tide of public drunkenness, violence, and family abandonment, and a spike in alcohol-related deaths," and he also links the current overproduction of grain with a "threat to public health." Although there are certainly other causes of our current problems with obesity, particularly among young children, Pollan's analogy makes sense. As long as farmers need to sell their overabundant crops, consumers will be presented with a "surfeit of cheap calories"—with potentially disastrous results.

Note: For information on writing a summary, **see 18a.** For information on synthesizing sources, **see Chapter 19.** For information on evaluating electronic and print texts, **see 16c and 17c.**

CHECKLIST
Analyzing Texts

As you read a text, keep the following questions in mind:

❑ Does the text provide any information about the writer's background? If so, how does this information affect your reading of the text?

❑ What is the writer's purpose? How can you tell?

❑ What audience is the text aimed at? How can you tell?

❑ What is the text's most important idea? What support does the writer provide for that idea?

❑ What information can you learn from the text's introduction and conclusion?

❑ What information can you learn from the thesis statement and topic sentences?

❑ What key words are repeated? What does this repetition tell you about the writer's purpose and emphasis?

❑ How would you characterize the writer's tone?

❑ Are there parallels between the writer's experiences and your own?

❑ Where do you agree with the writer? Where do you disagree?

❑ What, if anything, is not clear to you?

CHAPTER 3

Reading Visuals

The texts you read in college courses—books, newspapers, and periodical articles, in print or online—are often accompanied by visual images. For example, textbooks often include illustrations to make complex information more accessible, newspapers use photographs to break up columns of written text, and Web sites use graphics of all kinds to add visual appeal.

Close-Up READING VISUALS

Visuals are used to convey information to supplement written text; they may also be used to persuade as well as to amuse.

Fine Art

Photo © Christie's Images/The Bridgeman Art Library

Profile of a Woman Wearing a Jabot (pastel on paper) by Mary Stevenson Cassatt (1844–1926).

Photographs

Jeff Greenberg/Lonely Planet Images/Getty Images

Photo of university student preparing backstage at Beijing Opera.

(continued)

READING VISUALS *(continued)*

Maps

Map of Dublin, Ireland.

Cartoons

Cartoon by Stan Eales.

Scientific Diagrams

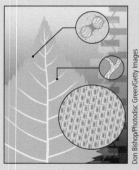

Plant engineering diagram.

Advertisements

THE SMELL OF ADVENTURE

MINI COOPER

GET A WHIFF OF MINI EXCITEMENT!

Mini Cooper ad.

Tables

Table 1

Relationship between Sleep Deprivation and Academic Performance

Grade Totals	Sleep Deprived	Not Sleep Deprived	Usually Sleep Deprived	Improved	Harmed	Continue Sleep Deprivation?
A = 10	4	6	1	4	0	4
B = 20	9	11	8	8	1	8
C = 10	10	0	6	5	4	7
D = 10	8	2	2	1	3	2
Total	31	19	17	18	8	21

Table from student paper.

Bar Graphs

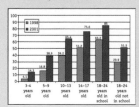

Bar graph from student paper.

3a Analyzing and Interpreting Visuals

Because the world audience is becoming increasingly visual, it is important for you to acquire the skills needed to read and interpret visuals as well as to use them in your own written work. (For information on incorporating visuals into your own writing, **see 6b2.**)

The powerful newspaper photograph shown in Figure 3.1, which depicts a Marine in front of the Vietnam Veterans Memorial, uses a variety of techniques to convey its message. To **analyze and interpret** this photograph, you need to determine what strategies it uses to achieve its effect.

You might notice right away that contrasts are very important in this picture. In the background is the list of soldiers who died in the war; in the foreground, a lone member of a Marine honor guard stands in silent vigil, seemingly as static as the names carved in granite. Still, those who view this photo know that the Marine is motionless only in the picture; when the photographer puts the camera down, the Marine lives on, in contrast to those whose names are listed behind him.

The large image of the Marine set against the smaller names in the background also suggests that the photographer's purpose is at least in

The whole world is watching

Member of Marine honor guard passes the Vietnam memorial on which names of casualties of the war are inscribed.

Bryan Grigsby

FIGURE 3.1 Newspaper photograph taken at the Vietnam Veterans Memorial.

part to capture the contrast between the past and the present, the dead and the living. Thus, the photograph has a persuasive purpose: it suggests, as its title states, that "the whole world is watching" (and, in fact, *should* be watching) this scene in order to remember the past and honor the dead.

To convey their ideas, visuals often rely on contrasting light and shadow and on the size and placement of individual images (as well as on the spatial relationship of these images to one another and to the whole). In addition, visuals often use words (captions, slogans, explanatory text), and they may also include color, animation, audio narration, and even musical soundtracks. Given the complexity of most visuals and the number of individual elements each one uses to convey its message, analyzing (or "reading") visual texts can be challenging. This task will be easier, however, if you follow the same **active reading** process you use when you read a written text.

3b Previewing a Visual

Just as with a written text, the first step in analyzing a visual text is to **preview** it, skimming it to get a sense of its subject and emphasis. At this stage, you may notice little more than the visual's major features: its central image, its dominant colors, its use of white space, and the most prominent blocks of written text. Still, even these elements can give you a general idea of what the focus of the visual is and what purpose it might have.

FIGURE 3.2 Magazine ad for New Balance sneakers.

For example, the New Balance ad shown in Figure 3.2 includes two large images—a foot and a shoe—both with the distinctive New Balance "N" logo. This logo also appears in the slogan "N is for fit," which has a prominent central position. The slogan is allowed to speak for itself, with the text that explains the visual message appearing in very small type at the bottom of the page. Yellow is used to highlight the logo, the shoe's tread, and the word *fit*.

3c Highlighting and Annotating a Visual

When you **highlight** a visual text, you mark it to help you identify key images and their relationship to one another. You might, for example, use arrows to point to important images, or you might circle key words or details. When you **annotate** a visual text, you record your reactions to the images and words you see. (If a visual's background is dark, or if you are not permitted to write directly on it, you can do your highlighting and annotating on small self-stick notes.)

A student in a composition class was asked to analyze the advertisement for Mini Cooper automobiles shown in Figure 3.3. When she visited the company Web site, she saw that Mini Cooper was appealing to consumers who value affordability and reliability as well as the company's commitment to "minimalism" and fuel efficiency. However, the Web site was also appealing to those looking for features like high performance, sporty design, and creativity—for example, the opportunity to "build your own" car by choosing features and colors. The student's highlighting and annotating focus on how the ad's written text and visuals work together to present the company's message: that the Mini Cooper is not just a practical choice but also one that offers possibilities for excitement and adventure.

FIGURE 3.3 Mini Cooper ad.

CHECKLIST

Analyzing Visuals

❑ Who has created the visual?

❑ For what purpose was the visual created? For example, does it seem to be designed primarily to inform? To persuade? To entertain or amuse?

❑ Where did the visual originally appear? What is the target audience for this publication?

❑ What scene does the visual depict?

❑ What individual images are shown in the visual? What associations do these images have for you?

❑ Do any people appear in the visual? What do they suggest about its target audience? What is their relationship to the scene and to one another? What are they doing?

❑ How would you describe the people's facial expressions? Their positions? Their body language?

❑ Does the visual include a lot of blank space?

❑ How large are the various elements (words and images)?

❑ Is the background light or dark? Clear or blurred? What individual elements stand out most clearly against this background?

❑ What general mood is suggested by the visual's use of color and shadow?

❑ Does the visual include any written text? What is its purpose?

❑ In general terms, what is the visual's message? How do its individual elements help to communicate this message?

❑ How would the visual's message or impact be different if something were added? If something were deleted?

Note: For information on writing a critical analysis of a visual, **see 11b4.** For information on using visuals (such as editorial cartoons, photos, charts, and graphs) to support an argument, **see 10a.**

CHAPTER **4**

Planning an Essay

4a Understanding the Writing Process

Writing is a complex process of decision making—of selecting, deleting, and rearranging material.

The Writing Process

The writing process includes the following stages:

Planning: Consider your purpose, audience, and tone; choose your topic; discover ideas to write about.

Shaping: Decide how to organize your material.

Drafting: Write your first draft.

Revising: "Re-see" what you have written; write additional drafts.

Editing: Check grammar, spelling, punctuation, and mechanics.

Proofreading: Reread every word, checking for any remaining errors.

Of course, the neatly defined stages listed above do not communicate the reality of the writing process. In practice, this process is neither a linear series of steps nor an isolated activity. (In fact, in an electronic classroom, a significant part of the writing process can take place in full view of an online audience.) Writing is also often interactive: the writing process can be interrupted (and supplemented) by emailing, blogging, chat room discussions, or surfing the Internet.

Moreover, the stages of the writing process actually overlap: as you look for ideas, you begin to shape your material; as you shape your material, you begin to write; as you write a draft, you reorganize your ideas; as you revise, you continue to discover new material. These stages may be repeated again and again throughout the writing process. During your college years and in the years that follow, you will develop your own version of the writing process and use it whenever you write, adapting it to the audience, purpose, and writing situation at hand.

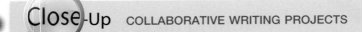

Close-Up   COLLABORATIVE WRITING PROJECTS

In school—and particularly in the workplace—you will find that writing is increasingly a collaborative effort. On a regular basis, you will work with others to plan projects, do research, draft different sections of a single document (or different components of a larger project), and offer suggestions for revision.

4b   Computers and the Writing Process

See
Ch. 30

See
31d2

Computers have changed the way we write and communicate in both academic and **workplace** settings. In addition to using word-processing applications for typical writing tasks, writers may rely on programs such as *PowerPoint*® for giving presentations, *Publisher*® for creating customized résumés or brochures, and Web-page authoring software such as *Dreamweaver*® or *HomeSite*® for creating Internet-accessible documents that include images, movies, and a wide range of visual effects.

With the prominent role of the Internet in professional, academic, and personal communication, it is increasingly likely that the feedback you receive on your writing will be electronic. For example, if your instructor uses course management software such as *WebCT*™ or *Blackboard*™, you may receive an email from your instructor about a draft that you have submitted to a digital drop box. Or, you may use discussion boards for attaching or sharing your documents with other students. Chat room and Net meeting software also allow you to discuss ideas collaboratively and to offer and receive feedback on drafts.

Although the tools you use may be course- or workplace-specific, you will still have to develop an efficient writing process. **Chapter 25** provides more comprehensive information on the options available to you as you write in a digital environment.

4c   Understanding Your Assignment

Planning your essay—thinking about what you want to say and how you want to say it—begins well before you actually start recording your thoughts in any organized way. This planning is as important a part of the writing process as the writing itself. During this planning stage, you determine your **purpose** for writing and identify your **audience.** Then, you go on to focus on your assignment, choose and narrow your topic, and gather ideas.

Before you start to write, be sure you understand the exact requirements of your **assignment.** Ask questions if necessary, and be sure you understand the answers.

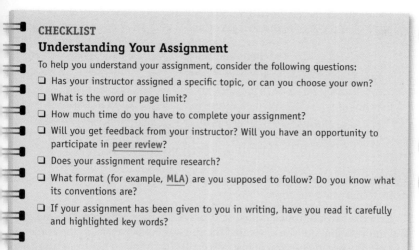

CHECKLIST

Understanding Your Assignment

To help you understand your assignment, consider the following questions:

❏ Has your instructor assigned a specific topic, or can you choose your own?

❏ What is the word or page limit?

❏ How much time do you have to complete your assignment?

❏ Will you get feedback from your instructor? Will you have an opportunity to participate in peer review?

❏ Does your assignment require research?

❏ What format (for example, MLA) are you supposed to follow? Do you know what its conventions are?

❏ If your assignment has been given to you in writing, have you read it carefully and highlighted key words?

See 6c2

See Ch. 18

Rebecca James, a first-year composition student, was given the following assignment.

The free online encyclopedia *Wikipedia* has become a common starting point for students seeking information on a topic. Because anyone can alter articles in this database, the reliability of *Wikipedia* as a valid source of information has been criticized by members of the academic community. In an essay of about 3–5 pages, evaluate the benefits and drawbacks of using *Wikipedia* in college research. To support your assessment, focus on a *Wikipedia* entry related to one of your courses.

The class was given three weeks to complete the assignment. Students were expected to do some research and to have the instructor and other students read and comment on at least one draft.

4d   Choosing a Topic

Sometimes your instructor will allow you to choose your own topic; more often, however, you will be given a general assignment, which you will have to narrow to a **topic** that suits your purpose and audience.

From Assignment to Topic

Course	Assignment	Topic
American History	Analyze the effects of a social program on one segment of American society.	How did the GI Bill of Rights affect American service-women?
Sociology	Identify and evaluate the success of one resource available to the homeless population of one major American city.	The role of the Salvation Army in meeting the needs of Chicago's homeless
Psychology	Write a three- to five-page paper assessing one method of treating depression.	Animal-assisted therapy for severely depressed patients

& **Note:** If your instructor permits you to do so, you can work with other students to narrow your topic.

Rebecca had no trouble thinking of ways she used *Wikipedia* to find general information, but she knew that the site was controversial in the academic community because several of her instructors discouraged her from using it as a research source. As she wrote her paper, she knew she would have to find a balance between the usefulness of *Wikipedia* on the one hand and its lack of reliability on the other.

Because her assignment was so specific, Rebecca was easily able to restate it in the form of a topic.

Topic: *Wikipedia* and college research

4e   Finding Something to Say

? Once you have a topic, you can begin to collect ideas for your paper, using one (or several) of the strategies discussed in the following pages.

1   Reading and Observing

As you read textbooks, magazines, and newspapers and browse the Internet, be on the lookout for ideas that relate to your topic. Films, television programs, interviews, telephone calls, letters, emails, and questionnaires can also provide material. But be sure your instructor permits such research—and remember to **document** ideas that are not your own. If you do not, you will be committing **plagiarism.**

See
Ch. 20

When students in Rebecca's composition class were assigned to read *Wikipedia*'s policy statement, "Researching with *Wikipedia*," in preparation for their paper assignment, she learned about the problems of using *Wikipedia* in college-level research. This reading assignment gave her a wider perspective on her topic and encouraged her to look beyond her own experience with *Wikipedia*.

> **ESL TIP**
> Don't use all your time making sure you are writing grammatically correct sentences. Remember, the purpose of writing is to communicate ideas. If you want to write an interesting, well-developed essay, you will need to devote plenty of time to the activities described in this section.

2 Keeping a Journal

Many professional writers keep print or electronic **journals** (sometimes in the form of blogs), writing in them regularly whether or not they have a specific project in mind. Journals, unlike diaries, do more than simply record personal experiences and reactions. In a journal, you explore ideas, ask questions, and draw conclusions. You might, for example, analyze your position on a political issue, try to solve an ethical problem, or trace the evolution of your ideas about an academic assignment.

One of Rebecca's journal entries appears below.

Journal Entry

I use *Wikipedia* all the time, whenever something comes up that I want to know more about. Once my roommate and I were talking about graffiti art, and I started wondering how and where it began. I went to *Wikipedia* and found a long article about graffiti's origins and development as an art form. Some of my instructors say not to use *Wikipedia* as a research source, so I try to avoid going to the site for paper assignments. Still, it can be really helpful when I'm trying to find basic information. There are a lot of business and financial terms that come up in my accounting class, and I can usually find simple explanations on *Wikipedia* of things I don't understand.

3 Freewriting

When you **freewrite,** you write nonstop about anything that comes to mind, moving as quickly as you can. Give yourself a set period of time—say, five minutes—and don't stop to worry about punctuation, spelling, or grammar, or about where your freewriting takes you. This strategy encourages your mind to make free associations; thus, it helps you to discover ideas you probably aren't even aware you have. When your time is up, look over what you have written, and underline, circle, bracket, star, boldface, or otherwise highlight the most promising ideas. You can then use one or more of these ideas as the center of a focused freewriting exercise.

When you do **focused freewriting,** you zero in on your topic. Here, too, you write without stopping to reconsider or reread, so you have no time to be self-conscious about style or form, to worry about the relevance of your ideas, or to count how many words you have (and panic about how many more you think you need). At its best, focused freewriting can suggest new details, a new approach to your topic, or even a more interesting topic.

Excerpts from Rebecca's freewriting and focused freewriting exercises appear below.

Freewriting (Excerpt)

I'm just going to list a bunch of things from my accounting class notes that I've recently looked up in *Wikipedia*: shareholder, stakeholder, strategic management, core competency, certified public accountant, certified management accountant, profit and loss. Not really sure which entry to focus on for this assignment. All the entries have strengths and weaknesses. I guess that's the point, but some *Wikipedia* articles are better than others. Maybe I'll choose an article that's sort of in the middle—one that provides some good basic info but could also be improved in some ways.

Focused Freewriting (Excerpt)

I think I'm going to use the "Certified Management Accountant" article as my focus for this paper. It explains this accounting term pretty clearly and concisely, which is good. However, it does have some problems, which are called out at the top of the article: poor writing, lack of cited sources, and not enough internal links. This article seems to represent a good balance of *Wikipedia's* benefits and drawbacks. I hope I can think of enough things to say about the article in my paper. I could start off with some background info on *Wikipedia* and then lead into the CMA example. That way, I can use the CMA article to support my points about *Wikipedia* in general.

4 Brainstorming

One of the most useful ways to collect ideas is by brainstorming (either on your own or in a group). This strategy enables you to recall bits of information and to see connections among them.

When you **brainstorm,** you list all the points you can think of that seem pertinent to your topic, recording ideas—comments, questions, single words, symbols, or diagrams—as quickly as you can, without pausing to consider their relevance or trying to understand their significance.

An excerpt from Rebecca's brainstorming notes appears below.

Brainstorming Notes (Excerpt)

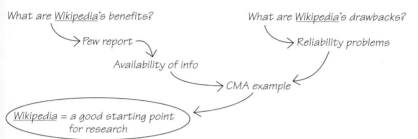

Topic: *Wikipedia* and College Research

What are *Wikipedia*'s benefits?

→ Pew report

Availability of info

→ CMA example ←

Wikipedia = a good starting point for research ←

What are *Wikipedia*'s drawbacks?

→ Reliability problems

Close-Up   COLLABORATIVE BRAINSTORMING   &

In addition to brainstorming on your own, you can also try **collaborative brainstorming,** working with other students to think of ideas to write about. If you and your classmates are working with similar but not identical topics—which is often the case—you will have the basic knowledge to help one another, and you can share your ideas without concern that you will all wind up focusing on the same few points.

Typically, collaborative brainstorming is an informal process. It can take place in person (in class or outside of class), on the phone, or in a chat room or class discussion board. Some instructors lead class brainstorming sessions; others arrange small-group brainstorming discussions in class.

Whatever the format, the exchange of ideas is likely to produce a lot of material that is not useful (and some that is irrelevant), but it will very likely also produce some ideas you will want to explore further. (Be sure you get your instructor's permission before you brainstorm with other students.)

---

5 Clustering

Clustering—sometimes called *webbing* or *mapping*—is similar to brainstorming. However, clustering encourages you to explore your topic in a more systematic (and more visual) manner.

Begin your cluster diagram by writing your topic in the center of a sheet of paper. Then, surround your topic with related ideas as they occur to you, moving outward from the general topic in the center and writing down increasingly specific ideas and details as you move toward the edges of the page. Following the path of one idea at a time, draw lines to create a diagram (often lopsided rather than symmetrical) that arranges ideas on spokes or branches radiating out from the center (your topic).

Rebecca's cluster diagram appears below.

Cluster Diagram

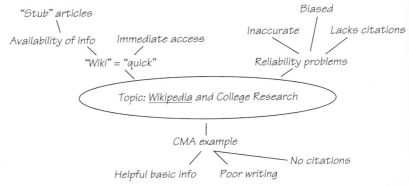

6   Asking Journalistic Questions

Journalistic questions offer an orderly, systematic way of finding material to write about. Journalists ask the questions *Who? What? Why? Where? When?* and *How?* to ensure that they have explored all angles of a story, and you can use these questions to make sure you have considered all aspects of your topic.

Rebecca's list of journalistic questions appears below.

Journalistic Questions

- <u>Who</u> uses *Wikipedia*, and for what purposes?

- <u>What</u> is a wiki? <u>What</u> are *Wikipedia's* benefits? <u>What</u> are its drawbacks?

- <u>When</u> was *Wikipedia* created? <u>When</u> did it become so popular among college students?

- <u>Where</u> do people go for more information after reading a *Wikipedia* article?

- <u>Why</u> are people drawn to *Wikipedia*? <u>Why</u> do some instructors discourage students from using it as a research source?

- <u>How</u> can *Wikipedia* be used responsibly? <u>How</u> can *Wikipedia* be improved?

CHAPTER **5**

Using a Thesis to Shape Your Material

Now it is time to start sifting through your ideas to choose those you can use. As you do this, you begin to **shape** your material into a thesis-and-support essay.

5a Understanding Thesis and Support

Your **thesis** is the main idea of your essay, the central point your ideas support. The concept of **thesis and support**—stating the thesis and then supplying information that explains and develops it—is central to much of the writing you will do in college.

As the following diagram illustrates, the essays you will write will consist of an <u>introductory paragraph,</u> which opens your essay and states your thesis; a number of **body paragraphs,** which provide the support for your thesis statement; and a <u>concluding paragraph,</u> which reviews your essay's major points and gives readers a sense of closure, perhaps summing up your main points or restating your thesis.

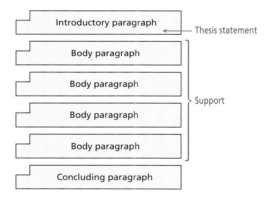

5b Developing a Thesis Statement

An effective **thesis statement** has four characteristics:

1. **An effective thesis statement clearly communicates your essay's main idea.** It tells readers what your essay's topic is and suggests

See 7e2–3

29

what you will say about it. Thus, your thesis statement reflects your essay's purpose.

2. **An effective thesis statement is more than a general subject, a statement of fact, or an announcement of your intent.**

Subject	Statement of Fact	Announcement
The Military Draft	The United States currently has no military draft.	In this essay, I will reconsider our country's need for a draft.

Thesis Statement: Although an all-volunteer force has replaced the draft, a draft may eventually be necessary if the US is to remain secure.

3. **An effective thesis statement is carefully worded.** Because it communicates your paper's main idea, your thesis statement should be clearly and accurately worded. Your thesis statement—usually expressed in a single concise sentence—should be direct and straightforward. It should not include abstract language, overly complex terminology, or unnecessary details that might confuse or mislead readers.

Be particularly careful to avoid vague, wordy phrases—*centers on, deals with, involves, revolves around, has a lot to do with, is primarily concerned with*, and so on.

The real problem in our schools ~~does~~ *is* not ~~revolve around~~ the absence of nationwide goals and standards; the problem is ~~primarily concerned with~~ the absence of resources.

Finally, an effective thesis statement should not include words or phrases such as "Personally," "I believe," "I hope to demonstrate," and "It seems to me," which weaken your credibility by suggesting that your conclusions are tentative or are based solely on opinion rather than on reading, observation, and experience.

4. **An effective thesis statement suggests your essay's direction, emphasis, and scope.** Your thesis statement should not make promises that your essay will not fulfill. It should suggest where you will place your emphasis and indicate in what order your major points will be discussed, as the following thesis statement does.

Effective Thesis Statement
Widely ridiculed as escape reading, romance novels are important as a proving ground for many never-before-published writers and, more significantly, as a showcase for strong heroines.

This thesis statement is effective because it tells readers that the essay to follow will focus on two major roles of the romance novel: providing markets for new writers and (more important) presenting strong female characters. It also suggests that the essay will briefly treat the role of the romance novel as escapist fiction. As the following diagram shows, this effective thesis statement also indicates the order in which the various ideas will be discussed.

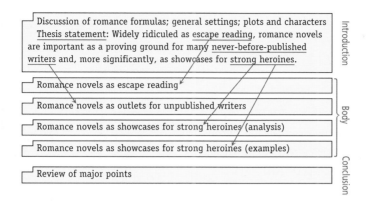

Rebecca James came up with the following thesis statement for her essay about *Wikipedia* and college research.

Thesis Statement: I have found *Wikipedia* to be a valuable tool for locating reliable research sources.

5c Revising Your Thesis Statement

At this point, your thesis statement is only **tentative.** As you write and re-write, you will think of new ideas and see new connections. As a result, you may change your essay's direction, emphasis, and scope, and if you do so, you must reword your thesis statement to reflect these modifications.

When Rebecca revised her essay, her thesis statement changed. Compare her tentative thesis above with her revised thesis statement in her paper's final draft in **6e.**

5d Constructing an Informal Outline

Once you have a tentative thesis statement, you may want to construct an informal outline to guide you as you write. An **informal outline** arranges your essay's main points and major supporting ideas in an orderly way.

Rebecca's informal outline appears below.

Informal Outline

<u>Thesis statement:</u> I have found *Wikipedia* to be a valuable tool for locating reliable research sources.

Definition of wiki and explanation of *Wikipedia*

- Fast and easy
- Range of topics

Wikipedia's benefits

- Internal links
- External links
- Comprehensive abstracts
- Current and popular culture topics
- "Stub" articles to be expanded

Wikipedia's potential

- Current quality control
- Future enhancements

Wikipedia's drawbacks

- Not accurate
- Bias
- Vandalism
- Lack of citations

CMA example: benefits

- Clear, concise
- Internal links
- External links

CMA example: drawbacks

- Writing style
- No citations
- Needs more internal links

At this stage of the writing process, Rebecca decided that her informal outline was all she needed to guide her as she wrote a first draft. (Later on, she might decide to construct a formal outline to check her paper's organization.)

Although you may be used to constructing outlines for your written work by hand, a number of software applications and formatting features can help in this process, including the outlining feature in some desktop publishing and word-processing programs (such as *Microsoft Word*). Another useful tool for outlining (particularly for **oral presentations**) is *Microsoft PowerPoint,* presentation software that enables you to format information on individual slides with major headings, subheadings, and bulleted lists.

See 31d2

Close-Up FORMAL OUTLINES

Sometimes—particularly when you are writing (or revising) a long or complex essay—you will need to construct a **formal outline,** which indicates both the exact order and the relative importance of all the ideas you will explore. (For information on how to construct a formal outline and for an example of a complete **sentence outline, see 6c4.** For an example of an excerpt from another sentence outline, **see 15j1.** For an example of a formal **topic outline, see 15h.**)

CHAPTER **6**

Drafting and Revising

6a Writing a Rough Draft

Once you are able to see a clear order for your ideas, you are ready to write a rough draft of your paper. A **rough draft** usually includes false starts, irrelevant information, and unrelated details. At this stage, though, the absence of focus and order is not a problem. You write your rough draft simply to get your ideas down so that you can react to them. You should expect to add or delete words, reword sentences, rethink ideas, and reorder paragraphs as you write. You should also expect to discover some new ideas—or even to take an unexpected detour.

CHECKLIST
Drafting Strategies

The following suggestions can help you as you draft and revise:

❑ **Prepare your work area.** Once you begin to write, you should not have to stop because you need better lighting, important notes, or anything else.

❑ **Fight writer's block.** An inability to start (or continue) writing, writer's block is usually caused by fear that you will not write well or that you have nothing to say. If you really don't feel ready to write, take a short break. If you decide that you really don't have enough ideas to get you started, use one of the strategies for finding something to say.

See 4e

❑ **Get your ideas down on paper as quickly as you can.** Don't worry about sentence structure, spelling and punctuation, or finding exactly the right word—just write. Writing quickly helps you uncover new ideas and new connections between ideas. You may find that following an informal outline enables you to move smoothly from one point to the next, but if you find this structure too confining, go ahead and write without consulting your outline.

See 5d

❑ **Write notes to yourself.** As you type your drafts, get into the habit of including bracketed, boldfaced notes to yourself. These comments, suggestions, and questions can help you when you write subsequent drafts.

❑ **Take regular breaks as you write.** Try writing one section of your essay at a time. When you have completed a section—for example, one paragraph—take a break. Your mind will continue to focus on your assignment while you do other things. When you return to your essay, writing will be easier.

❑ **Leave yourself enough time to revise.** All writing benefits from revision, so be sure you have time to reconsider your work and to write as many drafts as you need.

ESL TIP

Using your native language occasionally as you draft your paper may keep you from losing your train of thought. However, writing most or all of your draft in your native language and then translating it into English is generally not a good idea. This process will take a long time, and the translation into English may sound awkward.

When you write your rough draft, concentrate on the body of your essay, and don't waste time mapping out an introduction and conclusion. (These paragraphs are likely to change substantially in subsequent drafts.) For now, focus on drafting the support paragraphs of your essay.

Using her informal outline to guide her, Rebecca James wrote the following rough draft. Notice that she included boldfaced and bracketed notes to remind herself to add or check information when she revised her draft.

Rough Draft

Wikipedia and College Research

When given an assignment, students often turn first to *Wikipedia,* the popular free online encyclopedia that currently includes 10,000,000 articles. I have found *Wikipedia* to be a valuable tool for locating reliable research sources. **[Add more here]**

A wiki is an open-source Web site that allows users to edit or alter its content. Derived from a Hawaiian word meaning "quick," the term *wiki* conveys the swiftness and ease with which users can access information on such sites. **[Do I need to document this? Definition from *Britannica.com*]** *Wikipedia* is the most popular wiki. It includes a range of topics, such as . . . . **[Include a couple of examples here]** *Wikipedia*'s editing tools make it easy for users to add new entries or edit existing ones.

Wikipedia's slogan is "Making Life Easier." The site offers numerous benefits to its users. One benefit to *Wikipedia* over traditional print encyclopedias is its "wikilinks," or internal links to other content within *Wikipedia.* **[Use Pew report data on *Google* searches and wikilinks]** *Wikipedia* articles also often include external links to other sources as well as comprehensive abstracts. *Wikipedia* articles are constantly being updated and provide unmatched coverage of popular culture topics and current events. **[Make sure this is correct]** Finally, the site includes "stub" articles, which provide basic information that may be expanded by users.

Wikipedia claims that its articles "are continually edited and improved over time, and in general, this results in an upward trend of quality and a growing consensus over a fair and balanced representation of information." **["About" page—need full citation]** *Wikipedia* ranks its articles using the criteria of accuracy, neutrality, completeness, and style, letting users know which articles are among the site's best. In fact, some of *Wikipedia*'s best articles are comparable to those found in professionally edited online encyclopedias, such as *Encyclopaedia Britannica Online.* **[Check on this to make sure]** Although there's no professional editorial board to oversee the development of content within *Wikipedia,* users may be nominated into an editor role that allows them to manage the process by which content is added and updated. Users may also use the "Talk" page to discuss an article's content and make suggestions for improvement.

Wikipedia's popularity has also stimulated emergent technologies. Other companies are now trying to capitalize on *Wikipedia*'s success by enhancing users' experience of the site. Two examples include the online service *Pediaphon,* which converts *Wikipedia* articles into MP3 audio files, and the search-tool software *Powerset,* which allows users to more easily navigate *Wikipedia* articles.

Wikipedia concedes that "not everything in *Wikipedia* is accurate, comprehensive, or unbiased." **["Researching with Wikipedia" page—need full citation]** Because anyone can create or edit *Wikipedia* articles, they can be factually inaccurate, biased, and even vandalized. Many *Wikipedia* articles also lack citations to the sources that support their claims, revealing a lack of reliability. **[Need more here]**

Personally, I have benefited from using *Wikipedia* in learning more for my accounting class. For example, the *Wikipedia* article "Certified Management Accountant" describes the CMA's role in relation to other types of accounting positions. The article contains several internal links to related *Wikipedia* articles as well as a list of external links to additional resources. **[Give examples?]** In comparison, *Encyclopaedia Britannica Online* doesn't contain an article on CMAs.

Although the *Wikipedia* article on CMAs provides helpful, general information on this accounting term, it is limited in terms of reliability, scope, and style. **[Explain more here. Add a visual?]** The limitations of the CMA article indicate that *Wikipedia* should be used as a gateway to more reliable and comprehensive research sources.

Wikipedia articles should be used as a starting point for research and as a link to more in-depth sources. *Wikipedia* users should understand the current shortcomings of this popular online tool. **[Add more!]**

6b   Moving from Rough Draft to Final Draft

As you revise successive drafts of your essay, you should narrow your focus from larger elements, such as overall structure and content, to increasingly smaller elements, such as sentence structure and word choice.

1 Revising Your Drafts

After you finish your rough draft, set it aside for a day or two if you can. When you return to it, focus on only a few areas at a time. As you review this first draft, begin by evaluating your essay's thesis-and-support structure and general organization. Once you feel satisfied that your thesis statement says what you want it to say and that your essay's content supports this thesis and is logically arranged, you can turn your attention to other matters. For example, you can make sure that you have included all the **transitional words and phrases** that readers will need to follow your discussion.

See 7b2

As you review your drafts, you may want to look at the questions in the "Revising Your Essay" checklist on pages 48–49. If you have the opportunity for **peer review** or a **conference** with your instructor, consider your readers' comments carefully.

See 6c2, 6c3

Because it can be more difficult to read text on the computer screen than on hard copy, you should print out every draft. This will enable you to make revisions by hand on printed pages and then return to the computer to type these changes into your document. (As you type your draft, you may want to leave extra space between lines. This will make any errors or inconsistencies more obvious and at the same time give you plenty of room to write questions, add new material, or edit sentences.)

If you write your revisions by hand on hard copy, you may find it helpful to develop a system of symbols. For instance, you can circle individual words or box groups of words (or even entire paragraphs) that you want to relocate, using an arrow to indicate the new location. You can also use numbers or letters to indicate the order in which you want to rearrange ideas. When you want to add words, use a caret like *this*.

An excerpt from Rebecca's rough draft, with her handwritten revisions, appears below.

Draft with Handwritten Revisions (Excerpt)

The article contains several internal links to related *Wikipedia*
  (including the article "Certified Public Accountant")
articles as well as a list of external links to additional
  (such as the Web site for the Institute of Management Accountants)
resources. In comparison, *Encyclopaedia Britannica Online* doesn't

contain an article on CMAs.

2 Adding Visuals

As you write and revise, you should consider whether one or more **visuals** might strengthen your paper by providing support for the points you are making. Sometimes you may want to use a visual that appears in one of your sources; at other times, you may be able to create a visual (for example, a

Close-Up   MANAGING FILES

As you revise, it is important to manage your files carefully, following these guidelines:

- First, be sure to save your drafts. Using the Save option in your word processor's file menu saves only your most recent draft. If you prefer to save every draft you write (so you can return to an earlier draft to locate a different version of a sentence or to reconsider a section you have deleted), use the Save As option instead.
- Also, be sure to label your files. To help you keep track of different versions of your paper, label every file in your folder by content and date (for example, **First Draft, Nov 5**).
- Finally, be very careful not to delete material that you may need later; instead, move this material to the end of your document so that you can assess its usefulness later on and retrieve it if necessary.

photograph or a chart) yourself; at still other times, you may need to search *Google Images* or another image database to find an appropriate visual.

Once you have decided to add a particular visual to your paper, the next step is to determine where to insert it. (In general, you should place the visual in the part of the essay where it will have the greatest impact in terms of conveying information or persuading your audience.) Then, you need to format the visual. (Within *Microsoft Word*, you can double-click on an image to call up a picture-editing menu that allows you to alter the size, color, and position of the image within your essay—and even enables you to wrap text around the image.) Next, you should make sure that the visual stands out in your paper: surround it with white space, add ruled lines, or enclose it in a box.

CHECKLIST
Adding Visuals to Your Paper

To add a visual to your paper, follow these steps:

❑ Find an appropriate visual.

❑ Place the image in a suitable location.

❑ Format the image, and make sure it is clearly set off from the written text.

❑ Introduce the visual with a sentence (or refer to it in the text).

❑ Label the visual.

❑ Document the visual (if necessary).

After you have inserted the visual where you want it, you need to integrate it into your text. You can include a sentence that introduces the visual (**The following table illustrates the similarities between the two health plans**), or you can refer to it in your text (**Figure 1 shows Kennedy as a young man**) to give it some context and explain why you are using it. You should also identify the visual by labeling it (**Fig. 1. Photo of John F. Kennedy, 1937**). In addition, if the visual is not one you have created yourself, you must <u>document</u> it. In most academic disciplines, this means including full source information directly below the image and sometimes in the list of references as well. (To see how Rebecca integrated a visual into her paper, **see 6e.**)

See
Pts.
5–6

6c Using Specific Revision Strategies

Everyone revises differently, and every writing task calls for a slightly different process of revision. Five strategies in particular can help you revise at any stage of the writing process.

1 Using Word-Processing Tools

Your word-processing program includes a variety of tools designed to make the revision process easier. For example, *Microsoft Word*'s **Track Changes** feature allows you to make changes to a draft electronically and to see the original version of the draft and the changes simultaneously. Changes appear in color as underlined or crossed-out text (or as balloons in the margin), and you can view the changes on the screen or in print. This feature also allows you to accept or reject all changes or just specific changes.

Another useful tool is the **Compare Documents** feature. Whereas Track Changes allows you to keep track of changes to a single document, Compare Documents allows you to analyze the changes in two completely separate versions of a document, usually an original and its most recent update. Changes appear in color as highlighted text.

Rebecca used Track Changes as she revised her rough draft. An excerpt from her draft, along with her changes, appears below.

Draft with Track Changes (Excerpt)

A wiki is an open-source Web site that allows users to edit ~~or alter~~<u>and add to</u> its content. Derived from a Hawaiian word meaning "quick," the term *wiki* conveys the swiftness and ease with which users can access information on such sites~~.~~ <u>as well as contribute content ("Wiki").</u> With its slogan "Making Life Easier," *Wikipedia* ~~is~~<u>has</u> positioned itself as the most popular wiki. ~~It includes a range~~<u>, providing ever-increasing coverage</u> of topics~~, such as....~~<u>. ranging from contemporary rock bands to obscure scientific and technical concepts. In accordance with the site's policies, users can edit existing articles and add new articles using</u> *Wikipedia*'s editing tools ~~also make it easy for users to add new~~<u>, which do not require specialized programming knowledge</u> or ~~edit existing entries~~<u>expertise</u>.

Close-Up TRACK CHANGES VS. COMPARE DOCUMENTS

Where you are in the writing process can help you decide whether to track your changes or to compare one complete version of your document with another. **Track Changes** is especially useful in helping you follow sentence-level changes as you draft and revise; it can also be helpful later on, when you edit words and phrases. **Compare Documents** is most helpful when you are comparing global changes, such as paragraph unity and thesis-and-support structure, between one draft and another.

2 Participating in Peer Review

Peer review—a collaborative revision strategy that enables you to get feedback from your classmates—is another useful activity. With peer review, instead of trying to imagine an audience for your paper, you address a real audience, exchanging drafts with classmates and commenting on their drafts. Such collaborative work can be formal or informal, conducted in person or electronically. For example, you and a classmate may email drafts back and forth, using *Word*'s Comment tool (see page 41), or your instructor may conduct the class as a workshop, assigning students to work in groups to critique each other's essays. Students can also comment on classmates' drafts posted on a course discussion board or listserv.

Close-Up ELECTRONIC PEER REVIEW

Some software is particularly useful for peer-review groups. For example, *Word*'s **Comment** tool allows several readers to insert comments at any point or to highlight a particular portion of the text they would like to comment on and then insert annotations. With this tool, a single paper can receive comments from multiple readers. Comments are identified by the initials of the reviewer and by a color assigned to the reviewer.

Other online programs also facilitate the peer-review process. For example, *InSite* is a Web-based application that allows students to respond to each other's drafts with a set of peer-review questions, as shown on the facing page.

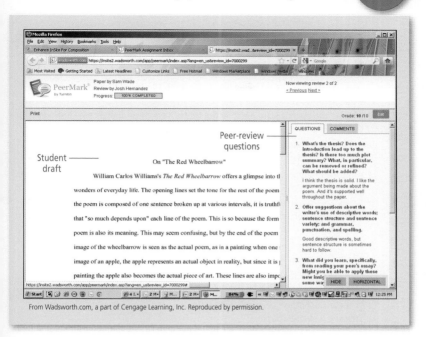

From Wadsworth.com, a part of Cengage Learning, Inc. Reproduced by permission.

An excerpt from Rebecca's rough draft with peer reviewers' comments appears above. (Note that her classmates used *Word*'s Comment tool to insert comments.)

Draft with Peer Reviewers' Comments (Excerpt)

Personally, I have benefited from using *Wikipedia* in learning more for my accounting class. For example, the *Wikipedia* article "Certified Management Accountant" describes the CMA's role in relation to other types of accounting positions. The article contains several internal links to related *Wikipedia* articles (including the article "Certified Public Accountant") as well as a list of external links to additional resources (such as the Web site for the Institute of Management Accountants). In comparison, *Encyclopaedia Britannica Online* doesn't contain an article on CMAs.

Comment [KL1]: It's also helpful for other classes outside my major.

Comment [KL2]: Why is this imp.? Maybe explain more??

Comment [BR3]: Yes! This is one of my fav. features of *Wikipedia*. ☺

Comment [CB4]: But sometimes these links don't lead to the best sources either . . .

CHECKLIST

Questions for Peer Review

The following questions can help guide you through the peer-review process:

❏ What is the essay about? Does the topic fulfill the requirements of the assignment?

❏ What is the essay's main idea? Is the thesis clearly worded? If not, how can the wording be improved?

❏ Is the essay arranged logically? Do the body paragraphs appear in an appropriate order?

❏ What ideas support the thesis? Does each body paragraph develop one of these ideas?

❏ Is any necessary information missing? Identify any areas that seem to need further development. Is any information irrelevant? If so, suggest possible deletions.

❏ Can you think of any ideas or examples from your own reading, experience, or observations that would strengthen the writer's essay?

❏ Can you follow the writer's ideas? If not, would clearer connections between sentences or paragraphs be helpful? Where are such connections needed?

❏ Is the introductory paragraph interesting to you? Would another opening strategy be more effective?

❏ Does the conclusion leave you with a sense of closure? Would another concluding strategy be more effective?

❏ Is anything unclear or confusing?

❏ What is the essay's greatest strength?

❏ What is the essay's greatest weakness?

For information on audience concerns for peer-review participants, **see 1b.**

3 Using Instructors' Comments

Instructors' comments—in correction symbols, in marginal comments, or in conferences—can also help you revise.

Correction Symbols Your instructor may indicate concerns about style, grammar, mechanics, or punctuation by using the correction symbols listed on the inside back cover of this book. Instead of correcting a problem, the instructor will simply identify it and supply the number of the section in this handbook that deals with the error. After reading the appropriate pages, you should be able to make the necessary corrections on your own. For example, the symbol and number noted within the following sentence referred a student to **44f2,** the section in this handbook that discusses sexist language.

Instructor's Comment: Equal access to jobs is a desirable goal for all
Sxt—see 44f2
(mankind.)

After reading the appropriate section in the handbook, the student made the following change.

Revised: Equal access to jobs is a desirable goal for everyone.

Marginal Comments   Instructors frequently write marginal comments on your essays to suggest changes in content or structure. These comments may ask you to add supporting information or to arrange paragraphs differently within the essay, or they may recommend stylistic changes, such as more varied sentences. Marginal comments may also question your logic, suggest a more explicit thesis statement, ask for clearer transitions, or propose a new direction for a discussion. In some cases, you can consider these comments to be suggestions rather than corrections. You may decide to incorporate these ideas into a revised draft of your essay, or you may not. In all instances, however, you should take your instructor's comments seriously.

An excerpt from Rebecca's rough draft, along with her instructor's comments, follows. (Note that her instructor used *Microsoft Word*'s Comment tool to insert comments.)

Draft with Instructor's Comments (Excerpt)

Personally, I have benefited from using *Wikipedia* in learning more for my accounting class. For example, the *Wikipedia* article "Certified Management Accountant" describes the CMA's role in relation to other types of accounting positions. The article contains several internal links to related *Wikipedia* articles (including the article "Certified Public Accountant") as well as a list of external links to additional resources (such as the Web site for the Institute of Management Accountants). In comparison, *Encyclopaedia Britannica Online* doesn't contain an article on CMAs.

> Comment [JB5]: Revise to eliminate use of "personally" and the first person ("*I*") in this paper. Use this ¶ to talk about *Wikipedia*'s benefits to college students, using the CMA article as an example.

> Comment [JB6]: In your final draft, edit out all contractions. (Contractions are too informal for most college writing.) See 48b1.

Conferences   Many instructors require or encourage one-on-one conferences, and you should certainly schedule a conference if you can. During a conference, you can respond to your instructor's questions and ask for clarification of marginal comments. If a certain section of your paper presents a problem, use your conference time to focus on it, perhaps asking for help in sharpening your thesis or choosing more accurate words.

CHECKLIST
Getting the Most Out of a Conference

To make your conference time as productive as possible, follow these guidelines:

❏ **Make an appointment.** If you are unable to keep your appointment, be sure to call or email your instructor to reschedule.

❏ **Review your work carefully.** Before the conference, reread your notes and drafts, and go over all your instructor's comments and suggestions. Make all the changes you can on your draft.

❏ **Bring a list of questions.** Preparing a list in advance will enable you to get the most out of the conference in the allotted time.

❏ **Bring your paper-in-progress.** If you have several drafts, you may want to bring them all, but be sure you bring any draft on which your instructor has commented.

❏ **Take notes.** As you discuss your paper, write down any suggestions that you think will be helpful so you won't forget them when you revise.

❏ **Participate actively.** A successful conference is not a monologue; it should be an open exchange of ideas.

Close-Up   WRITING CENTER CONFERENCES

If you are unable to meet with your instructor—and, in fact, even if you are—it is a good idea to make an appointment with a tutor in your school's writing center. A writing tutor (who may be either a professional or a student) is likely to know a good deal about what your instructor expects and is trained to help you produce an effective essay.

What a writing tutor can do is help you find ideas to write about and develop a thesis statement, identify parts of your essay that need more support (and help you decide what kind of support to include), and coach you as you revise your essay. What a tutor will *not* do is write your paper for you or act as a proofreader.

When you meet with a tutor, follow the guidelines in the checklist above—and always bring a copy of your assignment.

Conferences can also take place online—most commonly, through email. If you send emails to your instructor, to your writing center tutor, or to members of your peer-review group, include a specific subject line that clearly identifies the message as coming from a student writer (for example, "question about assignment" or "comments on my paper"). This is especially important if your email address does not include your name. When you attach a document to an email and send it for comments, mention the attachment in your subject line (for example, "first draft—see attachment")—and be sure your name appears on the attachment itself, not just on the email.

Close-Up COLLABORATION AND THE REVISION PROCESS

In a sense, the feedback you get from your instructor (or from a writing center tutor)—in conference, by email, or in written comments on a draft—opens a dialogue that is a form of collaboration. Like the comments you get from your classmates during peer review, these comments present ideas for you to react to, questions for you to answer, and answers to questions you may have. As you react to these comments, you engage in a collaboration that can help you revise your work.

4 Using a Formal Outline

Outlining can be helpful early in the revision process, when you are reworking the larger structural elements of your essay, or later on, when you are checking the logic of a completed draft. A formal outline reveals at once whether points are irrelevant or poorly placed—or, worse, missing. It also reveals the hierarchy of your ideas—which points are dominant and which are subordinate.

The Conventions of Outlining

Formal outlines conform to specific conventions of structure, content, and style. If you follow the conventions of outlining carefully, your formal outline can help you make sure that your paper presents all relevant ideas in an effective order, with appropriate emphasis.

Structure
- Outline format should be followed strictly.
  I. First major point of your paper
     A. First subpoint
     B. Next subpoint
        1. First supporting example
        2. Next supporting example
           a. First specific detail
           b. Next specific detail
  II. Second major point

(continued)

The Conventions of Outlining (*continued*)

- Headings should not overlap.
- No heading should have a single subheading. (A category cannot be subdivided into one part.)
- Each entry should be preceded by an appropriate letter or number, followed by a period.
- The first word of each entry should be capitalized.

Content
- The outline should include the paper's thesis statement.
- The outline should cover only the body of the essay, not the introductory or concluding paragraphs.
- Headings should be concise and specific.
- Headings should be descriptive, clearly related to the topic to which they refer.

Style
- Headings of the same rank should be grammatically parallel.
- A **sentence outline** should use complete sentences, with all verbs in the same tense.
- In a sentence outline, each entry should end with a period.
- A **topic outline** should use words or short phrases, with all headings of the same rank using the same parts of speech.
- In a topic outline, entries should not end with periods.

As part of her revision process, Rebecca made the following sentence outline of her rough draft (shown on pages 35–36) to help her check her paper's organization.

Sentence Outline

Thesis statement: I have found *Wikipedia* to be a valuable tool in locating reliable research sources.

    I. A wiki is an open-source Web site that allows users to edit or alter its content.

       A. *Wikipedia* is the most popular wiki.

       B. *Wikipedia* includes a range of topics.

    II. *Wikipedia* offers numerous benefits to its users.

       A. Many *Wikipedia* articles contain internal links.

       B. Many *Wikipedia* articles contain external links.

    C. Many *Wikipedia* articles contain comprehensive abstracts.

    D. Many *Wikipedia* articles cover current and popular culture topics.

    E. Site includes "stub" articles.

III. *Wikipedia* is making efforts to improve the quality of its content.

    A. *Wikipedia* ranks its articles using the criteria of accuracy, neutrality, completeness, and style.

    B. Users may serve as editors of the site's content.

    C. Users may use the "Talk" page to make suggestions for improvement.

IV. *Wikipedia*'s popularity has stimulated emergent technologies.

    A. The online service *Pediaphon* converts *Wikipedia* articles into MP3 audio files.

    B. The search-tool software *Powerset* allows users to more easily navigate *Wikipedia* articles.

 V. *Wikipedia* also has several drawbacks.

    A. *Wikipedia* articles may be factually inaccurate.

    B. *Wikipedia* articles may be biased.

    C. *Wikipedia* articles may be vandalized.

    D. Many *Wikipedia* articles lack citations.

VI. The *Wikipedia* article "Certified Management Accountant" offers certain benefits.

    A. It gives a clear, concise description of the CMA's role.

    B. It provides internal and external links to additional resources.

VII. *Wikipedia*'s "Certified Management Accountant" article is limited in the information it offers.

    A. It is unreliable.

    B. It is limited in scope.

    C. It is poorly written.

This outline revealed some problems in Rebecca's draft. For example, she saw that point IV was not relevant to her discussion, and she realized that she needed to develop the sections in which she discussed the benefits and drawbacks of the specific *Wikipedia* entry that she selected for this assignment. Thus, the outline helped her to revise her rough draft.

5 Using Checklists

The revision checklist that follows is keyed to sections of this text. Moving from global to specific concerns, it parallels the actual revision process. As your understanding of the writing process increases and you become better able to assess the strengths and weaknesses of your writing, you may want to add items to (or delete items from) this checklist. You can also use your instructors' comments to tailor the checklist to your own needs.

CHECKLIST

Revising Your Essay

The Whole Essay

❑ Do you understand your essay's purpose? (**See 1a.**)

❑ Have you taken your audience's needs into account? (**See 1b.**)

❑ Are your thesis and support logically related, with each body paragraph supporting your thesis statement? (**See 5a.**)

❑ Is your thesis statement clearly and specifically worded? (**See 5b.**)

❑ Have you discussed everything promised in your thesis statement? (**See 5b.**)

❑ Have you presented your ideas in a logical sequence? Can you think of a different arrangement that might be more appropriate for your purpose? (**See 5d.**)

Paragraphs

❑ Does each body paragraph have just one main idea? (**See 7a.**)

❑ Are topic sentences clearly worded and logically related to your thesis? (**See 7a1.**)

❑ Does each body paragraph have a clear organizing principle? (**See 7b1.**)

❑ Are the relationships between sentences within your paragraphs clear? (**See 7b2–4.**)

❑ Are your body paragraphs developed fully enough to support your points? (**See 7c.**)

❑ Does your introductory paragraph arouse reader interest and prepare readers for what is to come? (**See 7e2.**)

❑ Are your paragraphs arranged according to familiar patterns of development? (**See 7d.**)

❑ Have you provided transitional paragraphs where necessary? (**See 7e1.**)

❑ Does your concluding paragraph sum up your main points? (**See 7e3.**)

Sentences

❑ Have you avoided potentially confusing shifts in tense, voice, mood, person, or number? (**See 35a1–4.**)

❑ Are your sentences constructed logically? (**See 35b–d.**)

❑ Have you placed modifiers clearly and logically? (**See Ch. 36.**)

❑ Are your sentences varied? (**See Ch. 40.**)

❑ Have you combined sentences where ideas are closely related? (**See 40b.**)

❑ Have you used emphatic word order? (**See 41a.**)

❑ Have you used sentence structure to signal the relative importance of clauses in a sentence and their logical relationship to one another? (**See 41b.**)

❑ Have you strengthened your sentences with repetition, balance, and parallelism? (**See 41c–d, 43a.**)

❑ Have you eliminated nonessential words and unnecessary repetition? (**See 42a–b.**)

❑ Have you avoided overloading your sentences with too many words, phrases, and clauses? (**See 42c.**)

Words

❑ Is your level of diction appropriate for your audience and your purpose? (**See 44b.**)

❑ Have you selected words that accurately reflect your intentions? (**See 44c1.**)

❑ Have you chosen words that are specific, concrete, and unambiguous? (**See 44c3–4.**)

❑ Have you enriched your writing with figures of speech? (**See 44d.**)

❑ Have you eliminated jargon, neologisms, pretentious diction, clichés, and offensive language from your writing? (**See 44e–f.**)

Close-Up   CHOOSING A TITLE

When you are ready to decide on a title for your essay, keep these criteria in mind:

- A title should be descriptive, giving an accurate sense of your essay's focus. Whenever possible, use a key word or phrase that is central to your paper.
- A title can echo the wording of your assignment, reminding you (and your instructor) that you have not lost sight of it.
- Ideally, a title should arouse interest, perhaps by using a provocative question or a quotation or by taking a controversial position.

Assignment: Write about a problem on college campuses today.

Topic: Free speech on campus

Possible Titles:

Free Speech: A Problem for Today's Colleges (echoes wording of assignment and includes key words of essay)

How Free Should Free Speech on Campus Be? (provocative question)

The Right to "Shout 'Fire' in a Crowded Theater" (quotation)

Hate Speech: A Dangerous Abuse of Free Speech on Campus (controversial position)

6d   Editing and Proofreading

Once you have revised your drafts to your satisfaction, two final tasks remain: **editing** and **proofreading.**

1   Editing

When you **edit,** you concentrate on grammar and spelling, punctuation and mechanics. Although you have dealt with these issues as you revised previous drafts of your paper, editing is now your primary focus. As you proceed, read each sentence carefully, consulting the items on the editing checklist below. Keep your preliminary notes and drafts and your reference books (such as this handbook and a dictionary) nearby as you work. Some reference works (such as *Dictionary.com* and *Merriam-Webster Online*) are available online.

CHECKLIST
Editing Your Essay

Grammar

❑ Do subjects and verbs agree? (**See 34a.**)

❑ Do pronouns and antecedents agree? (**See 34b.**)

❑ Are verb forms correct? (**See 37a.**)

❑ Are tense, mood, and voice of verbs logical and appropriate? (**See 37b–d.**)

❑ Have you used the appropriate case for each pronoun? (**See 38a–b.**)

❑ Are pronoun references clear and unambiguous? (**See 38c.**)

❑ Are adjectives and adverbs used correctly? (**See Ch. 39.**)

Punctuation

❑ Is end punctuation used correctly? (**See Ch. 45.**)

❑ Are commas used correctly? (**See Ch. 46.**)

❑ Are semicolons used correctly? (**See Ch. 47.**)

❑ Are apostrophes used correctly? (**See Ch. 48.**)

❑ Are quotation marks used where they are required? (**See Ch. 49.**)

❑ Are quotation marks used correctly with other punctuation marks? (**See 49e.**)

❑ Are other punctuation marks—colons, dashes, parentheses, brackets, slashes, and ellipses—used correctly? (**See Ch. 50.**)

Spelling

❑ Are all words spelled correctly? (**See Ch. 51.**)

Mechanics

❑ Is capitalization consistent with standard English usage? (**See Ch. 52.**)

❑ Are italics used correctly? (**See Ch. 53.**)

❑ Are hyphens used where required and placed correctly within and between words? (**See Ch. 54.**)

❑ Are abbreviations used where convention calls for their use? (**See Ch. 55.**)

❑ Are numerals and spelled-out numbers used appropriately? (**See Ch. 56.**)

2 Proofreading

After you have completed your editing, print out a final draft and **proofread,** rereading every word carefully to make sure neither you nor your computer missed any typos or other errors.

Close-Up PROOFREADING STRATEGIES

To help you proofread more effectively, try using these strategies:

• Read your paper aloud.
• Have a friend read your paper aloud to you.
• Read silently word by word, using your finger or a sheet of paper to help you keep your place.
• Read your paper's sentences in reverse order, beginning with the last sentence.

Use the Search or Find command to look for usage errors you commonly make—for instance, confusing *it's* with *its, lay* with *lie, effect* with *affect, their* with *there,* or *too* with *to.* You can also uncover **sexist language** by searching for words like *he, his, him,* or *man.*

See 44f2

Keep in mind that neatness does not equal correctness. The clean text that your computer produces can mask flaws that might otherwise be apparent; for this reason, it is up to you to make sure no spelling errors or typos slip by.

When you have finished proofreading, check to make sure the final typed copy of your paper conforms to your instructor's format requirements.

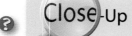

Close-Up USING SPELL CHECKERS AND GRAMMAR CHECKERS

Although spell checkers and grammar checkers can make the process of editing and proofreading your papers easier, they have limitations.

- **Spell Checkers** A spell checker simply identifies strings of letters it does not recognize; it does not distinguish between homophones or spot every typographical error. For example, it does not recognize *there* in "They forgot there books" as incorrect, nor does it identify a typo that produces a correctly spelled word, such as *word* for *work* or *thing* for *think*. Moreover, a spell checker may not recognize every technical term, proper noun, or foreign word you may use.
- **Grammar Checkers** Grammar checkers scan documents for certain features (the number of words in a sentence, for example); however, they are not able to read a document to see if it makes sense. As a result, grammar checkers are not always accurate. For example, they may identify a long sentence as a run-on when it is, in fact, grammatically correct, and they generally advise against using passive voice— even in contexts where it is appropriate. Moreover, grammar checkers do not always supply answers; often, they ask questions—for example, whether *which* should be *that* or whether *which* should be preceded by a comma—that you must answer. In short, grammar checkers can guide your editing and proofreading, but you must be the one who decides when a sentence is (or is not) correct.

6e Preparing a Final Draft

The annotated essay that follows is the final draft of Rebecca James's essay, which you first saw on pages 35–36. It incorporates the suggestions that her peer reviewers and her instructor made on her rough draft.

This final draft is very different from the rough draft of the essay. As she revised, Rebecca provided more examples to illustrate her points. She also moved from a focus on her own experiences using *Wikipedia* to a broader view of the issue, and she revised her thesis statement accordingly. In addition, she added specific information from sources to support her points, including parenthetical documentation and a works-cited list that conform to **MLA** documentation style. Finally, she added a **visual** (accompanied by a caption) to illustrate the specific shortcomings of the *Wikipedia* article she selected for the assignment.

See
Ch. 21

See
6b2

Final Draft

James 1

Rebecca James

Professor Burks

English 101

14 November 2010

Wikipedia: Friend or Foe?

When given a research assignment, students often turn first to *Wikipedia*, the popular free online encyclopedia. With 10,000,000 articles and counting, *Wikipedia* is a valuable source for anyone seeking general information on a topic. For college-level research, however, *Wikipedia* is most valuable when it is used not as an authoritative source but as a gateway to more reliable research sources.

A wiki is an open-source Web site that allows users to edit and add to its content. Derived from a Hawaiian word meaning "quick," the term *wiki* conveys the swiftness and ease with which users can access information on such sites as well as contribute content ("Wiki"). With its slogan "Making Life Easier," *Wikipedia* has become the most popular wiki, providing ever-increasing coverage of topics ranging from contemporary rock bands to obscure scientific and technical concepts. In accordance with the site's policies, users can edit existing articles and add new articles using *Wikipedia*'s editing tools, which do not require specialized programming knowledge or expertise.

Wikipedia offers several benefits to researchers seeking information on a topic. Longer *Wikipedia* articles often include comprehensive abstracts that summarize their content. Articles also often include links to other *Wikipedia* articles. In fact, *Wikipedia*'s internal links, or "wikilinks," are so prevalent that they significantly increase *Wikipedia*'s Web presence. According to a 2007 report by the Pew Internet &

Introduction

Thesis statement

Background on wikis and *Wikipedia*

Benefits of *Wikipedia*

American Life Project, Internet users conducting a *Google* search most frequently click first on the *Wikipedia* link, which usually appears at the top of *Google*'s list of search results (Rainie and Tancer 3). This suggests that most Internet users are satisfied with what they find on *Wikipedia*. In addition, many *Wikipedia* articles contain external links to other print and online sources, including reliable peer-reviewed sources. Finally, because its online format allows users to update its content at any time from any location, *Wikipedia* offers up-to-the-minute coverage of political and cultural events as well as information on popular culture topics that receive little or no attention in other sources. Even when the available information on a particular topic is limited, *Wikipedia* allows users to create "stub" articles, which provide basic information that other users can expand over time. In this way, *Wikipedia* offers an online forum for a developing bank of information on a range of topics.

Benefits of
Wikipedia

Another benefit of *Wikipedia* is that it has the potential to become a reliable and comprehensive database of information. As *Wikipedia*'s "About" page explains, the site's articles "are continually edited and improved over time, and in general, this results in an upward trend of quality and a growing consensus over a fair and balanced representation of information." Using the criteria of accuracy, neutrality, completeness, and style, *Wikipedia* classifies its best articles as "featured" and its second-best articles as "good." In addition, *Wikipedia*'s policy statements indicate that the information in its articles must be verifiable and must be based on documented preexisting research. Although no professional editorial board oversees the development of content within

James 3

Wikipedia, users may be nominated into an editor role that allows them to manage the process by which content is added and updated. Users may also use the "Talk" page to discuss an article's content and make suggestions for improvement. With these control measures in place, some *Wikipedia* articles are comparable to articles in professionally edited online encyclopedias, such as *Encyclopaedia Britannica Online.*

Despite its numerous benefits and its enormous potential, *Wikipedia* is not an authoritative research source. As the site's "Researching with *Wikipedia*" page concedes, "not everything in *Wikipedia* is accurate, comprehensive, or unbiased." Because anyone can create or edit *Wikipedia* articles, they can be factually inaccurate or biased—and they can even be vandalized. Many *Wikipedia* articles, especially those that are underdeveloped, do not supply citations to the sources that support their claims. This absence of source information should lead users to question the articles' reliability. Of course, many underdeveloped *Wikipedia* articles include labels to identify their particular shortcomings—for example, poor grammar or missing documentation. Still, users cannot always determine the legitimacy of information contained in the *Wikipedia* articles they consult.

For college students, *Wikipedia* can provide useful general information and links to helpful resources. For example, accounting students will find that the *Wikipedia* article "Certified Management Accountant" describes the CMA's role in relation to other types of accounting positions. This article can help students in introductory accounting classes to assess the basic differences in focus and responsibilities between a CMA and a CPA, or Certified Public Accountant. The article contains

Drawbacks of *Wikipedia*

Strengths of "CMA" *Wikipedia* entry

James 4

several internal links to related *Wikipedia* articles (including the article "Certified Public Accountant") as well as a list of external links to additional resources (such as the Web site for the Institute of Management Accountants). In comparison, *Encyclopaedia Britannica Online* does not contain an article on CMAs.

Weaknesses of "CMA" *Wikipedia* entry

    Although the *Wikipedia* article on CMAs provides helpful general information about this accounting term, it is limited in terms of its reliability, scope, and style. The top of the article displays three warning labels that identify the article's shortcomings. As fig. 1 illustrates, the article's problems include poor writing and a lack of cited sources. In addition, the article would benefit from more internal links to related *Wikipedia* articles. The specific limitations of the CMA article reinforce the sense that *Wikipedia* is best used not as a source but as a path to more reliable and comprehensive research sources.

Fig. 1. "Certified Management Accountant"; *Wikipedia;* Wikimedia Foundation, 2010; Web; 7 Nov. 2010.

Conclusion

    Like other encyclopedia articles, *Wikipedia* articles should be used only as a starting point for research and as a link to more in-depth sources. Moreover, users should keep in mind that *Wikipedia* articles can include more factual errors, bias, and inconsistencies than professionally edited encyclopedia articles. Although future enhancements to the site may make it more reliable, *Wikipedia* users should understand the current shortcomings of this popular online tool.

James 5

Works Cited

Rainie, Lee, and Bill Tancer. "Wikipedia Users." *Pew Internet & American Life Project*. Pew Research Center, 24 Apr. 2007. Web. 1 Nov. 2010.

"Wiki." *Encyclopaedia Britannica Online*. Encyclopaedia Britannica, 2010. Web. 27 Oct. 2010.

"*Wikipedia*: About." *Wikipedia*. Wikimedia Foundation, 2010. Web. 28 Oct. 2010.

"*Wikipedia*: Researching with *Wikipedia*." *Wikipedia*. Wikimedia Foundation, 2010. Web. 28 Oct. 2010.

CHAPTER 7

Writing Paragraphs

A **paragraph** is a group of related sentences. It may be complete in itself or part of a longer piece of writing.

CHECKLIST
When to Begin a New Paragraph

❏ Begin a new paragraph whenever you move from one major point to another.

❏ Begin a new paragraph whenever you move from one time period or location to another.

❏ Begin a new paragraph whenever you introduce a new step in a process.

❏ Begin a new paragraph when you want to emphasize an important idea.

❏ Begin a new paragraph every time a new person speaks.

❏ Begin a new paragraph to signal the end of your introduction and the beginning of your conclusion.

7a　Writing Unified Paragraphs

A paragraph is **unified** when it develops a single main idea. The **topic sentence** states the main idea of the paragraph, and the other sentences in the paragraph support that idea.

1　Using Topic Sentences

A topic sentence often comes at the beginning of a paragraph. Occasionally, however, a topic sentence may occur at the end of a paragraph, particularly if a writer wants to lead up to an unexpected conclusion.

Topic Sentence at the Beginning　A topic sentence at the beginning of a paragraph tells readers what to expect and helps them to understand your paragraph's main idea immediately.

> I was a listening child, careful to hear the very different sounds of Spanish and English. Wide-eyed with hearing, I'd listen to sounds more than words. First, there were English (*gringo*) sounds. So many words were still unknown that when the butcher or the lady at the drugstore said something to me, exotic polysyllabic sounds would bloom in the midst of their sentences. Often the speech of people in public seemed to me very loud, booming with confidence. The man behind the counter would literally ask, "What can I do for you?" But by being so firm and so clear, the sound of his voice said that he was a *gringo*; he belonged in public society. (Richard Rodriguez, *Aria: Memoir of a Bilingual Childhood*)

Aria: Memoir of a Bilingual Childhood by Richard Rodriguez. Copyright © 1980 by Richard Rodriguez. Originally appeared in *The American Scholar*. Reprinted by permission of Georges Borchardt, Inc., on behalf of the author.

Topic Sentence at the End　A topic sentence at the end of a paragraph is useful if you are presenting an unusual or hard-to-accept idea. By presenting a logical chain of reasoning before you state your main idea in your topic sentence, you are more likely to convince readers that your paragraph's main idea is reasonable.

> These sprays, dusts and aerosols are now applied almost universally to farms, gardens, forests, and homes—nonselective chemicals that have the power to kill every insect, the "good" and the "bad," to still the song of birds and the leaping of fish in the streams, to coat the leaves with a deadly film, and to linger on in soil—all this though the intended target may be only a few weeds or insects. Can anyone believe it is possible to lay down such a barrage of poisons on the surface without making it unfit for life? They should not be called "insecticides," but "biocides." (Rachel Carson, "The Obligation to Endure," *Silent Spring*)

Note:　In some narrative or descriptive paragraphs, a topic sentence may seem forced or unnatural. In these cases, the topic sentence may be implied rather than explicitly stated.

2 Testing for Unity

Each sentence in a paragraph should support the main idea that is stated in the topic sentence. The following paragraph is not unified because it includes sentences that do not support the main idea.

Paragraph Not Unified

One of the first problems I had as a college student was improving my computer skills. All students were required to buy a computer before school started. Throughout the first semester, we took a special course to teach us to use a computer. My laptop has a lot of memory and can do word processing and spreadsheets. It has a large screen and a DVD drive. My parents were happy that I had a computer, but they were concerned about the price. Tuition was high, and when they added in the price of the computer, it was almost out of reach. To offset expenses, I got a part-time job in the school library. (student writer)

> Sentences do not support main idea

When he revised, the writer deleted the sentences about his parents' financial situation and the computer's characteristics and added details related to the main idea.

Revised Paragraph

One of the first problems I had as a college student was improving my computer skills. All first-year students were required to buy a computer before school started. Throughout the first semester, we took a special course to teach us to use the computer. In theory this system sounded fine, but in my case it was a disaster. In the first place, I had never owned my own computer. The closest I had ever come to a computer was the computer I shared with my sister. Besides, I could not type well. To make matters worse, many of the students in my computer orientation course already knew how to work with spreadsheets, presentation software, and wikis. By the end of the first week, I was convinced that I would never be able to keep up with them.

> Sentences now support main idea

7b Writing Coherent Paragraphs

A paragraph is **coherent** when all its sentences clearly relate to one another. You can create coherence by arranging details or ideas according to an organizing principle, by using transitional words and phrases, by using parallel structure, and by repeating key words and phrases.

1 Arranging Details

Even if all its sentences are about the same subject, a paragraph lacks coherence if the sentences are not arranged according to a general organizing principle—that is, if they are not arranged *spatially, chronologically,* or *logically.*

See 7d2

Spatial order establishes the way in which readers will "see" details. For example, an object or scene can be viewed from top to bottom or from near to far. Spatial order is central to **descriptive paragraphs**.

See 7d1, 4

Chronological order presents events in sequence, using transitional words and phrases to establish the time order of events—*at first, yesterday, later, in 1930,* and so on. Chronological order is central to **narrative paragraphs** and **process paragraphs**.

See 7d3, 6

Logical order presents details or ideas in terms of their logical relationships to one another. For example, the ideas in a paragraph may move from *least important to most important.* Transitional words and phrases such as *the most important* and *the least important* or *first, second,* and *finally* establish these relationships and lead readers through the paragraph. Logical order is central to **exemplification paragraphs** and **comparison-and-contrast paragraphs**.

2 Using Transitional Words and Phrases

Transitional words and phrases link sentences by identifying the spatial, chronological, and logical organizing principles discussed above. The following paragraph, which has no transitional words and phrases, illustrates just how important these words and phrases are.

Paragraph without Transitional Words and Phrases

> Napoleon certainly made a change for the worse by leaving his small kingdom of Elba. He went back to Paris, and he abdicated for a second time. He fled to Rochefort in hope of escaping to America. He gave himself up to the English captain of the ship *Bellerophon*. He suggested that the Prince Regent grant him asylum, and he was refused. All he saw of England was the Devon coast and Plymouth Sound as he passed on to the remote island of St. Helena. He died on May 5, 1821, at the age of fifty-two.

In the narrative paragraph above, the topic sentence states the main idea of the paragraph, and the rest of the sentences support this idea. Because of the absence of transitional words and phrases, however, readers cannot tell exactly how one event in the paragraph relates to another in time. Notice how much easier it is to read this passage once transitional words and phrases (such as *after, finally, once again,* and *in the end*) have been added.

Paragraph with Transitional Words and Phrases

Napoleon certainly made a change for the worse by leaving his small kingdom of Elba. After Waterloo, he went back to Paris, and he abdicated for a second time. A hundred days after his return from Elba, he fled to Rochefort in hope of escaping to America. Finally, he gave himself up to the English captain of the ship *Bellerophon*. Once again, he suggested that the Prince Regent grant him asylum, and once again, he was refused. In the end, all he saw of England was the Devon coast and Plymouth Sound as he passed on to the remote island of St. Helena. After six years of exile, he died on May 5, 1821, at the age of fifty-two. (Norman Mackenzie, *The Escape from Elba*)

Frequently Used Transitional Words and Phrases

To Signal Sequence or Addition

again
also
besides
first . . . second . . . third
furthermore
in addition
moreover
one . . . another
too

To Signal Time

afterward
as soon as
at first
at the same time
before
earlier
finally
in the meantime
later
meanwhile
next
now
soon
subsequently
then
until

To Signal Comparison

also
in comparison
in the same way
likewise
moreover
similarly

To Signal Contrast

although
but
despite
even though
however
in contrast

(continued)

Frequently Used Transitional Words and Phrases (*continued*)

instead
meanwhile
nevertheless
nonetheless
on the contrary

on the one hand . . . on the other hand
still
whereas
yet

To Introduce Examples

for example
for instance
namely

in other words
thus

To Signal Narrowing of Focus

after all
indeed
in fact
in other words

in particular
specifically
that is

To Introduce Conclusions or Summaries

as a result
consequently
in conclusion
in other words

in summary
therefore
thus
to conclude

To Signal Concession

admittedly
certainly
granted

naturally
of course

To Introduce Causes or Effects

accordingly
as a result
because
consequently
hence

since
so
then
therefore

See
41c,
43a

3 Using Parallel Structure

Parallelism—the use of matching words, phrases, clauses, or sentence structures to emphasize similar ideas—can increase coherence in a paragraph. Note in the following paragraph how parallel constructions beginning with *He was* link Thomas Jefferson's accomplishments.

Thomas Jefferson was born in 1743 and died at Monticello, Virginia, on July 4, 1826. During his eighty-four years, he accomplished a number of things. Although best known for his draft of the Declaration of Independence, Jefferson was a man of many talents who had a wide intellectual range. He was a patriot who was one of the revolutionary founders of the United States. He was a reformer who, when he was governor of Virginia, drafted the Statute for Religious Freedom. He was an innovator who drafted an ordinance for governing the West and devised the first decimal monetary system. He was a president who abolished internal taxes, reduced the national debt, and made the Louisiana Purchase. And, finally, he was an architect who designed Monticello and the University of Virginia. (student writer)

4 Repeating Key Words and Phrases

Repeating **key words and phrases** throughout a paragraph connects the sentences to one another and to the paragraph's main idea. The following paragraph repeats the key word *mercury* to keep readers focused on the subject.

Mercury poisoning is a problem that has long been recognized. "Mad as a hatter" refers to the condition prevalent among nineteenth-century workers who were exposed to mercury during the manufacturing of felt hats. Workers in many other industries, such as mining, chemicals, and dentistry, were similarly affected. In the 1950s and 1960s, there were cases of mercury poisoning in Minamata, Japan. Research showed that there were high levels of mercury pollution in streams and lakes surrounding the village. In the United States, this problem came to light in 1969, when a New Mexico family got sick from eating food tainted with mercury. Since then, pesticides containing mercury have been withdrawn from the market, and chemical wastes can no longer be dumped into the ocean. (student writer)

Note: The same methods you use to link sentences within paragraphs may also be used to link the paragraphs in an essay.

7c Writing Well-Developed Paragraphs

A paragraph is **well developed** when it includes the **support**—examples, statistics, expert opinion, and so on—that readers need to understand its main idea. Keep in mind that length alone does not determine whether a paragraph is well developed. To determine the amount and kind of support you need, consider your audience, your purpose, and the scope of your paragraph's main idea.

The following paragraph is not adequately developed because it does not include enough support to convince readers that children and parents are "bombarded by ads for violent toys."

Underdeveloped Paragraph

From Thanksgiving until Christmas, children and their parents are bombarded by ads for violent toys and games. Toy manufacturers persist in thinking that only toys that appeal to children's aggressiveness will sell. Despite claims that they (unlike action toys) have educational value, video games have escalated the level of violence. The real question is why parents continue to buy these violent toys and games for their children. (student writer)

When the student writer revised her paragraph, she added specific examples to support her topic sentence.

Revised Paragraph (Examples Added)

From Thanksgiving until Christmas, children and their parents are bombarded by ads for violent toys and games. Toy manufacturers persist in thinking that only toys that appeal to children's aggressiveness will

Examples sell. One television commercial praises the merits of a commando team that attacks and captures a miniature enemy base. Toy soldiers wear realistic uniforms and carry automatic rifles, pistols, knives, grenades, and ammunition. Another commercial shows children playing with cars that turn into robots that shoot missiles and have projectile-launching wings. Despite claims that they (unlike action toys) have educational value,

Examples video games have escalated the level of violence. The most popular video games—such as *Grand Theft Auto* and *Resident Evil 5*—depict graphic violence, criminal behavior, nudity, and other objectionable material. One game allows players to hack up ghosts with a variety of weapons, such as ice picks, swords, and energy beams. Other best-selling games graphically simulate hand-to-hand combat on city streets and feature dismembered bodies and the sound of breaking bones. The real question is why parents continue to buy these violent toys and games for their children.

 ## 7d   Patterns of Paragraph Development

Patterns of paragraph development—*narration, exemplification,* and so on—reflect the way a writer arranges material to express ideas most effectively.

1 Narration

A **narrative** paragraph tells a story by presenting events in chronological (time) order. Most narratives move in a logical, orderly sequence from beginning to end, from first event to last. Clear transitional words and phrases (*later, after that*) and time markers (*in 1990, two years earlier, the next day*) establish the chronological sequence.

My academic career almost ended as soon as it began when, three weeks after I arrived at college, I decided to pledge a fraternity. By midterms, I was wearing a pledge cap and saying "Yes, sir" to every fraternity brother I met. When classes were over, I ran errands for the fraternity members, and after dinner I socialized and worked on projects with the other people in my pledge class. In between these activities, I tried to study. Somehow I managed to write papers, take tests, and attend lectures. By the end of the semester, though, my grades had slipped, and

Topic sentence identifies subject of narrative

Sequence of events

© Philip Gould/Corbis

I was exhausted. It was then that I began to ask myself some important questions. I realized that I wanted to be popular, but not at the expense of my grades and my future career. At the beginning of my second semester, I dropped out of the fraternity and got a job in the biology lab. Looking back, I realize that it was then that I actually began to grow up. (student writer)

FIGURE 7.1 Student in pledge cap; one event in narrative sequence.

2 Description

A **descriptive** paragraph communicates how something looks, sounds, smells, tastes, or feels. The most natural arrangement of details in a description reflects the way you actually look at a person, scene, or object: near to far, top to bottom, side to side, or front to back. This arrangement of details is made clear by transitions that identify precise spatial relationships: *next to, near, beside, under, above,* and so on.

Note: Sometimes a descriptive paragraph does not have a topic sentence. In such cases, it is unified by a **dominant impression**—the effect created by all the details in the description.

© Buddy Mays/Corbis

FIGURE 7.2 Vividly detailed close-up of Blue Morpho butterfly in Costa Rican rainforest.

When you are inside the jungle, away from the river, the trees vault out of sight. It is hard to remember to look up the long trunks and see the fans, strips, fronds, and sprays of glossy leaves. Inside the jungle you are more likely to notice the snarl of climbers and creepers round the trees' boles, the flowering bromeliads and epiphytes in every bough's crook, and the fantastic silk-cotton tree trunks thirty or forty feet across, trunks buttressed in flanges of wood whose curves can make

Details convey dominant impression

three high walls of a room—a shady, loamy-aired room where you would gladly live, or die. Butterflies, iridescent blue, striped, or clear-winged, thread the jungle paths at eye level. And at your feet is a swath of ants bearing triangular bits of green leaf. The ants with their leaves look like a wide fleet of sailing dinghies—but they don't quit. In either direction they wobble over the jungle floor as far as the eye can see. I followed them off the path as far as I dared, and never saw an end to ants or to those luffing chips of green they bore. (Annie Dillard, "In the Jungle")

3 Exemplification

An **exemplification** paragraph supports a topic sentence with a series of examples (or, sometimes, with a single extended example). These examples can be drawn from personal observation, experience, or research.

Topic sentence identifies paragraph's main idea

Series of examples

Illiterates cannot travel freely. When they attempt to do so, they encounter risks that few of us can dream of. They cannot read traffic signs and, while they often learn to recognize and to decipher symbols, they cannot manage street names which they haven't seen before. The same is true for bus and subway stops. While ingenuity can sometimes help a man or woman to discern directions from familiar landmarks, buildings, cemeteries, churches, and the like, most illiterates are virtually immobilized. They seldom wander past the streets and neighborhoods they know. Geographical paralysis becomes a bitter metaphor for their entire existence. They are immobilized in almost every sense we can imagine. They can't move up. They can't move out. They cannot see beyond. Illiterates may take an oral test for drivers' permits in most sections of America. It is a questionable concession. Where will they go? How will they get there? How will they get home? Could it be that some of us might like it better if they stayed where they belong? (Jonathan Kozol, *Illiterate America*)

Art Montes De Oca/Taxi/Getty Images

FIGURE 7.3 Street signs illustrate one area of confusion for illiterates.

4 Process

Process paragraphs describe how something works, presenting a series of steps in strict chronological order. The topic sentence identifies the process, and the rest of the paragraph presents the steps. Transitional words such as *first, then, next, after this,* and *finally* link steps in the process.

Topic sentence identifies process

Steps in process

Members of the court have disclosed, however, the general way the conference is conducted. It begins at ten A.M. and usually runs on until late afternoon. At the start each justice, when he enters the room, shakes hands with all others there (thirty-six handshakes altogether). The custom, dating back generations, is evidently designed to begin the meeting at a friendly level, no matter how heated the intellectual differences may be. The conference takes up, first, the applications for review—a few appeals, many more petitions for certiorari. Those on the Appellate Docket, the regular paid cases, are considered first, then the pauper's applications on the Miscella-

neous Docket. (If any of these are granted, they are then transferred to the Appellate Docket.) After this the justices consider, and vote on, all the cases argued during the preceding Monday through Thursday. These are tentative votes, which may be and quite often are changed as the opinion is written and the problem thought through more deeply. There may be further discussion at later conferences before the opinion is handed down. (Anthony Lewis, *Gideon's Trumpet*)

FIGURE 7.4 US Supreme Court justices after final step in process (handing down opinion in *Gideon v. Wainwright*, November 1962).

Bettmann/Corbis

Close-Up   INSTRUCTIONS

When a process paragraph presents **instructions** to enable readers to actually perform the process, it is written in the present tense and in the imperative mood—"*Remove* the cover . . . and *check* the valve."

5 Cause and Effect

A **cause-and-effect** paragraph explores causes or predicts or describes results; sometimes a single cause-and-effect paragraph does both. Clear, specific transitional words and phrases such as *one cause, another cause, a more important result, because,* and *as a result* convey the cause-and-effect relationships.

Paragraphs that examine causes explain why something happens or happened.

The main reason that a young baby sucks his thumb seems to be that he hasn't had enough sucking at the breast or bottle to satisfy his sucking needs. Dr. David Levy pointed out that babies who are fed every 3 hours don't suck their thumbs as much as babies fed every 4 hours, and that babies who have cut down on nursing time from 20 minutes to 10 minutes . . . are more likely to suck their thumbs than babies who still have to work for 20 minutes. Dr. Levy fed a litter of puppies with a medicine dropper so that they had no

Topic sentence establishes major cause

Cause explored in detail

FIGURE 7.5 Baby sucking thumb.

Richard Nowitz/Corbis

chance to suck during their feedings. They acted just the same as babies who don't get enough chance to suck at feeding time. They sucked their own and each other's paws and skin so hard that the fur came off. (Benjamin Spock, *Baby and Child Care*)

Paragraphs that focus on effects explain how a change is or was the result of a specific set of causes or actions.

Topic sentence establishes major effect

On December 8, 1941, the day after the Japanese attack on Pearl Harbor in Hawaii, my grandfather barricaded himself with his family—my grandmother, my teenage mother, her two sisters and two brothers—inside of his home in La'ie, a sugar plantation village on Oahu's North Shore. This was my maternal grandfather, a man most villagers called by his last name, Kubota. It could mean either "Wayside Field" or else "Broken Dreams," depending on which ideograms he used. Kubota ran La'ie's general store, and the previous night, after a long day of bad news on the radio, some locals had come by, pounded on the front door, and made threats. One was said to have brandished a machete. They were angry and shocked, as the whole nation was in the aftermath of the surprise attack. Kubota was one of the few Japanese Americans in the village and president of the local Japanese language school. He had become a target for their rage and suspicion. A wise man, he locked all his doors and windows and did not open his store the next day, but stayed closed and waited for news from some official. (Garrett Hongo, "Kubota")

Discussion of other effects

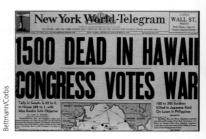
Bettmann/Corbis

FIGURE 7.6 Headline announcing attack on Pearl Harbor.

6 Comparison and Contrast

Comparison-and-contrast paragraphs examine the similarities and differences between two subjects. **Comparison** focuses on similarities; **contrast** emphasizes differences. Comparison-and-contrast paragraphs can be organized in one of two ways: **point-by-point** or **subject-by-subject.**

Point-by-point comparisons discuss two subjects together, alternating points about one subject with comparable points about the other.

Topic sentence establishes comparison

Alternating points about the two subjects

There are two Americas. One is the America of Lincoln and Adlai Stevenson; the other is the America of Teddy Roosevelt and the modern super-patriots. One is generous and humane, the other narrowly egotistical; one is self-critical, the other self-righteous; one is sensible, the other romantic; one is good-humored, the other solemn; one is inquiring, the other pontificating; one is moderate, the other filled with passionate intensity; one is judicious and the other arrogant in the use of great power. (J. William Fulbright, *The Arrogance of Power*)

FIGURE 7.7 Abraham Lincoln (left) and Theodore Roosevelt (right) symbolize the contrast between the two Americas.

Subject-by-subject comparisons treat one subject completely and then move on to the other subject. In the following paragraph, notice how the writer shifts from one subject to the other with the transitional word *however*.

FIGURE 7.8 Man using mute button to halt conversation (illustrates contrast between conversation styles of men and women).

First, it is important to note that men and women regard conversation quite differently. For women it is a passion, a sport, an activity even more important to life than eating because it doesn't involve weight gain. The first sign of closeness among women is when they find themselves engaging in endless, secretless rounds of conversation with one another. And as soon as a woman begins to relax and feel comfortable in a relationship with a man, she tries to have that type of conversation with him as well. However, the first sign that a man is feeling close to a woman is when he admits that he'd rather she please quiet down so he can hear the TV. A man who feels truly intimate with a woman often reserves for her and her alone the precious gift of one-word answers. Everyone knows that the surest way to spot a successful long-term relationship is to look around a restaurant for the table where no one is talking. Ah . . . now that's real love. (Merrill Markoe, "Men, Women, and Conversation")

Topic sentence establishes comparison

First subject discussed

Second subject introduced

7 Division and Classification

Division paragraphs take a single item and break it into its component parts.

FIGURE 7.9 Components of blood—blood cells and platelets—in vein.

The blood can be divided into four distinct components: plasma, red cells, white cells, and platelets. One component, plasma, is ninety percent water and holds a great number of substances in suspension. It contains proteins, sugars, fat, and inorganic salts. Plasma also contains urea and other by-products from the breaking down of proteins, hormones, enzymes,

Topic sentence identifies categories

Categories discussed

and dissolved gases. The red cells, another component of blood, give blood its distinctive color. The red cells are most numerous; they get oxygen from the lungs and release it in the tissues. The less numerous white cells are a component of blood that defends the body against invading organisms. Finally, the platelets, which occur in almost the same number as white cells, are responsible for clotting. (student writer)

Classification paragraphs take many separate items and group them into categories according to qualities or characteristics they share.

Topic sentence establishes categories

Charles Babbage, an English mathematician, reflecting in 1830 on what he saw as the decline of science at the time, distinguished among three major kinds of scientific fraud. He called the first "forging," by which he meant complete fabrication—the recording of observations that were never made. The second category he called "trimming"; this consists of manipulating

Categories discussed

the data to make them look better,

© 2008 Harvard University, Peabody Museum 97=39=70/72853 N1383

FIGURE 7.10 The FeJee mermaid illustrates "forging," one of three categories of scientific fraud.

or, as Babbage wrote, "clipping off little bits here and there from those observations which differ most in excess from the mean and in sticking them on to those which are too small." His third category was data selection, which he called "cooking"—the choosing of those data that fitted the researcher's hypothesis and the discarding of those that did not. To this day, the serious discussion of scientific fraud has not improved on Babbage's typology. (Morton Hunt, *New York Times Magazine*)

8 Definition

Definition paragraphs develop a definition by means of other patterns—for instance, defining *happiness* by telling a story (narration) or defining a diesel engine by telling how it works (process). The following definition paragraph is developed by means of exemplification: it begins with a straightforward definition of *gadget* and then cites an example.

Topic sentence gives general definition

A gadget is nearly always novel in design or concept and it often has no proper name. For example, the semaphore which signals the arrival of the mail in our rural mailbox certainly has no proper name. It is a contrivance consisting of a

Definition expanded with an example

piece of shingle. Call it what you like, it saves us frequent frustrating trips to the mailbox in winter when you have to dress up and wade through snow to get there. That's a gadget! (*Smithsonian*)

Alain Schein Photography/Corbis

FIGURE 7.11 Rural mailbox with semaphore (term defined by exemplification).

7e Writing Special Kinds of Paragraphs

So far, this chapter has focused on **body paragraphs,** the paragraphs that carry the weight of your essay's discussion. Other kinds of paragraphs—*transitional paragraphs, introductory paragraphs,* and *concluding paragraphs*—have special functions in an essay.

1 Transitional Paragraphs

A **transitional paragraph** connects one section of the essay to another. Writers often use transitional paragraphs to summarize what they have already said before they move on to a new point. The following transitional paragraph uses a series of questions to sum up some of the ideas the writer has been discussing. In the next part of his essay, he goes on to answer these questions.

> Can we bleed off the mass of humanity to other worlds? Right now the number of human beings on Earth is increasing by 80 million per year, and each year that number goes up by 1 and a fraction percent. Can we really suppose that we can send 80 million people per year to the Moon, Mars, and elsewhere, and engineer those worlds to support those people? And even so, nearly remain in the same place ourselves? (Isaac Asimov, "The Case against Man")

2 Introductory Paragraphs

An **introductory paragraph** prepares readers for the essay to follow. It typically introduces the subject, narrows it, and then states the essay's thesis.

> Christine was just a girl in one of my classes. I never knew much about her except that she was strange. She didn't talk much. Her hair was dyed black and purple, and she wore heavy black boots and a black turtleneck sweater, even in the summer. She was attractive—in spite of the ring she wore through her left eyebrow—but she never seemed to care what the rest of us thought about her. Like the rest of my classmates, I didn't really want to get close to her. It was only when we were assigned to do our chemistry project together that I began to understand why Christine dressed the way she did. (student writer)

To arouse their audience's interest, writers may vary this direct approach by using one of the following introductory strategies.

Strategies for Effective Introductions

Quotation or Series of Quotations

When Mary Cassatt's father was told of her decision to become a painter, he said: "I would rather see you dead." When Edgar Degas saw a show of Cassatt's etchings, his response was: "I am not willing to admit that a woman can draw that well." When she returned to Philadelphia after twenty-eight years abroad, having achieved renown as an Impressionist painter and the esteem of Degas, Huysmans, Pissarro, and Berthe Morisot, the *Philadelphia Ledger* reported: "Mary Cassatt, sister of Mr. Cassatt, president of the Pennsylvania Railroad, returned from Europe yesterday. She has been studying painting in France and owns the smallest Pekingese dog in the world." (Mary Gordon, "Mary Cassatt")

Question or Series of Questions

Of all the disputes agitating the American campus, the one that seems to me especially significant is that over "the canon." What should be taught in the humanities and social sciences, especially in introductory courses? What is the place of the classics? How shall we respond to those professors who attack "Eurocentrism" and advocate "multiculturalism"? This is not the sort of tedious quarrel that now and then flutters through the academy; it involves matters of public urgency. I propose to see this dispute, at first, through a narrow, even sectarian lens, with the hope that you will come to accept my reasons for doing so. (Irving Howe, "The Value of the Canon")

Definition

Moles are collections of cells that can appear on any part of the body. With occasional exceptions, moles are absent at birth. They first appear in the early years of life, between ages two and six. Frequently, moles appear at puberty. New moles, however, can continue to appear throughout life. During pregnancy, new moles may appear and old ones darken. There are three major designations of moles, each with its own unique distinguishing characteristics. (student writer)

Controversial Statement

Many Americans would probably be surprised to learn that Head Start has not been an unqualified success. Founded in 1965, the Head Start program provides early childhood education, social services, and medical check-ups to poor children across the US. In recent years, it has also focused on the children of migrant workers and on children who are homeless. For the most part, Americans view Head Start not just as a success but also as a model for other social programs.

What many people do not know, however, is that although Head Start is a short-term success for many children, the ambitious long-term goals of the program have not been met. For example, studies have shown that children who participate in Head Start do not see long-term increases in IQ or in academic achievement. For this reason, it may be time to consider making significant changes in the way Head Start is run. (student writer)

Close-Up INTRODUCTORY PARAGRAPHS

- Avoid introductions that begin by announcing your subject ("In my paper, I will talk about Lady Macbeth").
- Avoid introductions that undercut your credibility ("I don't know much about alternative energy sources, but I would like to present my opinion about the subject").
- Avoid introductions that discuss the difficulty of the topic ("I had trouble deciding what to write about, but I finally . . .").

CHECKLIST
Writing Effective Introductions

After you draft your introduction, check its effectiveness by asking the following questions:

❑ Does your introductory paragraph include a thesis statement?
❑ Does it lead naturally into the body of your essay?
❑ Does it create interest?
❑ Does it avoid statements that undercut your credibility?

3 Concluding Paragraphs

A **concluding paragraph** typically begins with specifics—reviewing the essay's main points, for example—and then moves to more general comments. Whenever possible, it should end with a sentence that readers will remember.

Keep in mind that an effective conclusion does not simply restate what was said in the introduction. It presents information in the context of what you have said in the body of your essay. Because your conclusion brings your essay to a close, it should never introduce new points or pursue new lines of thought.

> As an Arab-American, I feel I have the best of two worlds. I'm proud to be part of the melting pot, proud to contribute to the tremendous diversity of cultures, customs and traditions that makes this country unique. But Arab-bashing—public acceptance of hatred and bigotry—is something no American can be proud of. (Ellen Mansoor Collier, "I Am Not a Terrorist")

Writers may use any of the following concluding strategies to sum up their essay's ideas.

Strategies for Effective Conclusions

Prediction

Looking ahead, [we see that] prospects may not be quite as dismal as they seem. As a matter of fact, we are not doing so badly. It is something of a miracle that creatures who evolved as nomads in an intimate, small-band, wide-open-spaces context manage to get along at all as villagers or surrounded by strangers in cubicle apartments. Considering that our genius as a species is adaptability, we may yet learn to live closer and closer to one another, if not in utter peace, then far more peacefully than we do today. (John Pheiffer, "Seeking Peace, Making War")

Warning

The Internet is the twenty-first century's talking drum, the very kind of grassroots communication tool that has been such a powerful source of education and culture for our people since slavery. But this talking drum we have not yet learned to play. Unless we master the new information technology to build and deepen the forms of social connection that a tragic history has eroded, African-Americans will face a form of cyberseg-regation in the next century as devastating to our aspirations as Jim Crow segregation was to those of our ancestors. But this time, the fault will be our own. (Henry Louis Gates Jr., "One Internet, Two Nations")

From The New York Times, October 31, 1999. Reprinted by permission of Janklow & Nesbit, on behalf of the author.

Recommendation for Action

Computers have revolutionized learning in ways that we have barely begun to appreciate. We have experienced enough, however, to rec-ognize the need to change our thinking about our purposes, methods, and outcome of higher education. Rather than resisting or postponing change, we need to anticipate and learn from it. We must harness the technology and use it to educate our students more effectively than we have been doing. Otherwise, we will surrender our authority to those who can. (Peshe Kuriloff, "If John Dewey Were Alive Today, He'd Be a Webhead")

Quotation

Apart from what any critic had to say about my writing, I knew I had succeeded where it counted when my mother finished reading my book and gave me her verdict: "So easy to read." (Amy Tan, "Mother Tongue")

Close-Up CONCLUDING PARAGRAPHS

- Don't waste time repeating sentences from your introduction in different words.
- Don't apologize or undercut your credibility ("Of course, I am not an expert" or "At least, this is my opinion").
- Don't introduce any new points or go off in new directions.

CHECKLIST
Writing Effective Conclusions

After you draft your conclusion, check its effectiveness by asking the following questions:

❑ Does your concluding paragraph sum up your essay, perhaps by reinforcing the essay's main points?

❑ Does it do more than just repeat the introduction's wording?

❑ Does it avoid introducing new points?

❑ Does it avoid apologies?

❑ Does it end memorably?

Critical Thinking and Argumentation

PART **2**

Critical Thinking and Argumentation

❓ Frequently Asked Questions

CHAPTER 8

Thinking Critically

As you read (and write) essays, you should carefully consider the strengths and weaknesses of the ideas they present. This is especially true in **argumentative essays**—those that take a stand on a debatable topic.

See Ch. 9

Although many writers try to be fair, others attempt to manipulate readers by using emotionally charged language, by unfairly emphasizing certain facts over others, and by intentionally using flawed logic. For this reason, it is important that you **think critically** when you read (and when you write). Specifically, you need to distinguish fact from opinion, evaluate supporting evidence, detect bias, evaluate visuals, and understand the basic principles of inductive and deductive reasoning.

8a Distinguishing Fact from Opinion

A **fact** is a verifiable statement that something is true or that something occurred. An **opinion** is a personal judgment or belief that can never be substantiated beyond any doubt and is, therefore, debatable.

Fact: Measles is a potentially deadly disease.

Opinion: All children should be vaccinated against measles.

An opinion may be supported or unsupported.

Unsupported Opinion: All children in Pennsylvania should be vaccinated against measles.

Supported Opinion: Despite the fact that an effective measles vaccine is widely available, several unvaccinated Pennsylvania children have died of measles each year since 1992. States that have instituted vaccination programs have had no deaths in the same time period. For this reason, all children in Pennsylvania should be vaccinated against measles.

Note: Keep in mind that support can only make a statement more convincing; it cannot turn an opinion into a fact.

Opinions can be supported with **examples, statistics,** or **expert opinion.**

Examples
The American Civil Liberties Union is an organization that has been unfairly characterized as left wing. It is true that it has opposed prayer in the public schools, defended conscientious objectors, and challenged police methods of conducting questioning and searches of suspects. However, it has also backed the antiabortion group Operation Rescue in a police brutality suit and presented a legal brief in support of a Republican politician accused of violating an ethics law.

Statistics
A recent National Institute of Mental Health study concluded that mentally ill people account for more than 30 percent of the homeless population (Young 27). Because so many homeless people have psychiatric disabilities, the federal government should expand the state mental hospital system.

Expert Opinion
No soldier ever really escapes the emotional consequences of war. As William Manchester, noted historian and World War II combat veteran, observes in his essay "Okinawa: The Bloodiest Battle of All," "the invisible wounds remain" (72).

8b Evaluating Supporting Evidence

The examples, statistics, or expert opinion a writer uses to support a statement is called **evidence.** The more compelling the supporting evidence, the more likely readers will be to accept a statement.

Strong evidence convincingly supports a statement or assertion, while **weak evidence** does little to persuade readers that a point is worth considering. In general, evidence is strong if it is *accurate, sufficient, representative, relevant, authoritative,* and *documented.*

- Evidence is **accurate** if it comes from a reliable source. Such a source quotes exactly and does not present remarks out of context. It also presents examples, statistics, and expert testimony fairly, drawing them from other reliable sources.
- Evidence is **sufficient** if a writer presents an adequate amount of information. It is not enough, for instance, for a writer to cite just one example in an attempt to demonstrate that most poor women do not receive adequate prenatal care. Similarly, the opinions of just a single expert, no matter how reputable, are not enough to support this position.
- Evidence is **representative** if it reflects a fair range of sources and viewpoints. Writers should not just choose evidence that supports their position and ignore evidence that does not. For example, a writer who is

making the point that the United States Congress should pass a bill that grants limited amnesty to undocumented immigrants should not just present support from people who agree with this position. The writer should also address the arguments against this position and point out their weaknesses or inaccuracies.

- Evidence is **relevant** if it specifically applies to the case being discussed. For example, a writer cannot support the position that increased airport security in Europe has discouraged terrorist attacks by citing examples from US airports.
- Evidence is **authoritative** if it comes from experts. In other words, evidence should come from books, periodicals, and Web sites written by people who are generally recognized as experts in a particular field. Personal experience can also serve as evidence if the writer has special insight into the issue or problem being discussed.
- Evidence is **documented** if it is accompanied by the information readers need to identify its source. By supplying this source information, writers help readers determine whether the evidence is credible and whether the writer is trustworthy. (**See Parts 5–6** of this handbook for a discussion of different documentation formats.)

8c Detecting Bias

Bias is the tendency to base conclusions on preconceived ideas rather than on evidence. As a critical reader, you should be aware that bias may sometimes lead writers to see what they want to see and therefore to select only that evidence that supports their own positions.

Close-Up   DETECTING BIAS

When you read, check carefully to detect bias:

- **The Writer's Stated Beliefs** If a writer declares himself or herself to be skeptical about global warming, this statement should alert you to the possibility that the writer may not present a balanced view of the subject.
- **Sexist or Racist Statements** A writer who refers to all engineers as male or all nurses as female reflects a clear bias. Similarly, a researcher who assumes that certain racial or ethnic groups are intellectually superior to others is also likely to present a biased view.

(continued)

DETECTING BIAS (continued)

- **Slanted Language** Some writers use **slanted language**—language that contains value judgments—to influence readers' reactions. For example, "The senator gave an impassioned speech" gives one impression; "The senator delivered a diatribe" gives another.
- **Biased Tone** The tone of a piece of writing indicates a writer's attitude toward readers or toward his or her subject. An angry or sarcastic tone might indicate that the writer is not presenting his or her case fairly.
- **Biased Choice of Evidence** A writer's choice of examples and statistics should be balanced. When they are not, they reveal the writer's bias. For instance, a writer may include only examples that support a point and leave out examples that contradict it.
- **Biased Choice of Experts** A writer should cite experts who represent a fair range of opinion. If, for instance, a writer assessing a state government's policy on same-sex marriage includes only statements by experts who oppose this issue, he or she is presenting a biased case.

8d   Understanding Inductive Reasoning

Argumentative essays rely primarily on **logic.** Logical reasoning enables you to construct arguments that reach conclusions in a persuasive and systematic way. Before you can evaluate or write arguments, you should understand the basic principles of **inductive** and **deductive** reasoning.

1 Moving from Specific to General

Inductive reasoning moves from specific facts, observations, or experiences to a general conclusion. You can see how inductive reasoning operates by studying the following list of statements that focus on the relationship between SAT scores and admissions at one liberal arts college:

- The SAT is a requirement for all applicants.
- High school grades and rank in class are also examined.
- Nonacademic factors, such as sports, activities, and interests, are taken into account as well.
- Special attention is given to the applications of athletes, minorities, and children of alumni.
- Fewer than 52 percent of applicants for a recent class with SAT verbal scores between 600 and 700 were accepted.
- Fewer than 39 percent of applicants with similar math scores were accepted.
- Approximately 18 percent of applications with SAT verbal scores between 450 and 520 and about 19 percent of applicants with similar SAT math scores were admitted.

After reading the specific statements above, you could use inductive reasoning to reach the general conclusion that although they are important, SAT scores are not the single factor that determines whether a student is admitted to this college.

2 Making Inferences

No matter how much evidence is presented, an inductive conclusion is never certain, only probable. To reach an inductive conclusion a writer must make an **inference,** a conclusion about the unknown based on the known.

In order to bridge the gap that exists between the specific observations and the general conclusion, readers have to make an **inductive leap.** If enough specific evidence is presented, this gap will be relatively small, and readers will readily accept the conclusion. If the gap is too big, readers will see the conclusion as a <u>hasty generalization</u> and will not accept it.

See 8f

8e Understanding Deductive Reasoning

1 Moving from General to Specific

Deductive reasoning moves from a generalization believed to be true or self-evident to a more specific conclusion. The process of deduction has traditionally been illustrated with a **syllogism,** a three-part set of statements or propositions that includes a **major premise,** a **minor premise,** and a **conclusion.**

> **Major Premise:** All books from that store are new.
>
> **Minor Premise:** These books are from that store.
>
> **Conclusion:** Therefore, these books are new.

The **major premise** of a syllogism makes a general statement that the writer believes to be true. The **minor premise** presents a specific example of the belief that is stated in the major premise. If the reasoning is sound, the **conclusion** should follow from the two premises. (Note that the conclusion contains no terms that have not already appeared in the major and minor premises.) The strength of a deductive argument is that if readers accept the premises, they must grant the conclusion.

Note: When you write an argumentative essay, you can use a syllogism during the planning stage (to test the validity of your points), or you can use it as a revision strategy (to test your logic). In either case, the syllogism enables you to express your deductive argument in its most basic form and to see whether it makes sense.

2 Constructing Sound Syllogisms

A syllogism is **valid** (or logical) when its conclusion follows from its premises. A syllogism is **true** when it makes accurate claims—that is, when the information it contains is consistent with the facts. To be **sound,** a syllogism must be both valid and true. However, a syllogism may be valid without being true or true without being valid. The syllogism below, for example, is valid but not true.

> **Major Premise:** All politicians are male.
>
> **Minor Premise:** Senator Barbara Boxer is a politician.
>
> **Conclusion:** Therefore, Senator Barbara Boxer is male.

As odd as it may seem, this syllogism is valid. In the major premise, the phrase *all politicians* establishes that the entire class *politicians* is male. After Barbara Boxer is identified as a politician, the conclusion that she is male automatically follows—but, of course, she is not. Because the major premise of this syllogism is not true, no conclusion based on it can be true. Even though the logic of the syllogism is correct, its conclusion is not. Therefore, the syllogism is not sound.

3 Recognizing Enthymemes

An **enthymeme** is a syllogism in which one of the premises—often the major premise—is unstated. Enthymemes often occur as sentences containing words that signal conclusions—*therefore, consequently, for this reason, for, so, since,* or *because.*

> Melissa is on the Dean's List; therefore, Melissa is a good student.

The preceding sentence contains the minor premise and the conclusion of a syllogism. The reader must fill in the missing major premise in order to complete the syllogism and see whether or not the reasoning is logical.

> **Major Premise:** All those on the Dean's List are good students.
>
> **Minor Premise:** Melissa is on the Dean's List.
>
> **Conclusion:** Therefore, Melissa is a good student.

Note: Bumper stickers often take the form of enthymemes, stating just a conclusion ("Eating meat is murder") and leaving readers to supply both the major and minor premises. Careful readers, however, are not so easily fooled. They supply the missing premise (or premises), and then determine if the resulting syllogism is sound.

8f Recognizing Logical Fallacies

Fallacies are flawed arguments. A writer who inadvertently uses logical fallacies is not thinking clearly or logically; a writer who intentionally uses them is trying to deceive readers. Learn to recognize fallacies—to challenge them when you read and to avoid them when you write.

Logical Fallacies

- **Hasty Generalization** Drawing a conclusion based on too little evidence
  The person I voted for is not doing a good job in Congress. Therefore, voting is a waste of time. (One disappointing experience does not warrant the statement that you will never vote again.)

- **Sweeping Generalization** Making a generalization that cannot be supported no matter how much evidence is supplied
  Everyone should exercise. (Some people, for example those with severe heart conditions, might not benefit from exercise.)

- **Equivocation** Shifting the meaning of a key word or phrase during an argument
  It is not in the public interest for the public to lose interest in politics. (Although clever, the shift in the meaning of the term *public interest* clouds the issue.)

- **Non Sequitur (Does Not Follow)** Arriving at a conclusion that does not logically follow from what comes before it
  Kim Williams is a good lawyer, so she will make a good senator. (Kim Williams may be a good lawyer, but it does not necessarily follow that she will make a good senator.)

- **Either/Or Fallacy** Treating a complex issue as if it has only two sides
  Either we institute universal health care, or the health of all Americans will be at risk. (Good health does not necessarily depend on universal health care.)

- **Post Hoc** Establishing an unjustified link between cause and effect
  The United States sells wheat to China. This must be what caused the price of wheat to rise. (Other factors, unrelated to the sale, could have caused the price of wheat to rise.)

(continued)

Logical Fallacies (*continued*)

- **Begging the Question** (*circular reasoning*) Stating a debatable premise as if it were true

  Research on cloning should be banned because nothing good can come from something inherently evil. (Where is the evidence that cloning is "inherently evil"?)

- **False Analogy** Assuming that because things are similar in some ways, they are similar in other ways

  When forced to live in crowded conditions, people act like rats. They turn on each other and act violently. (Both people and rats might dislike living in crowded conditions, but unlike rats, people do not necessarily resort to violence in this situation.)

- **Red Herring** Changing the subject to distract readers from the issue

  Our company may charge high prices, but we give a lot to charity each year. (What does charging high prices have to do with giving to charity?)

- **Argument to Ignorance** Saying that something is true because it cannot be proved false, or vice versa

  How can you tell me to send my child to a school where there is a child who has AIDS? After all, doctors can't say for sure that my child won't catch AIDS, can they? (Just because a doctor cannot prove the speaker's claim to be false, it does not follow that the claim is true.)

- **Bandwagon** Trying to establish that something is true because everyone believes it is true

  Everyone knows that eating candy makes children hyperactive. (Where is the evidence to support this claim?)

- **Argument to the Person** (*Ad Hominem*) Attacking the person and not the issue

  Of course the former Vice President supports drilling for oil in the Arctic. He worked for an oil company. (By attacking his opponent, the speaker attempts to sidestep the issue.)

- **Argument to the People** (*Ad Populum*) Suggesting that because most people believe something, it must be true

  Since most people believe in global warming, it must be a threat. (By appealing to popular sentiment, the speaker attempts to distract the audience from the issue.)

CHECKLIST

Thinking Critically

❏ Are the writer's points supported primarily by fact or by opinion?

❏ Does the writer offer supporting evidence for his or her opinions?

❏ What kind of evidence is provided? How convincing is it?

❏ Is the evidence accurate? sufficient? representative? relevant? authoritative? documented?

❏ Does the writer display any bias? If so, is the bias revealed through language, tone, or choice of evidence?

❏ Does the writer present a balanced picture of the issue?

❏ Are any alternative viewpoints overlooked?

❏ Does the writer omit pertinent examples?

❏ Does the writer use logical reasoning?

❏ Does the writer use any logical fallacies?

❏ Does the writer oversimplify complex ideas?

❏ Does the writer make reasonable inferences?

❏ Does the writer represent the ideas of others accurately? fairly?

ESL TIP

In many cultures, people present arguments in order to persuade others to believe something. However, the rules for constructing such arguments are different in different cultures. In US academic settings, writers are discouraged from using the types of arguments outlined in section **8f** because they are not considered fair.

CHAPTER **9**

Writing Argumentative Essays

For most people, the true test of their critical thinking skills comes when they write an **argumentative essay,** one that takes a stand on an issue and uses logic and evidence to convince readers. When you write an argument, you follow the same process you use when you write any <u>essay</u>. However, because the purpose of an argument is to change the way readers think, you need to use some additional strategies to present your ideas to your audience.

See Chs. 4–6

9a Planning an Argumentative Essay

1 Choosing a Topic

As with any type of essay, choosing the right topic for your argumentative essay is important. First, you should choose a topic that you already know something about. The more you know about your topic, the easier it will be to gather the information you need to write your argumentative essay. You should also choose a topic that interests and challenges you, one in which you have an emotional and intellectual stake.

It stands to reason that the more you care about a topic, the more enthusiastically you will pursue it. Still, you should be willing to consider other people's viewpoints—even those that contradict your own beliefs. If you find that you cannot be open-minded, you should consider choosing another topic. Remember, in order to be persuasive, you will have to demonstrate to readers that your position is fair and that you have considered both the strengths and the weaknesses of opposing arguments.

Your topic should also be narrow enough so that you can write about it within the assigned page limit. If your topic is too broad, you will not be able to treat it in enough detail. Finally, your topic should be interesting to your readers. Keep in mind that some topics—such as "The Need for Gun Control" or "The Fairness of the Death Penalty"—have been discussed and written about so often that you may not be able to say anything new or interesting about them. Instead of relying on an overused topic, choose one that enables you to contribute something to the debate.

2 Taking a Stand

See 5b

After you have chosen a topic, your next step is to **take a stand**—to state your position in the form of a **thesis statement**. Properly worded, this thesis statement lays the foundation for the rest of your argument.

Now, you need to make sure that your thesis is **debatable**—that it presents an idea that at least some people will object to. A **factual statement**—a verifiable assertion about which reasonable people do *not* disagree—is not suitable as a thesis for an argumentative essay.

CHECKLIST
Developing an Effective Thesis

To make sure you have an effective thesis for your argumentative essay, ask the following questions:

❏ Does your thesis make clear to readers what position you are taking?

❏ Is your thesis one with which reasonable people might disagree?

❏ Can you formulate an antithesis?

❏ Can your thesis be supported by evidence?

Fact: First-year students are not required to purchase a meal plan from the university.

Thesis Statement: First-year students should not be required to purchase a meal plan from the university.

One way to make sure that your thesis statement actually is debatable is to formulate an **antithesis,** a statement that takes the opposite position. If you can state an antithesis, you can be certain that your thesis statement is debatable.

Thesis Statement: Term limits would improve government by bringing people with fresh ideas into office every few years.

Antithesis: Term limits would harm government because elected officials would always be inexperienced.

3 Defining Your Terms

You should always define the most significant terms you use in your argument—especially any key terms you use in your thesis statement. After all, the soundness of an entire argument may hinge on the definition of a word that may mean one thing to one person and another thing to someone else. For example, in the United States, *democratic* elections involve the selection of government officials by popular vote; in other countries, the word *democratic* may be used to describe elections in which only one candidate is running or in which all candidates represent the same party. For this reason, if your argument hinges on a key term like *democratic,* you should make sure that your readers know exactly what you mean.

Close-Up USING PRECISE LANGUAGE

Be careful to use precise language in your thesis statement. Avoid vague and judgmental words, such as *wrong, bad, good, right,* and *immoral.*

Vague: Censorship of the Internet would be wrong.

Clearer: Censorship of the Internet would unfairly limit free speech.

4 Considering Your Audience

As you plan your essay, keep a specific **audience** in mind. Are your readers unbiased observers or people deeply concerned about the issue you plan to discuss? Can they be cast in a specific role—concerned parents, victims of

See 1b

discrimination, irate consumers—or are they so diverse that they cannot be categorized?

Always assume a **skeptical audience**—one that is likely to question or even challenge your assumptions. Even sympathetic readers will need to be convinced that your argument is logical and that your evidence is solid. Skeptical readers will need reassurance that you understand their concerns and that you are willing to concede some of their points. However, no matter what you do, you may never be able to convince hostile readers that your conclusion is valid or even worth considering. The best you can hope for is that these readers will acknowledge the strengths of your argument even if they reject your conclusion.

5 | Refuting Opposing Arguments

As you develop your argument, you should briefly summarize and then **refute**—that is, disprove or call into question—opposing arguments by showing that they are untrue, unfair, illogical, irrelevant, or misguided. In the following paragraph, a student refutes the argument that Sea World is justified in keeping whales in captivity.

> Of course, some will say that Sea World wants to capture only a few whales, as George Will points out in his commentary in *Newsweek*. Unfortunately, Will downplays the fact that Sea World wants to capture a hundred whales, not just "a few." And, after releasing ninety of these whales, Sea World intends to keep ten for "further work." At hearings in Seattle last week, several noted marine biologists went on record as condemning Sea World's research program.

Note: When you acknowledge an opposing view, be careful not to distort or oversimplify it. This tactic, known as creating a **straw man,** can seriously undermine your credibility.

9b | Using Evidence Effectively

1 | Supporting Your Argument

Most arguments are built on **assertions**—statements that you make about your topic—backed by <u>evidence</u>—supporting information, in the form of examples, statistics, or expert opinion. Some of the most common sources of evidence are scholarly journals, magazines, newspapers, Web sites, and books. You may also get evidence from observations, interviews, surveys, and your own personal experience.

Keep in mind that all information—words and ideas—that you get from a source requires <u>**documentation**</u>. Only assertions that are **self-**

See
8b

See
Pts.
5–6

evident ("All human beings are mortal"), **true by definition** ("2 + 2 = 4"), or **factual** ("The Atlantic Ocean separates England and the United States") need no documentation.

Even though you support your points with evidence from your sources, your argument should not be a patchwork of other people's ideas. In other words, *your* voice—not those of your sources—should dominate the discussion. You should present your points, introduce and interpret your evidence, and make sure that readers know how your ideas relate to one another and to your thesis. In this way, you let readers know that you are in control of the argument and that you have something to add to the discussion.

Note: Remember that you can never prove a thesis conclusively; if you could, there would be no argument. The best you can do is to provide enough evidence to establish a high probability that your thesis is reasonable or valid.

Close-Up USING VISUALS AS EVIDENCE

A well-chosen visual can help support an argument—provided it conveys a clear message and is relevant to the discussion. For more on using visuals in your arguments, **see Chapter 10.**

2 Establishing Credibility

In order to convince readers, you have to satisfy them that you are someone they should listen to—in other words, that you have **credibility.**

Establishing Common Ground When you write an argument, it is tempting to go on the attack, emphasizing the differences between your position and those of your opponents. Writers of effective arguments, however, know they can gain a greater advantage by establishing common ground between their opponents and themselves.

One way to establish common ground is to use the techniques of **Rogerian argument,** based on the work of the psychologist Carl Rogers. According to Rogers, you should think of the members of your audience as colleagues with whom you must collaborate to find solutions to problems. Instead of verbally assaulting them, you should emphasize points of agreement. In this way, you establish common ground and work toward a resolution of the problem you are discussing.

Demonstrating Knowledge Including relevant personal experiences in your argumentative essay can show readers that you know a lot about your subject; demonstrating this kind of knowledge gives you authority.

You can also demonstrate knowledge by showing that you have done research into a subject. By referring to important and reliable sources of information and by providing accurate documentation, you show readers that you have done the necessary background reading.

Maintaining a Reasonable Tone Talk *to* your readers, not *at* them. Remember that readers are more likely to respond to a writer who seems sensible than to one who is strident or insulting. For this reason, you should use moderate language, qualify your statements, and avoid words and phrases such as *never, all,* and *in every case,* which can make your claims seem exaggerated and unrealistic.

Presenting Yourself as Someone Worth Listening To Present your argument in positive terms, and don't apologize for your views. For example, do not rely on phrases—such as "In my opinion" and "It seems to me"—that undercut your credibility. Be consistent, and be careful not to contradict yourself. Finally, avoid using first person pronouns, such as *I,* as well as slang and colloquialisms.

❓ ③ Being Fair

See
8c

Because argument promotes one point of view over another, it is seldom objective. However, college writing requires that you stay within the bounds of fairness and avoid **bias.** To be sure that the support for your argument is not misleading or distorted, you should take the following steps.

Avoid Distorting Evidence Writers sometimes intentionally misrepresent their opponents' views by exaggerating them and then attacking this extreme position, but you should avoid this unfair tactic in your college writing.

Avoid Quoting Out of Context Be careful not to take someone's words out of their original setting and use them in another. When you select certain statements and ignore others, you can change the meaning of what someone has said or suggested.

Avoid Slanting Slanting occurs when you select only information that supports your case and ignore information that does not. Slanting also occurs when you use **inflammatory language**—language calculated to arouse strong emotions—to create bias.

Avoid Using Unfair Appeals Traditionally, writers of arguments try to influence readers by appealing to their sense of reason. Problems arise when writers attempt to influence readers unfairly. For example, writers can use See
8f **fallacies** to fool readers into thinking that a conclusion is logical when it is not. These unfair appeals are unacceptable in colege writing.

9c Organizing an Argumentative Essay

In its simplest form, an argument consists of a thesis statement and supporting evidence. However, argumentative essays frequently use **inductive** and **deductive reasoning** and other strategies to win audience approval and overcome potential opposition.

See 8d–e

Elements of an Argumentative Essay

Introduction

The **introduction** of your argumentative essay acquaints readers with your subject. Here you can show how your subject concerns your audience, establish common ground with your readers, and perhaps explain how your subject has been misunderstood.

See 7e2

Thesis Statement

Your **thesis statement** can appear anywhere in your argumentative essay. Most often, you present your thesis in your introduction. However, if you are taking a highly controversial position—one to which you believe your readers might react negatively—you may delay stating your thesis until later in your essay.

See 5b–c

Background

In this section, you briefly present a narrative of past events, an overview of others' opinions on the issue, definitions of key terms, or a review of basic facts.

Arguments in Support of Your Thesis

Here you present your arguments and the evidence to support them. Most often, you begin with your weakest argument and work up to your strongest. If all your arguments are equally strong, you might begin with the one with which your readers are most familiar and therefore most likely to accept.

Refutation of Opposing Arguments

In this part of your essay, you summarize and **refute** the major arguments against your thesis. If the opposing arguments are relatively weak, refute them after you have made your case. However, if the opposing arguments are strong, you should concede their strengths and then discuss their limitations before you present your own arguments.

See 9a5

(continued)

See
7e3

Elements of an Argumentative Essay *(continued)*

Conclusion

Your <u>conclusion</u> should reinforce the stand you are taking in your argument. Here, you can summarize key points, paraphrase your thesis, remind readers of the weaknesses of opposing arguments, or underscore the logic of your position. Many writers end their arguments with a strong concluding statement, such as a relevant quotation or a statement that sums up their position on the issue.

9d   Writing and Revising an Argumentative Essay

The following student essay includes many of the elements discussed in this chapter. The student, Samantha Masterton, was asked to write an argumentative essay on a topic of her choice, drawing her supporting evidence from her own knowledge and experience as well as from other sources.

Masterton 1

Samantha Masterton

Professor Egler

English 102

14 April 2011

The Returning Student: Older Is Definitely Better

After graduating from high school, young people must
decide what they want to do with the rest of their lives. Many Introduction
graduates (often without much thought) decide to continue
their education uninterrupted, and they go on to college.
This group of teenagers makes up what many see as typical
first-year college students. Recently, however, this stereotype
has been challenged by an influx of older students, including
myself, into American colleges and universities. Not only do
these students make a valuable contribution to the schools
they attend, but they also offer an alternative to young people
who go to college simply because they do not know what else
to do. A few years off between high school and college can Thesis
statement
give many students the life experience they need to appreciate
the value of higher education and to gain more from it.

The college experience of an eighteen-year-old is quite Background
different from that of an older "nontraditional" student. The
typical high school graduate is often concerned with things
other than studying—for example, going to parties, dating,
and testing personal limits. However, older students—those
who are twenty-five years of age or older—are serious about
the idea of returning to college. Although many high school
students do not think twice about whether or not to attend
college, older students have much more to consider when
they think about returning to college. For example, they must
decide how much time they can spend getting their degree

Masterton 2

and consider the impact that attending college will have on their family and their finances.

Background (continued)

In the United States, the makeup of college students is changing. According to the US Department of Education report *Nontraditional Undergraduates*, the percentage of students who could be classified as "nontraditional" has increased over the last decade (7). So, despite the challenges that older students face when they return to school, more and more are choosing to make the effort.

Argument in support of thesis

Most older students return to school with clear goals. The *Nontraditional Undergraduates* report shows that more than one-third of nontraditional students decided to attend college because it was required by their job, and 87 percent enrolled in order to gain skills (10). Getting a college degree is often a requirement for professional advancement, and older students are therefore more likely to take college seriously. In general, older students enroll in college with a definite course of study in mind. For older students, college is an extension of work rather than a place to discover what they want to be when they graduate. A study by psychologists R. Eric Landrum, Je T'aime Hood, and Jerry M. McAdams concluded, "Nontraditional students seemed to be more appreciative of their opportunities, as indicated by their higher enjoyment of school and appreciation of professors' efforts in the classroom" (744).

Argument in support of thesis

Older students also understand the actual benefits of doing well in school; as a result, they take school seriously. The older students I know rarely cut classes or put off studying. This is because older students are often balancing the demands of home and work and because they know how

Masterton 3

important it is to do well. The difficulties of juggling school, family, and work force older students to be disciplined and focused—especially concerning their schoolwork. This pays off: older students tend to spend more hours per week studying and tend to have a higher GPA than younger students do (Landrum, Hood, and McAdams 742-43).

My observations of older students have convinced me that many students would benefit from delaying entry into college. Eighteen-year-olds are often immature and inexperienced. They cannot be expected to have formulated definite goals or developed firm ideas about themselves or about the world in which they live. In contrast, older students have generally had a variety of real-life experiences. Most have worked for several years, many have started families. Their years in the "real world" have helped them become more focused and more responsible than they were when they graduated from high school. As a result, they are better prepared for college than they would have been when they were younger.

Argument in support of thesis

Of course, postponing college for a few years is not for everyone. Certainly some teenagers have a definite sense of purpose and these individuals would benefit from an early college experience. Charles Woodward, a law librarian, went to college directly after high school, and for him the experience was positive. "I was serious about learning, and I loved my subject," he said. "I felt fortunate that I knew what I wanted from college and from life." Many younger students, however, are not like Woodward; they graduate from high school without any clear sense of purpose. For this reason, it makes sense for them to postpone college until they are mature enough to benefit from the experience.

Refutation of opposing argument

Masterton 4

Refutation of opposing argument

Granted, some older students have difficulties when they return to college. Because they have been out of school so long, these students may have problems studying and adapting to academic life. As I have seen, though, most of these problems disappear after a period of adjustment. Of course, it is true that many older students find it difficult to balance the needs of their family with college and to deal with the financial burden of tuition. However, this challenge is becoming easier with the growing number of online courses, the availability of distance education, and the introduction of governmental programs, such as educational tax credits (Agbo 164-65).

Conclusion

All things considered, higher education is often wasted on the young, who are either too immature or too unfocused to take advantage of it. Taking a few years off between high school and college would give these students the time they need to make the most of a college education. The increasing number of older students returning to college seems to indicate that many students are taking this path. According to a US Department of Education report, *Digest of Education Statistics, 2007*, 31.3 percent of students enrolled in American colleges in 2005 were twenty-five years of age or older (273). Older students such as these have taken time off to serve in the military, to gain valuable work experience, or to raise a

Concluding statement

family. In short, they have taken the time to mature. By the time they get to college, these students have defined their goals and made a firm commitment to achieve them.

Masterton 5

Works Cited

Agbo, S. "The United States: Heterogeneity of the Student Body and the Meaning of 'Nontraditional' in U.S. Higher Education." *Higher Education and Lifelong Learners: International Perspectives on Change*. Ed. Hans G. Schuetze and Maria Slowey. London: Routledge, 2000. 149-69. Print.

Landrum, R. Eric, Je T'aime Hood, and Jerry M. McAdams. "Satisfaction with College by Traditional and Nontraditional College Students." *Psychological Reports* 89.3 (2001): 740-46. Print.

United States. Dept. of Educ. Office of Educ. Research and Improvement. Natl. Center for Educ. Statistics. *Digest of Education Statistics, 2007*. By Thomas D. Snyder, Sally A. Dillow, and Charlene M. Hoffman. 2008. *National Center for Education Statistics*. Web. 5 Apr. 2011.

---. ---. ---. ---. *Nontraditional Undergraduates*. By Susan Choy. 2002. *National Center for Education Statistics*. Web. 7 Apr. 2011.

Woodward, Charles B. Personal interview. 21 Mar. 2011.

Works-cited list begins new page

Four sets of three unspaced hyphens indicate that *United States, Dept. of Educ., Office of Educ. Research and Improvement,* and *Natl. Center for Educ. Statistics* are repeated from the previous entry

CHECKLIST

Writing Argumentative Essays

❏ Does your essay have a debatable thesis?

❏ Have you adequately defined the terms you use in your argument?

❏ Have you considered the opinions, attitudes, and values of your audience?

❏ Have you supported your points with evidence?

❏ Have you summarized and refuted opposing arguments?

❏ Have you established your credibility?

❏ Have you been fair?

❏ Have you constructed your arguments logically?

❏ Have you avoided logical fallacies?

❏ Have you provided your readers with enough background information?

❏ Have you presented your points clearly and organized them logically?

❏ Have you written an interesting introduction and a strong conclusion?

❏ Have you documented all information that is not your own?

Using Transitions in Argumentative Essays

Argumentative essays should include transitional words and phrases to indicate which paragraphs are arguments in support of the thesis, which are refutations of arguments that oppose the thesis, and which are conclusions.

Arguments in Support of Thesis

accordingly	for instance	in general
because	generally	since
for example	given	

Refutations

admittedly	despite	naturally
although	granted	nonetheless
certainly	in all fairness	of course

Conclusions

all things considered	in conclusion	therefore
as a result	in summary	thus

CHAPTER 10

Using Visuals as Evidence

10a Using Visuals

See
6b2,
26d

Visuals can add a persuasive dimension to your argumentative essays. Because visual images can have such an immediate impact, they can make a good argumentative essay even more persuasive.

In this sense, visuals can serve as **evidence.** For example, the addition of a photograph of a roadway work zone choked with traffic (Figure 10.1) could help support your assertion that your township should provide more effective work zone strategies to reduce congestion. In addition, a graph or chart could easily establish the fact that traffic congestion has gotten considerably worse over the past twenty years (Figure 10.2).

FIGURE 10.1 Traffic jam in a roadway work zone.

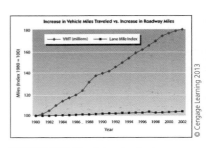

FIGURE 10.2 Chart showing the increase in vehicle miles traveled versus the increase in roadway miles from 1980 to 2002.

To persuade readers, visuals rely on elements such as images, written text, white space, and color. Consider, for example, the editorial cartoon in Figure 10.3, which comments on the high cost of a college education and on students' difficulties in meeting these costs. The structure of the cartoon is simple: graduating students are shown walking up a steep staircase that represents the challenges that they must meet in order to graduate. Once they receive their diplomas, however, they encounter two very large steps that represent the daunting challenges they face upon graduation. The use of written text is simple and direct. The person handing out diplomas congratulates the students and advises them to watch their step; the two

FIGURE 10.3 Cartoon by Jeff Parker from *Florida Today*.

CHECKLIST

Selecting Visuals

❑ What point does the visual make?

❑ Does the visual clearly support your argument?

❑ How do the various elements of the visual reinforce your point?

❑ Is the visual aimed at a particular type of audience?

❑ Could your use of the visual confuse or distract your readers in any way?

❑ Does the visual distort or misrepresent facts?

large steps are labeled "cost of college" and "sour job market." (In addition, muted blue and grey colors reinforce the somber message of the cartoon.) Thus, with very few words, the visual forcefully makes the cartoonist's point: that in spite of the challenges graduating students have already overcome, they face ever greater—and perhaps insurmountable—challenges in the future. If you were writing an argument that took the same position, this cartoon could certainly help you make your point.

When you select visuals, it is important to remember your purpose and audience and the tone you wish to establish. Just as you would with any other evidence in an argumentative essay, you should evaluate visuals to make sure that they are not taken out of context and that they do not make their points unfairly by distorting or misrepresenting facts to readers.

10b Evaluating Visuals

 Just as you have to think critically about the ideas you read, you also have to think critically about the visuals that accompany these texts.

Almost all photographs that appear in print have been altered in some way. The most common changes involve **cropping** a picture to eliminate distracting background objects, **recoloring** a background to emphasize subjects in the foreground, and **altering the brightness and contrast** of an image to enhance its overall quality.

Problems arise, however, when an overly zealous editor, reporter, or photographer alters a photograph in order to support a particular point of view. Problems also occur when a researcher or reporter misrepresents experimental data in a graph or chart. Occasionally, this kind of error is caused by carelessness, but sometimes it is a deliberate attempt to mislead or deceive.

Close-Up ALTERING IMAGES

Keep in mind that you are not allowed to alter copyrighted work. Even though the **fair use doctrine** permits you to use copyrighted visual material (with proper acknowledgement) in a research paper, it does not permit you to distort, misrepresent, or otherwise alter this material in order to mislead readers.

1 Recognizing Doctored Photographs

A photograph is **doctored** when it has been intentionally falsified or altered in some significant way. Consider the doctored photograph shown in Figure 10.4. The government of Iran posted this photograph on the Internet to announce the test of a new long-range missile. Within days, the photograph appeared in major newspapers around the world—including the *New York Times,* the *Chicago Tribune,* and the *Los Angeles Times.*

© Sepah News/Handout/Document Iran/Corbis

FIGURE 10.4 Doctored photograph of Iranian missiles.

Soon after its publication, however, people began to suspect that this image had been tampered with. Eventually, the Iranian government took down the doctored picture and released the original photograph shown in Figure 10.5. Apparently, the original photo had been manipulated to cover up the fact that one of the rockets in the test had failed to launch.

FIGURE 10.5 Undoctored photograph of Iranian missiles.

Unfortunately, incidents such as this one are becoming quite common. The Internet is full of misleading and altered images. For this reason, you should be very careful when you select photographs from the Internet to support your arguments. If you suspect that a picture has been altered, research it to determine its validity, just as you would for a print source.

2 Recognizing Staged Photographs

Another questionable tactic is the use of **staged photographs,** visual images that purport to be spontaneous when they are actually posed. Even the hint of staging can discredit a visual image.

One of the most famous debates about staged photographs concerns the flag-raising photograph at the battle of Iwo Jima during World War II (see Figure 10.6). Photographer Joe Rosenthal's Pulitzer Prize–winning image is perhaps the most famous war photograph ever taken. When it appeared in newspapers on February 25, 1945, it immediately captured the attention of the American public, so much so that it became the model for the Marine Corps monument in Washington, DC. Almost immediately, however, people began to question whether the photograph was staged. Rosenthal did not help matters when he seemed to admit to a correspondent that it was. Later, however, he said that he had been referring to a posed shot he took the same day (see Figure 10.7), not the famous flag-raising picture. Historians now agree that the flag-raising picture was not staged, but the charge that it was haunted Rosenthal his entire life and is still repeated by some as if it were fact.

FIGURE 10.6 Soldiers raise a flag at the battle of Iwo Jima, February 1945.

FIGURE 10.7 Soldiers pose before the camera at Iwo Jima, February 1945.

3 Recognizing Misleading Charts and Graphs

Charts and graphs are effective tools for showing relationships among statistical data in science, business, and other disciplines, where they are often used as supporting evidence. However, charts can skew results and mislead readers when their components (titles, labels, and so on) are manipulated—for example, to show just partial or mislabeled data. Whenever you encounter a chart or graph in a document, examine it carefully to be certain that visual information is labeled clearly and accurately and that data increments are large enough to be significant.

Consider, for example, the potentially misleading nature of the two salary charts below. At first glance, it appears as if the salaries in the "Salaries Up!" chart (Figure 10.8) rose dramatically while those in the "Salaries Stable!" chart (Figure 10.9) remained almost the same. A closer analysis of the two charts, however, reveals that the salaries in the two charts are nearly identical across the six-year period. The data in the two charts seem to differ dramatically because of the way each chart displays salary increases: in the first chart, salary increases are given in $500

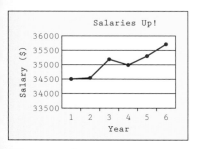

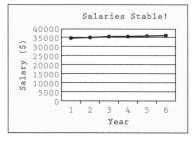

FIGURE 10.8 Salary chart 1 from the *CPIT Maths2Go* online tutorial.

FIGURE 10.9 Salary chart 2 from the *CPIT Maths2Go* online tutorial.

increments; in the second chart, salary increases are given in $5,000 increments. For this reason, a $1,000 increase in the first chart registers quite visibly, whereas in the second chart it hardly shows at all.

Close-Up INTEGRATING VISUALS

To make sure that your visuals are smoothly integrated into your argumentative essays, follow these guidelines:

- Place your visual as close as possible to the point in the essay where you discuss it.
- Include a specific reference to the visual—for example, *See Figure 3* or *See the figure below*.
- Explain the visual in the text of your paper so readers will understand what they are supposed to learn from it.
- Make sure the visual is large enough so readers can see its individual elements and read any words or numbers.
- If you take a visual from a source, be sure to document it.

Writing in the Disciplines

Writing in the Disciplines

❓ Frequently Asked Questions

CHAPTER 11

Writing in the Humanities

Humanities disciplines include art history, drama, film, history, languages, literature, music, philosophy, and religion. In these disciplines, research often involves analyzing or interpreting a **primary source**—a literary work, a historical document, a musical composition, or a painting or piece of sculpture—or making connections between one work and another. Scholars in humanities disciplines may also cite **secondary sources**—commentaries on primary sources—to support their points or develop new interpretations.

11a Understanding Purpose, Audience, and Tone

Writing assignments in the humanities may be formal or informal. While formal writing may require you to use academic discourse and **MLA documentation style** and format, informal writing assignments may call for no more than your personal responses to your reading and observations. Each of these two types of writing has a distinct purpose and tone.

See Ch. 21

   Informal writing assignments—for example, journals, reflections, or response papers—may use a relatively conversational, even colloquial, style and use the first person (*I*). Often, your instructor will specify an audience: your classmates, the instructor, or someone else. Sometimes you may be asked to share these writings, perhaps by posting regular responses to a class discussion board. At other times, you may keep these writings entirely private—for example, in a journal that reflects on your learning throughout a semester.

   More **formal** writing assignments—literary analyses, research papers, literature reviews, and so on—often require that you summarize, analyze, or evaluate print and electronic sources and **synthesize** information from a variety of sources. Because the purpose of a formal writing assignment is often to persuade an audience to accept a particular point of view or position, these assignments require a more objective tone and a more formal **level of diction** than informal assignments do.

See Ch. 19

See 44b

11b Writing Assignments

1 Response Paper

In some humanities disciplines (particularly literature, music, and art), you may be asked to write a **response paper,** an informal first-person account of your reactions to a literary work, a painting, a dance performance, or a concert.

Assignment (World Music)

Attend one of the performances offered by the Music and Drama Department during the upcoming month. Then, write an informal paper that communicates your response to the performance. What was memorable or remarkable? How did the audience react at particular moments? How did you feel as you were watching and listening, and how did you feel when the performance was over?

Sample Response Paper (Excerpt)

When I first arrived, I saw that the people in the audience were pretty much who I expected to see at a classical music recital, including quite a few faculty. (I'm sure they were shocked to see me there.) The audience was quiet as they waited for Chu's entrance; everyone just kind of sat looking at the darkened stage, which contained a very large grand piano and a cello. When Chu came on stage, the applause was almost deafening. I hadn't realized he was so famous. The audience quieted down when he sat down and picked up his bow. The first item on the program was a solo titled *Allegretto Minimoso.* I have to admit that once Chu started to play his cello, I didn't even notice what was going on in the audience anymore. His music made me think of tall cliffs towering over the ocean under a bright sky during a storm. I was hooked from the first moment.

2 Book and Film Review

Instructors in the humanities may require students to write **reviews** of books, films, or art exhibits. The purpose of a review is to evaluate a work, exhibit, or performance and perhaps make recommendations to readers.

Assignment (Journalism)

Write an informal review of a film you liked when you were a child, contrasting your reactions to the film then with your reactions to it now. In choosing a film, remember that your review will be submitted to our school newspaper, where your primary audience will be students about your age.

Sample Film Review

I have always been a fan of musicals, handsome boys, and history lessons. Kenny Ortega's 1992 film *Newsies* finds a way to incorporate all these elements into one entertaining (although flawed) package.

The film begins with a narrator describing New York City in 1899 through the eyes of the poor newspaper boys who sell papers on the street. The "newsies" walk the dirty streets of New York shoeless and homeless while the rich and powerful newspaper publishers squeeze as much money as they can from the public. *Newsies* focuses on two young boys who sell newspapers for some of the most famous publishers of the time, including Joseph Pulitzer.

When Pulitzer (Robert Duvall) decides to raise the cost of the boys' newspaper purchase by a tenth of a percent, they are outraged. Jack Kelly (Christian Bale) and David Jacobs (David Moscow) set out to rally the rest of their gang, as well as the "street rats" of the other boroughs, to help fight "old man Pulitzer." At the same time, Warden Snyder (Kevin Tighe), the operator of The Refuge, a poorly run and corrupt orphanage, is trying to find Jack to bring him back to the orphanage. While trying to start a strike and evade Warden Snyder, the boys attract the attention of Bryan Denton (Bill Pullman), a reporter for the New York *Sun* who finds their troubles newsworthy.

Musicals like *Newsies* are a guilty pleasure of mine because they are films I loved when I was growing up. The first time I saw this movie, I was swept up by the singing and dancing as well as by the glimpse into a time and place I knew nothing about. And, of course, I loved watching my former heartthrob, Christian Bale; with a handful of strappingly handsome young boys thrown into the mix, *Newsies* is basically the early 1990s version of the present-day *Twilight* films, where young girls' love is directed at Jacob and Edward.

Recently, I watched *Newsies* again, and it was not the pleasurable experience I remembered. Although the film is historically accurate and has a catchy soundtrack, I found it disappointing. The young actors are not always all that talented, and some of the singers and dancers are just not polished enough. And, with all the new advances in film and cinematography that have taken place since *Newsies* was made in 1992, it is startling to see backgrounds that are all too noticeably digitally imaged.

As much as I liked this movie when it first came out, I see now that it is not as good as I thought it was. Still, there are not enough drawbacks to make me completely write it off. It may be too cute for adults, but it helps me remember what it was like to be young.

3 Literature Review

See 15c2

When you are writing a research paper, your instructor may ask you to prepare an **annotated bibliography**—a list of sources (accompanied by full source information) followed by summary and evaluation. In some cases, you may also be asked to write a literature review that discusses these sources and their relevance to your research.

Assignment (Nineteenth-Century American History)

Write a literature review that discusses three of the sources you use in your research paper. Do not simply describe or summarize your sources; synthesize, compare, and contrast them, developing your own point of view. Be sure to include paraphrases and quotations from your sources as well as a works-cited list.

Sample Literature Review (Excerpt)

The women mill operatives of Lowell, Massachusetts, produced a variety of writings in different genres that portray the ways in which they negotiated their everyday urban experiences in their boardinghouses and on the factory production line. While their descriptions of daily life in the mill town can be read as a story of their journey to financial independence, these writings also reveal the women's collective coming of political age.

The *Lowell Offering*, first published in 1840, was a "monthly magazine, thirty pages long, priced at six and one-quarter cents an issue" (Eisler 33) that began as a corporately owned concern but later was bought, run, and edited by two women who were both former mill operatives. While the publishers of the *Offering* focused on presenting the working women's own creations, The Factory Girl's Garland, also begun in 1840 (only to fold less than a year later), was more of a "liberal reformist paper [that] spoke paternalistically in favor of the mill women, and at times even preached at them" (Vogel 791).

Jean Marie Lutes explains that some labor reformists among the operatives found the "sentimental tales, romantic stories, and poetic rhyme" of the *Offering* too "neutral," accusing it of having "neglected the operative as a working being" (8). Therefore, they chose to represent their concerns through the *Voice of Industry*, a newspaper whose "case for reform," Lutes argues, was only made possible through the preliminary cultural work performed by the less critical *Offering*: while the *Voice* explicitly called for recognition of working class women's rights, it was the *Offering* that "initiate[d] the discourse of female working-class culture" (9). These periodicals demonstrate various ways in which the operatives initiated change for white working-class women through both their physical and their literary labors.

Works Cited

Eisler, Benita. *The Lowell Offering: Writings by New England Mill Women (1840-1845)*. New York: Norton, 1998. Print.

Lutes, Jean Marie. "Cultivating Domesticity: Labor Reform and the Literary Culture of the Lowell Mill Girls." *Works and Days* 22.11 (1993): 7-27. Print.

Vogel, Lise. "Their Own Work: Two Documents from the Nineteenth-Century Labor Movement." *Signs: Journal of Women in Culture and Society* 1.3 (1976): 787-802. Print.

4 Critical Analysis

Instructors in various humanities disciplines often ask students to analyze texts. (For an example of a literary analysis, **see 12c**.) A critical analysis takes apart a print or visual text, considering its various components in order to make sense of the whole.

Assignment (Mass Communications)

Research an ad campaign for a specific product, service, or cause. Select a poster, billboard, or other visual from the campaign, and write an essay analyzing the ad's purpose, target audience, and overall message. Describe how the ad's words and images work together to reach the intended audience, and explain who benefits from the ad's message, and how.

Sample Critical Analysis (Excerpt)

The National Teen Dating Abuse Helpline, along with Texas Attorney General Greg Abbott, recently launched a multimedia campaign aimed at helping to prevent teen dating abuse. The "LOVE" campaign has produced posters as well as public service announcements, songs, Web site images, and other materials to alert teens to the prevalence and danger of dating abuse. One poster (see fig. 1) shows the word *Love* written in a graffiti style, superimposed over a photograph of a teen couple. This ad illustrates the techniques the campaign uses to promote respectful and supportive romantic relationships to its teen audience.

Courtesy of loveisrespect.org

Fig. 1. "LOVE" campaign poster; *loveisrespect.org;* Natl. Teen Dating Abuse Helpline, 2009; Web; 15 Oct. 2011.

The "LOVE" poster uses words and images to convey the campaign's overall message: that teens can prevent and stop dating abuse when they are given the resources they need to identify warning signs and to get help. The central image of a neon pink stylized "Love" logo, framed with splattered paint and a smaller, repeated version of the logo, emphasizes the ad's positive focus on what love should be: fun, exciting, and—above all—respectful. In addition, the text beneath the logo uses an informal, conversational style (rather than formal, grammatically correct language) to appeal to its young audience. The whitewashed image behind the logo, showing the close-up embrace of a teen couple, subtly supports the ad's message that teens should trust their own instincts and ask for help when "things don't feel right."

Together, the poster's words and images work to empower teens to build healthy, loving relationships and to recognize the signs of dating abuse in time to stop it. By focusing on *love* rather than *abuse,* the ad maintains an upbeat message that supports teen dating as long as it is loving and respectful. The concluding advice to "call us or chat online," along with the Helpline's contact information, gives teens a place to go when abuse happens, enabling them not just to recognize the problem but also to do something about it.

11c Conventions of Style, Format, and Documentation

1 Style and Format

Each humanities discipline has its own specialized vocabulary. You should use the technical terms used in the field, but be careful not to overuse such terminology. You can use the first person (*I*) when you are expressing your own reactions and convictions—for example, in a response paper or **reflective statement.** In other situations, however, avoid the first person.

See 27c

Although papers in the humanities do not usually include abstracts, internal headings, tables, or graphs, this situation is changing. Be sure you know what your instructor expects.

Note: When you write papers about **literature,** follow the special conventions that apply to literary analysis.

See Ch. 12

2 Documentation

Literature and modern and classical language scholars, as well as scholars in music and sometimes in art history, use **MLA documentation style**; history scholars generally use **Chicago style.**

See Ch. 21; Ch. 23

11d Avoiding Plagiarism

See Ch. 20

When **plagiarism** occurs in the humanities, it is often the result of inaccurate summarizing and paraphrasing, failure to use quotation marks where they are required, and confusion between your ideas and those of your sources.

Whenever you use sources, you must be careful to document them. In this way, you acknowledge the work of others who influenced your ideas or contributed to your conclusions. Take accurate notes, avoid cutting and pasting chunks of information from online sources directly into your paper, and whenever you quote, summarize, or paraphrase, do so honestly. Document ideas as well as words, no matter where they come from. "Borrowing"

See
Ch. 20

without acknowledgment is plagiarism, and the penalties for plagiarism can be severe. (You do not have to document **common knowledge.** If you have any questions about what constitutes common knowledge in a particular humanities discipline, be sure to check with your instructor.)

11e   Research Sources

Each discipline within the humanities has its own methodology, so it is important to know not only the sources or tools that are used by scholars in a particular field but also the way students and scholars conduct research.

In literature, for example, scholars may analyze, explain, interpret, or evaluate the text of a poem, short story, novel, or play or the work of a particular author. They study the text itself, but often they also consult other sources for evidence that will support their conclusions. They use the tools of their discipline: library resources (online catalogs, specialized databases, periodical indexes, bibliographies, and so on) and Internet resources to locate that evidence.

In other humanities disciplines—such as history—specialized databases, periodical indexes, reference works, and Web sites also exist. But **primary sources,** such as narratives, letters, diaries, or other original documents, also provide important evidence.

In some cases, you may be asked to provide your own analysis, interpretation, or evaluation of an original text, work of art, or musical composition, without reading what has already been written about it. More often, however, you will be asked to use **secondary sources** to reinforce your conclusions, especially when you are an undergraduate student, and you must be sure to **evaluate** those sources carefully before you use them.

See
Chs.
16, 17

Doing library research in the humanities does not usually require that you know what the latest thinking is about a particular work, author, idea, or theory. Older books and journal articles may be as valuable as recent ones. When you begin your research, you can consult the *Humanities Index*, a general resource that lists articles from more than two hundred scholarly journals in areas such as history, language, literary criticism, philosophy, and religion. It is available in print—with entries arranged alphabetically in yearly volumes according to author and subject—and in electronic form, which allows you to search multiple years at once.

Many specialized sources are also available for each humanities discipline. They include databases that cover the literature of that discipline and other sources that provide background information about people, creative works, literary or artistic movements, or historical time periods. Some of these specialized sources will be found in your library's reference collection; many will be available online, either on the Web or through your library's databases.

Close-Up FINDING ADDITIONAL SOURCES

Some online indexes offer citation searching, allowing you to search for any articles that cite articles you have found useful. Reading the lists of works cited at the ends of books, chapters, or journal articles may help you to identify other relevant sources. Reference works also frequently include lists of sources for further reading. Finally, annotated bibliographies can help you distinguish the useful sources from the irrelevant ones, saving you a good deal of time in the long run.

1 Reference Books

Library research is an important part of study in many humanities disciplines. When you do research in any subject area, the *Humanities Index* is one general source you can use. Another excellent index available in print and as a computer-searchable database is the *Arts and Humanities Citation Index*. *Grove's Dictionary of Music and Musicians*, available in print and online, offers full-text bibliographies, biographies, and articles on music and musicians.

2 Databases for Computer Searches

Some of the most helpful databases for humanities disciplines include *Arts and Humanities Citation Index; Art Abstracts/Art Index; MLA International Bibliography; JSTOR Scholarly Journal Archive; ARTStor Digital Image Collection; Religion Index; Philosopher's Index; Essay and General Literature Index; Art Bibliographies Modern; America: History and Life; Historical Abstracts; Linguistics and Language Behavior Abstracts (LLBA);* and *RILM Abstracts of Music Literature.* Ask a reference librarian about the availability of these and other databases in your library.

3 Other Sources of Information

Research in the humanities is not limited to print and electronic resources. For example, historians may do interviews and archival work; art historians visit museums and galleries; and music scholars attend concerts.

CHAPTER 12

Writing a Literary Analysis

12a Reading Literature

See
Ch. 2

When you read a literary work you plan to write about, you use the same critical thinking skills and <u>active reading</u> strategies you apply to other works you read: **preview** the work and **highlight** it to identify key ideas and cues to meaning; then, **annotate** it carefully.

As you read and take notes, focus on the special concerns of literary analysis, considering elements such as a short story's plot, a poem's rhyme or meter, or a play's staging. Look for *patterns*, related groups of words, images, or ideas that run through a work. Look for *anomalies*, unusual forms, unique uses of language, unexpected actions by characters, or original treatments of topics. Finally, look for *connections*, links with other literary works, with historical events, or with biographical information.

When you read a work of literature, keep in mind that you do not read to discover the one correct meaning the writer has hidden between the lines— there *is* no "one correct meaning." The meaning of a literary work is created by the interaction between a text and its readers. Do not assume, however, that a work can mean whatever you want it to mean; ultimately, your interpretation must be consistent with the stylistic signals, thematic suggestions, and patterns of imagery in the text.

12b Writing about Literature

When you have finished your reading and annotating, you decide on a topic, and then you **brainstorm** to find ideas to write about; next, you decide on a thesis and use it to help you organize your material. As you arrange related material into categories, you will begin to see a structure for your paper. At this point, you are ready to start drafting your essay.

When you write about literature, your goal is to make a point and support it with appropriate references to the work under discussion or to related works or secondary sources. In this sense, an essay on a literary topic is often a kind of <u>argumentative essay</u> in which you use sources and your own insights to support a thesis statement.

See
Ch. 9

As you write, you observe the conventions of literary criticism, which has its own specialized vocabulary and formats. You also respond to certain discipline-specific assignments. For instance, you may be asked to **analyze** a work, to take it apart and consider one or more of its elements—perhaps the plot or characters in a story or the use of language in a poem. Or, you may be asked to **interpret** a work, to explore its possible meanings. Finally, you may be called on to **evaluate** a work, to judge its strengths and weaknesses.

More specifically, you may be asked to trace the critical or popular reactions to a work, to compare two works by a single writer (or by two different writers), or to consider the relationship between a work of literature and a literary movement or historical period. You may also be asked to analyze a character's motives or the relationship between two characters or to comment on a story's setting or tone. Whatever the case, understanding exactly what you are expected to do will make your writing task easier.

Conventions of Writing about Literature

When you write about a literary work, keep the following conventions in mind:

- Use present-tense verbs when discussing works of literature (**The character of Mrs. Mallard's husband is not developed**).

- Use past-tense verbs only when discussing historical events (**Owen's poem conveys the destructiveness of World War I, which at the time the poem was written was considered to be. . . .**); when presenting historical or biographical data (**Her first novel, published in 1811 when Austen was thirty-six, . . .**); or when identifying events that occurred prior to the time of the story's main action (**Miss Emily is a recluse; since her father died she has lived alone except for a servant**).

- Support your points with specific, concrete examples from the work you are discussing, *briefly* summarizing key events, quoting dialogue or description, describing characters or setting, or paraphrasing ideas.

- Combine paraphrase, summary, and quotation with your own interpretations, weaving quotations smoothly into your paper (**see Ch. 18**).

- Be careful to acknowledge all the sources you use, including the literary work or works under discussion. Introduce the words or ideas of others with a reference to the source, and follow borrowed material with appropriate parenthetical documentation (**see 21a1**). Be sure you have quoted accurately and enclosed the words of others in quotation marks.

(continued)

See
21a2

Conventions of Writing about Literature (*continued*)

- Include a <u>works-cited list</u> in accordance with MLA documentation style.

- When citing a part of a short story or novel, supply the page number (**168**). For a poem, give the line numbers (**2-4**) if they are included in the text; in your first reference, include the word *line* or *lines* (**lines 2-4**). For a classic verse play, include act, scene, and line numbers (**1.4.29-31**). For other plays, supply act and/or scene numbers. (When quoting more than four lines of prose or more than three lines of poetry, follow the guidelines outlined in **49b**.)

- Avoid subjective expressions like *I feel, I believe, it seems to me,* and *in my opinion.* These weaken your paper by suggesting that its ideas are "only" your opinion and have no validity in themselves.

- Avoid unnecessary plot summary. Your goal is to draw a conclusion about one or more works and to support that conclusion with pertinent details. If a plot development supports a point you wish to make, a *brief* summary is acceptable, but plot summary is no substitute for analysis.

- Use literary terms accurately. For example, be careful not to confuse *narrator* or *speaker* with *writer.* Feelings or opinions expressed by a narrator or character do not necessarily represent those of the writer. You should not say, **In the poem's last stanza, Frost expresses his indecision,** when you mean the poem's *speaker* is indecisive.

- Italicize titles of books and plays (**see 53a**); enclose titles of short stories and poems in quotation marks (**see 49c**). Book-length poems are treated as long works, and their titles should be italicized.

12c Sample Literary Analysis

See
21a

Margaret Chase, a student in an introductory literature course, wrote the following analysis of Alice Walker's short story "Everyday Use." The paper uses <u>MLA documentation style</u> and cites three outside sources.

Chase 1

Margaret Chase

Professor Sierra

English 1001

6 February 2011

The Politics of "Everyday Use"

Alice Walker's "Everyday Use" focuses on a mother, Introduction
Mrs. Johnson, and her two daughters, Maggie and Dee, and
how they look at their African-American heritage. The story's
climax comes when Mrs. Johnson rejects Dee's request to take
a hand-stitched quilt away with her so that she can hang
it on her wall. Knowing that Maggie will put the quilt to
"everyday use," Dee is horrified, and she tells her mother and
Maggie that they do not understand their heritage. Although ⟶ Thesis
some literary critics see Dee's character as materialistic and   statement
shallow, a closer examination of the social and historical
circumstances in which Walker wrote this 1973 story supports
a different interpretation of Dee's behavior.

At several points in the story, Walker establishes that
Dee is quite different from Maggie. As the story opens, the   Dee contrasted
reader learns that Dee, the college-educated daughter, is   with Maggie;
   quotation
coming home to visit her mother and sister after an absence of   describes
   Maggie
several years. Maggie, Dee's younger, less ambitious sister, has
remained at home with her mother. Unlike Dee, Maggie is shy
and introverted. She is described as looking like a lame animal
that has been run over by a car. According to the narrator,
"She has been like this, chin in on chest, eyes on ground, feet
in shuffle" (485) ever since she was burned in a fire.

Dee is also very different from her mother. As Mrs.   Dee contrasted
Johnson waits for Dee to arrive, she thinks about a dream   with Mrs.
   Johnson;
she had about how Dee's homecoming might look on a   quotations
   used as
   support

Chase 2

television talk show. In her dream, Mrs. Johnson is slim and attractive, talking to the host with a "quick and witty tongue" (485). In reality, she acknowledges, she would never look "a strange white man in the eye" (485), but "Dee . . . would always look anyone in the eye. Hesitation was no part of her nature" (485). For Mrs. Johnson, looking a white man in the eye is dangerous; for Dee, it is an act of defiance and courage.

Contrast between Dee and others, continued; quotation analyzed to illustrate contrast

Later in the story, Mrs. Johnson says that unlike Dee, she never got an education. After second grade, she explains, the school closed down. She says, "Don't ask me why: in 1927 colored asked fewer questions than they do now" (486). Here, Mrs. Johnson concedes that she accepts the status quo even though she knows that it is unjust. This admission further establishes the difference between Mrs. Johnson and Dee. Mrs. Johnson has accepted her circumstances, while Dee has tried hard to change hers. Their differences are illustrated in the film version of the story by their contrasting dress. As shown in fig. 1, Dee and her boyfriend, Hakim, dress in the Afro-American style of the late 1960s, embracing their African roots; Mrs. Johnson and Maggie dress in plain, conservative clothing.

Dee's character (past); quotations from story and summary of interview blended to support student's point

Although Mrs. Johnson makes several statements that hint that she admires Dee's defiant character, she also points to incidents that highlight Dee's materialism and selfish ambition. When their first house burned down, Dee watched it burn while she stood under a tree with "a look of concentration" (485) rather than remorse. Mrs. Johnson knows how much Dee hated their small, dingy house, and she knows too that Dee must have been glad it was destroyed. In fact, as Walker acknowledges in an interview with her biographer, Evelyn C. White ("Stitches in Time"), Dee might

Chase 3

Bruce R. Schwartz

Fig. 1. Dee and Hakim arrive at the family home. *The Wadsworth Original Film Series in Literature: "Everyday Use,"* dir. Bruce R. Schwartz, Wadsworth, 2005; DVD.

even have set the fire that destroyed the house and scarred her sister. Even now, Dee is ashamed of the tin-roofed house her family lives in, and she has said that she would never bring her friends there. Mrs. Johnson has always known that Dee wanted "nice things" (486); even at sixteen, "she had a style of her own, and knew what style was" (486). With these observations by Mrs. Johnson, Walker indicates that Dee has always been materialistic and self-serving as well as strong willed.

When Dee arrives home with her new boyfriend, it is clear that her essential character is, for the most part, unchanged. As she eyes her mother's belongings and asks Mrs. Johnson if she can take the top of the butter churn home with her, it is clear that she is still materialistic. Moreover, her years away from home have also politicized her.

Dee's character (present); student's analysis of events in story

Chase 4

Dee now wants to be called "Wangero" because she believes (although mistakenly) that her given name comes from whites who owned her ancestors. She now wears African clothing and talks about how it is a new day for African Americans. Still selfish, she is determined to maintain her own independent identity even if doing so will estrange her from her mother and her sister.

Social and political context for Dee's behavior

The meaning and political importance of Dee's decision to adopt an African name and wear African clothing needs to be seen in the social and political context in which Walker's story is set. In her interview with Evelyn White, Walker explains that the late 1960s were a time of awakening for African Americans. Many turned ideologically and culturally to Africa, adopting the dress, hairstyles, and even the names of their African ancestors. Walker admits that as a young woman she too became interested in discovering her African heritage. (In fact, she herself was given the name *Wangero* during a visit to Kenya in the late 1960s.) Walker tells White that she considered keeping this new name but eventually realized that to do so would be to "dismiss" her family and her American heritage. When she researched her American family, she found that her great-great grandmother had walked from Virginia to Georgia carrying two children. "If that's not a Walker," she says in the interview, "I don't know what is." Thus, Walker realized that, over time, African Americans actually transformed the names they had originally taken from their enslavers. To respect the ancestors she knew, Walker says, she decided it was important to retain her name.

Social and political context, continued

Along with adopting symbols of their African heritage, many African Americans also worked to elevate symbols of

Chase 5

Fig. 2. Traditional hand-stitched quilt. Evelyn C. White, "Alice Walker: Stitches in Time," interview, *The Wadsworth Original Film Series in Literature: "Everyday Use,"* dir. Bruce R. Schwartz, Wadsworth, 2005, DVD.

their own families' heritage, such as the quilt shown in fig. 2, to the status of high art. One way of doing this was to put these objects in museums; another was to hang them on the walls of their homes (Salaam 42). Such acts were intended to convince racist whites that African Americans were indeed cultured and civilized and consequently deserved not only basic civil rights, but also respect (Salaam 43). These gestures also helped to improve self-esteem and pride within black communities (Salaam 42).

According to literary critics Houston Baker and Charlotte Pierce-Baker, when Mrs. Johnson chooses at the end of the story to give the quilt to Maggie, she is challenging Dee's simplistic understanding of heritage by recognizing that quilts signify "sacred generations of women who have made

Critics' analysis of Mrs. Johnson's decision

Chase 6

their own special kind of beauty separate from the traditional artistic world" (qtd. in Piedmont-Marton 45). According to Baker and Peirce-Baker, Mrs. Johnson's epiphany is that her daughter Maggie, whom she has long dismissed because of her quiet nature and shyness, understands the true meaning of the quilt in a way that Dee never will (Piedmont-Marton 45). Readers can tell that Maggie, unlike Dee, has paid close attention to the traditions and skills of her mother and grandmother: she has actually learned to quilt. More important, by staying with her mother instead of going away to school, she has gotten to know her family, as she clearly shows when she tells her mother that Dee can have the quilt because she does not need it to help her remember her grandmother.

Although Maggie's and Mrs. Johnson's views of heritage may be more emotionally profound than Dee's, it is important not to dismiss the significance of Dee's desire to elevate the quilt to the level of high art. The political stakes of defining such an object as art in the late 1960s and early 1970s were high, and the fight for racial equality went well beyond demanding basic civil rights. Clearly, Dee is a materialistic woman who does not understand the emotional significance of her heritage. Still, her desire to hang the quilt should not be seen as a completely selfish act. At the time the story was written, displaying the quilt would have been not only a personal gesture, but a political gesture as well.

Student's analysis of Maggie's final gesture

Conclusion

Defense of Dee's actions (student's opinion, based on analysis of story)

Chase 7

Works Cited

Piedmont-Marton, Elisabeth. "An Overview of 'Everyday Use.'"

    Short Stories for Students 2 (1997): 42-45. *Literature*

    Resource Center. Web. 20 Jan. 2011.

Salaam, Kalamu Ya. "A Primer of the Black Arts Movement:

    Excerpts from *The Magic of Juju: An Appreciation*

    of the Black Arts Movement." Black Renaissance/

    Renaissance Noire (2002): 40-59. *Expanded Academic*

    ASAP. Web. 21 Jan. 2011.

Walker, Alice. "Alice Walker: Stitches in Time." Interview

    by Evelyn C. White. *The Wadsworth Original Film Series*

    in Literature: "Everyday Use." Dir. Bruce R. Schwartz.

    Wadsworth, 2005. DVD.

---. "Everyday Use." *Literature: Reading, Reacting, Writing*.

    Ed. Laurie G. Kirszner and Stephen R. Mandell.

    8th ed. Boston: Wadsworth, 2013. 484-90. Print.

Writing in the Social Sciences

The **social sciences** include anthropology, business, criminal justice, economics, education, political science, psychology, social work, and sociology. When you approach an assignment in the social sciences, your purpose is often to study the behavior of individuals or groups. You may be seeking to understand causes; predict results; define a policy, habit, or trend; or analyze a problem.

Before you can consider a problem in the social sciences, you must develop a **hypothesis,** an educated guess about what you believe your research will suggest. Then, you can gather the data that will either prove or disprove that hypothesis. Data may be quantitative or qualitative. **Quantitative data** are numerical—the "countable" results of surveys and polls. **Qualitative data** are less exact and more descriptive—the results of interviews or observations, for example.

Many assignments in the social sciences call for responses to a problem. For this reason, a clear **problem statement** at the beginning of a piece of writing, such as a proposal or a case study, is necessary to define and guide the discussion. Not only does this statement keep the reader on track, but it also helps the writer stay focused. In this sense, a problem statement establishes the structure for the piece of writing and presents the rationale for the rest of the discussion.

13a Understanding Purpose, Audience, and Tone

Like writing assignments in the humanities, writing assignments in the social sciences can be *informal* or *formal*.

Informal writing assignments require you to examine ideas, phenomena, and data in the world around you. One example of an informal writing assignment is a personal experience essay, in which you are asked to relate your own observations of an event or an experience. Because you are being asked for your personal reactions, it is acceptable to use the first person (*I*) as well as a conversational tone.

Formal writing assignments—such as case studies, research essays, and proposals—use an objective tone and a technical vocabulary. These assignments often require you to examine similarities and differences between what you have observed and what you have read or to evaluate terms and concepts from your course readings and lectures. While the purpose of writing in the social sciences is often to **inform,** it may also be to **persuade**—for example, to propose changes in an after-school tutoring center or to convince readers that binge drinking is a problem on college campuses.

Sometimes your instructor will define an audience for your assignment—your classmates, a supervisor of a social agency, or a public official, for example—but at other times you have to come up with your own or assume that you are addressing a general audience of readers in your field.

Close-Up USING THE PASSIVE VOICE

Unlike writers in the humanities, writers in the social sciences often use the passive voice, particularly in the parts of the paper that describe the research methods. Passive voice allows writers to avoid the first person and to present their research in objective terms.

See 37d

13b Writing Assignments

1 Personal Reaction Report

In some social science disciplines (particularly psychology, education, and sociology), you may be asked to write an informal **personal reaction report,** an account of a site visit or a visit with a professional who works in your area of study. In this kind of assignment, you record specific details about your experience. For example, students in a sociology class might report on a visit to a state correctional facility or to a homeless shelter.

Assignment (Anthropology: Service Learning)

Write a personal reaction report in which you describe your first visit to your service-learning field site. What expectations did you have? Record your initial impressions of the site: How did you feel as you were walking in? What were the first things you noticed? What surprises did you find?

Sample Personal Reaction Report (Excerpt)

Working with animals was my first choice for the service-learning part of this course. I have loved animals ever since I was a child. However, normally I interact with the pets in people's homes, so I was not accustomed to the behaviors of the affection-starved animals that I encountered at the Humane Society. Each animal has its own sad story. Each has its own personality traits as well. On my first day at the Humane Society, I met Barney, a dog with an interesting personality. He had a bright blue collar around his neck and was full of energy. During our 30-minute walk, he purposely walked around me and tangled me up in his leash. He repeated this "game" as often as I would allow him to, and he reacted well to affection. Because he wasn't hand-shy, I concluded that his owner probably had not abused him. Barney and I have already formed a close bond.

2 Book Review

Instructors in the social sciences may ask you to write a book review. A **book review** should include a summary to familiarize your audience with the book's content. It should also include your evaluation of the book and your analysis of its contribution to the discipline. Be sure to include the author, date, and title of the book in your first paragraph.

Assignment (Political Science)

Write a book review summarizing the content and commenting on the usefulness to the field of Steven Kelman's *Making Public Policy: A Hopeful View of American Government.* (This book will be one of your sources for your group research project.) Reviews will be evaluated according to how well they demonstrate your understanding of the book, what insights they provide into your research topic, and how well they are written.

Sample Book Review (Excerpt)

In the next section of his book, Kelman effectively explores the relationship between the Presidency and the bureaucracy. Rather than dividing the Executive and the bureaucracy into the Senior Executive Service and the Civil Service, Kelman limits his discussion to the Executive Office of the President (EOP) and direct political appointments.

Kelman's observations concerning the importance of organizational structure, ground rules, and operating tradition are key. Particularly significant is how organizational characteristics affect the flow of debate, information, and decision making. For example, when a congressional committee debates legislation, the consequences of different organizational structures become visible and are subject to change. When a committee chair excludes an issue from debate, however, the different organizational structures never become visible. According to Kelman, political decision makers may not even be conscious of the exclusion.

3 Case Study

Social science courses, especially psychology, sociology, and anthropology, frequently require **case studies** that focus on individuals or small groups. Case studies often describe a problem and suggest solutions or treatments. In psychology, social work, and education, case studies typically focus on individuals and their interaction with peers or with agency professionals.

Assignment (Psychology of the Family)

Write a formal case study of the family you have been observing.

Sample Case Study

Family Profile

The Newberg family consists of Tom and Tina and their children David (8), Angela (6), and Cristina (4).

Problem

Tom has been laid off from his automobile production-line job. Tina is not employed outside the home. They have a mortgage on their home as well as $10,000 in credit card debt.

The loss of income when Tom was laid off from his job caused a change in the economic status of the Newberg family. Initially, Tom tried to maintain his traditional family role, wanting to be the sole provider, while Tina continued to stay at home with their children. Both Tom and Tina saw no way to alleviate their financial difficulties. Both were heavy smokers, and this habit increased their expenses.

Observations

Tom spent so much time looking for a job that he had little time with his family—especially the children. Eventually, Tina borrowed money from her parents to start a door-to-door beauty products business. When this failed, she found a job driving a school bus, but it was only part time. Tom and Tina's financial situation severely strained the family. Even so, the couple made no plans for the future; they just kept hoping things would improve.

Discussion

Even when the Newbergs both managed to get full-time jobs, they could not maintain the lifestyle they were used to. Image is very important to Tom and Tina: they thought they had to look like a traditional family in order to have self-esteem. This is especially important to Tom. The prognosis for the Newberg family is not promising unless they make some changes. They have to learn to cooperate, to set goals as a family, and to share responsibilities. Both debt counseling and family counseling are strongly recommended.

4 Field Research Report

See 17d

Social science instructors may ask you to write a **field research report.** **Field research** involves gathering information by observing people, places, or things. (It can also involve conducting an interview or carrying out a survey.) Field research reports often conform to guidelines established by your instructor, typically including how information was gathered, the information itself, and conclusions based on the information.

Assignment (Anthropology)

Groups of two or three students will engage in a firsthand observational exercise of present-day Philadelphia or its suburbs. Each group will walk along a major suburban or urban thoroughfare such as Lancaster Avenue or Market Street. While walking, group members should observe the shifting patterns of buildings as well as the landscape configurations. Beforehand, you will be given detailed maps and survey documents that will enable you to see the buildings and the property lines as they existed over a century ago. Then, in a two- to three-page paper, you will describe what you observe and discuss the changes that have taken place over the years—and, if possible, account for these changes.

Sample Field Research Report (Excerpt)

Our group walked southwest on Buck Lane, a small street that runs perpendicular to Lancaster Avenue. As we walked away from Lancaster Avenue, The Haverford School was on our left. The school was built in 1901 on a 25-acre tract that was purchased from Howell Evans. As the years went by, the school's prestige increased, and the campus grew (see Figure 1).

On our right, the houses were small and well kept, not particularly fancy or on large lots. In 1881, almost all of the land on the right side of the road was owned by Michael Gallagher, who sold the land between 1900 and 1913 to the Kerrigan family. The Kerrigan family held the land until 1948, when it was divided into smaller subplots (in Figure 1, this tract is called the "Kerrigan Heir Plan").

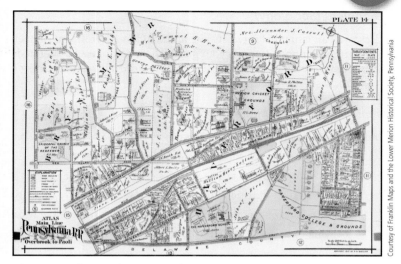

Courtesy of Franklin Maps and the Lower Merion Historical Society, Pennsylvania

Figure 1. Buck Lane (vertical) and Lancaster Avenue (diagonal) c. 1913.

At the turn of the century, many wealthy people, like the Kerrigan family, moved to the western suburbs to escape the noise and congestion of Philadelphia, which was experiencing an industrial boom. The development of the Philadelphia and Western Railroad (currently the Norristown High-Speed Line) in 1907 gave these individuals easy and inexpensive transportation into the city. They built houses on large plots of land. Eventually, these tracts were divided and developed for the middle-class families who were moving into the area. However, a few wealthy families chose not to subdivide, and even today, their houses occupy large plots of land. The major trends that affected the development of the suburbs northwest of Philadelphia were the expansion of train lines and the growth of the middle class after World War II. As the area changed, many of the older wealthy families sold their estates and moved farther from the city.

5 Annotated Bibliography and Literature Review

Social science instructors may ask you to write an **annotated bibliography** in which you summarize and evaluate each of your research sources. You may also be asked to write a **literature review,** an essay in which you discuss the entries in your annotated bibliography and perhaps compare them. (The literature review is often part of a social science research paper.)

Assignment (Sociology)

Research an issue that interests you and that has a significant impact on particular populations in your state. Then, compile an annotated bibliography of at least six sources. Finally, write a literature review that discusses these sources.

Sample Annotated Bibliography (Excerpt)

Adams, J. R. (2010). Farm bill funding boosts FMNP. *National Association of Farmers' Market Nutrition Programs*. Retrieved from http://www.nafmnp.org. This article provides current information on the Farmers' Market Nutrition Program (FMNP), with particular emphasis on its legislative appropriation status. The author stresses the need for lobbying to keep the FMNP program alive.

Sample Literature Review (Excerpt)

J. R. Adams (2010) discusses the successful efforts farmers and lobbyists have made in securing funding for the Farmers' Market Nutrition Program. For example, even though funding had originally been cut by half in the projected budget for 2010, this shortfall was corrected (Rosen, 2010). Farmers stand to benefit from this program and from the similar Seniors Farmers' Market Nutrition Program (SFMNP). Similarly, as S. Z. Greenberg et al. (2009) point out, these programs not only create a potential new market for farmers' products, but also may benefit from private grants to supplement government funding.

6 Proposal

A **proposal** is often the first stage of a research project. In a proposal, you define the scope and nature of the problem to be addressed, outline your research project, and suggest possible solutions. The proposal is where you make a convincing case for your research project.

Assignment (Psychology of Substance Abuse)

Write a proposal to solve a problem associated with alcohol abuse. Each source you use—including Web sites, journal articles, monographs, and interviews—should be documented in **APA style**.

See
22a

Sample Proposal (Excerpt)

Statement of the Problem

It is a fact that alcohol can impair coordination. The severity of this effect depends on an individual's Blood Alcohol Concentration (BAC), which is determined by the individual's weight, speed of alcohol consumption, and amount of alcohol consumed. If an individual's BAC is greater than .08, he or she can be charged with Driving Under the Influence (DUI).

As Figure 1 illustrates, the number of DUIs in Frewsdale is high, with 1067 DUI charges in the past 5 years. Of course, this number reflects only the individuals who were actually caught; the number of people driving with a BAC higher than .08 is probably much greater, as shown by our survey of Frewsdale University students, in which more than 80% of respondents—none of whom had ever received a DUI charge—indicated that they or someone they knew had driven drunk.

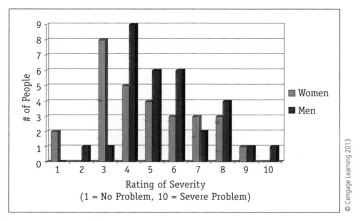

© Cengage Learning 2013

Figure 1. Drunk driving in Frewsdale.

An alternative transportation method for people who have been drinking would greatly reduce the number of DUIs in Frewsdale. Furthermore, such a program would reduce the number of people who walk home alone late at night and potentially put themselves at risk.

To address this problem, we propose a safe-ride program aimed primarily at providing a free ride home on weekends (when people most frequently go out, as Figure 2 shows) for residents of Frewsdale who have been drinking.

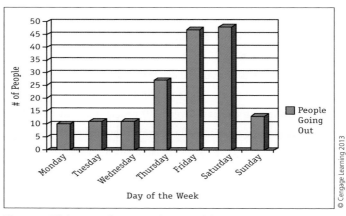

© Cengage Learning 2013

Figure 2. Nights people go out in Frewsdale.

13c   Conventions of Style, Format, and Documentation

1 Style and Format

Because you are addressing specialists, you should use the specialized vocabulary of the discipline and, when you discuss charts and tables, you should use statistical terms, such as *mean, percentage,* and *chi square.* Keep in mind, however, that you should use plain language to explain what *percentages, means*, and *standard deviations* signify in terms of your analysis.

See 22b

A social science research paper follows a specific format. For example, **APA manuscript guidelines** require a title page that includes a **running head** (if the paper is being submitted for publication)**, a title,** and a **by-line** (your name, school, and so on). Every page of the paper, including the title page, should have a **page header,** an abbreviated title and page number printed at the top. Social science papers also include **internal headings.** The body of the paper may present and discuss graphs, maps, photographs, flowcharts, or tables.

2 Documentation

See Ch. 22

Many of the journals in the various social science disciplines use **APA documentation style.**

13d Avoiding Plagiarism

When writing in the social sciences, it is important to avoid **plagiarism** by correctly documenting paraphrases, summaries, and quotations as well as the statistics and visuals of others that you use in your paper.

See Ch. 20

In addition, social scientists are bound by ethical considerations regarding the treatment of research subjects, the protection of privacy, and the granting of credit to those who have made substantial contributions to a research project.

13e Research Sources

Social scientists engage in both library and field research.

In **library research,** social scientists consult print and electronic compilations of statistics, government documents, and newspaper articles, in addition to scholarly books and articles. In **field research,** social scientists conduct **interviews** and surveys and observe individuals and groups. Because so much of their data are quantitative, social scientists must know how to analyze statistics and how to read and interpret tables.

See 17d

Social scientists may also review the literature on a topic to discover what research has already been done, or they may analyze research reports. Social scientists are particularly interested in case studies and published reports of surveys, opinion polls, interviews, experiments, and observations that may be useful in proving or disproving a theory.

Social scientists are expected to base their studies on the most current thinking surrounding a topic. For this reason, statistics must be up to date, and so researchers rely on electronic databases to locate the most recent scholarly journal articles and government publications.

Some excellent databases and print indexes cover the literature of the social sciences. *Social Sciences Citation Index* is available as a database titled *Web of Science.* Other databases and indexes cover specific disciplines within the social sciences. In addition to databases, the **Internet** may be very helpful to social scientists who are looking for government information, including census data, statistics, congressional reports, laws, and reports issued by government agencies.

See Ch. 16

1 Government Documents

Government documents are important resources for social scientists because they contain complete and up-to-date facts and figures on a wide variety of subjects. Government documents can be located through the *Monthly Catalog,* which contains the list of documents (in print and electronic form) published each month. Other useful indexes include *The Congressional Information Service Index, The American Statistics Index,* and *The Index to U.S. Government Periodicals.*

The Web site <www.gpoaccess.gov> provides direct access to the documents published by the Government Printing Office for all three branches of government without the intermediate step of searching through the print *Monthly Catalog.* In addition, <www.thomas.gov>, via the Library of Congress, is a good resource for federal legislative information and government documents. Finally, <http://www.fedstats.gov> is a central source for government statistics that also links to individual agencies and databases.

2 Newspaper Articles

Newspaper articles are particularly good resources for research topics in political science, economics, and business. Useful sources of information from newspapers are *NewsBank, National Newspaper Index,* and *LexisNexis Academic Universe.*

3 Databases for Computer Searches

Some of the more widely used databases for social science disciplines are *Cendata; General BusinessFile ASAP; JSTOR* Scholarly Journal Archive; *Social Sciences Citation Index; Social Sciences Index; PsycINFO; ERIC; Sociological Abstracts; Information Science Abstracts; PAIS International; Population Bibliography; EconLit; ABI/INFORM; Management Contents; LexisNexis Academic Universe;* and *Facts on File.*

4 Other Sources of Information

Interviews, surveys, and observations of the behavior of various groups and individuals are important nonlibrary sources for social science research.

CHAPTER **14**

Writing in the Natural and Applied Sciences

14a   Understanding Purpose, Audience, and Tone

Writing assignments in the natural and applied sciences—for example, in courses in biology, chemistry, geology, astronomy, physics, engineering, nursing, and computer science—use a formal, objective tone and follow documentation guidelines such as those published by the Council of Science Editors (<u>CSE</u>).

See
Ch. 24

Most scientific writing is aimed at readers who are familiar with the technical language and writing conventions of a particular scientific discipline, but occasionally it may be aimed at general readers. Its purpose is to report **empirical data** (data that are obtained through observations and experiments).

Writing Assignments

1 Observation

Some science instructors may ask you to write about and analyze your own observations of the natural world. This is one of the few assignments in the natural and applied sciences in which you will be encouraged to use the first person (*I*). In this type of assignment, you first record your observations (using scientific terminology where necessary) and then analyze the phenomena you describe.

Assignment (Ecology)

Write a report in which you describe a natural setting and then discuss the environmental impact of human beings on that setting.

Sample Observation (Excerpt)

Lake Wenatchee, part of the Alpine Lakes, is in the Wenatchee National Forest, where over 700 small freshwater lakes are scattered throughout the central Cascade region. The average annual precipitation is 40 inches; this heavy rainfall accounts for the mixed conifers—Douglas firs, grand firs, and cedars—that thrive there. The rain-shadow effect also causes the soils in the region to be rich in organic materials as well as in basalt, pumice, and volcanic ash. However, human activity—clear-cutting of old-growth forest, damming of rivers, and fire suppression—is altering the area's natural ecology. These activities lead to a build-up of debris, a higher number of forest fires, severe soil erosion, and the endangerment of local species of animals and fish.

While climbing one part of a barely distinguishable trail, I noticed a very large area on the side of the mountain that had no trees. This was an alarming sign. Because the terrain is sloped, clear-cutting the trees causes extreme soil erosion, including mudslides. Clear-cutting also destroys animal habitats, so many species of owl, woodpecker, and squirrel will very likely be threatened.

2 Biographical Report

In a science or math course, an instructor may ask you to write a report about a historical figure. When writing your essay, try to relate the information you find about your subject to the work you have been doing in the course—for example, you might consider how Mendel's ideas about genetics relate to your class's work on heredity.

Assignment (Geometry)

Select a figure whose life and work we have discussed in class. Then, write a biographical essay in which you summarize his or her contributions to geometry.

Sample Biographical Report (Excerpt)

Jean-Victor Poncelet was born in Metz, northeastern France, in July 1788. He studied calculus with Gaspard Monge at the École Polytechnique and then joined the army as a lieutenant of engineers, following Napoleon to Russia. While he was a prisoner of war in Saratoff on the River Volga, he began researching projective geometry, investigating the projective properties of figures later in his great work *Traité des Propriétés Projectives des Figures*.

Projective geometry is a branch of geometry concerned with properties of geometric figures that retain their character. The basic elements of projective geometry are points, lines, and planes. The concept of parallel does not exist in projective geometry because any pair of distinct lines intersects in a point, and if these lines are parallel in the sense of Euclidean geometry, then their point of intersection is at infinity.

3 Abstract

An **abstract**—a concise summary of a journal article—is a standard part of many assignments in the natural sciences. Abstracts are usually about two hundred words long. In the natural sciences, the purpose of an abstract is to summarize the goals, methods, and results of the research.

You begin writing an abstract after you have finished writing your paper. When writing an abstract, follow the organization of your paper, devoting a sentence or two to each of its major sections. State the purpose, the method of research, results, and conclusions in the order in which they appear in the paper, but include only essential information. Keep in mind that abstracts do not include quotations or paraphrases.

The following abstract was written as part of the assignment on page 142.

Sample Abstract

This project used Wisconsin Fast Plants to determine the effect of gibberellic acid on plants. Gibberellic acid is a growth hormone that stimulates a plant to grow taller by elongation of internode length. The research tested the hypothesis that plants that are treated with gibberellic acid will grow taller than plants that are untreated, and the internode length on treated plants will be longer than that on untreated plants. Results supported this hypothesis: the internode length on treated plants was longer than that on untreated plants. Furthermore, even the dwarf plants that were treated with gibberellic acid grew longer, reaching almost the same height as the control standard plants by the last day of measurement. Therefore, the results of this experiment indicate that gibberellic acid can stimulate the growth of plants by elongation of internode length, though not by internode number.

4 Literature Survey

Literature surveys are common in the sciences, often appearing as a section of a proposal or as part of a report or a research paper. A **literature survey** summarizes a number of studies and sometimes compares and contrasts them. By doing so, the literature survey provides a theoretical context for the paper's discussion.

Sometimes, however, a literature survey can be a paper on its own, and in this case it makes an argument about how to view the literature. In other words, a literature review paper doesn't simply survey the literature but also evaluates it.

Keep in mind that in the natural sciences *literature* means **peer-reviewed** primary sources. A literature review most often comments on **primary research literature**—articles reporting the results of original research. Typically, literature reviews do not discuss **secondary sources,** articles that comment on the work of others.

See 16c

A literature survey should have a formal tone and be aimed at readers who know the field. The purpose of a literature survey is to give these readers an overview of a range of scholarly publications about a subject. Although you may touch on the history of your topic, your primary focus should be on the most current research available.

Assignment (Biology)

Research an aspect of plant biology, and present your findings in a report that contains the following sections: Abstract, Introduction, Literature Survey, Materials, Methods, Results, Discussion, Conclusions, Reference List, and Appendix (if necessary).

Sample Literature Survey (Excerpt)

The cell *Myxococcus xanthus* responds to starvation by initiating a cycle that culminates with the cell forming spore-filled fruiting bodies. This developmental cycle, which is dependent upon changes in gene expression, ensures cell sporulation at the appropriate time and place. Thousands of cells are affected by this process. Recent studies strongly suggest that NtrC-like activators are a crucial component of the complex regulatory controls of *M. xanthus*' developmental program. Twelve NtrC activators were found to be most important in the process.[1] These findings led to further research that examined the specific developmental moments at which NtrC proteins activate specific sets of genes throughout the process.[2] In addition, Garza and others[3] identified two inductive components of the early part of the developmental process.

References

1. Gorski L, Kaiser D. Targeted mutagenesis of σ^{54} activator proteins in *Myxococcus xanthus*. J Bacteriol. 2010;180:5896-5905.

2. Keseler IM, Kaiser D. An early A-signal-dependent gene in *Myxococcus xanthus* has a σ^{54}-like promoter. J Bacteriol. 2007;177:4638-4644.

3. Garza AG, Pollack JS, Harris BZ, Lee A, Keseler IM, Licking EF, Singer M. SdeK is required for early fruiting body development in *Myxococcus xanthus*. J Bacteriol. 2010;180:4628-4637.

5 Lab Report

The **lab report** is one of the most frequently assigned writing tasks in the sciences. Lab reports typically contain the following sections: *Purpose, Apparatus, Method, Procedure, Data, Results,* and *Conclusion.* However, not every section will be necessary for every experiment, and some experiments may require additional components, such as an abstract or a reference list. In addition, lab reports may include tables, charts, graphs, and diagrams. The format for a lab report is usually defined by a course's lab manual.

14c Conventions of Style, Format, and Documentation

1 Style and Format

Because writing in the sciences focuses on experiments, not on those conducting the experiments, writers often use the passive voice.

Another stylistic convention concerns verb tense: a conclusion or a statement of generally accepted fact should be in the present tense ("Objects in motion *tend* to stay in motion"); a summary of a study, however, should be in the past tense ("Watson and Crick *discovered* the structure of DNA"). Finally, note that direct quotations are seldom used in scientific papers.

Keep in mind that each scientific discipline prescribes its own formats for **tables** and other visuals and the way they are to be presented.

See 26d1

Remember that different scientific journals may use different paper formats. For example, the *Journal of Immunology* might have a format different from that of the *Journal of Parasitology*. Your instructor may ask you to prepare your paper according to the style sheet of a particular journal to which you could submit your work. Although publication may seem a remote possibility to you, following a style sheet reminds you that writing in the sciences involves writing for a specific audience.

2 Documentation

Citation systems (documentation styles) within the sciences vary from one scientific discipline to another; even within a given discipline, the citation system may vary from one journal to another. For this reason, ask your instructor which system is required.

14d Avoiding Plagiarism

In the sciences, it is especially important to acknowledge the work of others who contributed to your research results. If many people contribute to a research project, the work of each one must be properly cited. Falsifying data or using the experimental results, computer codes, chemical formulas, graphs, images, ideas, or words of others without proper acknowledgment is particularly serious because it undermines the integrity of your work.

If you need more information about what constitutes **plagiarism** in the sciences or how to cite the work of individual collaborators in a research project, be sure to check with your instructor.

See Ch. 20

14e Research Sources

Although much scientific research takes place in the laboratory or in the natural world, it is also important that scientists know how to do library research. Literature surveys allow scientists to discover what research has already been done. Building on this research, they can conduct meaningful experiments that prove or disprove a theory or solve a problem. Much of this research is collaborative. It is not uncommon for several people to work on different aspects of a research problem in the laboratory or in the library and then jointly report on the results.

Scientists must always use the most current information. Although books may provide background material, scholarly journal articles, conference proceedings, technical reports, and research reports provide the most up-to-date information.

Numerous comprehensive databases cover the sciences. *Science Citation Index* covers all the natural and applied sciences. Others cover specific disciplines: *PubMed* (medicine), *Biological Abstracts* (biology), and *Chemical Abstracts* (chemistry) are examples of specialized databases.

1 Databases for Computer Searches

Helpful databases for research in the sciences include: *BIOSIS; Agricola; Aquatic Sciences and Fisheries Abstracts; Columbia Earthscape; CAB Abstracts; CINAHL; Compendex; NTIS; Inspec; PubMed; MATHSCI; Life Sciences Collection; GEOREF; Chemical Abstracts; Environmental Sciences and Pollution Management Abstracts; Science Citation Index; Wildlife and Ecology Studies Worldwide; GEOBASE; OceanBase; Web of Science;* and *Zoological Record Online.* Check with a reference librarian about the availability of these and other databases in your library.

2 Other Sources of Information

Opportunities for research outside the library vary widely because of the many ways in which scientists can gather information. In agronomy, for example, researchers collect soil samples; in toxicology, they test air or water quality; and in chemistry, they conduct experiments to identify unknown substances. Scientists also conduct surveys. And, of course, the Internet is an important source of up-to-date scientific information.

CHAPTER 15

Writing a Research Paper

Research is the systematic investigation of a topic outside your own knowledge and experience. However, doing research means more than just reading other people's ideas. When you undertake a research project, you become involved in a process that requires you to **think critically:** to evaluate and interpret the ideas explored in your sources and to develop ideas of your own.

See Ch. 8

Although the research process is much richer and more complex than the list of activities in the following box suggests, your research will be most efficient if you follow a systematic process.

The Research Process

Activity	Date Due	Date Completed
Move from an Assignment to a Topic, **15a**		
Do Exploratory Research and Formulate a Research Question, **15b**		
Assemble a Working Bibliography, **15c**		
Develop a Tentative Thesis, **15d**		
Do Focused Research, **15e**		
Take Notes, **15f**		
Fine-Tune Your Thesis, **15g**		
Outline Your Paper, **15h**		
Draft Your Paper, **15i**		
Revise Your Paper, **15j**		
Prepare Your Final Draft, **15k**		

147

15a Moving from Assignment to Topic

1 Understanding Your Assignment

Every research paper begins with an assignment. Before you can find a direction for your research, you must be sure you understand the exact requirements of the specific assignment.

CHECKLIST

Understanding Your Assignment

Asking yourself the following questions will help you focus on your research project:

❑ Has your instructor provided a list of possible topics, or are you expected to select a topic on your own?

❑ Is your purpose to explain, to persuade, or to do something else?

❑ Is your audience your instructor? Your fellow students? Both? Someone else?

❑ Can you assume that your audience knows a lot (or just a little) about your topic?

❑ When is the completed research paper due?

❑ About how long should it be?

❑ Will you be given a specific research schedule to follow, or are you expected to set your own schedule?

❑ Is peer review permitted? Is it encouraged? If so, at what stages of the writing process?

❑ Does your instructor expect you to prepare a formal outline?

❑ Are instructor–student conferences required? Are they encouraged?

❑ Will your instructor review notes, outlines, or drafts with you at regular intervals?

❑ Does your instructor require you to keep a research notebook?

❑ What manuscript guidelines and documentation style are you to follow?

❑ What help is available to you—from your instructor, from other students, from experts on your topic, from community resources, from your library staff?

In **Chapters 4–6** of this text, you followed the writing process of Rebecca James as she planned, drafted, and revised a short essay for her first-semester composition course. In her second-semester composition class, Rebecca was given the following assignment:

> Write a ten- to fifteen-page research paper that takes a position on any issue related to the Internet. Keep a research notebook that traces your progress.

Throughout this chapter, you will see examples of the work Rebecca did in response to this assignment.

2 Choosing a Topic

Once you understand the requirements and scope of your assignment, you need to decide on a topic. In many cases, your instructor will help you choose a topic, either by providing a list of suitable topics or by suggesting a general subject area—for example, a famous trial, an event that happened on the day you were born, a problem on college campuses. Keep in mind, though, that you will still need to narrow your topic to one you can write about: one trial, one event, one problem.

If your instructor requires you to select a topic on your own, you should consider several possible topics and weigh both their suitability for research and your interest in them. You decide on a topic for your research paper in much the same way you decide on a topic for a short essay: you read, brainstorm, talk to people, and ask questions. Specifically, you talk to friends and family, coworkers, and perhaps your instructor; read magazines and newspapers; take stock of your interests; consider possible topics suggested by your other courses (historical events, scientific developments, and so on); and, of course, browse the Internet. (Your search engine's **subject guides** can be particularly helpful as you look for a promising topic for your research or try to narrow a broad subject area.)

See 16a2

3 Starting a Research Notebook

Keeping a **research notebook,** a combination journal of your reactions and log of your progress, is an important part of the research process. A research notebook maps out your direction and keeps you on track; throughout the research process, it helps you define and redefine the boundaries of your assignment.

In your research notebook (which can be an actual notebook or a computer file), you can record lists of things to do, sources to check, leads to follow up on, appointments, possible community contacts, questions to which you would like to find answers, stray ideas, possible thesis statements or titles, and so on. (Be sure to date your entries and to check off and date work completed.)

As she began her research, Rebecca James set up a computer file in which she planned to keep all the electronic documents for her paper. In a *Word* document that she labeled "Research Notebook," she outlined her schedule and explored some preliminary ideas.

Here is an entry from Rebecca's research notebook in which she discusses how she chose a topic for her research paper.

Excerpt from Research Notebook

> Last semester, I wrote an essay for Professor Burks about using *Wikipedia* for college-level research. In class, we'd read *Wikipedia*'s policy statement, "Researching with *Wikipedia*," which helped me to understand *Wikipedia*'s specific limitations for college research. In that paper, I used a sample *Wikipedia* entry related to my accounting class to support my points about the site's strengths and weaknesses. For this research paper, which has to be about the Internet, I want to expand the paper I wrote for my first-semester composition course. This time, I want to talk more about the academic debate surrounding *Wikipedia*. (I asked Professor Burks if I could use this topic for her class this semester, and she said I could. In fact, she really liked the idea.)

15b Doing Exploratory Research and Formulating a Research Question

During **exploratory research,** you develop an overview of your topic, searching the Internet and perhaps also looking through general reference works such as encyclopedias, bibliographies, and specialized dictionaries (either in print or online). Your goal at this stage is to formulate a **research question** that you want your research paper to answer. A research question helps you to decide which sources to seek out, which to examine first, which to examine in depth, and which to skip entirely. (The answer to your research question will be your paper's **thesis statement.**)

See 15d

When developing a list of keywords to help you focus your online database searches, it is often helpful to see how others have framed questions about the same topic. To gather a list of words and phrases (paying particular attention to specific words that appear together), you can look at social-networking and collaboratively produced sites such as *Wikipedia* and *Twitter* and at social-bookmarking sites such as *Delicious* and *Diigo*. Searching for a broad term like *censorship* on these sites will help you see how it is used in a wide range of contexts.

Rebecca began her exploratory research with a preliminary search on *Google* (see Figure 15.1). When she entered the keywords *Wikipedia and academia*, they generated millions of hits, but she wasn't overwhelmed. She had learned in her library orientation that the first ten to twenty items would be most useful to her because the results of a *Google* search are listed in order of relevance to the topic, with the most relevant sites listed first. After a quick review of these items, she moved on to a keyword search on *InfoTrac College Edition*, a database to which her library subscribed (see Figure 15.2).

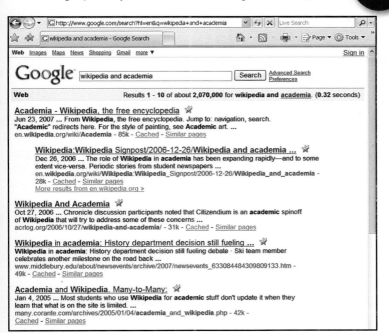

FIGURE 15.1 *Google* search engine. © Google, Inc.

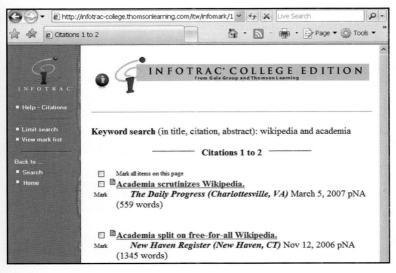

FIGURE 15.2 *InfoTrac College Edition*. © Cengage Learning.

When she finished her exploratory research, Rebecca was able to decide on a research question for her paper.

Research Question: What are the most recent developments in the academic debate surrounding *Wikipedia*?

15c Assembling a Working Bibliography

See
21a2

During your exploratory research, you begin to assemble a **working bibliography** of the sources you consult. This working bibliography will be the basis for your <u>works-cited list</u>, which will include all the sources you cite in your paper.

1 Recording Bibliographic Information

As you consider each potential source, record full and accurate bibliographic information in a separate computer file designated "Bibliography" (or, if you prefer, on individual index cards). Keep records of interviews (including telephone and email interviews), meetings, lectures, films, and electronic sources as well as articles and books. For each source, include basic identifying details—such as the date of an interview, the call number of a library book, the URL of an Internet source and the date you downloaded it (and perhaps the search engine you used to find it as well), or the author of an article accessed from a database. Also write up a brief evaluation that includes your comments about the kind of information the source contains, the amount of information offered, its relevance to your topic, and its limitations.

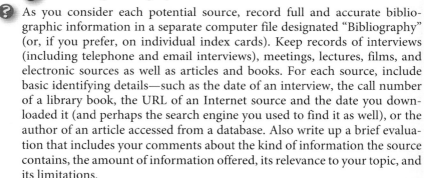

Close-Up ASSEMBLING A WORKING BIBLIOGRAPHY

As you record bibliographic information for your sources, include the following information:

- **Article** Author(s); title of article (in quotation marks); title of journal (italicized in computer file, underlined on index card); volume and issue numbers; date; inclusive page numbers; medium; date downloaded (if applicable); URL (if applicable); brief evaluation
- **Book** Author(s); title (italicized in computer file, underlined on index card); call number (for future reference); city of publication; publisher; date of publication; medium; brief evaluation

Figure 15.3 shows two of the sources Rebecca found as she put together her working bibliography.

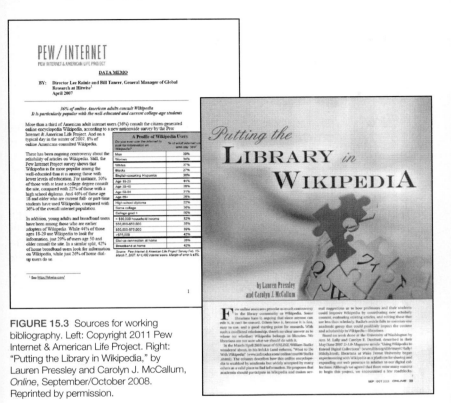

FIGURE 15.3 Sources for working bibliography. Left: Copyright 2011 Pew Internet & American Life Project. Right: "Putting the Library in Wikipedia," by Lauren Pressley and Carolyn J. McCallum, *Online*, September/October 2008. Reprinted by permission.

Following are examples of records Rebecca kept for her working bibliography.

Information for Working Bibliography (in Computer File)

Author —	Badke, William
Title —	"What to Do with *Wikipedia*"
Publication information and medium —	*Online* Mar.-Apr. 2008: 48-50. *Academic Search Elite*. Web. Accessed April 7, 2011.
URL —	http://www.infotoday.com/online/mar08/Badke.shtml
Evaluation —	Argues that it's important for the academic community to be involved in *Wikipedia*'s development. Notes that "36% of online American adults consult *Wikipedia*."

Information for Working Bibliography (on Index Card)

Author ———	Bauerlein, Mark
Title ———	The Dumbest Generation: How the Digital Age Stupefies Young Americans and Jeopardizes Our Future (or, Don't Trust Anyone Under 30)
Publication information ———	NY: Penguin, 2008.
Medium ———	Print
Evaluation ———	Book is several years old, so information may be dated. Chapter 4, "Online Learning and Non-Learning," includes useful discussion of poor writing in Wikipedia articles.

As you go about collecting sources and building your working bibliography, be careful to evaluate the quality and relevance of all the materials you examine. Making informed choices early in the research process will save you a lot of time in the long run. (For guidelines on evaluating Internet sources, **see 16c;** for more information on evaluating library sources, **see 17c.**)

❷ Preparing an Annotated Bibliography

Some instructors require an **annotated bibliography,** a list of all your sources accompanied by a brief summary and evaluation of each source. The following is an excerpt from Rebecca's annotated bibliography.

Annotated Bibliography (Excerpt)

Read, Brock. "Middlebury College History Department Limits Students' Use of
   Wikipedia." Chronicle of Higher Education 16 Feb. 2007: n. pag. *Academic
   Search Elite*. Web. 3 Apr. 2011. This article discusses the policy instituted
   in 2007 by the Middlebury College history department that prohibits
   students from citing *Wikipedia* as a research source. In the article, the
   Chronicle interviews Middlebury College history department chairman
   Don J. Wyatt.

   This article provides an important perspective on the problems
   of using *Wikipedia* in college-level research. Middlebury's history
   department has become a well-known example of the kinds of
   measures the academic community can take to limit students' use of
   Wikipedia as a research source.

15d Developing a Tentative Thesis

Your **tentative thesis** is a preliminary statement of the main point you think your research will support. This statement, which you will eventually refine into your paper's <u>thesis statement,</u> should answer your research question. Rebecca's progress from assignment to tentative thesis appears below.

See 15g

Tentative Thesis

Assignment	Topic	Research Question
Issue related to the Internet	Using *Wikipedia* for college-level research	What are the most recent developments in the academic debate surrounding *Wikipedia*?

Tentative Thesis: The debate surrounding *Wikipedia* has helped people in the academic community to consider how college-level research has changed in recent years.

Because your tentative thesis suggests the specific direction your research will take as well as the scope and emphasis of your argument, it can help you generate a list of the main points you plan to develop in your paper. This list can help you narrow the focus of your research so you can zero in on a few specific areas to explore as you read and take notes.

Rebecca used her tentative thesis to help her generate the following list of points to explore further.

Points to Explore

<u>Tentative thesis:</u> The debate surrounding *Wikipedia* has helped people in the academic community to consider how college-level research has changed in recent years.

- Give background about *Wikipedia;* explain its benefits and drawbacks.
- Talk about who uses *Wikipedia* and for what purposes.
- Explain possible future enhancements to the site.
- Explain college professors' resistance to *Wikipedia*.
- Talk about efforts made by librarians and others to incorporate *Wikipedia* into academic research.

15e Doing Focused Research

During exploratory research, you consult general reference works to get an overview of your topic. During **focused research,** you dig deeper into your topic: you consult periodical articles, books, and other sources (in print and online) to find the specific information—facts, examples, statistics, definitions, quotations—you need to support your points. Once you have decided on a tentative thesis and made a list of the points you plan to explore, you are ready to begin your focused research.

❶ Reading Sources

As you look for information, try to explore as many sources as possible. It makes sense to examine more sources than you actually intend to use so that you can proceed even if some of your sources turn out to be biased, outdated, unreliable, superficial, or irrelevant—in other words, not suitable.

As you explore various sources, quickly evaluate each source's potential usefulness. For example, if your source is a journal article, read the abstract; if your source is a book, skim the table of contents and the index. Then, if an article or a section of a book seems useful, photocopy it for future reference. As you explore sources online, you may find you have multiple windows open at once. If this is the case, be especially careful not to paste material you see onscreen directly into your paper. (This practice can lead to **plagiarism**.) Instead, print out promising material (or send yourself the link) so you can evaluate it further later on. (For information on evaluating electronic and print sources, **see 16c** and **17c**.)

See
Ch. 20

❓ ❷ Balancing Primary and Secondary Sources

See
17b

During your focused research, you will encounter both **primary sources** (original documents and observations) and **secondary sources** (interpretations of original documents and observations).

> **Primary Source:** United States Constitution, Amendment XIV (Ratified July 9, 1868). Section I.
>
> All persons born or naturalized in the United States, and subject to the jurisdiction thereof, are citizens of the United States and the state wherein they reside. No state shall make or enforce any law which shall abridge the privileges or immunities of citizens of the United States; nor shall any state deprive any person of life, liberty, or property, without the process of law; nor deny to any person within its jurisdiction the equal protection of the laws.

> **Secondary Source:** Paula S. Rothenberg, *Racism and Sexism: An Integrated Study.*
>
> Congress passed the Fourteenth Amendment . . . in July 1868. This amendment, which continues to play a major role in contemporary legal battles over discrimination, includes a number of important provisions. It explicitly extends citizenship to all those born or naturalized in the United States and guarantees all citizens due process and "equal protection" of the law.

For some research projects, primary sources are essential; however, most research projects in the humanities rely heavily on secondary sources, which provide scholars' insights and interpretations. Remember, though, that the further you get from the primary source, the more chances exist for inaccuracies caused by misinterpretations or distortions.

Primary and Secondary Sources

Primary Source	Secondary Source
Novel, poem, play, film	Criticism
Diary, autobiography	Biography
Letter, historical document, speech, oral history	Historical analysis
Newspaper article	Editorial
Raw data from questionnaires or interviews	Social science article; case study
Observation/experiment	Scientific article

15f Taking Notes

As you locate information, take notes to create a record of exactly what you found and where you found it.

1 Recording Source Information

Each piece of information you record in your notes (whether **summarized**, **paraphrased**, or **quoted** from your sources) should be accompanied by a short descriptive heading that indicates its relevance to one of the points you will develop in your paper. Because you will use these headings to guide you as you organize your notes, you should make them as specific as possible. For example, labeling every note for a paper on *Wikipedia* *Wikipedia* or **Internet** will not prove very helpful later on. More focused headings—for instance, ***Wikipedia*'s growth potential** or **college professors' objections**—will be much more useful.

See
Ch. 18

Also include brief comments that make clear your reasons for recording the information. These comments (enclosed in brackets so you will know they are your own ideas, not those of your source) should establish the purpose of your note—what you think it can explain, support, clarify, describe, or contradict—and perhaps suggest its relationship to other notes or other sources. Any questions you have about the information or its source can also be included in your comment.

Finally, each note should fully and accurately identify the source of the information you are recording. You do not have to write out the complete citation, but you do have to include enough information to identify your source. For example, **Rainie and Tancer** would be enough to send you back to your working bibliography, where you would be able to find the complete documentation for the authors' article.

Close-Up TAKING NOTES

When you take notes, your goal is flexibility: you want to be able to arrange and rearrange information easily and efficiently as your paper takes shape.

If you take notes at your computer, type each individual note (accompanied by source information) under a specific heading rather than listing all information from a single source under the same heading, and be sure to divide notes from one another with extra space or horizontal lines, as illustrated on page 159. (As you revise, you can move notes around so notes on the same topic are grouped together.)

If you take notes by hand, use the time-tested index-card system, taking care to write on only one side of the card and to use a separate index card for each individual note rather than running several notes together on a single card. (Later, you can enter the information from these notes into your computer file.)

CHECKLIST
Taking Notes

❑ **Identify the source of each piece of information,** including the page numbers for quotations from paginated sources.

❑ **Include everything now that you will need later** to understand your note— names, dates, places, connections with other notes—and to remember why you recorded it.

❑ **Distinguish quotations from paraphrases and summaries and your own ideas from those of your sources.** If you copy a source's words, place them in quotation marks. (If you take notes by hand, circle the quotation marks; if you type your notes, put the quotation marks in boldface.) If you write down your own ideas, enclose them in brackets—and, if you are typing, boldface them as well. These techniques will help you avoid accidental plagiarism in your paper.

See
Ch. 20

❑ **Put an author's ideas into your own words whenever possible,** summarizing and paraphrasing material as well as adding your own observations and analyses.

☐ **Copy quoted material accurately,** using the exact words, spelling, punctuation marks, and capitalization of the original.

☐ **Never paste information from a source directly into your paper.** This practice can lead to plagiarism.

Following are examples of notes that Rebecca took.

Notes (in Computer File)

Short heading   Source

Growth potential   Spinellis and Louridas 71

Note ——— (quotation)

"the apparently chaotic *Wikipedia* development process delivers growth at a sustainable rate."

Comment ———

[Does this mean *Wikipedia* will eventually become a reliable research source?]

Unreliability—vandalism   Spinellis and Louridas 68

Note ——— (paraphrase)

In 2006, 11% of *Wikipedia*'s articles were vandalized at least once, but only 0.13% of at-risk articles were locked.

Comment ———

[Are *Wikipedia*'s current control measures sufficient to prevent vandalism?]

Benefit—stubs   Spinellis and Louridas 71

Note ——— (summary)

"Stub" articles have the potential to become complete articles. Data show that, over time, the coverage of various topics in *Wikipedia* tends to even out.

Comment ———

[Do the benefits of stubs outweigh their drawbacks?]

Notes (on Index Card)

Short heading   Source

Note ——

Comment ——

Drawback — poor writing   Bauerlein 153–54
Bauerlein notes that Wikipedia articles are written in a "flat, featureless, factual style." He goes on to say that "Wikipedia prose sets the standard for intellectual style. Students relying on Wikipedia alone, year in and year out, absorb the prose as proper knowledge discourse, and knowledge itself seems blank and uninspiring."
[Does Wikipedia's poor writing actually influence students' writing?]

Note: Various note-taking programs, such as *Evernote* or *Notely*, can help you to keep track of your notes.

② Managing Photocopies and Downloaded Material

Much of the information you gather will be in the form of photocopies (of articles, book pages, and so on) and material downloaded (and perhaps printed out) from the Internet or from a library database. Learning to manage this source information efficiently will save you a lot of time.

> **ESL TIP**
>
> Taking notes in English (rather than in your native language) will make it easier for you to transfer the notes into a draft of your paper. However, you may find it faster and more effective to use your native language when writing your own comments about each note.

First, do not use the ease of copying and downloading as an excuse to postpone decisions about the usefulness of your sources. After all, you can easily accumulate so many pages that it will be almost impossible for you to keep track of all your information.

Also keep in mind that photocopies and downloaded articles are just raw material, not information that you have already interpreted and evaluated. Making copies of sources is only the first step in the process of taking thorough, careful notes. You still have to evaluate, paraphrase, and summarize your sources' ideas and make connections among them.

Moreover, photocopies and downloaded material do not give you much flexibility. For example, a single page of text may include information that should be earmarked for several different sections of your paper. This lack of flexibility makes it almost impossible for you to arrange source material into any meaningful order. Just as you would with any source, you will have to take notes on the information you read. These notes will give you the flexibility you need to write your paper.

Close-Up   AVOIDING PLAGIARISM

To avoid the possibility of accidental plagiarism, be sure to keep all down-loaded material in a separate file—not in your Notes file. After you read this material and decide how to use it, you can move the information you use into your Notes file (along with full source information).

See Ch. 20

CHECKLIST

Working with Photocopies and Downloaded Material

To get the most out of photocopies and material downloaded from the Internet, follow these guidelines:

❏ Record full and accurate source information, including the inclusive page numbers, electronic address (URL), and any other relevant information, on the first page of each copy.

❏ For printed material, clip or staple together consecutive pages of a single source.

❏ Do not photocopy or print out a source without reminding yourself—*in writing*—why you are doing so. In pencil or on removable self-stick notes, record your initial responses to the source's ideas, jot down cross-references to other works or notes, and highlight important sections.

❏ Photocopying can be time-consuming and expensive, so try to avoid copying material that is only marginally relevant to your paper.

❏ Keep photocopies and printouts in a separate file so you will be able to find them when you need them. Keep all electronic copies of source material together in one clearly labeled file.

Note: Many electronic tools give you other options for saving and organizing your source material. For example, you can use a program called *Zotero* to help you build your bibliography, and you can use a wiki to upload material, organize it into folders, and record your evaluations of various sources. **See 20b** for information on how using such resources can help you to avoid unintentional plagiarism.

15g   Fine-Tuning Your Thesis

After you have finished your focused research and note-taking, you should be ready to refine your tentative thesis into a carefully worded statement that expresses a conclusion your research can support. This **thesis statement**

See 5a–b

should be more precise than your tentative thesis, accurately conveying the direction, emphasis, and scope of your paper.

Compare Rebecca's tentative thesis with her final thesis statement.

Thesis Statement

Tentative Thesis

The debate surrounding *Wikipedia* has helped people in the academic community to consider how college-level research has changed in recent years.

Thesis Statement

Despite its contentious nature, the debate surrounding *Wikipedia* has overall been a positive development because it has led the academic community to confront the evolving nature of college-level research in the twenty-first century.

15h   Constructing an Outline

Once you have a thesis statement, you are ready to make an outline to guide you as you write your rough draft.

See 6c4

A formal outline is different from a list of the main points you tentatively plan to develop in your paper. A **formal outline**—which may be either a **topic outline** or a **sentence outline**—includes all the ideas you will develop in your paper, indicating both the exact order in which you will present these ideas and the relationship between main points and supporting details.

Note: The outline you construct at this stage is only a guide for you to follow as you draft your paper. During the revision process, you may want to construct another outline to check the logic of your paper's organization.

Rebecca James made the following topic outline to guide her as she wrote the first draft of her research paper.

Formal (Topic) Outline

Thesis statement: Despite its contentious nature, the debate surrounding *Wikipedia* has overall been a positive development because it has led the academic community to confront the evolving nature of college-level research in the twenty-first century.

    I. Definition of wiki and explanation of *Wikipedia*

        A. Fast and easy

        B. Range of topics

II. Introduction to *Wikipedia*'s drawbacks

    A. Warnings on "Researching with *Wikipedia*" page

    B. Criticisms of *Wikipedia* article

    C. Middlebury College history department example

III. *Wikipedia*'s unreliability

    A. Lack of citations, factual inaccuracy, and bias

    B. Vandalism

IV. *Wikipedia*'s poor writing

    A. *Wikipedia*'s coding system

    B. Bauerlein's point about *Wikipedia*'s influence on students' writing

 V. *Wikipedia*'s popularity and benefits

    A. Pew report statistic and table

    B. Comprehensive abstracts, internal and external links, and current and comprehensive bibliographies

VI. *Wikipedia*'s benefits over professionally edited online encyclopedias

    A. Current and popular culture topics

    B. "Stub" articles

VII. *Wikipedia*'s growth potential

    A. *Wikipedia*'s control measures

    B. Users as editors

    C. "Talk" page

VIII. Spinellis and Louridas

    A. Summary of their study

    B. Graph showing *Wikipedia*'s topic coverage

IX. Academia's reluctance to work with *Wikipedia*

    A. Academics' failure to keep up with technology

    B. Academics' qualifications to improve *Wikipedia*

 X. Librarians' efforts to use and improve *Wikipedia*

    A. Badke and Bennington's support of *Wikipedia*

    B. Pressley, McCallum, and other librarians' success stories

Close-Up   OUTLINING

Before you begin writing, create a separate file for each major section of your outline. Then, copy your notes into these files in the order in which you intend to use them.

Make sure that you label the files clearly for later reference. Each file name should include a reference to the class and assignment for which it was written. For instance, Rebecca's file for the section of her English 102 essay on *Wikipedia*'s growth potential is called "102 Wikipedia Growth Potential." The individual files relating to this paper are all collected in a folder titled "Eng 102 Wikipedia." By organizing your files in this way, you can print out each file as you need it and use it as a guide as you write.

15i   Writing a Rough Draft

See 6a

When you are ready to write your **rough draft,** check to be sure you have arranged your notes in the order in which you intend to use them. Follow your outline as you write, using your notes as needed. As you draft, write notes to yourself in brackets, jotting down questions and identifying points that need further clarification and areas that need more development. You can also use *Microsoft Word*'s Comment tool to add notes.

As you move along, leave space for material you plan to add, and identify phrases or whole sections that you think you may later decide to move or delete. In other words, lay the groundwork for revision.

As your draft takes shape, be sure to supply transitions between sentences and paragraphs to indicate how your points are related. To make it easy for you to revise later on, you might want to triple-space your draft. Also be careful to copy source information fully and accurately in this and every subsequent draft, placing documentation as close as possible to the material it identifies.

1   Shaping the Parts of the Paper

Like any other essay, a research paper has an introduction, a body, and a conclusion. In your rough draft, as in your outline, you focus on the body of your paper. Don't spend too much time planning your introduction or conclusion at this stage; your ideas will change as you write, and you will need to revise and expand your opening and closing paragraphs later to reflect those changes.

Introduction   In your **introduction,** you identify your topic and establish how you will approach it, perhaps presenting an overview of the problem you will discuss or summarizing research already done on your topic. Your **introduction** also includes your thesis statement, which presents the position you will support in the rest of the paper.

See 7e2

Body   As you draft the **body** of your paper, you lead readers through your discussion with clearly worded <u>topic sentences</u> that correspond to the divisions of your outline.

See 7a1

> Without a professional editorial board to oversee its development, *Wikipedia* has several shortcomings that ultimately limit its trustworthiness as a research source.

You can also use <u>headings</u> if they are a convention of the discipline in which you are writing.

See 26b

> <u>*Wikipedia*'s Advantages</u>
>
> *Wikipedia* has advantages over other, professionally edited online encyclopedias.

Use different <u>patterns of development</u> to shape the individual sections of your paper, and be sure to connect your sentences and paragraphs with clear transitions. If necessary, connect two sections of your paper with a <u>transitional paragraph</u> that shows their relationship.

See 7d

See 7e1

Conclusion   In the **conclusion** of your research paper, you may want to restate your thesis. This is especially important in a long paper because by the time your readers get to the end, they may have lost sight of your paper's main idea. Your <u>conclusion</u> can also include a summary of your key points, a call for action, or perhaps an apt quotation. (Remember, however, that in your rough draft, your concluding paragraph is usually very brief.)

See 7e3

2 **Working Source Material into Your Paper**

In the body of your paper, you evaluate and interpret your sources, comparing different ideas and assessing various points of view. As a writer, your job is to draw your own conclusions, blending information from various sources into a paper that coherently and forcefully presents your own original viewpoint.

Be sure to <u>integrate source material</u> smoothly into your paper, clearly and accurately identifying the relationships among various sources (and between those sources' ideas and your own). If two sources present conflicting interpretations, you should be especially careful to use precise language and accurate transitions to make the contrast apparent (for instance, **Although some academics believe that** *Wikipedia* **should not be a part of college-level research, Pressley and McCallum argue . . .**). When two sources agree, you should make this clear (for example, **Like Badke, Bennington claims . . .** or **Spinellis and Louridas's findings support Pressley and McCallum's point**). Such phrasing will provide a context for your own comments and conclusions. If different sources present complementary information about a subject, blend details from the sources carefully, keeping track of which details come from which source.

See 18d

? ③ Integrating Visuals

See
Ch. 3,
26d

Photographs, diagrams, graphs, and other <u>visuals</u> can be very useful in your research paper because they can provide additional support for the points you make. You can create a visual on your own (for example, by taking a photograph or creating a bar graph). You can also scan an appropriate visual from a book or magazine or access an image database. When you add a visual to a paper, be sure to provide a caption that identifies the name of the person who created it. This will enable readers to find full source information in your works-cited list.

When Rebecca searched *Google*'s image database, she found a visual to include in her paper (see Figure 15.4).

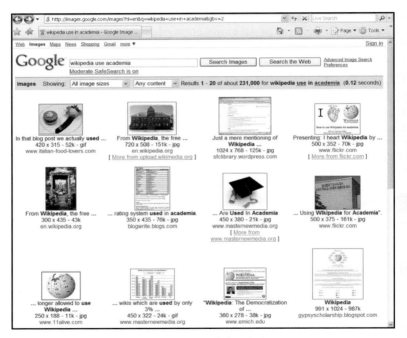

FIGURE 15.4 Image database search results. © Google, Inc.

15j Revising Your Drafts

As you review your drafts, you follow the revision procedures that apply to any paper (**see 6b–c**). In addition, you should review the questions in the checklist on page 169, which apply specifically to research papers.

1 Outlining

A good way to begin revising is to make a formal <u>outline</u> of your draft to
check the logic of its organization and the relationships among sections.
When Rebecca began to revise, the first thing she did was construct a
sentence outline to check the structure of her paper. An excerpt from her
sentence outline is shown below.

See 6c4, 15h

Sentence Outline (Excerpt)

<u>Thesis statement:</u> Despite its contentious nature, the debate surrounding
Wikipedia has overall been a positive development because it has led the
academic community to confront the evolving nature of college-level
research in the twenty-first century.

    I. *Wikipedia* is the most popular wiki.

        A. Users can edit existing articles and add new articles using
Wikipedia's editing tools.

        B. *Wikipedia* has grown into a huge collection of articles on a vast
range of topics.

    II. *Wikipedia* has several shortcomings that ultimately limit its
trustworthiness as a research source.

        A. Many *Wikipedia* articles lack reliability.

            1. Many *Wikipedia* articles do not supply citations to the
sources that support their claims.

            2. *Wikipedia* articles can be factually inaccurate, biased, and
even targeted for vandalism.

2 Instructor's Comments

Your instructor's suggestions for revisions can come in a conference or in
handwritten comments on your paper. Your instructor can also use *Microsoft Word*'s Comment tool to make comments electronically on a draft that
you email to him or her. When you revise, you can incorporate these suggestions into your paper, as Rebecca did.

Draft with Instructor's Comments (Excerpt)

    Emory University English professor Mark Bauerlein
asserts that *Wikipedia* articles are written in a "flat,
featureless, factual style" (153). *Wikipedia* has instituted
a coding system in which it labels the shortcomings of its

Comment [JB1]: You need a
transition sentence before
this one to show that this
¶ is about a new idea.
See 7b2.

Comment [JB2]: Wordy.
See 42a.

less-developed articles, but a warning about an article's poor writing style is likely to go unnoticed by the typical user.

Revision Incorporating Instructor's Suggestions

Because their content is open to public editing, *Wikipedia* articles also often suffer from poor writing. Emory University English professor Mark Bauerlein asserts that *Wikipedia* articles are written in a "flat, featureless, factual style" (153). *Wikipedia* has instituted a coding system to label the shortcomings of its less developed articles, but a warning about an article's poor writing style is likely to go unnoticed by the typical user.

 3 Peer Review

See
6c2

Feedback you get from **peer review**—other students' comments, handwritten or electronic—can also help you revise. As you incorporate your classmates' suggestions, as well as your own changes and any suggested by your instructor, you can use *Microsoft Word*'s Track Changes tool to help you keep track of the revisions you make on your draft.

Following are two versions of an excerpt from Rebecca's paper. The first version includes comments (inserted with *Microsoft Word*'s Comment tool) from three peer reviewers. The second uses the Track Changes tool to show the revisions Rebecca made in response to these comments.

Draft with Peer Reviewers' Comments (Excerpt)

Because users can update articles in real time from any location, *Wikipedia* offers up-to-the-minute coverage of political and cultural events as well as timely information on popular culture topics that receive little or no attention from other sources. Even when the available information on a particular topic is sparse, *Wikipedia* allows users to create "stub" articles, which provide minimal information that users can expand over time. According to a 2008 study, approximately 20% of *Wikipedia*'s articles are classified as stubs. Thus, *Wikipedia* can be a valuable first step in finding reliable research sources.

Comment [RS1]: I think you need a better transition here.

Comment [TG2]: I think an example here would really help.

Comment [DL3]: I agree. Maybe talk about a useful *Wikipedia* article you found recently.

Comment [RS4]: Which study?

Comment [DL5]: Do you need a pg. #?

Comment [RS6]: I think you need a better transition here.

Revision with Track Changes

Wikipedia has advantages over other, professionally edited online encyclopedias. Because users can update articles in real time from any location, *Wikipedia* offers up-to-the-minute coverage of political and cultural events as well as timely information on popular culture topics that receive little or no attention from other sources. For example, a student researching the history of video gaming would find *Wikipedia*'s "Wii" article, with its numerous pages of information and nearly 150 external links to additional sources, to be a valuable resource. *Encyclopaedia Britannica Online* does not contain a comparable article on this popular game console. Even when the available information on a particular topic is sparse, *Wikipedia* allows users to create "stub" articles, which provide minimal information that users can expand over time. According to a̶ ̶2̶0̶0̶8̶ Spinellis and Louridas's study, approximately 20% of *Wikipedia*'s articles are classified as stubs. ̶T̶h̶u̶s̶ (70). By offering immediate access to information on relatively obscure topics, *Wikipedia* can be a valuable first step in finding reliable research sources on such topics.

CHECKLIST
Revising a Research Paper

As you revise your research paper, consider the following questions:

❑ Should you do more research to find support for certain points?
❑ Do you need to reorder the major sections of your paper?
❑ Should you rearrange the order in which you present your points within sections?
❑ Do you need to add section headings? transitional paragraphs?
❑ Have you **integrated source material** smoothly into your paper?

See 18d

❑ Have you chosen visuals carefully and integrated them smoothly into your paper?
❑ Are quotations blended with paraphrase, summary, and your own observations and reactions?
❑ Have you avoided **plagiarism** by carefully documenting all borrowed ideas?

See Ch. 20

❑ Have you analyzed and interpreted the ideas of others rather than simply stringing those ideas together?
❑ Do your own ideas—not those of your sources—define the focus of your discussion?

Note: You will probably take your paper through several drafts, changing different parts of it each time or working on one part over and over again. After revising each draft thoroughly, print out a corrected version, and label it *First Draft, Second Draft*, and so on. Then, make additional corrections by hand on that draft before typing in your changes to create the next draft. Be sure to save and clearly label every electronic draft of your paper so you can go back to a previous draft if necessary.

Close-Up PREPARING YOUR WORKS-CITED LIST

When you finish revising your paper, copy the file that contains your working bibliography and insert it at the end of your paper. Keep the original file for your working bibliography as a backup in case any data is lost in the process. Delete any irrelevant entries, and then create your works-cited list. (Make sure the format of the entries in your works-cited list conforms to the documentation style you are using.)

If you save multiple drafts of your works-cited list, be sure to name each file with the date or some other label so that it is readily identifiable. Keep all files pertaining to a single project in a folder dedicated to that paper or assignment.

Note: You can use citation software programs such as *Zotero, CiteMe, Endnote,* and *EasyBib* to create your bibliography and to make sure all the sources you used—and only those sources—appear in your works-cited list.

15k Preparing a Final Draft

See 6d

See 1a

Before you print out the final version of your paper, **edit and proofread** hard copy of both your paper and your works-cited list. Next, consider (or reconsider) your paper's **title.** It should be descriptive enough to tell your readers what your paper is about, and it should create interest in your subject. Your title should also be consistent with the **purpose** and tone of your paper. (You would hardly want a humorous title for a paper about the death penalty or world hunger.) Finally, your title should be engaging and to the point—and perhaps even provocative. Often, a quotation from one of your sources will suggest a likely title.

When you are satisfied with your title, read your paper one last time, proofreading for grammar, spelling, or typing errors you may have missed. Pay particular attention to parenthetical documentation and works-cited entries. (Remember that every error undermines your credibility.) Once you are satisfied that your paper is as accurate as you can make it, print out your final draft. Then, fasten the pages with a paper clip (do not staple the pages or fold the corners together), and hand it in. Some instructors will allow you to email your final draft. (For the final draft of Rebecca's research paper, along with her works-cited list, **see 21c.**)

CHAPTER 16

Finding and Evaluating Web Sources

The **Web** (which is part of the Internet) is the research tool of choice for most college students. This strategy is not without its drawbacks, however. Because no one is responsible for checking Web documents to make sure they are trustworthy, factually accurate, or current, you have to use them with care.

Of course, there are many trustworthy sources of information on the Internet. For example, *Google Scholar* provides links to many scholarly sources that are as often as reliable as those found in your college library's databases. In addition, *The Directory of Open Access Journals* <doaj.org> lists almost six thousand open-access scientific and scholarly journals—many of which are highly respected—in its directories. Even so, because so much information on the Web is untrustworthy, it is important to carefully <u>evaluate</u> the material you find before you use it in your papers.

See
16c

16a Using the Web for Research

To carry out a Web search, you need a **Web browser,** an application—such as *Microsoft Internet Explorer, Mozilla Firefox, Safari, Opera*, or *Chrome*—that enables you to view information on the Web.

Close-Up   USING A BROWSER TO MANAGE YOUR RESEARCH

In addition to connecting you to the Web, a browser can help you keep track of your research.

- By using the browser's Bookmark function, you can save useful URLs.
- By using the browser's History function, you can view a list of the sites you have accessed during a research session.

Every document on the Web has an electronic address called a **URL** (uniform resource locator). Once you paste this URL into your browser's location field and click on Search, you will be connected to the Web site you want. (Figure 16.1 on page 172 shows a location field.)

Location
field
(enter URL)

FIGURE 16.1 Entering an address in *Internet Explorer*. © 2009 Netscape
Communications Corporation.

Close-Up TROUBLESHOOTING

If you cannot connect to a particular Web site, try the following strategies:

- Wait a short period of time, and try again. If a Web site is extremely
  busy, it may block users.
- Make sure that you have typed in the URL correctly. Adding a space or
  omitting a punctuation mark will send you to the wrong site—or to no
  site at all.
- If the URL is very long, delete a section at the end of the URL—from
  slash to slash—and try again.
- Try using just the base URL, deleting everything after *.com* or *.gov,* for
  example. If this abbreviated URL does not take you where you want to
  go, you have an incorrect address.
- If you are following a link from one document to another and cannot
  connect, type the URL of the link into the location field of your search
  engine, and try again.

A Web site's URL provides a good deal of information about how the files in a Web site are organized. For example, consider the following URL.

http://www.google.com

The *http* indicates that the file is in hypertext transfer protocol. After the colon and the two slashes is the name of the server on which the file is stored (www.google.com). The *www* tells you that the site is on the World Wide Web, *google* is the domain name, and *com* shows that this is a commercial site.

Longer URLs with more slashes usually indicate additional folders. So, the URL <http://www.drexel.edu/academic/coas/engphil/writingcontest.asp> indicates that the page you are looking at (*writingcontest.asp*) is inside a folder called *engphil,* which is inside another folder called *coas,* which in turn is inside a folder called *academic.* All these folders are located on the Drexel University server, *www.drexel.edu.*

Once you are connected to the Web, you use your browser to access a **search engine,** an application such as *Google, Yahoo!,* or *Ask.com* that searches for and retrieves documents. When you do research on the Web, your goal is to find information about your topic. There are two ways to use search engines to find the information you want: *by doing a keyword search* and *by using subject guides.*

❶ Doing a Keyword Search

The most common method of locating information is through a **keyword** **search.** You do this by entering a keyword (or words) into your search engine's search field. (Figure 16.2 shows a search engine's keyword search page.) The search engine will identify any site in its database on which the

FIGURE 16.2 *Google* keyword search page. © Google, Inc.

keyword (or words) you have typed appears. (These are called **hits.**) If, for example, you simply type *Civil War* (say, in hope of finding information on Fort Sumter during the Civil War), the search engine will generate an enormous list of hits. In addition to sites that might be relevant to your research, this list will also include many irrelevant sites, such as the Civil War Reenactors home page and sites that focus on Civil War music.

You can develop a list of useful keywords by looking online at the subject catalog of your college library and using its headings as keywords. You can also find keywords by looking at the list of subject headings in the *Library of Congress Subject Headings* (available electronically or at the reference desk of your school library). Finally, you can access an online general encyclopedia, such as *Wikipedia,* and look at the category list that follows each article. These categories make excellent keywords that you can use as you search. (Keep in mind, however, that articles from general encyclopedias are not acceptable for college-level research.)

Because keyword searching can yield thousands of irrelevant hits, you need to focus your search by using **search operators,** words and symbols that tell a search engine how to interpret your keywords. One way to focus your search is to put quotation marks around your search term (type *"Fort Sumter"* rather than *Fort Sumter*). This will direct the search engine to locate only documents containing this phrase.

Another way to focus your search is to carry out a **Boolean search,** a process named after George Boole, a nineteenth-century British logician and mathematician. You carry out a Boolean search by combining keywords with AND, OR, NOT (typed in all capital letters), or a plus or minus sign to eliminate irrelevant hits from your search. (To do this type of search, you may have to select a search engine's Advanced Search option.)

Close-Up　USING SEARCH OPERATORS

" " (quotation marks) Use quotation marks to search for a specific phrase: *"Baltimore Economy"*

AND Use AND to search for sites that contain both terms: *Baltimore* AND *Economy*

OR Use OR to search for sites that contain either term: *Baltimore* OR *Economy*

NOT Use NOT to exclude the term that comes after the NOT: *Baltimore* AND *Economy* NOT *Agriculture*

* (asterisk) Use an asterisk after a word to tell the search engine to look for a word plus any ending. For example, the term *photo** will yield *photograph, photographer, photojournalist, photoactive, photosynthesis,* and so on.

? (question mark) Use a question mark to tell the search engine to look for a group of letters plus one varying character. For example, *?at* will yield *hat, bat, cat, fat, mat,* and so on.

Note: Many search engines offer advanced options that allow you to tailor your search even further.

② Using Subject Guides

Most search engines, such as *Yahoo!, About.com,* and *Google,* contain a **subject guide** (or **search directory**)—a list of general categories from which you can choose. (Figure 16.3 shows the *Yahoo!* directory.) Each general category will lead you to a more specific list of categories and subcategories until you get to the topic you want. For example, clicking on *Society and Culture* might lead you to *Activism* and then to *Animal Rights* and eventually to an article focusing on cruelty to animals on factory farms. Although

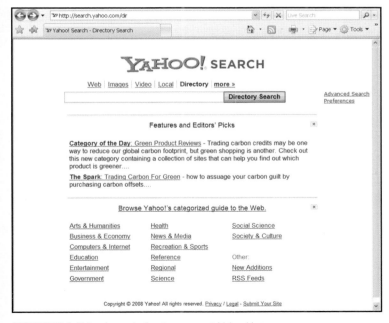

FIGURE 16.3 *Yahoo!* search directory page. © Yahoo! Inc.

See
17a

using subject guides is a time-consuming strategy for finding specific information, it can be an excellent tool during **exploratory research,** when you want to find or narrow a topic.

Note: You can access *Google's* directory by going to <google.com/dirhp>.

❸ Choosing the Right Search Engine

General-Purpose Search Engines   The most widely used search engines are **general-purpose search engines** that focus on a wide variety of topics. Some of these search engines are more user-friendly than others; some allow for more sophisticated searching functions; some are updated more frequently; and some are more comprehensive than others. As you try out various search engines, you will probably settle on a favorite that you will turn to first whenever you need to find information.

Close-Up   POPULAR SEARCH ENGINES

AltaVista <altavista.com>: Good, precise engine for focused searches. Fast and easy to use. Large database.

Ask.com <ask.com>: Allows you to narrow your search by asking questions, such as *Are dogs smarter than pigs?*

Bing <bing.com>: Currently the third most widely used search engine on the Web, *Bing* has a variety of specialized functions that sort responses into categories. By clicking on progressively narrower categories, you get more specific results. In some searches, a single "Best Match" response may appear. Excellent image and video functions.

Excite <excite.com>: Good for general topics. Because it searches over 250 million Web sites, you often receive more information than you need.

Google <google.com>: Arguably the best search engine available, it accesses a large database that includes both text and graphics. It is easy to navigate, and searches usually yield a high percentage of useful hits. (See page 177 for more information about *Google* resources.)

HotBot <hotbot.com>: Excellent, fast search engine for locating specific information. Good search options allow you to fine-tune your searches.

Lycos <lycos.com>: Enables you to search for specific media (graphics, for example). A somewhat small index of Web pages.

Yahoo! <yahoo.com>: Good for exploratory research. Enables you to search using either subject headings or keywords. Searches its own indexes as well as the Web.

Because even the best search engines search only a fraction of what is on the Web, if you use only one search engine, you will most likely miss much valuable information. It is therefore a good idea to repeat each search with several different search engines or to use one of the **metasearch** or **metacrawler** engines that uses several search engines simultaneously.

Close-Up   METASEARCH ENGINES

Dogpile <dogpile.com>
Ixquick <ixquick.com>
Metacrawler <metacrawler.com>
Zworks <zworks.com>

Specialized Search Engines   In addition to the popular general-purpose search engines and metasearch engines, there are also numerous **specialized search engines** devoted entirely to specific subject areas, such as literature, business, sports, and women's issues. Hundreds of such specialized search engines are indexed at *The Search Engine List* <thesearchenginelist.com>. These sites are especially useful during <u>focused research</u>, when you are looking for in-depth information about your topic.

See 17b

Close-Up   *GOOGLE* RESOURCES

Google is the most-used search engine on the Internet. In fact, many people now say that they are going to "Google" a subject rather than search it. Few people who use *Google,* however, actually know its full potential. Following are just a few of the resources that *Google* offers:

- ***Blog Search***   Enables users to find blogs on specific subjects
- ***Blogger***   A tool for creating and posting blogs online
- ***Book Search***   A database that allows users to access the full text of thousands of books
- ***Google Earth***   A downloadable, dynamic global map that enables users to see satellite views of almost any place on the planet
- ***Finance***   Business information, news, and interactive charts
- ***News***   Enables users to search thousands of news stories

(continued)

GOOGLE RESOURCES *(continued)*

- *Patent Search* Enables users to search the full text of US patents
- *Google Scholar* Searches scholarly literature, including peer-reviewed papers, books, and abstracts

You can access these tools by going to the *Google* home page, clicking on MORE in the upper left of your screen, and then clicking on EVEN MORE on the pull-down menu.

Even though all search engines rank results according to relevance, they have different ways of "deciding" what is relevant. For this reason, search engines have strengths and weakness. *NoodleTools* <noodletools.com> is a useful Web site that lists a large number of search engines (some general and some specialized) and helps you choose the one that is best suited for finding the information you need.

Close-Up   *GOOGLE SCHOLAR*

Although *Google Scholar* gives you access to some high-quality resources and often indicates how many Web sites have cited these sources, it does have some drawbacks:

- First, because it does not clearly define *scholar,* you have to make sure any articles you use conform to academic standards of reliability and scholarship.
- Second, the *Google Scholar* database will list some articles that you must pay to read. (You can often access these articles without charge from your college library's databases.)

16b Surveying Specialized Web Resources

The Web provides a number of specialized resources that you can use in your research. These Web sites often give you access to more focused and more authoritative resources than you get when you do a general keyword or subject search.

General Research
- *Librarians' Internet Index*—A search engine that lists sites judged reliable by librarians <lii.org>

- *Infomine*—A search engine with links to over 8,500 librarian-selected scholarly and educational Internet resources <ariadne.ac.uk/issue8/infomine>
- *Smithsonian Institution Libraries*—A collection of twenty libraries from the world's largest museum complex <sil.si.edu>
- *The National Archives*—A list of all of the National Archives' research tools and databases <archives.gov/research/tools/index.html>
- *Encyclopaedia Britannica*—The reliable encyclopedia, searchable with full text online <britannica.com>

Art
- *Guggenheim Museum*—A collection of over 160 artists, searchable by artist name, title, date, movement, medium, concept, and museum <guggenheimcollection.org/index.html>
- *The National Gallery of Art*—A searchable catalog of the museum's 110,000 objects, with more than 6,000 images available online <nga.gov/collection/index.shtm>

Books Online
- *Project Gutenberg*—A searchable catalog of more than 19,000 full-text books <gutenberg.org/wiki/Main_Page>

Business
- *Explorit Now!*—A Web site that gives access to numerous business journals and databases <business.exploritnow.com>
- *CBDNet*—A searchable database of materials published by the US Department of Commerce <cbdnet.access.gpo.gov/search2.html>

Government
- *American FactFinder*—A collection of census bureau data searchable by city, county, or ZIP code <factfinder.census.gov/home/saff/main.html>
- *FedStats*—A gateway to statistics from over one hundred US federal agencies <fedstats.gov>
- *Historical Census Browser*—A repository of historical US census data dating back to 1790, compiled by the University of Virginia <fisher.lib.virginia.edu/collections/stats/histcensus>
- *United States Government Printing Office (GPO)*—A search engine for multiple government databases <gpoaccess.gov/multidb.html>

Humanities
- *Voice of the Shuttle*—A comprehensive humanities search engine <vos.ucsb.edu>
- *World Wide Web Subject Catalog*—A catalog of annotated Internet resources maintained by the University of Kentucky Libraries <uky.edu/Libraries/guide.php?lsub_id=79&1tab_id=1400>
- *Humanities Web*—A Web site that shows the interconnections between history, arts, and culture <humanitiesweb.org>

Library of Congress

- *Library of Congress*—A searchable catalog that contains over 130 million items <loc.gov/search/new>
- *Library of Congress Digital Collections*—A searchable database of the LOC's items that have been digitized and are available online <loc.gov/library/libarch-digital.html>

CHECKLIST

Tips for Effective Web Searches

❑ **Choose the right search engine.** No one all-purpose search engine exists. Review the list of search engines in the boxes on pages 176–177.

❑ **Choose your keywords carefully.** A search engine is only as good as the keywords you use.

❑ **Include enough terms.** If you are looking for information on housing, for example, search for several variations of your keyword: *housing, houses, home buyer, buying houses, residential real estate,* and so on.

❑ **Use more than one search engine.** Because different search engines index different sites, try several. If one does not yield results after a few tries, try another. Also, don't forget to try a metasearch engine like *Metacrawler*.

❑ **Add useful sites to your Bookmark or Favorites list.** Whenever you find a particularly useful Web site, **bookmark** it by selecting this option on the menu bar of your browser (with some browsers, such as *Microsoft Explorer*, this option is called Favorites).

Using *Wikipedia* as a Research Source

Wikipedia is an open-source general encyclopedia created through the collaborative efforts of its users. Anyone registered with the site can write an article, and anyone who views the site can edit an article.

Although *Wikipedia* can give you a good general overview of your subject, you should not use it (or any other general encyclopedia) as a source. In addition, because *Wikipedia* has no editorial staff responsible for checking entries for accuracy, you should not rely on it for factual information. However, not all instructors share this view of *Wikipedia*. They point out that over time, *Wikipedia* entries usually get better. In addition, they say that *Wikipedia* not only provides up-to-date information but also includes bibliographic citations that enable students to link to more reliable sources. Keep in mind, however, that this is a minority opinion. For most instructors, *Wikipedia* is simply not an acceptable research source.

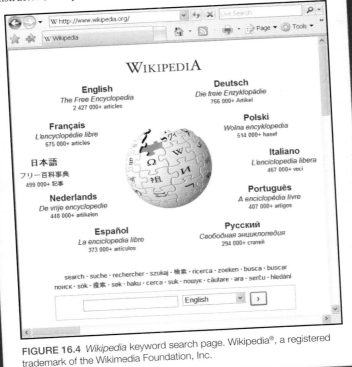

FIGURE 16.4 *Wikipedia* keyword search page. Wikipedia®, a registered trademark of the Wikimedia Foundation, Inc.

16c Evaluating Web Sites

Because anyone can post information on the Web, determining the quality of a Web site is crucial if you plan to use it as a source for your research. For this reason, you should evaluate the content of any Web site for *accuracy, credibility, objectivity, currency,* and *scope of coverage.*

Accuracy **Accuracy** refers to the reliability of the material itself and to its use of proper documentation.

Factual errors—especially errors in facts that are central to the main idea of the source—should cause you to question the reliability of the material you are reading. To evaluate a site's accuracy, ask these questions:

- Is the text free of basic grammatical and mechanical errors?
- Does the site contain factual errors?
- Does the site provide a list of references?
- Are working links available to other sources?
- Can information be verified by print or other sources?

Credibility   **Credibility** refers to the credentials of the person or organization responsible for the site.

Web sites operated by well-known institutions (the Smithsonian or the Library of Congress, for example) have a high degree of credibility. Those operated by individuals (personal Web pages or blogs, for example) are often less reliable. To evaluate a site's credibility, ask these questions:

- Does the site list an author (or authors)? Are credentials (for example, professional or academic affiliations) provided for the author?
- Is the author a recognized authority in his or her field?
- Is the site **refereed?** That is, does an editorial board or a group of experts determine what material appears on the Web site?
- Can you determine how long the Web site has existed?

Objectivity   **Objectivity** refers to the degree of bias that a Web site exhibits.

Some Web sites strive for objectivity, but others make no secret of their biases. They openly advocate a particular point of view or action, or they clearly try to sell something. Some Web sites may try to hide their biases. For example, a Web site may present itself as a source of factual information when it is actually advocating a political point of view. To evaluate a site's objectivity, ask these questions:

- Does advertising appear in the text?
- Does a business, a political organization, or a special interest group sponsor the site?
- Does the site express a particular viewpoint?
- Does the site contain links to other sites that express a particular viewpoint?

Currency   **Currency** refers to how up to date the Web site is.

The easiest way to assess a site's currency is to see when it was last updated. Keep in mind, however, that even if the date on the site is current, the information that the site contains may not be. To evaluate a site's currency, ask these questions:

- Does the site include the date when it was last updated?
- Are all the links to other sites still functioning?
- Is the actual information on the page up to date?
- Does the site clearly identify the date it was created?

CHECKLIST

Determining the Legitimacy of an Anonymous or Questionable Web Source

When a Web source is anonymous (or has an author whose name is not familiar to you), you have to take special measures to determine its legitimacy:

❑ **Follow the links.** Follow the hypertext links in a document to other documents. If the links take you to legitimate sources, you know that the author is aware of these sources of information.

❑ **Find out what Web pages link to the site.** You can go to <alexa.com> to find information about a Web site. Type the Web site's URL into *Alexa*'s search box, and you will be given the volume of traffic to the site, the ownership information for the site, and the other sites visited by people who visited the URL. In addition, you will be also be given a link to the "Wayback Machine," an archive that shows what the page looked like in the past.

❑ **Do a keyword search.** Do a search using the name of the sponsoring organization or the author as keywords. Other documents (or citations in other works) may identify the author.

❑ **Verify the information.** Check the information you find against a reliable source—a textbook or a reputable Web site, for example. Also, see if you can find information that contradicts what you have found.

❑ **Check the quality of the writing.** Review the writing on the Web site to see if there are typos, misspellings, and errors in grammar or word choice. If the writer is careless about these things, he or she has probably not spent much time checking facts.

❑ **Look at the URL.** Although a Web site's URL is not a foolproof guide to the site's purpose, it does give you some useful information. The last part of a Web site's URL (immediately following the **domain name**) can tell you whether the site is sponsored by a commercial entity (*.com*), a nonprofit organization (*.org*), an educational institution (*.edu*), the military (*.mil*), or a government agency (*.gov*). Knowing this information can help you assess its legitimacy.

Scope of Coverage **Scope of coverage** refers to the comprehensiveness of the information on a Web site.

More coverage is not necessarily better, but some sites may be incomplete. Others may provide information that is no more than common knowledge. Still others may present discussions that are not suitable for college-level research. To evaluate the scope of a site's coverage, ask these questions:

• Does the site provide in-depth coverage?
• Does the site provide information that is not available elsewhere?
• Does the site identify a target audience? Does this target audience suggest the site is appropriate for your research needs?

Close-Up EVALUATING MATERIAL FROM ONLINE FORUMS

Be especially careful with material posted on listservs, blogs, newsgroups, discussion boards, and other online forums. Unless you can adequately evaluate this material—for example, determine its accuracy and the credibility of the author or authors—you should not use it in your paper. In most cases, online forums are not good sources of high-quality information.

CHAPTER **17**

Finding and Evaluating Library Sources

Even though the Internet has changed the nature of research, your library should still be a part of any research project. A college library offers re-sources—electronic and print—that you cannot find on the free Internet. In addition, the library's sources are more reliable than much of what you find on the Internet. In the long run, it is a good idea to make your college library part of your research process.

Close-Up WHY USE THE LIBRARY?

- Many important publications are available only in print or through the databases to which the library subscribes.
- The information in your college library will usually be more focused and more useful than information you find by searching the Internet.
- Unlike the sites in your library's databases, the sites you access on the Internet may not be available when you try to access them again later.
- Because librarians screen the material in your college library, you can be reasonably certain that it meets standards for academic research. There-fore, you do not have to spend a great deal of time evaluating it for reliability.
- The authorship and affiliation of Internet documents can often be difficult to determine, but this is seldom the case with the resources in your college library.

17a Doing Exploratory Library Research

During **exploratory research,** your goal is to formulate a research question that you want your paper to answer. At this stage, you search the library's resources to get a general sense of what they include. (Later, during your **focused research,** you will look for specific source material to use in your paper.)

See
17b

1 Consulting Your Library's Web Site

The best way to start your exploratory research is to visit your college library's **Web site.** The Web site's home page is a gateway to a vast amount of information—for example, the library's catalog, specialized holdings, lists of full-text databases to which the library subscribes, special library services, and general information about the library. Many libraries also offer online help to students—for example, study guides on a wide variety of topics and email answers to research questions. Figure 17.1 shows the home page of a university library's online catalog.

FIGURE 17.1 Home page of a university library's online catalog. © Southeastern Louisiana University.

2 Searching Your Library's Online Catalog

The library's **online catalog** is a database that lists all the material held by the library in its collections. You can access this online catalog through the library's Web site. When you search the online catalog for information, you may conduct either a *keyword search* or a *subject search.* (Later on, when you know exactly what you are looking for, you can search for a particular book by title, author, or call number.)

Conducting a Keyword Search When you carry out a keyword search, you enter into the Search box of the online catalog a word (or words) associated with your topic. The computer then displays a list of articles that contain these words in their titles or in their bibliographic citations. The more precise your keywords are, the more specific and useful the information you retrieve will be.

Keyword searching also allows you to link terms using **Boolean operators** (**AND, OR, NOT**). For example, *elderly* **AND** *abuse* would identify books and articles that mention both elderly people and abuse; *elderly* **OR** *aged* **OR** *senior citizens* would identify books and articles that mention any of these terms. Keyword searching is especially useful when you want to narrow or expand the focus of your search.

> **CHECKLIST**
> ## Keyword Dos and Don'ts
>
> When conducting a keyword search, follow these guidelines:
>
> ❑ Use precise, specific keywords to distinguish your topic from similar topics.
>
> ❑ Enter both singular and plural keywords when appropriate—*printing press* and *printing presses*, for example.
>
> ❑ Enter both abbreviations and their full-word equivalents (for example, *US* and *United States*).
>
> ❑ Try variant spellings (for example, *color* and *colour*).
>
> ❑ Don't use too long a string of keywords. (If you do, you will retrieve large amounts of irrelevant material.)

Conducting a Subject Search When you carry out a **subject search,** you enter specific subject headings into the online catalog. Although it may be possible to guess at a subject heading, your search will be more successful if you consult the *Library of Congress Subject Headings,* either online or at the reference desk of your library, to help you identify the exact words you need. Figure 17.2 shows the results of a search in a university's online catalog.

Close-Up KEYWORD SEARCHING VERSUS SUBJECT SEARCHING

Keyword Searching
- Searches many subject areas

- Any significant word or phrase can be used

- Retrieves large number of items
- May retrieve many irrelevant items

Subject Searching
- Searches only a specific subject area
- Only the specific words listed in the *Library of Congress Subject Headings* can be used

- Retrieves small number of items
- Retrieves few irrelevant items

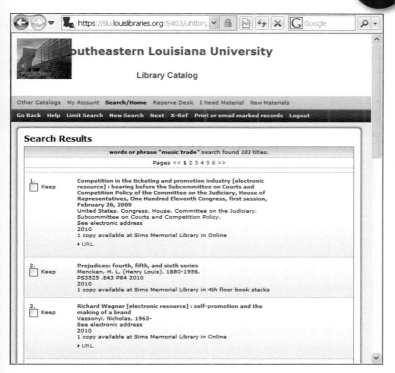

FIGURE 17.2 Online catalog search results for the subject heading *Music Trade.*
© Southeastern Louisiana University.

3 Consulting the Library's General Reference Works

General reference works—encyclopedias, bibliographies, and so on—that provide broad overviews of particular subjects can be helpful when you are doing exploratory research. From these sources, you can get an overview of your topic as well as find dates, places, and names. In addition, general reference works often include bibliographies that you can use later on when you do focused research.

Close-Up GENERAL REFERENCE WORKS

General Encyclopedias Many general multivolume encyclopedias are available in electronic format. For example, *The Encyclopaedia Britannica* is available on CD-ROM and DVD as well as on the World Wide Web at <http://www.britannica.com>.

(continued)

> **GENERAL REFERENCE WORKS** (continued)
>
> **Specialized Encyclopedias, Dictionaries, and Bibliographies** These specialized reference works contain in-depth articles focusing on a single subject area.
>
> **General Bibliographies** General bibliographies—such as *Books in Print* and *The Bibliographic Index*—list books available in a wide variety of fields.
>
> **General Biographical References** Biographical reference books—such as *Who's Who in America, Who's Who*, and *Dictionary of American Biography*—provide information about people's lives as well as bibliographic listings.

Note: Keep in mind that most instructors do not accept encyclopedias as research sources. Although a general encyclopedia is a good place to get an overview of a topic, and the works-cited lists that follow many entries may give you leads, encyclopedia articles are not detailed enough for college-level research. Check with your instructor if you have any questions about his or her policy concerning this issue.

❹ Using Library Databases

Your college library's Web site also enables you to access a variety of other electronic databases.

Online Databases   **Online databases** are collections of digital information—bibliographic citations of books, articles, and abstracts as well as full-text databases—arranged for easy access and retrieval. (You search the library's databases the same way you search the online catalog: by conducting a **keyword search** or a **subject search**.) One of your first tasks should be to determine what databases your library offers. Visit your library's Web site, or ask a reference librarian for more information. Figure 17.3 shows a partial list of databases to which one college library subscribes.

See 17a2

Most libraries subscribe to information service companies such as DIALOG or Gale Group Databases, which provide access to hundreds of databases not available on the Internet. Some library databases cover many subject areas (*Expanded Academic ASAP* or *LexisNexis Academic Universe,* for example); others cover a single subject area in great detail (*PsycINFO* or *Sociological Abstracts*, for example).

Assuming that your library offers a variety of databases, how do you know which ones will be best for your research topic? One strategy is to begin by searching a general database that includes full-text articles and then move on to a more specialized database that covers your subject in more detail. The specialized databases are more likely to include scholarly and professional sources as well as **abstracts** (short summaries) that can

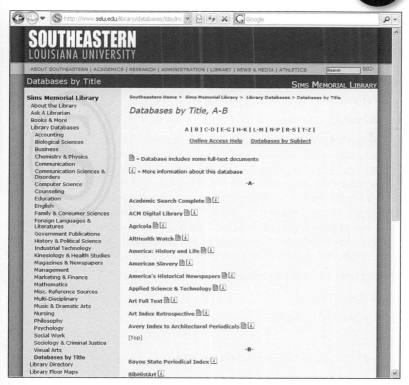

FIGURE 17.3 Excerpt from list of databases to which one college library subscribes.
© Southeastern Louisiana University.

help you determine the usefulness of a source. (Figure 17.4 on page 190 shows a printout from a library subscription database.)

Note: Remember that an article's abstract, such as the one shown in Figure 17.4, is not an acceptable research source. It can, however, help you decide if you want to read the full article.

17b Doing Focused Library Research

Once you have formulated your research question, you move on to **focused research.** During focused research, you examine *primary* and *secondary sources* in order to answer your research question and to gather information related to your topic.

Primary sources are original documents. They include diaries, letters, speeches, manuscripts, memoirs, autobiographies, government records, first-hand accounts, newspaper articles, and even books written at the time an event occurred. Primary sources can also include photographs, films,

Date | Volume number | Issue number | First page of article | Total number of pages

Title: The Supply Side of the Digital Divide: Is There Equal Availability in the Broadband Internet Access Market?

Periodical: *Economic Inquiry,* April 2003 v41 i2 p346(18).

Author: James E. Prieger

Author's Abstract: The newest dimension of the digital divide is access to broadband (high-speed) Internet service. Using comprehensive US data covering all forms of access technology (chiefly DSL and cable modem), I look for evidence of unequal broadband availability in areas with high concentrations of poor, minority, or rural households. There is little evidence of unequal availability based on income or on black or Hispanic concentration. There is mixed evidence concerning availability based on Native American or Asian concentration. Other findings: Rural location decreases availability; market size, education, Spanish language use, commuting distance, and Bell presence increase availability. (JEL L96, J78, L51)

Subjects: Digital Divide (Technology) = Demographic Aspects

Internet = Usage

Features: tables; figures

FIGURE 17.4 Library subscription database printout.

maps, audio and video recordings, statistics and other research data, novels, short stories, poems, and plays. **Secondary sources** are descriptions, interpretations, or analyses of primary sources. Secondary sources include textbooks, journal articles, criticisms, commentaries, and encyclopedia articles.

As you do focused research, you find periodical articles and books, consult specialized reference works, and make use of special library services.

1 Finding Periodical Articles

A **periodical** is a newspaper, magazine, scholarly journal, or other publication published at regular intervals (weekly, monthly, or quarterly). Articles in **scholarly journals** are often the most reliable sources you can find on a subject; they provide current information and are written by experts on the topic. And, because these journals focus on a particular subject area, they can provide in-depth analysis. However, because journal articles are written for experts, they can sometimes be difficult to understand.

Periodical indexes are databases that list articles from a selected group of magazines, newspapers, or scholarly journals. Most college libraries offer these indexes online. They are updated frequently and provide the most current information available.

Close-Up FREQUENTLY USED PERIODICAL INDEXES

Academic libraries usually subscribe to the following periodical indexes. (Be sure to check your library's Web site or ask a librarian about those available to you.)

General Indexes	Description
EBSCOhost	Includes thousands of periodical articles on many subjects
Expanded Academic ASAP	Covers all subjects in thousands of magazines and scholarly journals
FirstSearch	Includes full-text articles from many popular and scholarly periodicals
LexisNexis Academic Universe	Includes full-text articles from national, international, and local newspapers. Also includes large legal and business sections.
Readers' Guide Full-Text Mega Edition	Contains full-text articles for over two hundred journals from as far back as 1994. Indexes over four hundred popular periodicals from as far back as 1983.

Specialized Indexes	Description
Dow Jones Interactive	Includes full-text articles from US newspapers and trade journals
ERIC	Includes education-related journal articles and reports
General BusinessFile ASAP	Includes full-text articles on business topics
PubMed (MEDLINE)	Covers articles in medical journals
PsycINFO	Covers psychology and related fields
Sociological Abstracts	Covers the social sciences

2 Finding Books

The online catalog gives you the information you need—the call numbers—for locating specific titles. A **call number** is like a book's address in the library: it tells you exactly where to find the book you are looking for.

Once you become familiar with the physical layout of the library and the classification system your library uses, you should find it quite simple to locate the books you need.

CHECKLIST

Tracking Down a Missing Source

Problem	Possible Solution
1. Book has been checked out of library.	❑ Consult person at circulation desk.
	❑ Check other nearby libraries.
2. Book is not in library's collection.	❑ Ask instructor if he or she owns a copy.
	❑ Arrange for interlibrary loan (if time permits).
3. Periodical is not in library's collection/ article is ripped out of journal.	❑ Arrange for interlibrary loan (if time permits).
	❑ Check to see whether article is available in a full-text database.
	❑ Ask librarian whether article has been reprinted as part of a collection.

3 **Consulting Specialized Reference Works**

During your exploratory research, you use general reference works to help you narrow your topic. Now, you can access **specialized reference works**— unabridged dictionaries, special dictionaries, yearbooks, almanacs, atlases, and so on—to find facts, examples, statistics, definitions, and expert opinion. (Note that many of these works are available online as well as in print.)

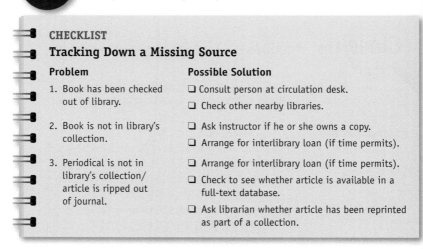

Close-Up SPECIALIZED REFERENCE WORKS

Unabridged Dictionaries Unabridged dictionaries, such as the *Oxford English Dictionary,* are comprehensive works that give detailed information about words.

Special Dictionaries These dictionaries focus on topics such as usage, synonyms, slang and idioms, etymologies, and foreign terms; some focus on specific disciplines such as accounting or law.

Yearbooks and Almanacs A **yearbook** is an annual publication that updates factual and statistical information already published in a reference source. An **almanac** provides lists, charts, and statistics about a wide variety of subjects.

World Almanac. Includes statistics about government, population, sports, and many other subjects. Published annually since 1868.

Information Please Almanac. Includes information unavailable in the *World Almanac.* Published annually since 1947.

Facts on File. Covering 1940 to the present, this work offers digests of important news stories from metropolitan newspapers.

Atlases An **atlas** contains maps and charts as well as historical, cultural, political, and economic information.

National Geographic Atlas of the World. Published by the National Geographic Society. The most up-to-date atlas available.

We the People: An Atlas of America's Ethnic Diversity. Presents information about specific ethnic groups. Maps show immigration routes and settlement patterns.

---

4 **Using Special Library Services**

As you do focused research, consult a reference librarian if you plan to use any of the following special services.

CloseUp SPECIAL LIBRARY SERVICES

- **Interlibrary Loans** Your library may be part of a library system that allows loans of books from one location to another.
- **Special Collections** Your library may house special collections of books, manuscripts, or documents.
- **Government Documents** A large university library may have a separate government documents area with its own catalog or index.
- **Vertical File** The vertical file includes pamphlets from a variety of organizations and interest groups, newspaper clippings, and other material collected by librarians.

17c **Evaluating the Library's Print and Electronic Sources**

Whenever you find a source (print or electronic), take the time to **evaluate** it—to assess its usefulness and its reliability. To determine the usefulness of a library source, ask the following questions:

- **Does the source discuss your topic in enough detail?** To be useful, a source should treat your topic comprehensively. For example, a book should include a section or chapter on your topic, not simply a footnote or a brief reference. For an article, either read the abstract or skim the entire article for key facts, looking closely at section headings, information set in boldface type, and topic sentences. An article should have your topic as its central subject (or at least one of its main concerns).

- **Is the source current?** The date of publication tells you whether the information in a book or article is up to date. A source's currency is particularly important for scientific and technological subjects, but even in the humanities, new discoveries and new ways of thinking lead scholars to reevaluate and modify their ideas.

- **Is the source respected?** A contemporary review of a source can help you make this assessment. *Book Review Digest,* available in print and online, lists popular books that have been reviewed in at least three newspapers or magazines and includes excerpts from representative reviews as well as abstracts.

- **Is the source reliable?** Is the source largely fact or unsupported opinion? Does the writer support his or her conclusions? Does the writer include documentation and a bibliography? Is the writer objective, or does he or she have a particular agenda to advance? Compare a few statements from the source with a neutral source—a textbook or an encyclopedia, for instance—to see whether a writer seems to be slanting facts.

In general, **scholarly publications**—books and journals aimed at an audience of expert readers—are more reliable than **popular publications**—books, magazines, and newspapers aimed at an audience of general readers. However, assuming they are current, written by reputable authors, and documented, articles from substantive popular publications (such as the *Atlantic* and *Scientific American*) may be appropriate for your research. Other popular publications—especially sensational tabloids such as the *Globe* and the *National Enquirer*—are almost never appropriate for your research. Check with your instructor to be sure.

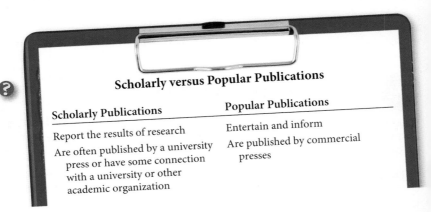

Scholarly versus Popular Publications

Scholarly Publications	Popular Publications
Report the results of research	Entertain and inform
Are often published by a university press or have some connection with a university or other academic organization	Are published by commercial presses

Scholarly Publications	Popular Publications
Are usually peer reviewed—that is, reviewed by other experts in the author's field before they are published	Are usually not peer reviewed
Are usually written by someone who is a recognized authority in the field	May be written by experts in a particular field but more often are written by freelance or staff writers
Are written for a scholarly audience so often use technical vocabulary and include challenging content	Are written for general readers so tend to use an accessible vocabulary and do not include challenging content
Nearly always contain extensive documentation as well as a bibliography of works consulted	Rarely cite sources or use documentation
Are published primarily because they make a contribution to a particular field of study	Are published primarily to make a profit

Close-Up EVALUATING POPULAR PERIODICALS

To find out how reliable a popular periodical is, go to the reference desk of your college library and find out if the library owns (or has access to) the following book:

LaGuardia, Cheryl, ed. *Magazines for Libraries.* 18th ed. Created by Bill Katz. New York: Bowker, 2011.

This book lists over six thousand periodicals by subject. Each entry includes an abstract that identifies the political orientation and scope of the publication. To locate a periodical, use the index at the end of the book.

17d Doing Field Research

In addition to using the library's resources, you can find valuable information by doing **field research** (sometimes called **primary research**). Field research involves gathering your own information by making observations (of people, places, objects, and events); by conducting an interview; or by conducting a survey.

❶ Making Observations

Your own observations can be a useful source of information. For example, an art or music paper can be enriched by information gathered during a visit to a museum or attending a concert. An education paper may include an account of a classroom visit, and a psychology or sociology paper may include observations (as well as photographs) of an individual's or a group's behavior.

❷ Conducting an Interview

Interviews (conducted in person or by email) often give you material that you cannot find in a library—for instance, biographical information, a first-hand account of an event, or the opinions of an expert.

The kinds of questions you ask in an interview depend on the information you want. **Open-ended questions**—questions designed to elicit general information—allow a respondent great flexibility in answering: *"Do you think students today are motivated? Why or why not?"* **Closed-ended questions**—questions intended to elicit specific information—zero in on a particular detail about a subject: *"How much money did the government's cost-cutting programs actually save?"*

❏ Allow the person you are interviewing to complete an answer before you ask another question.

❏ Take notes, but continue to pay attention as you do so.

❏ Pay attention to the reactions of your interview subject.

❏ Be willing to depart from your prepared list of questions to ask follow-up questions.

❏ At the end of the interview, thank your subject for his or her time and cooperation.

❏ Send a brief note of thanks.

Close-Up   CONDUCTING AN EMAIL INTERVIEW

Using email to conduct an interview can save you a great deal of time. Before you email your questions, make sure the person is willing to cooperate. If the person agrees to be interviewed, send a short list of specific questions. After you have received the answers, send an email thanking the person for his or her cooperation. When you conduct an email interview, make sure you follow the guidelines for writing emails.

See 25b1

3 Conducting a Survey

If your research project is examining a contemporary social, political, or economic issue, a **survey** of attitudes or opinions could be very useful. You begin conducting a survey by identifying the group of individuals that you will poll. This group can be a **convenient sample**—for example, people in your composition class—or a **random sample**—names chosen from the campus directory or a class roster. When you identify a sample, your goal is to select a population that is both *representative*—that accurately reflects the group you are studying—and *significant*—that includes enough respondents to convince people that your results are valid. If you poll ten people in your French class about a college policy and your university has ten thousand students, you cannot expect your conclusion to be convincing.

You should also make sure that your questions are clearly worded and designed to elicit the information you want. For example, multiple-choice questions or closed-ended questions that require a simple "yes" or "no"

CHECKLIST
Conducting a Survey
- ❏ Determine what you want to know.
- ❏ Select your sample.
- ❏ Design your questions.
- ❏ Distribute questionnaires.
- ❏ Collect the responses.
- ❏ Analyze the responses.
- ❏ Decide how you will use the results in your paper.

will yield more usable data than questions that call for paragraph-length answers. Also, be sure that you do not ask so many questions that respondents lose interest and stop answering. Finally, be careful not to ask biased or leading questions.

For an example of a student paper that uses information from a survey, **see 22c.**

CHAPTER **18**

Summarizing, Paraphrasing, and Quoting Sources

See
15f

Although it may seem like a good strategy, copying down the exact words of a source is the least efficient way of **taking notes.** Experienced researchers know that a better strategy is to take notes that combine summary and paraphrase with direct quotation. By doing so, they make sure they understand the material and see its relevance to their research.

18a Writing a Summary

A **summary** is a brief restatement of the main idea of a passage or an article. A summary is always much shorter than the original because it omits the examples, asides, analogies, and rhetorical strategies that writers use to add emphasis and interest.

See
Ch. 20

When you summarize, *use your own words*, not the exact language or phrasing of your source. If you think it is necessary to reproduce a distinctive word or phrase, place it in quotation marks; otherwise, you will be committing **plagiarism.** Remember that your summary should include only the main idea of your source, not your own interpretations or opinions. Finally, be sure to include parenthetical documentation.

Summaries

- **Summaries are original.** They should use your own language and phrasing, not the language and phrasing of your source.
- **Summaries are concise.** They should always be much shorter than the original.
- **Summaries are accurate.** They should express the main idea of your source.
- **Summaries are objective.** They should not include your opinions.
- **Summaries are complete.** They should convey a sense of the entire passage, not just a part of it.

Compare the following three passages. The first is an original source; the second, an acceptable summary; and the third, an unacceptable summary.

Original Source

Today, the First Amendment faces challenges from groups who seek to limit expressions of racism and bigotry. A growing number of legislatures have passed rules against "hate speech"—[speech] that is offensive on the basis of race, ethnicity, gender, or sexual orientation. The rules are intended to promote respect for all people and protect the targets of hurtful words, gestures, or actions.

Legal experts fear these rules may wind up diminishing the rights of all citizens. "The bedrock principle [of our society] is that government may never suppress free speech simply because it goes against what the community would like to hear," says Nadine Strossen, president of the American Civil Liberties Union and professor of constitutional law at New York University Law School. In recent years, for example, the courts have upheld the right of neo-Nazis to march in Jewish neighborhoods; protected cross-burning as a form of free expression; and allowed protesters to burn the American flag. The offensive, ugly, distasteful, or repugnant nature of expression is not reason enough to ban it, courts have said.

But advocates of limits on hate speech note that certain kinds of expression fall outside of First Amendment protection. Courts have ruled that "fighting words"—words intended to provoke immediate violence—or speech that creates a clear and present danger are not protected forms of expression. As the classic argument goes, freedom of speech does not give you the right to yell "Fire!" in a crowded theater. (Sudo, Phil. "Freedom of Hate Speech?")

The following acceptable summary gives an accurate, objective overview of the original without using its exact language or phrasing.

Acceptable Summary: The right to freedom of speech, guaranteed by the First Amendment, is becoming more difficult to defend. Some people think that stronger laws against the use of hate speech weaken the First Amendment. But others argue that some kinds of speech remain exempt from this protection (Sudo 17).

The following unacceptable summary uses words and phrases from the original without placing them in quotation marks. This use constitutes plagiarism. In addition, the unacceptable summary expresses the student writer's opinion (**Other people have the sense to realize . . .**).

See Ch. 20

Unacceptable Summary: Today, the First Amendment faces challenges from lots of people. Some of these people are legal experts who want to let Nazis march in Jewish neighborhoods. Other people have the sense to realize that some kinds of speech fall outside of First Amendment protection because they create a clear and present danger (Sudo 17).

CHECKLIST
Writing a Summary
- ❏ Reread your source until you understand it.
- ❏ Write a one-sentence restatement of the main idea.
- ❏ Write your summary, using the one-sentence restatement as your topic sentence. Use your own words and phrasing, not those of your source. Include quotation marks where necessary.
- ❏ Add appropriate documentation.

18b Writing a Paraphrase

A summary conveys just the main idea of a source; a **paraphrase** gives a *detailed* overview of a source's important ideas. It not only presents the source's main points, but it also reflects its tone and emphasis.

When you paraphrase, make certain that you use your own words, except when you want to quote to give readers a sense of the original. Try not to look at the source as you write, use language and syntax that come naturally to you, and avoid duplicating the phrasing or sentence structure of the original. Whenever possible, use synonyms that accurately convey the meaning of the original word or phrase. If you cannot think of a synonym for an important term, quote it. Remember that your paraphrase should reflect the ideas of your source—not your analysis or interpretation of those ideas. Finally, be sure to include parenthetical documentation.

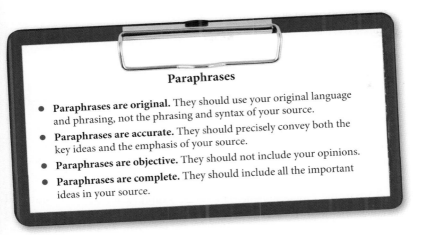

Paraphrases

- **Paraphrases are original.** They should use your original language and phrasing, not the phrasing and syntax of your source.
- **Paraphrases are accurate.** They should precisely convey both the key ideas and the emphasis of your source.
- **Paraphrases are objective.** They should not include your opinions.
- **Paraphrases are complete.** They should include all the important ideas in your source.

Compare the following three passages. The first is an original source, the second is an acceptable paraphrase, and the third is an unacceptable paraphrase.

Original Source

When you play a video game, you enter into the world of the programmers who made it. You have to do more than identify with a character on a screen. You must act for it. Identification through action has a special kind of hold. Like playing a sport, it puts people into a highly focused and highly charged state of mind. For many people, what is being pursued in the video game is not just a score, but an altered state.

The pilot of a race car does not dare to take . . . attention off the road. The imperative of total concentration is part of the high. Video games demand the same level of attention. They can give people the feeling of being close to the edge because, as in a dangerous situation, there is no time for rest and the consequences of wandering attention [are] dire. With pinball, a false move can be recuperated. The machine can be shaken, the ball repositioned. In a video game, the program has no tolerance for error, no margin for safety. Players experience their every movement as instantly translated into game action. The game is relentless in its demand that all other time stop and in its demand that the player take full responsibility for every act, a point that players often sum up [with] the phrase "One false move and you're dead." (Turkle, Sherry. *The Second Self: Computers and the Human Spirit.*)

The following acceptable paraphrase conveys the key ideas and emphasis of the source and maintains an objective tone. It quotes a key phrase, but its wording and sentence structure are very different from those of the source.

Acceptable Paraphrase: The programmer defines the reality of the video game. The game forces a player to merge with the character who is part of the game. The character becomes an extension of the player, who determines how he or she will think and act. According to Turkle, like sports, video games put a player into a very intense "altered state" of mind that is the most important part of the activity (83).

The total involvement they demand is what attracts many people to video games. These games can simulate the thrill of participating in a dangerous activity without any of the risks. There is no time for rest and no opportunity to correct errors of judgment. Unlike video games, pinball games are forgiving. A player can—within certain limits—manipulate a pinball game to correct minor mistakes. With video games, however, every move has immediate consequences. The game forces a player to adapt to its rules and to act carefully. One mistake can cause the death of the character on the screen and the end of the game (Turkle 83–84).

See Ch. 20

The following unacceptable paraphrase simply echoes the phrasing and syntax of the original, borrowing words and expressions without enclosing them in quotation marks. This constitutes **plagiarism.** In addition, the paraphrase digresses into a discussion of the student writer's own opinions about the relative merits of pinball and video games (**That is why I like . . .**).

Unacceptable Paraphrase: Playing a video game, you enter into a new world—one the programmer of the game made. You can't just play a video game; you have to identify with it. Your mind goes to a new level, and you are put into a highly focused state of mind.

Just as you would if you were driving a race car or piloting a plane, you must not let your mind wander. Video games demand complete attention. But the sense that at any time you could make one false move and lose is their attraction—at least for me. That is why I like video games more than pinball. Pinball is just too easy. You can always recover. By shaking the machine or quickly operating the flippers, you can save the ball. Video games, however, are not so easy to control. Usually, one slip and you're dead (Turkle 83–84).

CHECKLIST
Writing a Paraphrase
- ❏ Reread your source until you understand it.
- ❏ Write your paraphrase, following the tone and emphasis of the original.
- ❏ Avoid using the words or phrasing of the original. (Enclose any borrowed material within quotation marks.)
- ❏ Add appropriate documentation.

18c Quoting Sources

When you **quote,** you copy a writer's statements exactly as they appear in a source, word for word and punctuation mark for punctuation mark, enclosing the borrowed material in quotation marks. As a rule, you should not quote extensively in a research paper. Numerous quotations interrupt the flow of your discussion and give readers the impression that your paper is just a collection of other people's ideas.

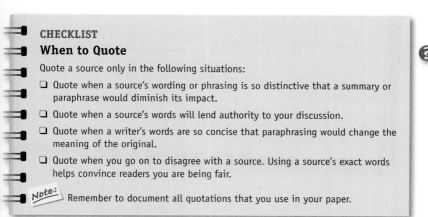

CHECKLIST

When to Quote

Quote a source only in the following situations:

❑ Quote when a source's wording or phrasing is so distinctive that a summary or paraphrase would diminish its impact.

❑ Quote when a source's words will lend authority to your discussion.

❑ Quote when a writer's words are so concise that paraphrasing would change the meaning of the original.

❑ Quote when you go on to disagree with a source. Using a source's exact words helps convince readers you are being fair.

Note: Remember to document all quotations that you use in your paper.

18d Integrating Source Material into Your Writing

Weave quotations, paraphrases, and summaries smoothly into your discussion, adding your own analysis or explanation to increase coherence and to show the relevance of your source material to the points you are making.

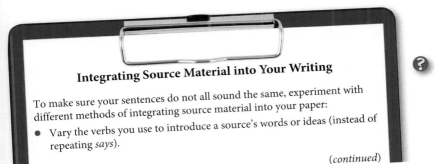

Integrating Source Material into Your Writing

To make sure your sentences do not all sound the same, experiment with different methods of integrating source material into your paper:

- Vary the verbs you use to introduce a source's words or ideas (instead of repeating *says*).

(continued)

Integrating Source Material into Your Writing (*continued*)

acknowledges	concludes	implies	proposes
admits	concurs	indicates	reports
affirms	discloses	insists	speculates
believes	explains	notes	suggests
claims	finds	observes	summarizes
comments	illustrates	predicts	warns

- Vary the placement of the **identifying tag** (the phrase that identifies the source), putting it in the middle or at the end of the quoted material instead of always at the beginning.

Quotation with Identifying Tag in Middle: "A serious problem confronting Amish society from the viewpoint of the Amish themselves," observes Hostetler, "is the threat of absorption into mass society through the values promoted in the public school system" (193).

Paraphrase with Identifying Tag at End: The Amish are also concerned about their children's exposure to the public school system's values, notes Hostetler (193).

❶ Integrating Quotations

Be sure to work quotations smoothly into your sentences. Quotations should never be awkwardly dropped into your paper, leaving the relationship between the quoted words and your point unclear. Use brief introductory remarks to provide a context for the quotation, and quote only those words you need to make your point.

Acceptable: For the Amish, the public school system is a problem because it represents "the threat of absorption into mass society" (Hostetler 193).

Unacceptable: For the Amish, the public school system represents a problem. "A serious problem confronting Amish society from the viewpoint of the Amish themselves is the threat of absorption into mass society through the values promoted in the public school system" (Hostetler 193).

Whenever possible, use an identifying tag to introduce the source of the quotation.

Identifying Tag: As John Hostetler points out, the Amish see the public school system as a problem because it represents "the threat of absorption into mass society" (193).

Close-Up PUNCTUATING IDENTIFYING TAGS

Whether or not to use a comma with an identifying tag depends on where you place the tag in the sentence. If the identifying tag immediately precedes a quotation, use a comma.

> As Hostetler points out, "The Amish are successful in maintaining group identity" (56).

If the identifying tag does not immediately precede a quotation, do not use a comma.

> Hostetler points out that the Amish frequently "use severe sanctions to preserve their values" (56).

Note: Never use a comma after *that:* Hostetler says that/ Amish society is "defined by religion" (76).

Substitutions or Additions within Quotations   Indicate changes or additions that you make to a quotation by enclosing your changes in brackets.

Original Quotation: "Immediately after her wedding, she and her husband followed tradition and went to visit almost everyone who attended the wedding" (Hostetler 122).

Quotation Edited to Make Verb Tenses Consistent: Nowhere is the Amish dedication to tradition more obvious than in the events surrounding marriage. Right after the wedding celebration, the Amish bride and groom "visit almost everyone who [has] attended the wedding" (Hostetler 122).

Quotation Edited to Supply an Antecedent for a Pronoun: "Immediately after her wedding, [Sarah] and her husband followed tradition and went to visit almost everyone who attended the wedding" (Hostetler 122).

Quotation Edited to Change an Uppercase to a Lowercase Letter: The strength of the Amish community is illustrated by the fact that "[i]mmediately after her wedding, she and her husband followed tradition and went to visit almost everyone who attended the wedding" (Hostetler 122).

Omissions within Quotations   When you delete unnecessary or irrelevant words, substitute an **ellipsis** (three spaced periods) for the deleted words.

See 50f1

Original Quotation: "Not only have the Amish built and staffed their own elementary and vocational schools, but they have gradually organized on local, state, and national levels to cope with the task of educating their children" (Hostetler 206).

Quotation Edited to Eliminate Unnecessary Words: "Not only have the Amish built and staffed their own elementary and vocational schools, but they have gradually organized . . . to cope with the task of educating their children" (Hostetler 206).

Close-Up OMISSIONS WITHIN QUOTATIONS

Be sure you do not misrepresent or distort the meaning of quoted material when you shorten it. For example, do not say, "the Amish have managed to maintain . . . their culture" when the original quotation is "the Amish have managed to maintain *parts of* their culture."

Note: If the passage you are quoting already contains ellipses, MLA style requires that you place brackets around any ellipses you add.

See 49b *Long Quotations* Set off a quotation of more than four typed lines of **prose** (or more than three lines of **poetry**) by indenting it one inch from the margin. Double-space, and do not use quotation marks.

If you are quoting a single paragraph, do not indent the first line. If you are quoting more than one paragraph, indent the first line of each complete paragraph an additional one-quarter inch. Integrate the quotation into your paper by introducing it with a complete sentence followed by a colon. Place parenthetical documentation one space after the end punctuation.

> According to Hostetler, the Amish were not always hostile to public education:
>
>> The one-room rural elementary school served the Amish community well in a number of ways. As long as it was a public school, it stood midway between the Amish community and the world. Its influence was tolerable, depending upon the degree of influence the Amish were able to bring to the situation. (196)

2 Integrating Paraphrases and Summaries

Introduce your paraphrases and summaries with identifying tags, and end them with appropriate documentation. By doing so, you make certain that your readers are able to see the boundaries of the source material so they can differentiate your ideas from those of your sources.

Correct (Identifying Tag Differentiates Ideas of Source from Ideas of Writer): Art can be used to uncover many problems that children have at home, in school, or with their friends. For this reason, many therapists use art therapy extensively. According to William Alschuler in *Art and Self-Image,* children's views of themselves in society are often reflected by their art style. For example, a cramped, crowded art style using only a portion of the paper shows a child's limited role (260).

Misleading (Ideas of Source Blend with Ideas of Writer): Art can be used to uncover many problems that children have at home, in school, or with their friends. For this reason, many therapists use art therapy extensively. Children's views of themselves in society are often reflected by their art style. For example, a cramped, crowded art style using only a portion of the paper shows their limited role (Alschuler 260).

CHAPTER **19**

Synthesizing Sources

19a Understanding Synthesis

A **synthesis** integrates information from two or more sources. In a synthesis, you draw ideas from your sources together and create something new. In the process, you try to make sense of your sources and help readers understand them in some meaningful way.

In academic settings, writers often need to synthesize information from several sources in a single paper—or even in a single paragraph. For this reason, knowing how to synthesize sources is an important skill. While summaries and paraphrases rephrase a source's main ideas, and quotations reproduce a source's exact language, syntheses use all these strategies to create an essay or paragraph that develops the writer's own viewpoint. An effective synthesis establishes a context for the source material it uses, showing the relevance of each source to the writer's points.

The following synthesis from a student research paper uses paraphrase and quotation to define the term *outsider art*.

Sample Student Synthesis

Topic sentence states student's main point

Summary of Karlins article

Paraphrase from one-page Glueck article

Bill Traylor is one of America's leading outsider artists. According to *Raw Vision* magazine, Traylor is one of the foremost artists of the twentieth century (Karlins). Born on a cotton plantation as a slave in the 1850s and illiterate all his life, Traylor was self-taught and did not consider himself an artist. He created work for himself rather than for the public (Glueck). The term *outsider art* refers to works of art created by individuals who are by definition outside society. Because of their mental condition, lack of education, criminal behavior, or physical handicaps, they are not part of the mainstream of society. According to Louis-Dreyfus, outsider artists also possess the following characteristics:

Long quotation from introduction to exhibit pamphlet

Few have formal training of any kind. They do their work absent from the self-consciousness that necessarily comes from being an artist in the ordinarily accepted circumstance. The French call it "Art Brut." But here in America, "Outsider Art" also refers to work done by the poor, illiterate, and self-taught African Americans whose artistic product is not the result of a controlling mental or behavioral factor but of their untaught and impoverished social conditions. (iv)

Conclusion summarizes student writer's position

As a Southern African-American man with few resources and little formal training, Traylor fits the definition of an outsider artist whose works are largely defined by the hardships he faced.

As this example demonstrates, an effective synthesis weaves key passages of source material together, establishing the relationship between the sources and the writer's own ideas.

19b Writing a Synthesis

The first step in synthesizing material is to determine how your sources are alike and different, where they agree and disagree, and whether they reach the same conclusions. As you identify connections between one source and another or between a source and your own ideas, you will develop your own perspective on your subject. It is this viewpoint, summarized in a thesis statement (in the case of an entire paper) or in a topic sentence (in the case of a paragraph), that becomes the focus of your synthesis.

In the following synthesis, a student effectively blends material from different sources to support his own ideas.

Assignment: Choose an area related to your major that you think others would benefit from learning more about. Then, using three sources, write a synthesis that defines and explains this topic to an audience unfamiliar with the field. Use MLA (Modern Language Association) documentation style.

Effective Synthesis

Computers carry out many of the tasks that make our way of life possible. For example, computer billing, with all its faults, makes modern business possible, and without computers we would not have access to the cellular services and cable or satellite

sen-
states
nt's
point

television that we take for granted. But computers are more than just fast calculators; they are also equipped with artificial intelligence (AI), which has transformed fields such as medicine, agriculture, and manufacturing. One technology writer defines artificial intelligence

ation
Haven-
article

(AI) as "a field that attempts to provide machines with humanlike reasoning and language-processing capabilities" (Havenstein). Farming

Source

There's no precise definition of AI, but broadly, it's a field that attempts to provide machines with humanlike reasoning and language-processing capabilities.

hrase of
ned
e's text
isual
nt

is an industry that is now using AI technology: with new, high-tech agricultural sprayers that treat crops precisely and accurately, farmers are able to improve the output and quality of their yield ("More Machine Intelligence"). AI has also made

Source

Researchers at Oklahoma State University, meanwhile, have demonstrated the potential for adding machine intelligence to agricultural sprayers (photo). Enhanced with sensors and computers, the field sprayers dramatically increased the application efficiency by applying fertilizers and herbicides only where needed, reports John B. Solie, professor, power and machinery at Oklahoma State.

F. Schussler/PhotoLink/Getty Images

Summary of Howell article

possible numerous medical advances—for example, helping scientists to generate human tissue, bone, and organs for patients in need

Conclusion summarizes student writer's position

(Howell). Given the importance of AI technology, it seems certain that computers will change our lives even more in the future.

Source

> **Human 2.0**
> News that an artificial pancreas has been developed, which could help millions of diabetes patients, is only the tip of the iceberg as far as augmentation of the human body goes. We can already grow skin, cartilage, bone, ears and bladders.

This synthesis effectively defines the term *artificial intelligence (AI)* and uses information from three short articles to explain AI and briefly describe its use in various fields. The writer introduces his paragraph with a summary of computer applications familiar to his readers and then moves into a discussion of AI.

The sources selected for the above synthesis could have been used far less carefully and effectively. In the following ineffective synthesis, source material dominates the discussion, all but eliminating the writer's voice.

Ineffective Synthesis

Begins with out-of-context quotation from source, not student writer's own position

Heather Havenstein defines artificial intelligence (AI) as "a field that attempts to provide machines with humanlike reasoning and language-processing capabilities." As reported in *IndustryWeek* magazine, the farming community is using

Source's exact words used without quotation marks, resulting in plagiarism

AI technology by adding machine intelligence to agricultural sprayers, dramatically increasing their application efficiency and improving the output and quality of crops ("More Machine Intelligence"). In the medical field, scientists have used AI to

Quotation used where paraphrase is more appropriate

"grow skin, cartilage, bone, ears and bladders" (Howell). AI technology has changed our lives in important ways, and it seems obvious that it will continue to do so in the future.

Vague conclusion

This example does not include a topic sentence that states the writer's position; it also lacks supporting examples and has a vague conclusion. Moreover, the paragraph **plagiarizes** its source's words.

See Ch. 20

CHAPTER **20**

Avoiding Plagiarism

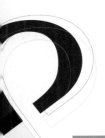

20a Defining Plagiarism

Plagiarism is presenting another person's ideas or words as if they were your own. Most plagiarism is **unintentional plagiarism**—for example, inadvertently pasting a quoted passage into a paper and forgetting to include the quotation marks and documentation.

There is a difference, however, between an honest mistake and **intentional plagiarism**—for example, copying a passage word for word from a journal article or submitting a paper that someone else has written. The penalties for unintentional plagiarism may sometimes be severe, but intentional plagiarism is almost always dealt with harshly: students who intentionally plagiarize can receive a failing grade for the paper (or the course) or can even be expelled from school.

Close-Up DETECTING PLAGIARISM

The same technology that has made unintentional plagiarism more common has also made plagiarism easier to detect. By doing a *Google* search, an instructor can quickly find the source of a phrase that has been plagiarized from an Internet source. In addition, plagiarism detection services, such as Turnitin.com, can search scholarly databases and identify plagiarized passages in student papers.

20b Avoiding Unintentional Plagiarism

The most common cause of unintentional plagiarism is sloppy research habits. To avoid this problem, start your research paper early. Do not cut and paste text from a Web site or full-text database directly into your paper. If you paraphrase, do so correctly by following the advice in **18b.**

> **ESL TIP**
>
> Plagiarism is a difficult concept for many ESL students to grasp because it is not a concern in all countries. In cultures that value the group over the individual, including some Asian, African, and Latin American cultures, plagiarism is less of a concern because the group is thought to own the original work.
>
> In places such as the United States, however, where the individual is valued over the group, plagiarism is considered stealing because the individual who originally developed the idea or work is considered to be its owner. Although you may be tempted to closely follow the syntax and word choice of your sources, be aware that this practice constitutes plagiarism.

In addition, take care to manage your sources—especially those you download—so that they do not overwhelm you. Unintentional plagiarism often occurs when students use source material thinking that it is their own. If you are writing a short paper, keep source material in a file. For longer papers, create separate files for each section of your paper.

A number of Web-based tools can help you manage your sources. For example, *Delicious* <delicious.com> enables you to tag and keep track of your research sources. *Zotero* <zotero.org> helps you to collect, organize, store, and share your research sources. Other programs can also be helpful. For example, *Evernote* <evernote.com> enables you to take notes and synchronize them with a calendar, and *Backpack* <backpackit.com> is a wiki page that lets you keep files, images, and notes in a single place.

See Chs. 21–24 Another cause of unintentional plagiarism is failure to use proper **documentation.** In general, you must document the following information:

- Direct quotations, summaries, and paraphrases of material in sources (including Web sources)

- Images that you borrow from a source (print or electronic)
- Facts and opinions that are another writer's original contributions
- Information that is the product of an author's original research
- Statistics, charts, graphs, or other compilations of data that are not yours

Material that is considered **common knowledge** (information most readers probably know) need not be documented. This includes facts available from a variety of reference sources, familiar sayings, and well-known quotations. Your own original research (interviews and surveys, for example) also does not require documentation.

So, although you do not have to document the fact that John F. Kennedy graduated from Harvard in 1940 or that he was elected president in 1960, you do have to document information from a historian's evaluation of his presidency. The best rule to follow is if you have doubts, document.

Close-Up   WHY DOCUMENT SOURCES?

There are a number of reasons to document sources:

- **To give credit**   By documenting your sources, you acknowledge the original work of others.
- **To become part of a conversation**   When you discuss the work of other scholars, you join an ongoing intellectual discussion.
- **To establish your credibility**   By indicating what sources you have consulted, you show readers that your conclusions should be taken seriously.
- **To differentiate your ideas from the ideas of your sources**   Documentation enables readers to identify the original ideas you have contributed to the discussion.

20c   Avoiding Intentional Plagiarism

When students **intentionally plagiarize,** they make a decision to misappropriate the ideas or words of others—and this is no small matter. Not only does intentional plagiarism deprive the student of a valuable educational experience (instructors assign research for a reason), it also subverts the educational goals of other students as well as of the institution as a whole. Because academic honesty is absolutely central to any college or university, intentional plagiarism is taken very seriously.

So why do some students engage in this unethical (and risky) behavior? Research has shown that many students who intentionally plagiarize do so out of procrastination and fear. They put off working on their writing projects until they have no time to complete them. Or, they have trouble finding source materials. Some students find that as they do their research, their ideas change. As a result, they discover at the last minute that they have to shift the focus of their papers, and they panic. Finally, other students think that they are not up to the job of writing a research paper. The easiest way to deal with all these types of problems is to ask for help. The chart below lists some of the most common reasons for intentional plagiarism along with some possible solutions.

Strategies for Avoiding Intentional Plagiarism

Problem	Solution
You run out of time	Ask your instructor for an extension.
You have a job or a heavy course load	Get help with time-management skills. Talk to your instructors.
You have weak writing skills	Go to the writing center.
You are unsure of what constitutes plagiarism	Ask your instructor for clarification. Review the discussion in this handbook.
You panic	Talk to your instructor. Get help from the counseling center.
Your topic is boring	Get permission to change your topic.

Of course, some students plagiarize out of laziness or because they mistakenly believe that buying a paper from a paper mill or paying someone to write a paper is "no big deal." Fortunately, these students are in the minority. Most, if not all, students realize that plagiarism is simply wrong.

20d Avoiding Other Kinds of Plagiarism

When instructors assign a research paper, they expect it to be your original work. They also expect your paper to be written in response to specific assignments they give. For this reason, you should not submit a paper that you have written for another course. (This is considered **self-plagiarism.**) If you intend to substantially rework or expand the paper, however, you may be able to use it. Check with your instructor before doing so.

A paper prepared in collaboration with other students can also present challenges. It is not uncommon in some courses to do work as part of a team. This collaborative work is acceptable in the course for which it was assigned. Even so, each member of the group should clearly identify the sections on which he or she worked.

Finally, although your instructors may encourage you to go the writing center for help, they do not expect your paper to include passages written by a tutor. Passages written (or revised and edited) by a friend or a family member are also unacceptable. If you present material contributed by others as if it were your own, you are committing plagiarism.

20e Revising to Eliminate Plagiarism

You can avoid plagiarism by using documentation wherever it is required and by following these guidelines.

1 Enclose Borrowed Words in Quotation Marks

Original: Historically, only a handful of families have dominated the fireworks industry in the West. Details such as chemical recipes and mixing procedures were cloaked in secrecy and passed down from one generation to the next. . . . One effect of familial secretiveness is that, until recent decades, basic pyrotechnic research was rarely performed, and even when it was, the results were not generally reported in scientific journals. (Conkling, John A. "Pyrotechnics.")

Plagiarism: John A. Conkling points out that until recently, little scientific research was done on the chemical properties of fireworks, and when it was, the results were not generally reported in scientific journals (96).

Even though the preceding example includes documentation, the student writer uses the source's exact words without placing them in quotation marks.

The writer can correct this problem either by putting the borrowed words in quotation marks or by paraphrasing them.

Correct (Borrowed Words in Quotation Marks): John A. Conkling points out that until recently, little scientific research was done on the chemical properties of fireworks, and when it was, "the results were not generally reported in scientific journals" (96).

Correct (Paraphrase): John A. Conkling points out that the little research conducted on the chemical composition of fireworks was seldom reported in the scientific literature (96).

Close-Up   PLAGIARISM AND INTERNET SOURCES

Any time you download text from the Internet, you run the risk of committing unintentional plagiarism. To avoid the possibility of plagiarism, follow these guidelines:

- Download information into individual files so that you can keep track of your sources.
- Do not cut and paste blocks of downloaded text directly into your paper; first summarize or paraphrase this material.
- If you record the exact words of your source, enclose them in quotation marks.
- Even if your information is from emails, online discussion groups, blogs, or Web sites, provide appropriate documentation.
- Always document figures, tables, charts, and graphs obtained from the Internet or from any other electronic source.

---

❷ Do Not Imitate a Source's Syntax and Phrasing

Original: Let's be clear: this wish for politically correct casting goes only one way, the way designed to redress the injuries of centuries. When Pat Carroll, who is a woman, plays Falstaff, who is not, casting is considered a stroke of brilliance. When Josette Simon, who is black, plays Maggie in *After the Fall,* a part Arthur Miller patterned after Marilyn Monroe and which has traditionally been played not by white women, but by blonde white women, it is hailed as a breakthrough.

But when the pendulum moves the other way, the actors' union balks. (Quindlen, Anna. "Error, Stage Left.")

Plagiarism: Let us be honest. The desire for politically appropriate casting goes in only one direction, the direction intended to make up for the damage done over hundreds of years. When Pat Carroll, a female, is cast as Falstaff, a male, the decision is a brilliant one. When Josette Simon, a black

woman, is cast as Maggie in *After the Fall*, a role that Arthur Miller based
on Marilyn Monroe and that has usually been played by a woman who is
not only white but also blonde, it is considered a major advance.

But when the shoe is on the other foot, the actors' union resists
(Quindlen 21).

Although the student example above does not use the exact words of the
source, the writer closely follows the original's syntax and phrasing, simply
substituting synonyms for the author's words.

In the revised passage below, the writer uses her own syntax and phrasing and puts a borrowed phrase in quotation marks.

Correct (Paraphrase): According to Anna Quindlen, the actors' union
supports "politically appropriate casting" only when it means casting
a woman or minority group member in a role created for a male or a
Caucasian. Thus, it is acceptable for actress Pat Carroll to play Falstaff or
for black actress Josette Simon to play Marilyn Monroe; in fact, casting
decisions such as these are praised. But when it comes to casting a
Caucasian in a role intended for an African American, Asian, or Hispanic,
the union objects (21).

Note: When it is clear that all information in a passage is from the same
source, only one parenthetical reference is needed. For this reason, the brief
quotation in the passage above does not require separate documentation.

3 Document Statistics Obtained from a Source

Although many people assume that statistics are common knowledge, they
are usually the result of original research and must, therefore, be documented.
Moreover, providing the source of the statistics helps readers to assess their
validity.

Correct: According to one study, male drivers between the ages of
sixteen and twenty-four accounted for the majority of accidents. Of
303 accidents recorded almost one half took place before the drivers
were legally allowed to drive at eighteen (Schuman et al. 1027).

4 Differentiate Your Words and Ideas from Those of Your Source

Original: At some colleges and universities traditional survey courses of
world and English literature . . . have been scrapped or diluted. At others they
are in peril. At still others they will be. What replaces them is sometimes a mere
option of electives, sometimes "multicultural" courses introducing material
from Third World cultures and thinning out an already thin sampling of Western writings, and sometimes courses geared especially to issues of class, race,

and gender. Given the notorious lethargy of academic decision-making, there has probably been more clamor than change; but if there's enough clamor, there will be change. (Howe, Irving. "The Value of the Canon.")

Plagiarism: Debates about expanding the literary canon take place at many colleges and universities across the United States. At many universities, the Western literature survey courses have been edged out by courses that emphasize minority concerns. These courses are "thinning out an already thin sampling of Western writings" in favor of courses geared especially to issues of "class, race, and gender" (Howe 40).

Because the student example above does not differentiate the writer's ideas from those of his source, it appears that only the quotations in the last sentence are borrowed when, in fact, the second sentence also owes a debt to the original.

In the revised passage below, the writer clearly identifies the boundaries of the borrowed material by introducing it with an identifying tag and ending with documentation.

Correct: Debates about expanding the literary canon take place at many colleges and universities across the United States. According to critic Irving Howe, at many universities the Western literature survey courses have been edged out by courses that emphasize minority concerns. These courses, says Howe, are "thinning out an already thin sampling of Western writings" in favor of "courses geared especially to issues of class, race, and gender" (40).

CHECKLIST

Avoiding Plagiarism

❑ **Take careful notes.** Be sure you have recorded information from your sources carefully and accurately.

❑ **Keep track of your sources.** Place all source material, along with pertinent bibliographic information, in the appropriate files.

❑ **In your notes, clearly identify summaries, paraphrases, and quotations.** In handwritten notes, put all words borrowed from your sources inside circled quotation marks. In typed notes, boldface all quotation marks. Always enclose your own comments within brackets.

❑ **In your paper, differentiate your ideas from those of your sources** by clearly introducing borrowed material with an identifying tag and by following it with parenthetical documentation.

❑ **Enclose all direct quotations** used in your paper within quotation marks.

❑ **Review all paraphrases and summaries** in your paper to make certain that they use your own phrasing and syntax and that any distinctive words and phrases from a source are quoted.

- ❏ **Document all quoted material and all paraphrases and summaries** of your sources.
- ❏ **Document all information** that is not common knowledge.
- ❏ **Document all opinions, conclusions, figures, tables, statistics, graphs, and charts** taken from a source.
- ❏ **Never submit the work of another person as your own.** Do not buy a paper from a term-paper site or hand in a paper written by a friend. In addition, never include passages that have been written by a friend, relative, or writing tutor. If you run into trouble, get help.
- ❏ **Never use sources that you have not actually read (or invent sources that do not exist).**

PART 5

Documenting Sources: MLA Style

Documenting Sources: MLA Style

? Frequently Asked Questions

Directory of MLA Parenthetical References

Directory of MLA Works-Cited List Entries

PRINT SOURCES: *Entries for Articles*

Articles in Scholarly Journals

Articles in Magazines and Newspapers

PRINT SOURCES: *Entries for Books*

Authors

Articles, Books, Reviews, Letters, and Reference
Works on the Internet

Paintings, Photographs, Cartoons, and Maps on the Internet

OTHER ELECTRONIC SOURCES

DVD-ROMs and CD-ROMs

Digital Files

CHAPTER 21

MLA Documentation Style

Documentation is the formal acknowledgment of the sources you use in your paper. This chapter explains and illustrates the documentation style recommended by the Modern Language Association (MLA). Chapter 22 discusses the documentation style of the American Psychological Association (APA), Chapter 23 gives an overview of the format recommended by *The Chicago Manual of Style,* and Chapter 24 presents the format recommended by the Council of Science Editors (CSE) and the formats used by organizations in other disciplines.

Close-Up CITATION GENERATORS

A number of Web sites can help you generate properly formatted citations for the most commonly used documentation styles. The most popular are *CiteMe* <citeme.com>, *Easybib* <easybib.com>, *Zotero* <zotero.org>, and *Endnote* (available free of charge at some schools).

Although these sites can save you time and effort, most have limitations. For example, most citation generators occasionally make basic formatting errors. For this reason, you still have to proofread bibliographic entries carefully before you submit your paper.

21a Using MLA Style

MLA style* is required by instructors of English and other languages as well as by many instructors in other humanities disciplines. MLA documentation has three parts: *parenthetical references in the body of the paper (also known as in-text citations), a works-cited list,* and *content notes.*

---

*MLA documentation style follows the guidelines set in the *MLA Handbook for Writers of Research Papers*, 7th ed. (New York: MLA, 2009).

1 Parenthetical References

MLA documentation uses parenthetical references in the body of the paper keyed to a works-cited list at the end of the paper. A typical parenthetical reference consists of the author's last name and a page number.

> The colony appealed to many idealists in Europe (Kelley 132).

If you state the author's name or the title of the work in your discussion, do not also include it in the parenthetical reference.

> Penn's political motivation is discussed by Joseph J. Kelley in *Pennsylvania,*
>
> *The Colonial Years, 1681-1776* (44).

To distinguish two or more sources by the same author, include a shortened title after the author's name. When you shorten a title, begin with the word by which the work is alphabetized in the list of works cited.

> Penn emphasized his religious motivation (Kelley, *Pennsylvania* 116).

Close-Up PUNCTUATING WITH MLA PARENTHETICAL REFERENCES

Paraphrases and Summaries   Parenthetical references are placed *before* the sentence's end punctuation.

> Penn's writings epitomize seventeenth-century religious thought (Dengler and Curtis 72).

Quotations Run In with the Text   Parenthetical references are placed *after* the quotation but *before* the end punctuation.

> As Ross says, "Penn followed his conscience in all matters" (127).

> According to Williams, "Penn's utopian vision was informed by his Quaker beliefs . . ." (72).

Quotations Set Off from the Text   When you quote more than four lines of prose or more than three lines of poetry, parenthetical references are placed one space after the end punctuation.

> According to Arthur Smith, William Penn envisioned a state based on his religious principles:
>
>> Pennsylvania would be a commonwealth in which all individuals would follow God's truth and develop according to God's law. For Penn, this concept of government was self-evident. It would be a mistake to see Pennsylvania as anything but an expression of Penn's religious beliefs. (314)

See 49b

Sample MLA Parenthetical References

1. A Work by a Single Author

Fairy tales reflect the emotions and fears of children (Bettelheim 23).

2. A Work by Two or Three Authors

The historian's main job is to search for clues and solve mysteries (Davidson and Lytle 6).

With the advent of behaviorism, psychology began a new phase of inquiry (Cowen, Barbo, and Crum 31-34).

3. A Work by More Than Three Authors

List only the first author, followed by **et al.** ("and others").

Helping each family reach its goals for healthy child development and overall family well-being was the primary approach of Project EAGLE (Bartle et al. 35).

Or, list the last names of all authors in the order in which they appear on the work's title page.

Helping each family reach its goals for healthy child development and overall family well-being was the primary approach of Project EAGLE (Bartle, Couchonnal, Canda, and Staker 35).

4. A Work in Multiple Volumes

If you list more than one volume of a multivolume work in your works-cited list, include the appropriate volume and page number (separated by a colon followed by a space) in the parenthetical citation.

Gurney is incorrect when he says that a twelve-hour limit is negotiable (6: 128).

5. A Work without a Listed Author

Use the full title (if brief) or a shortened version of the title (if long), beginning with the word by which it is alphabetized in the works-cited list.

The group later issued an apology ("Satire Lost" 22).

6. A Work That Is One Page Long

Do not include a page reference for a one-page article.

Sixty percent of Arab Americans work in white-collar jobs (El-Badru).

7. An Indirect Source

If you use a statement by one author that is quoted in the work of another author, indicate that the material is from an indirect source with the abbreviation **qtd. in** ("quoted in").

> According to Valli and Lucas, "the form of the symbol is an icon or picture of some aspect of the thing or activity being symbolized" (qtd. in Wilcox 120).

8. More Than One Work

Cite each work as you normally would, separating one citation from another with a semicolon.

> The Brooklyn Bridge has been used as a subject by many American artists (McCullough 144; Tashjian 58).

Note: Long parenthetical references can distract readers. Whenever possible, present them as **content notes**.

See 21a3

9. A Literary Work

When citing a work of **fiction,** it is often helpful to include more than the author's name and the page number in the parenthetical citation. Follow the page number with a semicolon, and then include any additional information that might be helpful.

> In *Moby-Dick,* Melville refers to a whaling expedition funded by Louis XIV of France (151; ch. 24).

Parenthetical references to **poetry** do not include page numbers. In parenthetical references to *long poems,* cite division and line numbers, separating them with a period.

> In the *Aeneid,* Virgil describes the ships as cleaving the "green woods reflected in the calm water" (8.124).

(In this citation, the reference is to book 8, line 124 of the *Aeneid.*)

When citing *short poems,* identify the poet and the poem in the text of the paper, and use line numbers in the citation.

> In "My mistress' eyes are nothing like the sun," Shakespeare's speaker says, "I have seen roses damasked red and white, / But no such roses see I in her cheeks," (lines 5-6).

Note: When citing lines of a poem, include the word **line** (or **lines**) in the first parenthetical reference; use just the line numbers in subsequent references.

When citing a **play,** include the act, scene, and line numbers (in arabic numerals), separated by periods. Titles of well-known dramatic works (such as Shakespeare's plays) are often abbreviated (**Mac. 2.2.14-16**).

10. Sacred Texts

When citing sacred texts, such as the Bible or the Qur'an, include the version (italicized) and the book (abbreviated if longer than four letters, but not italicized or enclosed in quotation marks), followed by the chapter and verse numbers (separated by a period).

> The cynicism of the speaker is apparent when he says, "All things are
>
> wearisome; no man can speak of them all" (*New English Bible,* Eccles. 1.8).

Note: The first time you cite a sacred text, include the version in your parenthetical reference; after that, include only the book. If you are using more than one version of a sacred text, however, include the version in each in-text citation.

11. An Entire Work

When citing an entire work, include the author's name and the work's title in the text of your paper rather than in a parenthetical reference.

> Lois Lowry's *Gathering Blue* is set in a technologically backward village.

12. Two or More Authors with the Same Last Name

To distinguish authors with the same last name, include their initials in your parenthetical references.

> Increases in crime have caused thousands of urban homeowners to install
>
> alarms (L. Cooper 115). Some of these alarms use sophisticated sensors that
>
> were developed by the army (D. Cooper 76).

13. A Government Document or a Corporate Author

Cite such works using the organization's name (usually abbreviated) followed by the page number (**Amer. Automobile Assn. 34**). You can avoid long parenthetical references by working the organization's name (not abbreviated) into your discussion.

> According to the President's Commission for the Study of Ethical Problems
>
> in Medicine and Biomedical and Behavioral Research, the issues relating to
>
> euthanasia are complicated (76).

14. A Legal Source

Titles of acts or laws that appear in the text of your paper or in the works-cited list should not be italicized or enclosed in quotation marks. In the parenthetical reference, titles are usually abbreviated, and the act or law is referred to by sections. Include the USC (United States Code) and the year the act or law was passed (if relevant).

> Such research should include investigations into the cause, diagnosis, early detection, prevention, control, and treatment of autism (42 USC 284q, 2000).

Names of legal cases are usually abbreviated (**Roe v. Wade**). They are italicized in the text of your paper but not in the works-cited list.

> In *Goodridge v. Department of Public Health*, the court ruled that the Commonwealth of Massachusetts had not adequately provided a reasonable constitutional cause for barring homosexual couples from civil marriages (2003).

15. An Electronic Source

If a reference to an electronic source includes paragraph numbers rather than page numbers, use the abbreviation **par.** or **pars.** followed by the paragraph number or numbers.

> The earliest type of movie censorship came in the form of licensing fees, and in Deer River, Minnesota, "a licensing fee of $200 was deemed not excessive for a town of 1000" (Ernst, par. 20).

If the electronic source has no page or paragraph numbers, cite the work in your discussion rather than in a parenthetical reference. By consulting your works-cited list, readers will be able to determine that the source is electronic and may therefore not have page numbers.

> In her article "Limited Horizons," Lynne Cheney observes that schools do best when students read literature not for practical information but for its insights into the human condition.

2 Works-Cited List

The **works-cited list,** which appears at the end of your paper, is an alphabetical listing of all the research materials you cite. Double-space within and between entries on the list, and indent the second and subsequent lines of each entry one-half inch. (**See 21b** for full manuscript guidelines.)

MLA PRINT SOURCES Entries for Articles

Article citations include the author's name; the title of the article (in quotation marks); the title of the periodical (italicized); the volume and issue numbers (when applicable; see page 233); the year or date of publication; the pages on which the full article appears, without the abbreviation *p.* or *pp.*; and the publication medium (**Print**). Figure 21.1 shows where you can find this information.

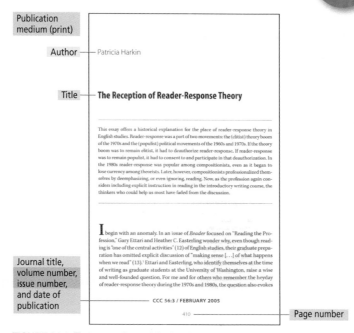

Publication medium (print)

Author — Patricia Harkin

Title — **The Reception of Reader-Response Theory**

This essay offers a historical explanation for the place of reader-response theory in English studies. Reader-response was a part of two movements: the (elitist) theory boom of the 1970s and the (populist) political movements of the 1960s and 1970s. If the theory boom was to remain elitist, it had to deauthorize reader-response. If reader-response was to remain populist, it had to consent to and participate in that deauthorization. In the 1980s reader-response was popular among compositionists, even as it began to lose currency among theorists. Later, however, compositionists professionalized themselves by deemphasizing, or even ignoring, reading. Now, as the profession again considers including explicit instruction in reading in the introductory writing course, the thinkers who could help us most have faded from the discussion.

I begin with an anomaly. In an issue of *Reader* focused on "Reading the Profession," Gary Ettari and Heather C. Easterling wonder why, even though reading is "one of the central activities" (12) of English studies, their graduate preparation has omitted explicit discussion of "making sense [...] of what happens when we read" (13).[1] Ettari and Easterling, who identify themselves at the time of writing as graduate students at the University of Washington, raise a wise and well-founded question. For me and for others who remember the heyday of reader-response theory during the 1970s and 1980s, the question also evokes

Journal title, volume number, issue number, and date of publication — CCC 56:3 / FEBRUARY 2005

410 — Page number

FIGURE 21.1 First page of an article showing the location of the information needed for documentation. © College Composition and Communication/ National Council of Teachers of English.

Author's last name First name   Title of article (in quotation marks)

Harkin, Patricia. "The Reception of Reader-Response Theory."

College Composition and Communication 56.3 (2005): 410-25. Print.

Title of periodical (italicized)   Volume and issue number   Year of publication   Inclusive page numbers   Publication medium

Articles in Scholarly Journals

1. An Article in a Scholarly Journal

MLA guidelines recommend that you include both the volume number and the issue number (separated by a period) for all scholarly journal articles that you cite, regardless of whether they are paginated continuously through an annual volume or separately in each issue. Follow the volume and issue numbers with the year of publication (in parentheses), the inclusive page numbers, and the publication medium.

Siderits, Mark. "Perceiving Particulars: A Buddhist Defense." *Philosophy East and West* 54.3 (2004): 367-83. Print.

Articles in Magazines and Newspapers

2. An Article in a Weekly Magazine (Signed)

For signed articles, start with the author, last name first. In dates, the day precedes the month (abbreviated except for May, June, and July).

> Corliss, Richard. "His Days in Hollywood." *Time* 14 June 2004: 56-62. Print.

3. An Article in a Weekly Magazine (Unsigned)

For unsigned articles, start with the title of the article.

> "Ronald Reagan." *National Review* 28 June 2004: 14-17. Print.

4. An Article in a Monthly Magazine

> Thomas, Evan. "John Paul Jones." *American History* Aug. 2003: 22-25. Print.

5. An Article That Does Not Appear on Consecutive Pages

When, for example, an article begins on page 120 and then skips to page 186, include only the first page number, followed by a plus sign.

> Di Giovanni, Janine. "The Shiites of Iraq." *National Geographic* June 2004:
>
> 62+. Print.

6. An Article in a Newspaper (Signed)

> Krantz, Matt. "Stock Success Not Exactly Unparalleled." *Wall Street Journal*
>
> 11 June 2004: B1+. Print.

7. An Article in a Newspaper (Unsigned)

> "A Steadfast Friend on 9/11 Is Buried." *New York Times* 6 Aug. 2002,
>
> late ed.: B8. Print.

Note: Omit the article *the* from the title of a newspaper even if the newspaper's actual title includes the article.

8. An Editorial in a Newspaper

> "The Government and the Web." Editorial. *New York Times* 25 Aug. 2009,
>
> late ed.: A20. Print.

9. A Letter to the Editor of a Newspaper

> Chang, Paula. Letter. *Philadelphia Inquirer* 10 Dec. 2010, suburban ed.:
>
> A17. Print.

10. A Book Review in a Newspaper

> Straw, Deborah. "Thinking about Tomorrow." Rev. of *Planning for the*
>
> *21st Century: A Guide for Community Colleges,* by William A.

Wojciechowski and Dedra Manes. *Community College Week* 7 June 2004:

15. Print.

11. An Article with a Title within Its Title

If the article you are citing contains a title that is normally enclosed in quotation marks, use single quotation marks for the interior title.

Zimmerman, Brett. "Frantic Forensic Oratory: Poe's 'The Tell-Tale Heart.'"

Style 35 (2001): 34-50. Print.

If the article you are citing contains a title that is normally italicized, use italics for the title in your works-cited entry.

Lingo, Marci. "Forbidden Fruit: The Banning of *The Grapes of Wrath* in the

Kern County Free Library." *Libraries and Culture* 38 (2003): 351-78.

Print.

MLA PRINT SOURCES Entries for Books

Book citations include the author's name; book title (italicized); and publication information (place, publisher, date, publication medium). Figures 21.2 and 21.3 on page 236 show where you can find this information.

Close-Up   PUBLISHERS' NAMES

MLA requires that you use abbreviated forms of publishers' names in the works-cited list. In general, omit articles; abbreviations, such as *Inc.* and *Corp.*; and words such as *Publishers, Books,* and *Press*. If the publisher's name includes a person's name, use the last name only. Finally, use standard abbreviations whenever you can—*UP* for University Press and *P* for Press, for example.

Name	Abbreviation
Basic Books	Basic
Government Printing Office	GPO
The Modern Language Association of America	MLA
Oxford University Press	Oxford UP
Alfred A. Knopf, Inc.	Knopf
Random House, Inc.	Random
University of Chicago Press	U of Chicago P

In each works-cited entry, capitalize all major words of the book's title except articles, coordinating conjunctions, prepositions, and the *to* of an infinitive (unless such a word is the first or last word of the title or subtitle). Do not italicize the period that follows a book's title.

Author's First name and   Italicized title (all major words and first
last name middle initial   word of subtitle capitalized)

Kleiner, Fred S. *Gardner's Art through the Ages: A Global History.*

Enhanced 13th ed. Boston: Wadsworth, 2011. Print.

     Edition   City   Publisher's   Year of   Publication
                                name   publication medium
                             (abbreviated)

FIGURE 21.2 Title page from a book showing the location of the information needed for documentation. © Cengage Learning, 2011.

Publication medium (print)

GARDNER'S
ART
THROUGH THE
AGES

Title

A GLOBAL HISTORY

Subtitle

ENHANCED THIRTEENTH EDITION

Edition

Copyright year

Author

FRED S. KLEINER

City of publication

Publisher

FIGURE 21.3 Copyright page from a book showing the location of the information needed for documentation. © Cengage Learning, 2011.

Authors

12. A Book by One Author

> Bettelheim, Bruno. *The Uses of Enchantment: The Meaning and Importance of*
>
> *Fairy Tales*. New York: Knopf, 1976. Print.

13. A Book by Two or Three Authors

List the first author with last name first. List subsequent authors with first name first in the order in which they appear on the book's title page.

> Peters, Michael A., and Nicholas C. Burbules. *Poststructuralism and*
>
> *Educational Research*. Lanham: Rowman, 2004. Print.

14. A Book by More Than Three Authors

List the first author only, followed by **et al.** ("and others").

> Badawi, El Said, et al. *Modern Written Arabic*. London: Routledge, 2004. Print.

Or, include all the authors in the order in which they appear on the book's title page.

> Badawi, El Said, Daud A. Abdu, Mike Carfter, and Adrian Gully. *Modern*
>
> *Written Arabic*. London: Routledge, 2004. Print.

15. Two or More Books by the Same Author

List books by the same author in alphabetical order by title. After the first entry, use three unspaced hyphens followed by a period in place of the author's name.

> Ede, Lisa. *Situating Composition: Composition Studies and the Politics of*
>
> *Location*. Carbondale: Southern Illinois UP, 2004. Print.
>
> ---. *Work in Progress*. 6th ed. Boston: Bedford, 2004. Print.

Note: If the author is the editor or translator of the second entry, place a comma and the appropriate abbreviation after the hyphens (**---, ed.**). See entry 17 for more on edited books and entry 25 for more on translated books.

16. A Book by a Corporate Author

A book is cited by its corporate author when individual members of the association, commission, or committee that produced it are not identified on the title page.

> American Automobile Association. *Western Canada and Alaska*. Heathrow:
>
> AAA, 2004. Print.

17. An Edited Book

An edited book is a work prepared for publication by a person other than the author. If your focus is on the *author's* work, begin your citation with the author's name. After the title, include the abbreviation **Ed.** ("Edited by"), followed by the editor or editors.

> Twain, Mark. *Adventures of Huckleberry Finn*. Ed. Michael Patrick Hearn.
>
> New York: Norton, 2001. Print.

If your focus is on the *editor's* work, begin your citation with the editor's name followed by the abbreviation **ed.** ("editor") if there is one editor or **eds.** ("editors") if there is more than one. After the title, give the author's name, preceded by the word **By.**

> Hearn, Michael Patrick, ed. *Adventures of Huckleberry Finn*. By Mark Twain.
>
> New York: Norton, 2001. Print.

Editions, Multivolume Works, Graphic Narratives, Forewords, Translations, and Sacred Works

18. A Subsequent Edition of a Book

When citing an edition other than the first, include the edition number that appears on the work's title page.

> Wilson, Charles Banks. *Search for the Native American Purebloods*. 3rd ed.
>
> Norman: U of Oklahoma P, 2000. Print.

19. A Republished Book

Include the original publication date after the title of a republished book—for example, a paperback version of a hardcover book.

> Wharton, Edith. *The House of Mirth*. 1905. New York: Scribner's, 1975. Print.

20. A Book in a Series

If the title page indicates that the book is a part of a series, include the series name, neither italicized nor enclosed in quotation marks, and the series number, followed by a period, after the publication information. Use the abbreviation **Ser.** if *Series* is part of the series name.

> Davis, Bertram H. *Thomas Percy*. Boston: Twayne, 1981. Print. Twayne's
>
> English Authors Ser. 313.

21. A Multivolume Work

When all volumes of a multivolume work have the same title, include the number of the volume you are using.

> Fisch, Max H., ed. *Writings of Charles S. Peirce: A Chronological Edition*. Vol. 4.
>
> Bloomington: Indiana UP, 2000. Print.

If you use two or more volumes that have the same title, cite the entire work.

Fisch, Max H., ed. *Writings of Charles S. Peirce: A Chronological Edition*.

6 vols. Bloomington: Indiana UP, 2000. Print.

When the volume you are using has an individual title, you may cite the title without mentioning any other volumes.

Mareš, Milan. *Fuzzy Cooperative Games: Cooperation with Vague Expectations*.

New York: Physica-Verlag, 2001. Print.

If you wish, however, you may include supplemental information, such as the number of the volume, the title of the entire work, the total number of volumes, or the inclusive publication dates.

22. An Illustrated Book or a Graphic Narrative

An **illustrated book** is a work in which illustrations accompany the text. If your focus is on the *author's* work, begin your citation with the author's name. After the title, include the abbreviation **Illus.** ("Illustrated by") followed by the illustrator's name and then the publication information.

Frost, Robert. *Stopping by Woods on a Snowy Evening*. Illus. Susan Jeffers.

New York: Dutton-Penguin, 2001. Print.

If your focus is on the *illustrator's* work, begin your citation with the illustrator's name followed by the abbreviation **illus.** ("illustrator"). After the title, give the author's name, preceded by the word **By**.

Jeffers, Susan, illus. *Stopping by Woods on a Snowy Evening*. By Robert

Frost. New York: Dutton-Penguin, 2001. Print.

A **graphic narrative** is a work in which text and illustrations work together to tell a story. Cite a graphic narrative as you would cite a book.

Bechdel, Alison. *Fun Home: A Family Tragicomic*. Boston: Houghton, 2006.

Print.

23. The Foreword, Preface, or Afterword of a Book

Campbell, Richard. Preface. *Media and Culture: An Introduction to Mass*

Communication. By Bettina Fabos. Boston: Bedford, 2005. vi-xi. Print.

24. A Book with a Title within Its Title

If the book you are citing contains a title that is normally italicized (a novel, play, or long poem, for example), do not italicize the interior title.

Fulton, Joe B. *Mark Twain in the Margins: The Quarry Farm Marginalia*

and A Connecticut Yankee in King Arthur's Court. Tuscaloosa:

U of Alabama P, 2000. Print.

If the book you are citing contains a title that is normally enclosed in quotation marks, keep the quotation marks.

> Hawkins, Hunt, and Brian W. Shaffer, eds. *Approaches to Teaching Conrad's "Heart of Darkness" and "The Secret Sharer."* New York: MLA, 2002. Print.

25. A Translation

> García Márquez, Gabriel. *One Hundred Years of Solitude*. Trans. Gregory Rabassa. New York: Avon, 1991. Print.

26. The Bible

> *The New English Bible with the Apocrypha*. Oxford Study ed. New York: Oxford UP, 1976. Print.

27. The Qur'an

> *Holy Qur'an*. Trans. M. H. Shakir. Elmhurst: Tahrike Tarsile Qur'an, 1999. Print.

Parts of Books

28. A Short Story, Play, Poem, or Essay in a Collection of an Author's Work

> Bukowski, Charles. "lonely hearts." *The Flash of Lightning behind the Mountain: New Poems*. New York: Ecco, 2004. 115-16. Print.

Note: The title of the poem in the entry above is not capitalized because it appears in lowercase letters in the original.

29. A Short Story, Play, or Poem in an Anthology

> Chopin, Kate. "The Storm." *Literature: Reading, Reacting, Writing*. Ed. Laurie G. Kirszner and Stephen R. Mandell. 8th ed. Boston: Wadsworth, 2013. 306-09. Print.

> Shakespeare, William. *Othello, the Moor of Venice*. *Shakespeare: Six Plays and the Sonnets*. Ed. Thomas Marc Parrott and Edward Hubler. New York: Scribner's, 1956. 145-91. Print.

30. An Essay in an Anthology or Edited Collection

> Crevel, René. "From *Babylon*." *Surrealist Painters and Poets: An Anthology*. Ed. Mary Ann Caws. Cambridge: MIT P, 2001. 175-77. Print.

Note: Supply inclusive page numbers for the entire essay, not just for the page or pages you cite in your paper.

31. More Than One Essay from the Same Anthology

List each essay from the same anthology separately, followed by a cross-reference to the entire anthology. Also list complete publication information for the anthology itself.

Agar, Eileen. "Am I a Surrealist?" Caws 3-7.

Caws, Mary Ann, ed. *Surrealist Painters and Poets: An Anthology*. Cambridge:

MIT P, 2001. Print.

Crevel, René. "From *Babylon*." Caws 175-77.

32. A Scholarly Article Reprinted in a Collection

Booth, Wayne C. "Why Ethical Criticism Can Never Be Simple." *Style* 32.2

(1998): 351-64. Rpt. in *Mapping the Ethical Turn: A Reader in Ethics,*

Culture, and Literary Theory. Ed. Todd F. Davis and Kenneth Womack.

Charlottesville: UP of Virginia, 2001. 16-29. Print.

33. An Article in a Reference Book (Signed/Unsigned)

For a **signed** article, begin with the author's name. For unfamiliar reference books, include full publication information.

Drabble, Margaret. "Expressionism." *The Oxford Companion to English*

Literature. 6th ed. New York: Oxford UP, 2000. Print.

If the article is **unsigned,** begin with the title. For familiar reference books, do not include full publication information.

"Cubism." *The Encyclopedia Americana*. 2004 ed. Print.

Note: Omit page numbers when the reference book lists entries alphabetically. If you are listing one definition among several from a dictionary, include the abbreviation **Def.** ("Definition") along with the letter and/or number that corresponds to the definition.

"Justice." Def. 2b. *The Concise Oxford Dictionary*. 11th ed. 2008. Print.

Dissertations, Pamphlets, Government Publications, and Legal Sources

34. A Dissertation (Published)

Cite a published dissertation the same way you would cite a book, but add relevant dissertation information before the publication information.

Rodriguez, Jason Anthony. *Bureaucracy and Altruism: Managing the*

Contradictions of Teaching. Diss. U of Texas at Arlington, 2003.

Ann Arbor: UMI, 2004. Print.

Note: University Microfilms, which publishes most of the dissertations in the United States, is also available online by subscription. For the proper format for citing online databases, see entries 53–58.

35. A Dissertation (Unpublished)

Use quotation marks for the title of an unpublished dissertation.

> Bon Tempo, Carl Joseph. "Americans at the Gate: The Politics of American
>
> Refugee Policy." Diss. U of Virginia, 2004. Print.

36. A Pamphlet

Cite a pamphlet as you would a book. If no author is listed, begin with the title (italicized).

> *The Darker Side of Tanning*. Schaumburg: The American Academy of
>
> Dermatology, 2010. Print.

37. A Government Publication

If the publication has no listed author, begin with the name of the government, followed by the name of the agency. You may use an abbreviation if its meaning is clear: **United States. Cong. Senate.**

> United States. Office of Consumer Affairs. *2003 Consumer's Resource*
>
> *Handbook*. Washington: GPO, 2003. Print.

When citing two or more publications by the same government, use three unspaced hyphens (followed by a period) in place of the name for the second and subsequent entries. When you cite more than one work from the same agency of that government, use an additional set of unspaced hyphens in place of the agency name.

> United States. FAA. *Passenger Airline Safety in the Twenty-First Century*.
>
> Washington: GPO, 2003. Print.
>
> ---. ---. *Recycled Air in Passenger Airline Cabins*. Washington: GPO, 2002.
>
> Print.

38. A Historical or Legal Document

In general, you do not need a works-cited entry for familiar historical documents. Parenthetical references in the text are sufficient—for example, **(US Const., art. 3, sec. 2)**.

If you cite an act in the works-cited list, include the name of the act, its Public Law (Pub. L.) number, its Statutes at Large (Stat.) cataloging number, its enactment date, and its publication medium.

> Children's Health Act. Pub. L. 106-310. 114 Stat. 1101. 17 Oct. 2000. Print.

In works-cited entries for **legal cases,** abbreviate names of cases, but spell out the first important word of each party's name. Include the volume number, abbreviated name (not italicized), and inclusive page numbers of the law report; the name of the deciding court; the decision year; and publication information for the source. Do not italicize the case name in the works-cited list.

Abbott v. Blades. 544 US 929. Supreme Court of the US. 2005. *United States Reports*. Washington: GPO, 2007. Print.

MLA ENTRIES FOR MISCELLANEOUS PRINT AND NONPRINT SOURCES

Lectures and Interviews

39. A Lecture

Grimm, Mary. "An Afternoon with Mary Grimm." Visiting Writers Program. Dept. of English, Wright State U, Dayton. 16 Apr. 2004. Lecture.

40. A Personal Interview

West, Cornel. Personal interview. 28 Dec. 2008.

Tannen, Deborah. Telephone interview. 8 June 2009.

41. A Published Interview

Huston, John. "The Outlook for Raising Money: An Investment Banker's Viewpoint." *NJBIZ* 30 Sept. 2002: 2-3. Print.

Letters

42. A Personal Letter

Include the abbreviation **TS** (for "typescript") after the date of a typed letter.

Tan, Amy. Letter to the author. 7 Apr. 2010. TS.

43. A Published Letter

Joyce, James. "Letter to Louis Gillet." 20 Aug. 1931. *James Joyce*. By Richard Ellmann. New York: Oxford UP, 1965. 631. Print.

44. A Letter in a Library's Archives

Include the abbreviation **MS** (for "manuscript") after the date of a handwritten letter.

Stieglitz, Alfred. Letter to Paul Rosenberg. 5 Sept. 1923. MS. Stieglitz Archive. Yale U Arts Lib., New Haven.

Films, Videotapes, Radio and Television Programs, and Recordings

45. A Film

Include the title of the film (italicized), the distributor, and the date, along with other information that may be useful to readers, such as the names of the performers, the director, and the screenwriter. Conclude with the publication medium.

> *Citizen Kane*. Dir. Orson Welles. Perf. Welles, Joseph Cotten, Dorothy
>
> Comingore, and Agnes Moorehead. RKO, 1941. Film.

If you are focusing on the contribution of a particular person, begin with that person's name.

> Welles, Orson, dir. *Citizen Kane*. Perf. Welles, Joseph Cotten, Dorothy
>
> Comingore, and Agnes Moorehead. RKO, 1941. Film.

46. A Videotape, DVD, or Laser Disc

Cite a videotape, DVD, or laser disc as you would cite a film, but include the original release date (when available).

> *Bowling for Columbine*. Dir. Michael Moore. 2002. United Artists and Alliance
>
> Atlantis, 2003. DVD.

47. A Radio or Television Program

> "War Feels Like War." *P.O.V.* Dir. Esteban Uyarra. PBS. WPTD, Dayton, 6 July
>
> 2004. Television.

48. A Recording

List the composer, conductor, or performer (whomever you are focusing on), followed by the title, publisher, year of issue, and publication medium (**CD-ROM**, **MP3 file**, and so on).

> Boubill, Alain, and Claude-Michel Schönberg. *Miss Saigon*. Perf. Lea Salonga,
>
> Claire Moore, and Jonathan Pryce. Cond. Martin Koch. Geffen, 1989.
>
> CD-ROM.
>
> Marley, Bob. "Crisis." *Kaya*. Kava Island, 1978. LP.

Paintings, Photographs, Cartoons, and Advertisements

49. A Painting

> Hopper, Edward. *Railroad Sunset*. 1929. Oil on canvas. Whitney Museum of
>
> American Art, New York.

50. A Photograph

Cite a photograph in a museum's collection in the same way you cite a painting.

Stieglitz, Alfred. *The Steerage.* 1907. Photograph. Los Angeles County

Museum of Art, Los Angeles.

51. A Cartoon or Comic Strip

Trudeau, Garry. "Doonesbury." Comic strip. *Philadelphia Inquirer* 15 Sept.

2003, late ed.: E13. Print.

52. An Advertisement

Microsoft. Advertisement. *National Review* 8 June 2010: 17. Print.

MLA ELECTRONIC SOURCES — Entries for Sources from Online Databases

To cite information from an online database, supply the publication information (including page numbers, if available; if unavailable, use **n. pag.**) followed by the name of the database (italicized), the publication medium (**Web**), and the date of access. Figure 21.4 shows where you can find this information.

| Author's last name | First name | Title of short story (in quotation marks) | Title of periodical (italicized) | Date of publication | Inclusive page numbers |

Keillor, Garrison. "Love Me: A Short Story." *Atlantic* July-Aug. 2003: 115-22.

Academic Search Elite. Web. 2 May 2011.

| Name of database (italicized) | Publication medium | Date of access |

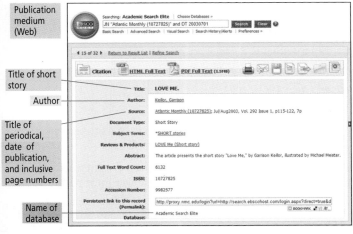

FIGURE 21.4 Opening screen from an online database showing the location of the information needed for documentation. © EBSCO.

Journal Articles, Magazine Articles, News Services,
and Dissertations from Online Databases

53. A Scholarly Journal Article with a Print Version

Schaefer, Richard J. "Editing Strategies in Television News Documentaries."

Journal of Communication 47.4 (1997): 69-89. *InfoTrac OneFile Plus*.

Web. 2 Oct. 2011.

54. A Scholarly Journal Article with No Print Version

Maeseele, Thomas. "From Charity to Welfare Rights? A Study of Social Care

Practices." *Social Work and Society: The International Online-Only*

Journal 8.1 (2010): n. pag. Web. 20 May 2011.

55. A Monthly Magazine Article

Livermore, Beth. "Meteorites on Ice." *Astronomy* July 1993: 54-58. *Expanded*

Academic ASAP Plus. Web. 12 Nov. 2010.

Wright, Karen. "The Clot Thickens." *Discover* Dec. 1999: n. pag. *MasterFILE*

Premier. Web. 10 Oct. 2010.

56. A News Service

Ryan, Desmond. "Some Background on the Battle of Gettysburg." *Knight*

Ridder/Tribune News Service 7 Oct. 1993: n. pag. *InfoTrac OneFile Plus*.

Web. 16 Nov. 2011.

57. A Newspaper Article

Meyer, Greg. "Answering Questions about the West Nile Virus." *Dayton Daily*

News 11 July 2002: Z3-7. *LexisNexis*. Web. 17 Feb. 2006.

58. A Published Dissertation

Rodriguez, Jason Anthony. *Bureaucracy and Altruism: Managing the*

Contradictions of Teaching. Diss. U of Texas at Arlington, 2003.

ProQuest. Web. 4 Mar. 2009.

MLA ELECTRONIC SOURCES   Entries for Sources from
Internet Sites

❓ MLA style* recognizes that full source information for Internet sources is
not always available. Include in your citation whatever information you can

---

*The documentation style for Internet sources presented here conforms to the most recent
guidelines published in the *MLA Handbook for Writers of Research Papers* (7th ed.) and
found online at <http://www.mlahandbook.org>.

reasonably obtain: the author or editor of the site (if available); the name of the site (italicized); the version number of the source (if applicable); the name of any institution or sponsor (if unavailable, include the abbreviation **N.p.** for "no publisher"); the date of electronic publication or update (if unavailable, include the abbreviation **n.d.** for "no date of publication"); the publication medium (**Web**); and the date you accessed the source. MLA recommends omitting the URL from the citation unless it is necessary to find the source (as in entry 62). Figure 21.5 shows where you can find this information.

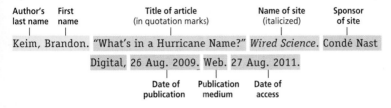

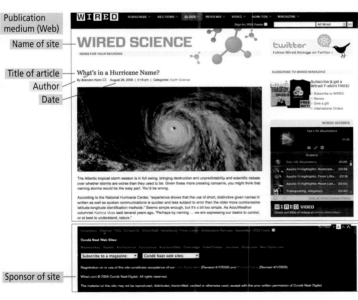

FIGURE 21.5 Part of an online article showing the location of the information needed for documentation. Wired.com © 2009 Condé Nast Digital. All rights reserved. Image from NOAA.

Internet-Specific Sources

59. An Entire Web Site

Nelson, Cary, ed. *Modern American Poetry*. Dept. of English, U of Illinois, Urbana-Champaign, 2002. Web. 26 May 2009.

60. A Document within a Web Site

"D-Day: June 6, 1944." *History.com*. History Channel, 1999. Web. 7 June
2010.

61. A Home Page for a Course

Walker, Janice R. "ENGL 1101-Composition I, Fall 2010." Course home page.
Georgia Southern University. Dept. of Writing and Linguistics, Georgia
Southern U, 6 Aug. 2010. Web. 8 Sept. 2011.

62. A Personal Home Page

Gainor, Charles. Home page. U of Toronto, 22 July 2010. Web. 10 Nov. 2011.
<http://www.chass.utoronto.ca:9094/~char>.

Note: If an electronic address (URL) is necessary, MLA requires that you
enclose the URL within angle brackets to distinguish the address from the
punctuation in the rest of the citation. If a URL will not fit on a line, the
entire URL will be automatically carried over to the next line. If you prefer
to divide the URL, divide it only after a slash. (Do not insert a hyphen.)

63. A Radio Program Accessed from an Internet Archive

"Teenage Skeptic Takes on Climate Scientists." Narr. David Kestenbaum.
Morning Edition. Natl. Public Radio. WNYC, New York, 15 Apr. 2008.
Transcript. *NPR*. Web. 30 Mar. 2010.

64. An Email

Mauk, Karen R. Message to the author. 28 June 2011. E-mail.

65. A Posting on an Online Forum or Blog

Schiller, Stephen. "Paper Cost and Publishing Costs." *New York Times*.
New York Times, 24 Apr. 2002. Web. 17 May 2002.

Merry. "The Way We Roll. . . ." *EnviroMom*. EnviroMom, 27 June 2008. Web.
3 July 2009.

*Articles, Books, Reviews, Letters, and Reference Works
on the Internet*

66. An Article in a Scholarly Journal

When you cite an article you accessed from an electronic source that also
has a print version, include the publication information for the print
source, the inclusive page numbers (if available), the publication medium
(**Web**), and the date you accessed it.

DeKoven, Marianne. "Utopias Limited: Post-Sixties and Postmodern
American Fiction." *Modern Fiction Studies* 41.1 (1995): 75-97. Web.
20 Jan. 2005.

67. An Article in a Magazine

Weiser, Jay. "The Tyranny of Informality." *Time*. Time, 26 Feb. 1996. Web.
1 Mar. 2009.

68. An Article in a Newspaper

Bilton, Nick. "Three Reasons Why the iPad Will Kill Amazon's Kindle."
New York Times. New York Times, 27 Jan. 2010. Web. 16 Feb. 2011.

69. An Article in a Newsletter

Sullivan, Jennifer S., comp. "Documentation Preserved, New Collections."
AIP Center for History of Physics 39.2 (2007): 2-3. Web. 26 Feb. 2009.

70. A Book

Douglass, Frederick. *My Bondage and My Freedom*. Boston, 1855. *Google Book
Search*. Web. 8 June 2011.

71. A Review

Ebert, Roger. Rev. of *Star Wars: Episode I—The Phantom Menace,* dir. George
Lucas. *Chicago Sun-Times*. Digital Chicago, 8 June 2000. Web. 22 June
2007.

72. A Letter to the Editor

Chen-Cheng, Henry H. Letter. *New York Times*. New York Times, 19 July
1999. Web. 1 Jan. 2011.

73. An Article in an Encyclopedia

Include the article's title, the title of the database (italicized), the version
number (if available), the sponsor, the date of electronic publication, the
publication medium (**Web**), and the date of access.

"Hawthorne, Nathaniel." *Encyclopaedia Britannica Online*. Encyclopaedia
Britannica, 2010. Web. 16 May 2011.

74. A Government Publication

Cite an online government publication as you would cite a print version;
end with the information required for an electronic source.

United States. Dept. of Justice. Office of Justice Programs. *Violence against
Women: Estimates from the Redesigned National Crime Victimization
Survey*. By Ronet Bachman and Linda E. Saltzman. Aug. 1995. *Bureau
of Justice Statistics*. Web. 10 July 2009.

Paintings, Photographs, Cartoons, and Maps on the Internet

75. A Painting

Seurat, Georges-Pierre. *Evening, Honfleur*. 1886. Museum of Mod. Art,
New York. *MoMA.org*. Web. 8 Jan. 2010.

76. A Photograph

Brady, Mathew. *Ulysses S. Grant 1822-1885*. 1864. *Mathew Brady's National
Portrait Gallery*. Web. 2 Oct. 2010.

77. A Cartoon

Stossel, Sage. "Star Wars: The Next Generation." Cartoon. *Atlantic Unbound*.
Atlantic Monthly Group, 2 Oct. 2002. Web. 14 Nov. 2009.

78. A Map

"Philadelphia, Pennsylvania." Map. *U.S. Gazetteer*. US Census Bureau, n.d.
Web. 17 July 2011.

MLA OTHER ELECTRONIC SOURCES

DVD-ROMs and CD-ROMs

79. A Nonperiodical Publication on DVD-ROM or CD-ROM

Cite a nonperiodical publication on DVD-ROM or CD-ROM the same way
you would cite a book, but include the appropriate medium of publication.

"Windhover." *The Oxford English Dictionary*. 2nd ed. Oxford: Oxford UP,
2001. DVD-ROM.

"Whitman, Walt." *DiskLit: American Authors*. Boston: Hall, 2000. CD-ROM.

80. A Periodical Publication on DVD-ROM or CD-ROM

Zurbach, Kate. "The Linguistic Roots of Three Terms." *Linguistic Quarterly*
37 (1994): 12-47. CD-ROM. *InfoTrac: Magazine Index Plus*. Information
Access. Jan. 2009.

Digital Files

81. A Word-Processing Document

Russell, Brad. "Work Trip Notes." File last modified on 22 Mar. 2009.
Microsoft Word file.

82. An MP3 File

U2. "Beautiful Day." *All That You Can't Leave Behind*. Universal-Island, 2000.
MP3 file.

Close-Up HOW TO CITE SOURCES NOT LISTED IN THIS CHAPTER

The sources listed in this chapter are the ones you will most likely encounter in your research. If you encounter a source that is not listed here, find the model that most closely matches it, and adapt the guidelines for your use.

For example, suppose you wanted to include **an obituary** from a print newspaper in your list of works cited. The models that most closely resemble this type of entry are *an editorial in a newspaper* (entry 8) and *a letter to the editor* (entry 9). If you used these models as your guide, your entry would look like this:

> Boucher, Geoff, and Elaine Woo. "Michael Jackson's Life Was Infused
>
>> with Fantasy and Tragedy." Obituary. *Los Angeles Times* 2 July
>>
>> 2009: 4. Print.

Follow the same procedure for an electronic source. Suppose you wanted to include a posting from a social networking site, such as *Facebook*. The models that most closely resemble this type of entry are a *personal home page* (entry 62) and a *blog posting* (entry 65). If you used these models as your guide, your entry would look like this:

> Branagh, Kenneth. Wall post. *Facebook.com*. 15 Mar. 2010.
>
>> Web. 16 Mar. 2010.

3 Content Notes

Content notes—multiple bibliographic citations or other material that does not fit smoothly into your paper—are indicated by a **superscript** (raised numeral) in the text. Notes can appear either as footnotes at the bottom of the page or as endnotes on a separate sheet entitled **Notes**, placed after the last page of the paper and before the works-cited list. Content notes are double-spaced within and between entries. The first line is indented one-half inch, and subsequent lines are typed flush left.

For Multiple Citations

In the Paper

Many researchers emphasize the necessity of having dying patients share their experiences.[1]

In the Note

1. Kübler-Ross 27; Stinnette 43; Poston 70; Cohen and Cohen 31-34; Burke 1: 91-95.

For Other Material

In the Paper

The massacre during World War I is an event the survivors could not easily forget.[2]

In the Note

2. For a firsthand account of these events, see Bedoukian 178-81.

21b MLA-Style Manuscript Guidelines

Although MLA papers do not usually include abstracts or internal headings, this situation is changing. Be sure you know what your instructor expects.

The guidelines in the three checklists that follow are based on the latest version of the *MLA Handbook for Writers of Research Papers.*

CHECKLIST
Typing Your Paper

When typing your paper, use the student paper in **21c** as your model.

❏ Leave a one-inch margin at the top and bottom and on both sides of the page. Double-space your paper throughout.

❏ Capitalize all important words in your title, but not prepositions, articles, coordinating conjunctions, or the *to* in infinitives (unless they begin or end the title or subtitle). Do not italicize your title or enclose it in quotation marks. Never put a period after the title, even if it is a sentence.

❏ Number all pages of your paper consecutively—including the first—in the upper right-hand corner, one-half inch from the top, flush right. Type your last name followed by a space before the page number on every page.

❏ Set off quotations of more than four lines of prose or more than three lines of poetry by indenting the whole quotation one inch. If you quote two or more paragraphs, indent the first line of each paragraph an additional quarter inch. (If the first sentence does not begin a paragraph, do not indent it. Indent the first line only in successive paragraphs.)

See 21a

❏ Citations should follow **MLA documentation style**.

CHECKLIST
Using Visuals

See 26d

❏ Insert **visuals** into the text as close as possible to where they are discussed.

❏ For **tables**, follow these guidelines: *Above the table*, label each table with the word **Table** followed by an arabic numeral (for instance, **Table 1**). Double-space, and type a descriptive caption, with the first line flush with the left-hand margin; indent subsequent lines one-quarter inch. Capitalize the caption as if it were a title.

Below the table, type the word **Source,** followed by a colon and all source information. Type the first line of the source information flush with the left-hand margin; indent subsequent lines one-quarter inch.

❑ Label other types of visual material—graphs, charts, photographs, drawings, and so on—**Fig.** (Figure) followed by an arabic numeral (for example, **Fig. 2**). Directly below the visual, type the label and a title or caption on the same line, followed by source information. Type all lines flush with the left-hand margin.

❑ Do not include the source of the visual in the works-cited list unless you use other material from that source elsewhere in the paper.

CHECKLIST
Preparing the MLA Works-Cited List

When typing your works-cited list, follow these guidelines:

❑ Begin the works-cited list on a new page after the last page of text or <u>content notes</u>, numbered as the next page of the paper.

See 21a3

❑ Center the title **Works Cited** one inch from the top of the page. Double-space between the title and the first entry.

❑ Each entry on the works-cited list has three divisions: author, title, and publication information. Separate divisions with a period and one space.

❑ List entries alphabetically, with last name first. Use the author's full name as it appears on the title page. If a source has no listed author, alphabetize it by the first word of the title (not counting the article).

❑ Type the first line of each entry flush with the left-hand margin; indent subsequent lines one-half inch.

❑ Double-space within and between entries.

21c Sample MLA-Style Research Paper

The following student paper, "The Great Debate: *Wikipedia* and College-Level Research," by Rebecca James, uses MLA documentation style. It ⸱des MLA-style in-text citations, a line graph, a notes page, and a works-

Title Pages

Although MLA does not require a separate title page, some instructors prefer that you include one. If so, follow this format:

About ⅓ page down

Title

The Great Debate:

Wikipedia and College-Level Research

2"

by

Name

Rebecca James

2"

Instructor

Professor Burks

Course

English 102

Double-space

Date submitted

24 April 2011

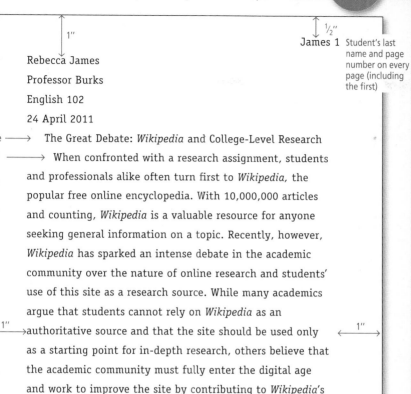

James 1 Student's last name and page number on every page (including the first)

½"

Rebecca James

Professor Burks

English 102

24 April 2011

er title → The Great Debate: *Wikipedia* and College-Level Research

nt ½" → When confronted with a research assignment, students

ole-
e → and professionals alike often turn first to *Wikipedia,* the

popular free online encyclopedia. With 10,000,000 articles

and counting, *Wikipedia* is a valuable resource for anyone

seeking general information on a topic. Recently, however,

Wikipedia has sparked an intense debate in the academic

community over the nature of online research and students'

use of this site as a research source. While many academics

argue that students cannot rely on *Wikipedia* as an

1" → authoritative source and that the site should be used only ← 1" →

as a starting point for in-depth research, others believe that

the academic community must fully enter the digital age

and work to improve the site by contributing to *Wikipedia*'s

database of articles. Despite its contentious nature, the
Thesis statement
debate surrounding *Wikipedia* has overall been a positive

development because it has led the academic community to

confront the evolving nature of college-level research in the

twenty-first century.

With its slogan "Making Life Easier," *Wikipedia* has

positioned itself as the most popular wiki, an open-source

Web site that allows users to edit as well as contribute

content. Derived from a Hawaiian word meaning "quick," the
Parenthetical documentation refers to material accessed from a Web site
term *wiki* conveys the swiftness and ease with which users

can access information on and contribute content to a site

("Wiki"). In accordance with the site's policies, users can edit

1"

James 2

Student's original conclusions; no documentation necessary

existing articles and add new articles using *Wikipedia*'s editing tools, which do not require specialized programming knowledge or expertise. Since its creation in 2001, *Wikipedia* has grown into a huge database of articles on topics ranging from contemporary rock bands to obscure scientific and technical concepts. Because anyone can edit or add content to the site, however, *Wikipedia* has been labeled unreliable by many members of the academic community.

Quotations from Internet source, introduced by author's name, are not followed by a paragraph or page number because this informtion was not provided in the electronic text

Without a professional editorial board to oversee its development, *Wikipedia* has several shortcomings that limit its trustworthiness as a research source. As *Wikipedia*'s own "Researching with *Wikipedia*" page concedes, "not everything in *Wikipedia* is accurate, comprehensive, or unbiased." "Reliability of *Wikipedia*," an article on *Wikipedia*, lists and discusses the many problems that have been identified, presenting criticisms under categories such as "areas of reliability," "susceptibility to bias," and "false biographical information."Academics have similar objections. Referring to the collaborative, open-source nature of the wiki format, Bart Ehrman, a professor at the University of North Carolina at Chapel Hill, observes,

Qtd. in indicates that Ehrman's comments were quoted in Philips's article

"Democratization isn't necessarily good for scholarship" (qtd. in Philips). Similarly, Middlebury College history department chairman Don J. Wyatt notes the danger of relying on *Wikipedia* for factual information: "From the standpoint of access, it's a marvelous thing. But from the standpoint of maintaining quality, it's much less so" (qtd. in Read). In fact, Middlebury's history department instituted a policy in 2007 that prohibits students from citing *Wikipedia* as a research source.

Most academics agree that many *Wikipedia* articles are unreliable. Although many *Wikipedia* articles include citations, many others—especially those that are underdeveloped—

James 3

do not supply citations to the sources that support their claims. In addition, because anyone can create or edit them, *Wikipedia* articles can be factually inaccurate, biased, and even targeted for vandalism. For example, some *Wikipedia* users tamper with the biographies of especially high-profile political or cultural figures.[1] According to a 2008 study that examines *Wikipedia* data from 2006, 11% of *Wikipedia*'s articles were vandalized at least once (Spinellis and Louridas 68). *Wikipedia* administrators can lock articles that are likely to be vandalized, preventing the ordinary user from editing them, but Spinellis and Louridas's study found that only 0.13% of at-risk articles were locked (68). As William Badke, associate librarian at Trinity Western University, notes, *Wikipedia* can be "an environment for shallow thinking, debates over interpretation, and the settling of scores" (50).

> Superscript number identifies content note

Because their content is open to public editing, *Wikipedia* articles also often suffer from poor writing. Emory University English professor Mark Bauerlein asserts that *Wikipedia* articles are written in a "flat, featureless, factual style" (153). *Wikipedia* has instituted a coding system to label the shortcomings of its less-developed articles, but a warning about an article's poor writing style is likely to go unnoticed by the typical user. Bauerlein argues that the poor writing of many *Wikipedia* articles reaffirms to students that sloppy writing and grammatical errors are acceptable in their own writing as well: "*Wikipedia* prose sets the standard for intellectual style. Students relying on *Wikipedia* alone, year in and year out, absorb the prose as proper knowledge discourse, and knowledge itself seems blank and uninspiring" (153-54). Thus, according to Bauerlein, *Wikipedia* articles have actually

James 4

set a new, lower standard for what constitutes acceptable college-level writing.

Despite *Wikipedia*'s drawbacks, there is no denying the popularity of the site among both college students and professionals. According to a 2007 report by the Pew Internet & American Life Project, 36% of American adults use *Wikipedia,* with the majority of users having or pursuing higher-education degrees (Rainie and Tancer 1). Table 1 shows a breakdown of the people who most commonly consult *Wikipedia*.

Table 1

Wikipedia User Profile

A Profile of Wikipedia Users	
Do you ever use the internet to look for information on Wikipedia?	% of adult internet users who say "yes"
Men	39%
Women	34%
Whites	37%
Blacks	27%
English-speaking Hispanics	36%
Age 18-29	44%
Age 30-49	38%
Age 50-64	31%
Age 65+	26%
High school diploma	22%
Some college	36%
College grad +	50%
< $30,000 household income	32%
$30,000-$50,000	35%
$50,000-$75,000	39%
>$75,000	42%
Dial-up connection at home	26%
Broadband at home	42%

Source: Pew Internet & American Life Project Survey Feb. 15-March 7, 2007. http://www.pewinternet.org/Reports/2007/Wikipedia=users/ Data=Memo.aspx. N=1,492 internet users. Margin of error is ±3%.

Source: Lee Rainie and Bill Tancer; "*Wikipedia* Users"; *Pew Internet & American Life Project*; Pew Research Center, 24 Apr. 2007; Web; 7 Apr. 2011; 1.

Table summarizes relevant data. Source information is typed directly below the table.

There are good reasons to explain why so many educated adults are using *Wikipedia*. The site offers numerous benefits to researchers seeking information on a topic. Longer *Wikipedia* articles often include comprehensive abstracts that summarize their content. *Wikipedia* articles also often include hyperlinks, or "wikilinks," to other *Wikipedia* articles, allowing users to navigate quickly through related content. In addition, many *Wikipedia* articles contain external links to other print and online sources, including reliable peer-reviewed sources. Another benefit, noted by Middlebury College's Don J. Wyatt, is the inclusion of current and comprehensive bibliographies in some *Wikipedia* articles (Read). Assuming that *Wikipedia* users make the effort to connect an article's content with more reliable, traditional research sources (including print sources), *Wikipedia* can be a valuable resource for serious researchers.

Wikipedia has advantages over other, professionally edited online encyclopedias. Because users can update articles in real time from any location, *Wikipedia* offers up-to-the-minute coverage of political and cultural events as well as timely information on popular culture topics that receive little or no attention in other reference sources. For example, a student researching the history of video gaming would find *Wikipedia*'s "Wii" article, with its numerous pages of information and nearly 150 external links to additional sources, to be a valuable resource. *Encyclopaedia Britannica Online* does not contain a comparable article on this popular game console. Even when the available information on a particular topic is sparse, *Wikipedia* allows users to create "stub" articles, which provide minimal information that users can expand over time. According to Spinellis and

James 6

Louridas's study, approximately 20% of *Wikipedia*'s articles are classified as stubs (70). By offering immediate access to information on relatively obscure topics, *Wikipedia* can be a valuable first step in finding reliable research sources on such topics.

As Spinellis and Louridas's study suggests, *Wikipedia* is poised to become an even more comprehensive database of information that could eventually gain acceptance in the academic community. *Wikipedia*'s "About" page claims that the site's articles "are continually edited and improved over time, and in general, this results in an upward trend of quality and a growing consensus over a fair and balanced representation of information." In fact, *Wikipedia* has instituted control measures to help weed out inaccurate or biased information and to make its content more reliable. For example, evaluating articles on the basis of accuracy, neutrality, completeness, and style, *Wikipedia* ranks its best articles as "featured" and its second-best articles as "good."[2] Although no professional editorial board oversees the development of content within *Wikipedia,* experienced users may become editors, and this role allows them to monitor the process by which content is added and updated. Users may also use the "Talk" page to discuss an article's content and make suggestions for improvement. With such control measures in place, some *Wikipedia* articles are comparable in scope and accuracy to articles in professionally edited online encyclopedias.

Although some critics argue that the collaborative nature of the wiki format does not necessarily help improve content, Spinellis and Louridas's study seems to confirm just the opposite.

Superscript number identifies content note

James 7

In examining trends of content development in *Wikipedia,* Spinellis and Louridas affirm that the coverage of various topics in *Wikipedia* tends to become more balanced over time:

> *Wikipedia*'s topic coverage has been criticized as too reflective of and limited to the interests of its young, tech-savvy contributors, covering technology and current affairs disproportionably more than, say, world history or the arts. We hypothesize that the addition of new *Wikipedia* articles is not a purely random process following the whims of its contributors but that references to nonexistent articles trigger the eventual creation of a corresponding article. Although it is difficult to claim that this process guarantees even and unbiased coverage of topics (adding links is also a subjective process), such a mechanism could eventually force some kind of balance in *Wikipedia* coverage. (71)

Spinellis and Louridas summarize their findings with a positive conclusion: "the apparently chaotic *Wikipedia* development process delivers growth at a sustainable rate" (71). Fig. 1 supports this conclusion, illustrating how, in recent years, *Wikipedia* has achieved a relative balance between complete and incomplete (or stub) articles. In offering increasingly more consistent (as well as broader) coverage, *Wikipedia* is positioning itself as a more reliable source of information than some of its critics might like to admit.

Some argue that the academic community's rejection of *Wikipedia* has less to do with *Wikipedia*'s shortcomings and more to do with academia's resistance to emergent digital

Quotation of more than four lines is typed as a block, indented 1", and double-spaced, with no quotation marks

Parenthetical documentation is placed one space after end punctuation

Graph summarizes relevant data. Source information is typed directly below the figure.

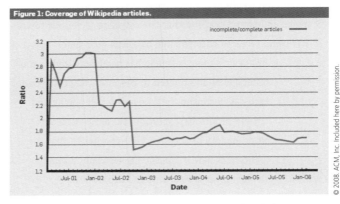

Fig. 1. Diomidis Spinellis and Panagiotis Louridas, "The Collaborative Organization of Knowledge"; *Communications of the ACM* 51.8 (2008): 71; *Academic Search Elite*; Web; 3 Apr. 2011.

research technologies. Harvard Law professor Jonathan L. Zittrain suggests that academia has, in effect, fallen behind:

> It's to academia's enduring disappointment that *Wikipedia* had to be invented by a [private entrepreneur] named Jimbo. So many projects by universities and libraries are about knowledge and information online, and they just couldn't get *Wikipedia* going, or anything like it. I don't see academia rising to the challenge and trying to figure out how this wonderful network can meet its goals of bringing information to the world. (qtd. in Foster)

William Badke, the Trinity Western University librarian, agrees, stating, "*Wikipedia* is an affront to academia, because

James 9

it undercuts what makes academics the elite in society. . . . *Wikipedia* doesn't depend on elite scholars" (49). Although he acknowledges that *Wikipedia* should serve only as a starting point for more in-depth research, Jimmy Wales, cofounder of *Wikipedia,* calls for the academic community to recognize *Wikipedia* as one of several new, important digital platforms that change the way people learn and disseminate knowledge: "Instead of fearing the power, complexity, and extraordinary potential of these new platforms, we should be asking how we can gain from their success" (qtd. in Goldstein). As Badke and others argue, members of the academic community are uniquely qualified to improve *Wikipedia* by expanding stub articles and by writing new articles about their areas of expertise. As Badke suggests, "The most daring solution would be for academia to enter the world of *Wikipedia* directly" (50). According to Badke, academics should not be asking whether or not college students should use *Wikipedia* in their research but rather how academia can work to improve this bank of information that is, and will continue to be, consulted before any other research source.

In recent years, librarians across the country have committed their time and resources to enhancing *Wikipedia* articles that pertain to their own special collections and areas of expertise. Like William Badke, Adam Bennington, a librarian at the State Farm Insurance Corporate Library in Bloomington, Illinois, argues that the *Wikipedia* phenomenon presents a "teachable moment" that enables librarians and other members of the academic community to develop students' information literacy skills (47). In their article "Putting the Library in *Wikipedia*," Wake Forest University librarians Lauren Pressley

Ellipsis indicates that the student has omitted words from the quotation

and Carolyn J. McCallum explain their own learning curve in contributing content to *Wikipedia* that directs users back to their library's special collections. Pressley and McCallum argue that librarians can play a pivotal role in making *Wikipedia* a more reliable and scholarly source of information, as demonstrated by their own contributions as well as by those made by librarians at the University of Washington Digital Initiatives, the University of North Texas, and Villanova University. "Through this type of collaboration," Pressley and McCallum suggest, "perhaps we will reach a whole new group of users that wouldn't have come through our doors another way" (42). Badke, Bennington, Pressley, McCallum, and other librarians believe that it is the responsibility of the academic community to bridge the divide between traditional research sources and the digital tools and technologies students are increasingly using to conduct college-level research.

With emerging research on *Wikipedia* use, and with new efforts by colleges and universities around the country to incorporate *Wikipedia* into academic research, the debate surrounding *Wikipedia* has shifted. While previously instructors tended to seek ways to prevent students from using *Wikipedia* as a research source, the academic community now seems to be acknowledging not only the undeniable popularity but also the importance and usefulness of this online resource in students' lives. Many former critics are now starting to acknowledge that *Wikipedia* offers academics an opportunity to participate in emergent digital technologies that have changed the ways students conduct research. In an interview with the *Chronicle of Higher Education,* Jimmy Wales explains future proposed enhancements to *Wikipedia,*

Paragraph synthesizes several sources cited in paper

Conclusion restates the thesis and summarizes key points

James 11

including a "flagging" feature that would allow instructors
to approve certain *Wikipedia* articles as acceptable research
sources (Young). Eventually, *Wikipedia* may become an
approved college-level research source. At the very least,
it will provide new insight into the evolving nature of
college-level research in the twenty-first century.

1″

½″

Center title —————————→ Notes

Indent ½″ ————————→ 1. In one well-known example, the reputation of journalist

John Seigenthaler was tarnished when a *Wikipedia* user edited

his biography to claim inaccurately that Seigenthaler was

involved in the Kennedy assassination, a lie that spread to

Double-
space   other online sources.

2. In addition, *Wikipedia*'s policies state that the

1″ information in its articles must be verifiable and must be   1″

based on documented, preexisting research.

1″ ½″
James 13

er title ⟶ Works Cited

Badke, William. "What to Do with *Wikipedia*." *Online*
    Mar.-Apr. 2008: 48-50. *Academic Search Elite*. Web.
    7 Apr. 2011.

Bauerlein, Mark. *The Dumbest Generation: How the Digital
    Age Stupefies Young Americans and Jeopardizes Our
    Future (or, Don't Trust Anyone Under 30)*. New York:
    Penguin, 2008. Print.

1″ →Bennington, Adam. "Dissecting the Web through *Wikipedia*."   1″
    American Libraries Aug. 2008: 46-48. Print.

Foster, Andrea L. "Professor Predicts Bleak Future for the
    Internet." *Chronicle of Higher Education* 18 Apr. 2008:
    A29. *Academic Search Elite*. Web. 3 Apr. 2011.

Goldstein, Evan R. "The Dumbing of America?" *Chronicle of
    Higher Education* 21 Mar. 2008: B4. *Academic Search
    Elite*. Web. 3 Apr. 2011.

Philips, Matthew. "God's Word, According to *Wikipedia*."
    Newsweek 23 June 2008: 14. Print.

Pressley, Lauren, and Carolyn J. McCallum. "Putting the
    Library in *Wikipedia*." *Online* Sept.-Oct. 2008: 39-42.
    Academic Search Elite. Web. 3 Apr. 2011.

Rainie, Lee, and Bill Tancer. *"Wikipedia* Users." *Pew
    Internet & American Life Project*. Pew Research
    Center, 24 Apr. 2007. Web. 7 Apr. 2011.

Read, Brock. "Middlebury College History Department
    Limits Students' Use of *Wikipedia*." *Chronicle of
    Higher Education* 16 Feb. 2007: n. pag. *Academic
    Search Elite*. Web. 3 Apr. 2011.

"Reliability of *Wikipedia*." *Wikipedia*. Wikimedia Foundation,
    2011. Web. 25 Mar. 2011.

Newspaper
article
accessed
from an
online
database

Signed
article in
a weekly
magazine

Newspaper
article
without
pagination
accessed from
an online
database

1″

Spinellis, Diomidis, and Panagiotis Louridas. "The
    Collaborative Organization of Knowledge."
    Communications of the ACM 51.8 (2008): 68-73.
    Academic Search Elite. Web. 3 Apr. 2011.

"Wiki." *Encyclopaedia Britannica Online*. Encyclopaedia
    Britannica, 2011. Web. 25 Mar. 2011.

"*Wikipedia*: About." *Wikipedia*. Wikimedia Foundation,
    2011. Web. 25 Mar. 2011.

"*Wikipedia*: Researching with *Wikipedia*." *Wikipedia*.
    Wikimedia Foundation, 2011. Web. 25 Mar. 2011.

Young, Jeffrey R. "*Wikipedia*'s Co-Founder Wants to Make
    It More Useful to Academe." *Chronicle of Higher
    Education* 13 June 2008: n. pag. *Academic Search
    Elite*. Web. 3 Apr. 2011.

Article in an online encyclopedia

Unsigned document within a Web site

PART 6

Documenting Sources: APA and Other Styles

PART 6

Documenting Sources: APA and Other Styles

? Frequently Asked Questions

Directory of APA In-Text Citations

1. A work by a single author (p. 274)
2. A work by two authors (p. 274)
3. A work by three to five authors (p. 274)
4. A work by six or more authors (p. 274)
5. Works by authors with the same last name (p. 275)
6. A work by a corporate author (p. 275)
7. A work with no listed author (p. 275)
8. A personal communication (p. 275)
9. An indirect source (p. 275)
10. A specific part of a source (p. 275)
11. An electronic source (p. 276)
12. Two or more works within the same parenthetical reference (p. 276)
13. A table (p. 276)

Directory of APA Reference List Entries

PRINT SOURCES: *Entries for Articles*

Articles in Scholarly Journals

1. An article in a scholarly journal with continuous pagination throughout an annual volume (p. 278)
2. An article in a scholarly journal with separate pagination in each issue (p. 278)
3. A book review in a scholarly journal (unsigned) (p. 278)

Articles in Magazines and Newspapers

4. A magazine article (p. 278)
5. A newspaper article (p. 278)
6. A newspaper editorial (unsigned) (p. 279)
7. A letter to the editor of a newspaper (p. 279)

PRINT SOURCES: *Entries for Books*

Authors

8. A book with one author (p. 279)
9. A book with more than one author (p. 279)
10. A book with no listed author or editor (p. 280)
11. A book with a corporate author (p. 280)
12. An edited book (p. 281)

Editions, Multivolume Works, and Forewords

13. A work in several volumes (p. 281)
14. The foreword, preface, or afterword of a book (p. 281)

Parts of Books

Government and Technical Reports

ENTRIES FOR MISCELLANEOUS PRINT SOURCES

Letters

ENTRIES FOR OTHER SOURCES

Television Broadcasts, Films, CDs, Audiocassette Recordings, and Computer Software

ELECTRONIC SOURCES: *Entries for Sources from Internet Sites*

Internet-Specific Sources

Abstracts and Newspaper Articles

CHAPTER **22**

APA Documentation Style

APA style* is used extensively in the social sciences. APA documentation has three parts: *parenthetical references in the body of the paper*, a *reference list*, and optional *content footnotes*.

1 Parenthetical References

APA documentation uses short parenthetical references in the body of the paper keyed to an alphabetical list of references at the end of the paper. A typical parenthetical reference consists of the author's last name (followed by a comma) and the year of publication.

> Many people exhibit symptoms of depression after the death of a pet
>
> (Russo, 2009).

If the author's name appears in an introductory phrase, include the year of publication there as well.

> According to Russo (2009), many people exhibit symptoms of depression
>
> after the death of a pet.

When quoting directly, include the page number, preceded by **p.** in parentheses after the quotation.

> According to Weston (2006), children from one-parent homes read at
>
> "a significantly lower level than those from two-parent homes" (p. 58).

Note: A long quotation (forty words or more) is not set in quotation marks. It is set as a block, and the entire quotation is double-spaced and indented one-half inch from the left margin. Parenthetical documentation is placed one space after the final punctuation.

---

*APA documentation format follows the guidelines set in the *Publication Manual of the American Psychological Association*, 6th ed. Washington, DC: APA, 2010.

Sample APA In-Text Citations

1. A Work by a Single Author

Many college students suffer from sleep deprivation (Anton, 2009).

2. A Work by Two Authors

There is growing concern over the use of psychological testing in elementary schools (Albright & Glennon, 2010).

3. A Work by Three to Five Authors

If a work has more than two but fewer than six authors, mention all names in the first reference; in subsequent references in the same paragraph, cite only the first author followed by **et al.** ("and others"). When the reference appears in later paragraphs, include the year.

First Reference

(Sparks, Wilson, & Hewitt, 2009)

Subsequent References in the Same Paragraph

(Sparks et al.)

References in Later Paragraphs

(Sparks et al., 2009)

4. A Work by Six or More Authors

When a work has six or more authors, cite the name of the first author followed by **et al.** and the year in all references.

(Miller et al., 2008)

Close-Up   CITING WORKS BY MULTIPLE AUTHORS

When referring to multiple authors in the text of your paper, join the last two names with **and**.

According to Rosen, Wolfe, and Ziff (2009). . . .

Parenthetical references (as well as reference list entries) require an **ampersand (&)**.

(Rosen, Wolfe, & Ziff, 2009)

5. Works by Authors with the Same Last Name

If your reference list includes works by two or more authors with the same last name, use each author's initials in all in-text citations.

Both F. Bor (2010) and S. D. Bor (2009) concluded that no further study was needed.

6. A Work by a Corporate Author

If the name of a corporate author is long, abbreviate it after the first citation.

First Reference

(National Institute of Mental Health [NIMH], 2010)

Subsequent Reference

(NIMH, 2010)

7. A Work with No Listed Author

If a work has no listed author, cite the first two or three words of the title (followed by a comma) and the year. Use quotation marks around titles of periodical articles and chapters of books; use italics for titles of books, periodicals, brochures, reports, and the like.

("New Immigration," 2009)

8. A Personal Communication

Cite letters, memos, telephone conversations, personal interviews, emails, messages from electronic bulletin boards, and so on only in the text of your paper—*not* in the reference list.

(R. Takaki, personal communication, October 17, 2009)

9. An Indirect Source

Cogan and Howe offer very different interpretations of the problem (cited in Swenson, 2009).

10. A Specific Part of a Source

Use abbreviations for the words *page* (**p.**), and *pages* (**pp.**), but spell out *chapter* and *section*.

These theories have an interesting history (Lee, 2010, chapter 2).

11. An Electronic Source

For an electronic source that does not show page numbers, use the paragraph number preceded by the abbreviation **para.**

Conversation at the dinner table is an example of a family ritual (Kulp, 2010, para. 3).

In the case of an electronic source that has neither page nor paragraph numbers, cite both the heading in the source and the number of the paragraph following the heading in which the material is located.

Healthy eating is a never-ending series of free choices (Shapiro, 2008, Introduction section, para. 2).

If the source has no headings, you may not be able to specify an exact location.

12. Two or More Works within the Same Parenthetical Reference

List works by different authors in alphabetical order, separated by semicolons.

This theory is supported by several studies (Barson & Roth, 1995; Rose, 2001; Tedesco, 2010).

List two or more works by the same author or authors in order of date of publication (separated by commas), with the earliest date first.

This theory is supported by several studies (Rhodes & Dollek, 2008, 2009, 2010).

For two or more works by the same author published in the same year, designate the work whose title comes first alphabetically *a*, the one whose title comes next *b*, and so on; repeat the year in each citation.

This theory is supported by several studies (Shapiro, 2009a, 2009b).

13. A Table

If you use a table from a source, give credit to the author in a note at the bottom of the table. Do not include this information in the reference list.

Note. From "Predictors of Employment and Earnings Among JOBS Participants," by P. A. Neenan and D. K. Orthner, 1996, *Social Work Research*, *20*(4), p. 233.

❷ Reference List

The **reference list** gives the publication information for all the sources you cite. It should appear at the end of your paper on a new numbered page titled **References**. Entries in the reference list should be arranged alphabetically. Double-space within and between reference list entries. The first line of each entry should start at the left margin, with the second and subsequent lines indented one-half inch. (**See 22b** for full manuscript guidelines.)

APA PRINT SOURCES Entries for Articles

Article citations include the author's name (last name first); the date of publication (in parentheses); the title of the article; the title of the periodical (italicized); the volume number (italicized); the issue number, if any (in parentheses); and the inclusive page numbers (including all digits). Figure 22.1 shows where you can find this information.

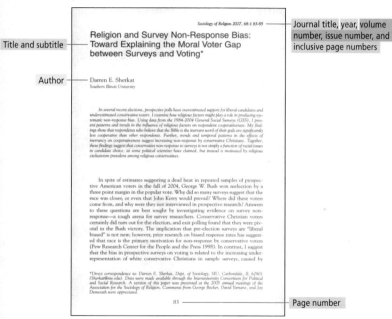

FIGURE 22.1 First page of an article showing the location of the information needed for documentation. © Association for the Sociology of Religion.

Capitalize the first word of the article's title and subtitle as well as any proper nouns. Do not underline or italicize the title of the article or enclose it in quotation marks. Give the periodical title in full, and capitalize all words except articles, prepositions, and conjunctions of fewer than four letters. Use **p.** or **pp.** when referring to page numbers in newspapers, but omit this abbreviation when referring to page numbers in journals and popular magazines.

Articles in Scholarly Journals

1. An Article in a Scholarly Journal with Continuous Pagination throughout an Annual Volume

Miller, W. (1969). Violent crimes in city gangs. *Journal of Social Issues, 27,* 581–593.

2. An Article in a Scholarly Journal with Separate Pagination in Each Issue

Williams, S., & Cohen, L. R. (2004). Child stress in early learning situations. *American Psychologist, 21*(10), 1–28.

 Note: Do not leave a space between the volume and issue numbers.

3. A Book Review in a Scholarly Journal (Unsigned)

A review with no author should be listed by title, followed by a description of the reviewed work in brackets.

Coming of age and joining the cult of thinness [Review of the book *The cult of thinness,* by Sharlene Nagy Hesse-Biber]. (2008, June). *Psychology of Women Quarterly, 32*(2), 221–222.

Articles in Magazines and Newspapers

4. A Magazine Article

McCurdy, H. G. (2003, June). Brain mechanisms and intelligence. *Psychology Today, 46,* 61–63.

5. A Newspaper Article

If an article appears on nonconsecutive pages, give all page numbers, separated by commas (for example, **A1, A14**). If the article appears on consecutive pages, indicate the full range of pages (for example, **A7–A9**).

James, W. R. (1993, November 16). The uninsured and health care. *Wall Street Journal,* pp. A1, A14.

6. A Newspaper Editorial (Unsigned)

An editorial with no author should be listed by title, followed by the label **Editorial** in brackets.

> The plight of the underinsured [Editorial]. (2008, June 12). *The New York Times,* p. A30.

7. A Letter to the Editor of a Newspaper

> Williams, P. (2006, July 19). Self-fulfilling stereotypes [Letter to the editor]. *Los Angeles Times,* p. A22.

APA PRINT SOURCES Entries for Books

Book citations include the author's name (last name first); the year of publication (in parentheses); the book title (italicized); and publication information. Figures 22.2 and 22.3 on page 280 show where you can find this information.

Capitalize only the first word of the title and subtitle and any proper nouns. Include any additional necessary information—edition, report number, or volume number, for example—in parentheses after the title. In the publication information, write out in full the names of associations, corporations, and university presses. Include the words **Book** and **Press**, but do not include terms such as **Publishers, Co.,** or **Inc.**

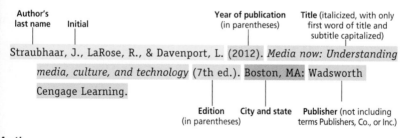

Author's last name · Initial · Year of publication (in parentheses) · Title (italicized, with only first word of title and subtitle capitalized)

Straubhaar, J., LaRose, R., & Davenport, L. (2012). *Media now: Understanding media, culture, and technology* (7th ed.). Boston, MA: Wadsworth Cengage Learning.

Edition (in parentheses) · City and state · Publisher (not including terms Publishers, Co., or Inc.)

Authors

8. A Book with One Author

> Maslow, A. H. (1974). *Toward a psychology of being.* Princeton, NJ: Van Nostrand.

9. A Book with More Than One Author

List up to seven authors by last name and initials, using an ampersand (&) to connect the last two names. For more than seven authors, insert an ellipsis (three spaced periods) and add the last author's name.

> Wolfinger, D., Knable, P., Richards, H. L., & Silberger, R. (2007). *The chronically unemployed.* New York, NY: Berman Press.

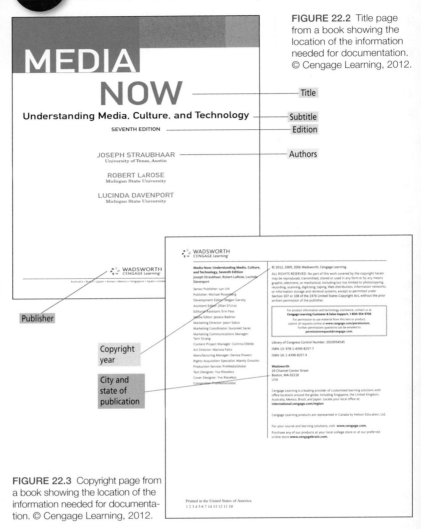

FIGURE 22.2 Title page from a book showing the location of the information needed for documentation. © Cengage Learning, 2012.

Title
Subtitle
Edition
Authors
Publisher
Copyright year
City and state of publication

FIGURE 22.3 Copyright page from a book showing the location of the information needed for documentation. © Cengage Learning, 2012.

10. A Book with No Listed Author or Editor

Teaching in a wired classroom. (2010). Philadelphia, PA: Drexel Press.

11. A Book with a Corporate Author

When the author and the publisher are the same, include the word **Author** at the end of the citation instead of repeating the publisher's name.

League of Women Voters of the United States. (2008). *Local league*

handbook. Washington, DC: Author.

12. An Edited Book

Lewin, K., Lippitt, R., & White, R. K. (Eds.). (1985). *Social learning and imitation*. New York, NY: Basic Books.

Editions, Multivolume Works, and Forewords

13. A Work in Several Volumes

Jones, P. R., & Williams, T. C. (Eds.). (1990–1993). *Handbook of therapy* (Vols. 1–2). Princeton, NJ: Princeton University Press.

14. The Foreword, Preface, or Afterword of a Book

Taylor, T. (1979). Preface. In B. B. Ferencz, *Less than slaves* (pp. ii–ix). Cambridge, MA: Harvard University Press.

Parts of Books

15. A Selection from an Anthology

Give inclusive page numbers preceded by **pp.** (in parentheses) after the title of the anthology. The title of the selection is not enclosed in quotation marks.

Lorde, A. (1984). Age, race, and class. In P. S. Rothenberg (Ed.), *Racism and sexism: An integrated study* (pp. 352–360). New York, NY: St. Martin's Press.

Note: If you cite two or more selections from the same anthology, give the full citation for the anthology in each entry.

16. An Article in a Reference Book

Edwards, P. (Ed.). (2006). Determinism. In *The encyclopedia of philosophy* (Vol. 2, pp. 359–373). New York, NY: Macmillan.

Government and Technical Reports

17. A Government Report

U.S. Department of Health and Human Services, National Institutes of Health, National Institute of Mental Health. (2007). *Motion pictures and violence: A summary report of research* (DHHS Publication No. ADM 91-22187). Washington, DC: Government Printing Office.

18. A Technical Report

Attali, Y., & Powers, D. (2008). *Effect of immediate feedback and revision on psychometric properties of open-ended GRE® subject test items* (ETS GRE

Board Research Report No. 04-05). Princeton, NJ: Educational Testing
Service.

APA ENTRIES FOR MISCELLANEOUS PRINT SOURCES

Letters

19. A Personal Letter

References to unpublished personal letters, like references to all other personal communications, should be included only in the text of the paper, not
in the reference list.

20. A Published Letter

Joyce, J. (1931). Letter to Louis Gillet. In Richard Ellmann, *James Joyce*

(p. 631). New York, NY: Oxford University Press.

APA ENTRIES FOR OTHER SOURCES

Television Broadcasts, Films, CDs, Audiocassette Recordings, and Computer Software

21. A Television Broadcast

Murphy, J. (Executive Producer). (2006, March 4). *The CBS evening news*

[Television broadcast]. New York, NY: Columbia Broadcasting Service.

22. A Television Series

Sorkin, A., Schlamme, T., & Wells, J. (Executive Producers). (2002). *The west*

wing [Television series]. Los Angeles, CA: Warner Bros. Television.

23. A Film

Spielberg, S. (Director). (1994). *Schindler's list* [Motion picture]. United

States: Universal.

24. A CD Recording

Marley, B. (1977). Waiting in vain. On *Exodus* [CD]. New York, NY: Island

Records.

25. An Audiocassette Recording

Skinner, B. F. (Speaker). (1972). *Skinner on Skinnerism* [Cassette recording].

Hollywood, CA: Center for Cassette Studies.

26. Computer Software

Sharp, S. (2009). Career Selection Tests (Version 7.0) [Software]. Chico, CA:

Avocation Software.

APA ELECTRONIC SOURCES | Entries for Sources from Internet Sites

APA guidelines for documenting electronic sources focus on Web sources, which often do not include all the bibliographic information that print sources do. For example, Web sources may not include page numbers or a place of publication. At a minimum, a Web citation should have a title, a date (the date of publication, update, or retrieval), and a Digital Object Identifier (DOI) (when available) or an electronic address (URL). If possible, also include the author(s) of a source. Figure 22.4 on page 284 shows where you can find this information.

When you need to divide a URL at the end of a line, break it after a double slash or before most other punctuation (do not add a hyphen). Do not add a period at the end of the URL.

Author's last name Initials | Year of publication (in parentheses) | Title of article (only first word of title and subtitle as well as proper nouns capitalized)

Yip, T., Gee, G. C., & Takeuchi, D. T. (2008). Racial discrimination and

psychological distress: The impact of ethnic identity and age among

immigrant and United States-born Asian adults. *Developmental*

Psychology, 44(3), 787–800. doi:10.1037/0012-1649.44.3.787

Volume number (italicized) | Issue number (in parentheses) | Inclusive page numbers (include all digits) | DOI (without period at end) | Title of periodical (italicized)

Internet-Specific Sources

27. An Internet Article Based on a Print Source

If the article has a DOI, you do not need to include the retrieval date or the URL. Always include the volume number (italicized) and the issue number (in parentheses, if available).

Rutledge, P. C., Park, A., & Sher, K. J. (2008). 21st birthday drinking:

Extremely extreme. *Journal of Consulting and Clinical Psychology,*

76(3), 511–516. doi:10.1037/0022-006X.76.3.511

28. An Article in an Internet-Only Journal

If the article does not have a DOI, include the URL. Always include the URL (when available) for the archived version of the article. If you accessed the article through an online database, include the URL for the home page of the journal. (If a single URL links to multiple articles, include the URL for the journal's home page.) No retrieval date is needed for content that is not likely to be changed or updated—for example, a journal article or a book.

Journal title, year, volume number, issue number, and inclusive page numbers

DOI

Title and subtitle

Authors

Page number

FIGURE 22.4 Part of an online article showing the location of the information needed for documentation. © American Psychological Association. Reprinted with permission of Elsevier.

Hill, S. A., & Laugharne, R. (2006). Patient choice survey in general adult psychiatry. *Psychiatry On-Line*. Retrieved from http://www.priory .co.uk/psych.htm

29. A Document from a University Web Site

Beck, S. E. (2008, April 3). *The good, the bad & the ugly: Or, why it's a good idea to evaluate web sources*. Retrieved July 7, 2008, from New Mexico State University Library website: http://lib.nmsu.edu/instruction /evalcrit.html

30. A Web Document (No Author Identified, No Date)

A document with no author or date should be listed by title, followed by the abbreviation **n.d.** (for "no date"), the retrieval date, and the URL.

The stratocaster appreciation page. (n.d.). Retrieved July 27, 2008, from http://members.tripod.com/~AFH

31. An Email

As with all other personal communications, citations for email should be included only in the text of your paper, not in the reference list.

32. A Posting to a Newsgroup

List the author's full name—or, if that is not available, the author's screen name. In brackets after the title, provide information that will help readers access the posting.

> Silva, T. (2007, March 9). Severe stress can damage a child's brain [Online
>
> forum comment]. Retrieved from http://groups.google.com/group
>
> /sci.psychology.psychotherapy.moderated

33. A Posting to a Blog

> Jamie. (2010, June 26). Re: Trying to lose 50 million pounds [Web log
>
> comment]. Retrieved from http://blogs.wsj.com/numbersguy

34. A Searchable Database

Include the database name only if the material you are citing is obscure, out of print, or otherwise difficult to locate. No retrieval date is needed.

> Murphy, M. E. (1940, December 15). When war comes. *Vital Speeches of the*
>
> *Day, 7*(5), 139–144. Retrieved from http://www.vsotd.com

Abstracts and Newspaper Articles

35. An Abstract

> Qiong, L. (2008, July). After the quake: Psychological treatment following
>
> the disaster. *China Today, 57*(7), 18–21. Abstract retrieved from
>
> http://www.chinatoday.com.cn/ctenglish/index.htm

36. An Article in a Daily Newspaper

> Fountain, H. (2008, July 1). In sleep, we are birds of a feather. *The New York*
>
> *Times*. Retrieved from http://www.nytimes.com

❸ Content Footnotes

APA format permits content notes, indicated by **superscripts** in the text. The notes are listed on a separate numbered page, titled **Footnotes**, after the reference list and before any appendices. Double-space all notes, indenting the first line of each note one-half inch and beginning subsequent lines flush left. Number the notes with superscripts that correspond to the numbers in your text.

22b APA-Style Manuscript Guidelines

Social science papers label sections with headings. Sections may include an introduction (untitled), followed by headings like **Background**, **Method**, **Results**, and **Conclusion**. Each section of a social science paper is a complete unit with a beginning and an end so that it can be read separately and still make sense out of context. The body of the paper may include charts, graphs, maps, photographs, flowcharts, or tables.

CHECKLIST

Typing Your Paper

When you type your paper, use the student paper in **22c** as your model.

❏ Leave one-inch margins at the top and bottom and on both sides. Double-space your paper throughout.

❏ Indent the first line of every paragraph and the first line of every content footnote one-half inch from the left-hand margin.

❏ Set off a **long quotation** (more than forty words) in a block format by indenting the entire quotation one-half inch from the left-hand margin. Do not indent the first line further.

❏ Number all pages consecutively. Each page should include a **page header** (an abbreviated title and a page number) typed one-half inch from the top of the page. Type the page header flush left and the page number flush right.

See 26b

❏ Center major headings, and type them with uppercase and lowercase letters. Place minor headings flush left, typed with uppercase and lowercase letters. Use boldface for both major and minor headings.

See 26c

❏ Format items in a series as a numbered list.

❏ Arrange the pages of the paper in the following order:

    ❏ **Title page** (page 1) with a running head (in all uppercase letters), page number, title, your name, and the name of your school. (Your instructor may require additional information.)

    ❏ **Abstract and keywords** (page 2)

    ❏ **Text of paper** (beginning on page 3)

    ❏ **Reference list** (new page)

    ❏ **Content footnotes** (new page)

    ❏ **Appendices** (start each appendix on a new page)

See 22a

❏ Citations should follow **APA documentation style**.

CHECKLIST
Using Visuals

APA style distinguishes between two types of visuals: **tables** and **figures** (charts, graphs, photographs, and diagrams). In manuscripts not intended for publication, tables and figures are included in the text. A short table or figure should appear on the page where it is discussed; a long table or figure should be placed on a separate page just after the page where it is discussed.

Tables

Number all **tables** consecutively. Each table should have a *label* and a *title*.

❑ The **label** consists of the word **Table** (not in italics), along with an arabic numeral, typed flush left above the table.

❑ Double-space and type a brief explanatory **title** for each table (in italics) flush left below the label. Capitalize the first letters of principal words of the title.

Table 7

Frequency of Negative Responses of Dorm Students to Questions Concerning

Alcohol Consumption

Figures

Number all **figures** consecutively. Each figure should have a *label* and a *caption*.

❑ The **label** consists of the word **Figure** (typed flush left below the figure) followed by the figure number (both in italics).

❑ The **caption** explains the figure and serves as a title. Double-space the caption, but do not italicize it. Capitalize only the first word and any proper nouns, and end the caption with a period. The caption follows the label (on the same line).

Figure 1. Duration of responses measured in seconds.

Note: If you use a table or figure from an outside source, include full source information in a note at the bottom of the table or figure. This information does not appear in your reference list.

CHECKLIST
Preparing the APA Reference List

When typing your reference list, follow these guidelines:

❑ Begin the reference list on a new page after the last page of text, numbered as the next page of the paper.

❑ Center the title **References** at the top of the page.

❑ List the items in the reference list alphabetically (with author's last name first).

continued

Preparing the APA Reference List *(continued)*

❑ Type the first line of each entry at the left margin. Indent subsequent lines one-half inch.

❑ Separate the major divisions of each entry with a period and one space.

❑ Double-space the reference list within and between entries.

Close-Up   ARRANGING ENTRIES IN THE APA REFERENCE LIST

● Single-author entries precede multiple-author entries that begin with the same name.

Field, S. (1987).

Field, S., & Levitt, M. P. (1984).

● Entries by the same author or authors are arranged according to date of publication, starting with the earliest date.

Ruthenberg, H., & Rubin, R. (1985).

Ruthenberg, H., & Rubin, R. (1987).

● Entries with the same author or authors and date of publication are arranged alphabetically according to title. Lowercase letters (*a, b, c,* and so on) that indicate the order of publication are placed within parentheses.

Wolk, E. M. (1996a). Analysis . . .

Wolk, E. M. (1996b). Hormonal . . .

22c   Model APA-Style Research Paper

The following student paper, "Sleep Deprivation in College Students," uses APA documentation style. It includes a title page, an abstract, a reference list, a table, and a bar graph. The Web citations in this student paper do not have DOIs, so URLs have been provided instead.

½″

Running head: SLEEP DEPRIVATION   1

Sleep Deprivation in College Students

Andrew J. Neale

University of Texas

Psychology 215, Section 4

Dr. Reiss

April 12, 2011

Page header on every page

1"

Center heading

Abstract

Abstract typed as a single paragraph in block format (not indented)

A survey was conducted of 50 first-year college students in an introductory biology class. The survey consisted of five questions regarding the causes and results of sleep deprivation and specifically addressed the students' study methods and the grades they received on the fall midterm. The study's hypothesis was that although students believe that forgoing sleep to study will yield better grades, sleep deprivation may actually cause a decrease in performance. The study concluded that while only 43% of the students who received either an A or a B on the fall midterm deprived themselves of sleep in order to cram for the test, 90% of those who received a C or a D were sleep deprived.

Keywords: sleep disorders, sleep deprivation, grade performance, grades and sleep, forgoing sleep

An optional list of keywords helps readers find your work in databases. Check with your instructor to see if this list is required.

SLEEP DEPRIVATION   3

tle
ered)→   Sleep Deprivation in College Students
t ½" →   For many college students, sleep is a luxury they feel

they cannot afford. Bombarded with tests and assignments
le-space
→   and limited by a 24-hour day, students often attempt

to make up time by doing without sleep. Unfortunately,

students may actually hurt their academic performance

by failing to get enough sleep. According to several

psychological and medical studies, sleep deprivation can

lead to memory loss and health problems, both of which are

likely to harm a student's academic performance.

Background

        Sleep is often overlooked as an essential part of a

←—1"—→healthy lifestyle. Millions of Americans wake up daily to

alarm clocks when their bodies have not gotten enough sleep.

This fact indicates that for many people, sleep is viewed as a

luxury rather than a necessity. As National Sleep Foundation

Executive Director Richard L. Gelula observes, "Some of the

problems we face as a society—from road rage to obesity—

may be linked to lack of sleep or poor sleep" (National Sleep

Foundation, 2002, para. 3). In fact, according to the National

Sleep Foundation, sleep deprivation causes "impairment in

mood, attention and memory, behavior control and quality of

life; lower academic performance and a decreased motivation

to learn; and health-related effects including increased risk

of weight-gain, lack of exercise and use of stimulants" (2010,

para. 5).

        Sleep deprivation is particularly common among college

students, many of whom have busy lives and are required to

memorize a great deal of material before their exams. It is

common for college students to take a quick nap between

Introduction

Thesis
statement

Heading
(centered and
boldfaced)

Literature
review (paras.
2–7)

Quotation
requires its
own docu-
mentation
and a page
number (or
a paragraph
number for
Internet
sources)

classes or fall asleep while studying in the library because they are sleep deprived. Approximately 44% of young adults experience daytime sleepiness at least a few days a month (National Sleep Foundation, 2002, para. 6). In particular, many students face daytime sleepiness on the day of an exam because they stayed up all night studying. These students believe that if they read and review immediately before taking a test—even though this usually means losing sleep—they will remember more information and thus get better grades. However, this is not the case.

A study conducted by professors Mary Carskadon at Brown University in Providence, Rhode Island, and Amy Wolfson at the College of the Holy Cross in Worcester, Massachusetts, showed that high school students who got adequate sleep were more likely to do well in their classes (Carpenter, 2001). According to this study, students who went to bed earlier on both weeknights and weekends earned mainly A's and B's. The students who received D's and F's averaged about 35 minutes less sleep per day than the high achievers (cited in Carpenter). The results of this study suggest that sleep is associated with high academic achievement.

Once students reach college and have the freedom to set their own schedules, however, many believe that sleep is a luxury they can do without. For example, students believe that if they use the time they would normally sleep to study, they will do better on exams. A survey of 144 undergraduate students in introductory psychology classes contradicted this assumption. According to this study, "long sleepers," those individuals who slept 9 or more hours out of a 24-hour day,

---

Student uses past tense when discussing other researchers' studies

Cited in indicates an indirect source

had significantly higher grade point averages (GPAs) than "short sleepers," individuals who slept less than 7 hours out of a 24-hour day. Therefore, contrary to the belief of many college students, more sleep is often associated with a high GPA (Kelly, Kelly, & Clanton, 2001).

Many students believe that sleep deprivation is not the cause of their poor performance, but rather that a host of other factors are to blame. A study in the *Journal of American College Health* tested the effect that several factors have on a student's performance in school, as measured by students' GPAs. Some of the factors considered included exercise, sleep, nutritional habits, social support, time management techniques, stress management techniques, and spiritual health (Trockel, Barnes, & Egget, 2000). The most significant correlation discovered in the study was between GPA and the sleep habits of students. Sleep deprivation had a more negative impact on GPAs than any other factor did (Trockel et al.).

First reference includes all three authors; *et al.* replaces second and third authors in subsequent reference in same paragraph

Despite these findings, many students continue to believe that they will be able to remember more material if they do not sleep at all before an exam. They fear that sleeping will interfere with their ability to retain information. Pilcher and Walters (1997), however, showed that sleep deprivation actually impaired learning skills. In this study, one group of students was sleep deprived, while the other got 8 hours of sleep before the exam. Each group estimated how well it had performed on the exam. The students who were sleep deprived believed their performance on the test was better than did those who were not sleep deprived, but actually the performance of the sleep-deprived students was significantly worse than that of

SLEEP DEPRIVATION   6

those who got 8 hours of sleep prior to the test (Pilcher &
Walters, 1997, cited in Bubolz, Brown, & Soper, 2001). This study
supports the hypothesis that sleep deprivation harms cognitive
performance even though many students believe that the less
sleep they get, the better they will do.

A survey of students in an introductory biology class at
the University of Texas, which demonstrated the effects of
sleep deprivation on academic performance, also supported
the hypothesis that despite students' beliefs, forgoing sleep
does not lead to better test scores.

Method

To determine the causes and results of sleep
deprivation, a study of the relationship between sleep and
test performance was conducted. Fifty first-year college
students in an introductory biology class were surveyed, and
their performance on the fall midterm was analyzed.

Each student was asked to complete a survey consisting
of the following five questions about their sleep patterns and
their performance on the fall midterm:

1. Do you regularly deprive yourself of sleep when
   studying for an exam?
2. Did you deprive yourself of sleep when studying for
   the fall midterm?
3. What was your grade on the exam?
4. Do you feel your performance was helped or harmed
   by the amount of sleep you had?
5. Will you deprive yourself of sleep when you study for
   the final exam?

To maintain confidentiality, the students were asked not
to put their names on the survey. Also, to determine whether

Student uses past tense when discussing his own research study

Numbered list is indented ½" and set in block format

the students answered question 3 truthfully, the group grade distribution from the surveys was compared to the number of A's, B's, C's, and D's shown in the instructor's record of the test results. The two frequency distributions were identical.

Results

Analysis of the survey data indicated a significant difference between the grades of students who were sleep deprived and the grades of those who were not. The results of the survey are presented in Table 1.

Table 1 introduced

The grades in the class were curved so that out of 50 students, 10 received A's, 20 received B's, 10 received C's, and 10 received D's. For the purposes of this survey, an A or B on the exam indicates that the student performed well. A grade of C or D on the exam is considered a poor grade.

Table 1

Results of Survey of Students in University of Texas Introduction to Biology Class Examining the Relationship between Sleep Deprivation and Academic Performance

Table placed on page where it is discussed

Grade totals	Sleep deprived	Not sleep deprived	Usually sleep deprived	Improved	Harmed	Continue sleep deprivation?
A = 10	4	6	1	4	0	4
B = 20	9	11	8	8	1	8
C = 10	10	0	6	5	4	7
D = 10	8	2	2	1	3	2
Total	31	19	17	18	8	21

Table created by student; no documentation necessary

Of the 50 students in the class, 31 (or 62%) said they deprived themselves of sleep when studying for the fall midterm. Of these students, 17 (or 34% of the class) answered

Statistical findings in table discussed

yes to the second question, reporting that they regularly deprive themselves of sleep before an exam.

Of the 31 students who said they deprived themselves of sleep when studying for the fall midterm, only 4 earned A's, and the majority of the A's in the class were received by those students who were not sleep deprived. Even more significant was the fact that of the 4 students who were sleep deprived and got A's, only one student claimed to usually be sleep deprived on the day of an exam. Thus, assuming the students who earn A's in a class do well in general, it is possible that sleep deprivation did not help or harm these students' grades. Not surprisingly, of the 4 students who received A's and were sleep deprived, all said they would continue to use sleep deprivation to enable them to study for longer hours.

The majority of those who deprived themselves of sleep in an effort to obtain a higher grade received B's and C's on the exam. A total of 20 students earned a grade of B on the exam. Of those students, only 9, or 18% of the class, said they were deprived of sleep when they took the test.

Students who said they were sleep deprived when they took the exam received the majority of the poor grades. Ten students got C's on the midterm, and of these 10 students, 100% said they were sleep deprived when they took the test. Of the 10 students (20% of the class) who got D's, 8 said they were sleep deprived. Figure 1 shows the significant relationship that was found between poor grades on the exam and sleep deprivation.

Figure 1 introduced

Conclusion

For many students, sleep is viewed as a luxury rather than as a necessity. Particularly during exam periods,

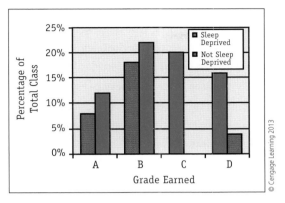

Figure 1. Results of a survey of students in a University of Texas Introduction to Biology class, examining the relationship between sleep deprivation and academic performance.

students use the hours in which they would normally sleep to study. However, this method does not seem to be effective. The survey discussed here reveals a clear correlation between sleep deprivation and lower exam scores. In fact, the majority of students who performed well on the exam, earning either an A or a B, were not deprived of sleep. Therefore, students who choose studying over sleep should rethink their approach and consider that sleep deprivation may actually lead to impaired academic performance.

Figure placed as close as possible to discussion in paper

Label and caption

(No source information needed for graph based on student's original data)

SLEEP DEPRIVATION   1″   10

Center
heading ─────────→   References

Indent ½″ ─────→ Bubolz, W., Brown, F., & Soper, B. (2001). Sleep habits and

Double-space ───→   patterns of college students: A preliminary study.

                        Journal of American College Health, 50, 131–135.

Entries listed   Carpenter, S. (2001). Sleep deprivation may be
in alphabetical
order   undermining teen health. *Monitor on Psychology,*

URL is pro-   *32*(9). Retrieved from http://www.apa.org/monitor
vided for Web
citation that   /oct01/sleepteen.html
does not have
a DOI   Kelly, W. E., Kelly, K. E., & Clanton, R. C. (2001). The

                        relationship between sleep length and grade-point

                        average among college students. *College Student*

                        Journal, 35(1), 84–90.

                  National Sleep Foundation. (2002, April 2). *Epidemic of*

                        daytime sleepiness linked to increased feelings of

                        anger, stress and pessimism. Retrieved from

                        http://www.sleepfoundation.org

                  National Sleep Foundation. (2010, July 6). *Later school*

                        start times improved adolescent alertness. Retrieved

                        from http://www.sleepfoundation.org

                  Trockel, M., Barnes, M., & Egget, D. (2000). Health-related

                        variables and academic performance among first-year

                        college students: Implications for sleep and other

                        behaviors. *Journal of American College Health, 49,*

                        125–131.

Directory of Chicago-Style Endnotes and Bibliography Entries

PRINT SOURCES: *Entries for Articles*

Articles in Scholarly Journals

1. An article in a scholarly journal with continuous pagination throughout an annual volume (p. 303)
2. An article in a scholarly journal with separate pagination in each issue (p. 303)

Articles in Magazines and Newspapers

3. An article in a weekly magazine (signed/unsigned) (p. 303)
4. An article in a monthly magazine (signed) (p. 304)
5. An article in a monthly magazine (unsigned) (p. 304)
6. An article in a newspaper (signed) (p. 304)
7. An article in a newspaper (unsigned) (p. 304)
8. A letter to the editor of a newspaper (p. 305)
9. A book review in a newspaper (p. 305)

PRINT SOURCES: *Entries for Books*

Authors and Editors

10. A book by one author or editor (p. 305)
11. A book by two or three authors or editors (p. 306)
12. A book by more than three authors or editors (p. 306)
13. A book with no listed author or editor (p. 306)
14. A book by a corporate author (p. 307)
15. A book with an author and an editor (p. 307)
16. A book quoted in a secondary source (p. 307)

Editions and Multivolume Works

17. A subsequent edition of a book (p. 307)
18. A multivolume work (p. 308)

Parts of Books

19. A chapter in a book (p. 308)
20. An essay in an anthology (p. 308)

Religious Works

21. Sacred texts (p. 308)

ENTRIES FOR MISCELLANEOUS PRINT AND NONPRINT SOURCES

Interviews

Letters and Government Documents

Videotapes, DVDs, and Recordings

ELECTRONIC SOURCES: *Entries for Sources from Online Publications*

Articles, Books, and Reference Works on the Internet

ELECTRONIC SOURCES: *Entries for Sources from an Online Database*

Sources from an Online Database

ELECTRONIC SOURCES: *Entries for Sources from Internet Sites*

Internet-Specific Sources

CHAPTER 23

Chicago Documentation Style

23a Using Chicago Humanities Style

The Chicago Manual of Style includes two citation methods, a notes-bibliography style used in history, in the humanities, and in some social science disciplines and an author-date style used in the sciences and social sciences. **Chicago humanities style*** has two parts: *notes at the end of the paper* (**endnotes**) and usually *a list of bibliographic citations* (**bibliography**). (Chicago style encourages the use of endnotes, but allows the use of footnotes at the bottom of the page.)

1 Endnotes and Footnotes

The notes format calls for a **superscript** (raised numeral) in the text after source material you have either quoted or referred to. This numeral, placed after all punctuation marks except dashes, corresponds to the numeral that precedes the endnote or footnote.

Endnote and Footnote Format: Chicago Style

In the Text

By November of 1942, the Allies had proof that the Nazis were engaged in the systematic killing of Jews.[1]

In the Note

    1. David S. Wyman, *The Abandonment of the Jews: America and the Holocaust 1941–1945* (New York: Pantheon Books, 1984), 65.

---

*Chicago humanities style follows the guidelines set in *The Chicago Manual of Style*, 16th ed. Chicago: University of Chicago Press, 2010. The manuscript guidelines and sample research paper at the end of this chapter follow guidelines set in Kate L. Turabian's *A Manual for Writers of Research Papers, Theses, and Dissertations*, 7th ed. Chicago: University of Chicago Press, 2007. Turabian style, which is based on Chicago style, addresses formatting concerns specific to college writers.

Close-Up SUBSEQUENT REFERENCES TO THE SAME WORK

In a paper with no bibliography, use the full citation in the first note for a work; in subsequent references to the same work, list only the author's last name, a comma, an abbreviated title, another comma, and a page number. In a paper with a bibliography, you may use the short form for all notes.

First Note on Espinoza

1. J. M. Espinoza. *The First Expedition of Vargas in New Mexico, 1692* (Albuquerque: University of New Mexico Press, 1949), 10–12.

Subsequent Note

5. Espinoza, *First Expedition*, 29.

Note: You may use the abbreviation *ibid.* ("in the same place") for subsequent references to the same work as long as there are no intervening references. *Ibid.* takes the place of the author's name, the work's title, and the page number if they are the same as those in the previous note. If the page number is different, cite *Ibid.* and the page number.

First Note on Espinoza

1. J. M. Espinoza. *The First Expedition of Vargas in New Mexico, 1692* (Albuquerque: University of New Mexico Press, 1949), 10–12.

Next Note

2. Ibid., 23.

2 Bibliography

The **bibliography** provides complete publication information for the works consulted. Bibliography entries are arranged alphabetically by the author's last name or the first major word of the title (if there is no author). Single-space within an entry; double-space between entries.

Sample Chicago-Style Endnotes and Bibliography Entries

CHICAGO PRINT SOURCES Entries for Articles

Article citations generally include the name of the author (last name first); the title of the article (in quotation marks); the title of the periodical (in italics); the volume number, issue number, and date; and the page reference. Months are spelled out in full, not abbreviated.

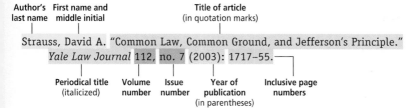

Articles in Scholarly Journals

1. An Article in a Scholarly Journal with Continuous Pagination throughout an Annual Volume

Endnote

> 1. John Huntington, "Science Fiction and the Future," *College English* 37 (Fall 1975): 341.

Bibliography

> Huntington, John. "Science Fiction and the Future." *College English* 37 (Fall 1975): 340–58.

2. An Article in a Scholarly Journal with Separate Pagination in Each Issue

Endnote

> 2. R. G. Sipes, "War, Sports, and Aggression: An Empirical Test of Two Rival Theories," *American Anthropologist* 4, no. 2 (1973): 80.

Bibliography

> Sipes, R. G. "War, Sports, and Aggression: An Empirical Test of Two Rival Theories." *American Anthropologist* 4, no. 2 (1973): 65–84.

Articles in Magazines and Newspapers

3. An Article in a Weekly Magazine (Signed/Unsigned)

Endnote
Signed
> 3. Pico Iyer, "A Mum for All Seasons," *Time,* April 8, 2002, 51.

Unsigned
> 3. "Burst Bubble," *NewScientist,* July 27, 2002, 24.

Although both endnotes above specify page numbers, the corresponding bibliography entries include page numbers only when the pages are consecutive (as in the second example that follows).

Bibliography
Signed

>Iyer, Pico. "A Mum for All Seasons." *Time,* April 8, 2002.

Unsigned

>"Burst Bubble." *NewScientist,* July 27, 2002, 24–25.

4. An Article in a Monthly Magazine (Signed)

Endnote

>4. Tad Suzuki, "Reflecting Light on Photo Realism," *American Artist,* March 2002, 47.

Bibliography

>Suzuki, Tad. "Reflecting Light on Photo Realism." *American Artist,* March 2002, 46–51.

5. An Article in a Monthly Magazine (Unsigned)

Endnote

>5. "Repowering the U.S. with Clean Energy Development," *BioCycle,* July 2002, 14.

Bibliography

>"Repowering the U.S. with Clean Energy Development." *BioCycle,* July 2002, 14.

6. An Article in a Newspaper (Signed)

Endnote

Because the pagination of newspapers can change from edition to edition, Chicago style recommends not giving page numbers for newspaper articles.

>6. Francis X. Clines, "Civil War Relics Draw Visitors, and Con Artists," *New York Times,* August 4, 2002, national edition.

Bibliography

>Clines, Francis X. "Civil War Relics Draw Visitors, and Con Artists." *New York Times,* August 4, 2002, national edition.

7. An Article in a Newspaper (Unsigned)

Endnote

>7. "Feds Lead Way in Long-Term Care," *Atlanta Journal-Constitution,* July 21, 2002, sec. E.

Note: Omit the initial article *the* from the newspaper's title, but include a city name in the title, even if it is not part of the actual title.

If you provide a note or mention the name of the newspaper and publication date in your text, you do not need to list unsigned articles or other newspaper items in your bibliography.

8. A Letter to the Editor of a Newspaper

Endnote

8. Arnold Stieber, letter to the editor, *Seattle Times,* July 4, 2009.

Bibliography

Stieber, Arnold. Letter to the editor. *Seattle Times,* July 4, 2009.

9. A Book Review in a Newspaper

Endnote

9. Janet Maslin, "The Real Lincoln Bedroom: Love in a Time of Strife," review of *The Lincolns: Portrait of a Marriage,* by Daniel Mark Epstein, *New York Times*, July 3, 2008.

Bibliography

Maslin, Janet. "The Real Lincoln Bedroom: Love in a Time of Strife." Review of *The Lincolns: Portrait of a Marriage,* by Daniel Mark Epstein. *New York Times,* July 3, 2008.

CHICAGO PRINT SOURCES Entries for Books

Capitalize the first, last, and all major words of titles and subtitles. Chicago style italicizes book titles.

| Author's last name | First name and middle Initial | Title (italicized, all major words capitalized) | City and state (to clarify unfamiliar or ambiguous city) | | |

Wartenberg, Thomas E. *The Nature of Art.* Belmont, CA: Wadsworth, 2002.

Publisher's name | Year of publication

Authors and Editors

10. A Book by One Author or Editor

Endnote

10. Robert Dallek, *An Unfinished Life: John F. Kennedy, 1917–1963* (New York: Little, Brown, 2003), 213.

Bibliography

Dallek, Robert. *An Unfinished Life: John F. Kennedy, 1917–1963*. New York: Little, Brown, 2003.

If the book has an editor rather than an author, add a comma and **ed.** after the name: **John Fields, ed.** Follow with a comma in a note.

11. A Book by Two or Three Authors or Editors
Endnote
Two Authors

> 11. Jack Watson and Grant McKerney, *A Cultural History of the Theater* (New York: Longman, 1993), 137.

Three Authors

> 11. Nathan Caplan, John K. Whitmore, and Marcella H. Choy, *The Boat People and Achievement in America: A Study of Economic and Educational Success* (Ann Arbor: University of Michigan Press, 1990), 51.

Bibliography
Two Authors

> Watson, Jack, and Grant McKerney. *A Cultural History of the Theater*. New York: Longman, 1993.

Three Authors

> Caplan, Nathan, John K. Whitmore, and Marcella H. Choy. *The Boat People and Achievement in America: A Study of Economic and Educational Success*. Ann Arbor: University of Michigan Press, 1990.

12. A Book by More Than Three Authors or Editors
Endnote
Chicago style favors **et al.** rather than **and others** after the first name in endnotes. Add a comma and **eds.** after the names of the editors in both the endnotes and the bibliography.

> 12. Robert E. Spiller et al., eds., *Literary History of the United States* (New York: Macmillan, 1953), 24.

Bibliography

List all authors' or editors' names in the bibliography.

> Spiller, Robert E., Willard Thorp, Thomas H. Johnson, and Henry Seidel Canby, eds. *Literary History of the United States*. New York: Macmillan, 1953.

13. A Book with No Listed Author or Editor
Endnote

> 13. *Merriam-Webster's Guide to Punctuation and Style,* 4th ed. (Springfield, MA: Merriam-Webster, 2008), 22.

Bibliography

> *Merriam-Webster's Guide to Punctuation and Style.* 4th ed. Springfield,
> MA: Merriam-Webster, 2008.

14. A Book by a Corporate Author

If a publication issued by an organization does not identify a person as the author, the organization is listed as the author even if its name is repeated in the title, in the series title, or as the publisher.

Endnote

> 14. National Geographic Society, *National Parks of the United States,*
> 6th ed. (Washington, DC: National Geographic Society, 2009), 77.

Bibliography

> National Geographic Society. *National Parks of the United States.* 6th ed.
> Washington, DC: National Geographic Society, 2009.

15. A Book with an Author and an Editor

Endnote

> 15. William Bartram, *The Travels of William Bartram,* ed. Mark Van
> Doren (New York: Dover Press, 1955), 85.

Bibliography

> Bartram, William. *The Travels of William Bartram.* Edited by Mark Van Doren.
> New York: Dover Press, 1955.

16. A Book Quoted in a Secondary Source

Endnote

> 16. Henry Adams, *Mont Saint-Michel and Chartres* (New York: Penguin
> Books, 1986), 296, quoted in Karen Armstrong, *A History of God: The 4000-
> Year Quest of Judaism, Christianity and Islam* (New York: Ballantine Books,
> 1993), 203–4.

Bibliography

> Adams, Henry. *Mont Saint-Michel and Chartres,* 296. New York: Penguin
> Books, 1986. Quoted in Armstrong, *A History of God,* 203–4.

> Armstrong, Karen. *A History of God: The 4000-Year Quest of Judaism,
> Christianity, and Islam.* New York: Ballantine Books, 1993.

Editions and Multivolume Works

17. A Subsequent Edition of a Book

Endnote

> 17. Laurie G. Kirszner and Stephen R. Mandell, *The Wadsworth Handbook,*
> 9th ed. (Boston: Wadsworth, 2010), 52.

Bibliography

> Kirszner, Laurie G., and Stephen R. Mandell. *The Wadsworth Handbook.*
> 9th ed. Boston: Wadsworth, 2010.

18. A Multivolume Work

Endnote

> 18. Kathleen Raine, *Blake and Tradition* (Princeton, NJ: Princeton
> University Press, 1968), 1:143.

Bibliography

> Raine, Kathleen. *Blake and Tradition.* Vol. 1. Princeton, NJ: Princeton
> University Press, 1968.

Parts of Books

19. A Chapter in a Book

Endnote

> 19. Roy Porter, "Health, Disease, and Cure," in *Quacks: Fakers and
> Charlatans in Medicine* (Stroud, UK: Tempus Publishing, 2003), 188.

Bibliography

> Porter, Roy. "Health, Disease, and Cure." In *Quacks: Fakers and Charlatans in
> Medicine,* 182–205. Stroud, UK: Tempus Publishing, 2003.

20. An Essay in an Anthology

Endnote

> 20. G. E. R. Lloyd, "Science and Mathematics," in *The Legacy of Greece,* ed.
> Moses Finley (New York: Oxford University Press, 1981), 270.

Bibliography

> Lloyd, G. E. R. "Science and Mathematics." In *The Legacy of Greece,* edited
> by Moses Finley, 256–300. New York: Oxford University Press, 1981.

Religious Works

21. Sacred Texts

References to religious works (such as the Bible or Qur'an) are usually
limited to the text or notes and not listed in the bibliography. In citing the
Bible, include the book (abbreviated), the chapter (followed by a colon),
and the verse numbers. Identify the version, but do not include a page
number.

Endnote

> 21. Phil. 1:9–11 (King James Version).

CHICAGO ENTRIES FOR MISCELLANEOUS PRINT AND NONPRINT SOURCES

Interviews

22. A Personal Interview

Endnote

> 22. Cornel West, interview by author, tape recording, June 8, 2011.

Personal interviews are cited in the notes or text but are usually not listed in the bibliography.

23. A Published Interview

Endnote

> 23. Gwendolyn Brooks, interview by George Stavros, *Contemporary Literature* 11, no. 1 (Winter 1970): 12.

Bibliography

> Brooks, Gwendolyn. Interview by George Stavros. *Contemporary Literature* 11, no. 1 (Winter 1970): 1–20.

Letters and Government Documents

24. A Personal Letter

Endnote

> 24. Julia Alvarez, letter to the author, April 10, 2009.

Personal letters are mentioned in the text or a note but are not listed in the bibliography.

25. A Government Document

Endnote

> 25. US Department of Transportation, *The Future of High-Speed Trains in the United States: Special Study, 2007* (Washington, DC: Government Printing Office, 2008), 203.

Bibliography

> US Department of Transportation. *The Future of High-Speed Trains in the United States: Special Study, 2007*. Washington, DC: Government Printing Office, 2008.

Videotapes, DVDs, and Recordings

26. A Videotape or DVD

Endnote

> 26. *Interview with Arthur Miller,* directed by William Schiff (Mequon, WI: Mosaic Group, 1987), videocassette (VHS), 17 min.

Bibliography

> *Interview with Arthur Miller.* Directed by William Schiff. Mequon, WI: Mosaic Group, 1987. Videocassette (VHS), 17 min.

27. A Recording

Endnote

> 27. Bob Marley and the Wailers, "Crisis," *Kaya,* Kava Island Records 423 095-3, 1978, compact disc.

Bibliography

> Marley, Bob, and the Wailers. "Crisis." *Kaya.* Kava Island Records 423 095-3, 1978, compact disc.

CHICAGO ELECTRONIC SOURCES   Entries for Sources from Online Publications

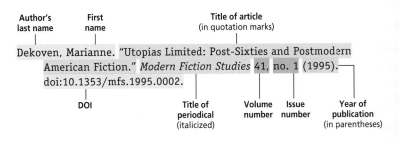

Author's last name | First name | Title of article (in quotation marks)

Dekoven, Marianne. "Utopias Limited: Post-Sixties and Postmodern American Fiction." *Modern Fiction Studies* 41, no. 1 (1995). doi:10.1353/mfs.1995.0002.

DOI | Title of periodical (italicized) | Volume number | Issue number | Year of publication (in parentheses)

Citations of sources from online publications usually include the author's name; the title of the article; the title of the publication; the publication information and date; the page numbers (if applicable); and the DOI (digital object identifier), a permanent identifying number, or URL. If no publication date is available or if your instructor or discipline requires one, include an access date before the DOI or URL.

You may break a DOI or URL that continues to a second line after a colon or double slash; before a comma, a period, a hyphen, a question mark, a percent symbol, a number sign, a tilde, or an underscore; or before or after an ampersand or equals sign.

Articles, Books, and Reference Works on the Internet

28. An Article in an Online Scholarly Journal

Endnote

> 28. Richard J. Schaefer, "Editing Strategies in Television Documentaries," *Journal of Communication* 47, no. 4 (1997): 80, doi:10.1111/j1460-2446.1997.tb02726.x.

Bibliography

> Schaefer, Richard J. "Editing Strategies in Television Documentaries." *Journal of Communication* 47, no. 4 (1997): 69–89. doi:10.1111 /j1460-2446.1997.tb02726.x.

29. An Article in an Online Magazine

Endnote

> 29. Steven Levy, "I Was a Wi-Fi Freeloader," *Newsweek,* October 9, 2002, http://www.msnbc.com/news/816606.asp.

If there is no DOI for a source, cite the URL.

Bibliography

> Levy, Steven. "I Was a Wi-Fi Freeloader." *Newsweek,* October 9, 2002. http://www.msnbc.com/news/816606.asp.

30. An Article in an Online Newspaper

Endnote

> 30. William J. Broad, "Piece by Piece, the Civil War *Monitor* Is Pulled from the Atlantic's Depths," *New York Times on the Web,* July 18, 2002, http://query.nytimes.com.

Bibliography

> Broad, William J. "Piece by Piece, the Civil War *Monitor* Is Pulled from the Atlantic's Depths." *New York Times on the Web,* July 18, 2002. http:// query.nytimes.com.

31. An Article in an Encyclopedia

If the reference book lists entries alphabetically, put the abbreviation **s.v.** (Latin for *sub verbo*, "under the word") before the entry name. If there is no publication or revision date for the entry, give the date of access before the DOI or URL.

Endnote

> 31. *Encyclopaedia Britannica Online,* s.v. "Adams, John," accessed July 5, 2010, http://www.britannica.com/EBchecked/topic/5132/John-Adams.

Dictionary and encyclopedia entries are not listed in the bibliography.

32. A Book

Endnote

> 32. Frederick Douglass, *My Bondage and My Freedom* (Boston, 1855), http://etext.virginia.edu/toc/modeng/public/DouMybo.html.

Bibliography

> Douglass, Frederick. *My Bondage and My Freedom*. Boston, 1855. http://
> etext.virginia.edu/toc/modeng/public/DouMybo.html.

Older works available online may not have all publication information.
Give the DOI as the last part of the citation.

33. A Government Publication

Endnote

> 33. US Department of Transportation, Federal Motor Carrier Safety
> Administration, *Safety Belt Usage by Commercial Motor Vehicle Drivers
> (SBUCMVD) 2007 Survey, Final Report* (Washington, DC: Government Printing
> Office, 2008), http://www.fmcsa.dot.gov/safety-security/safety-belt/exec
> -summary-2007.htm.

Bibliography

> US Department of Transportation. Federal Motor Carrier Safety
> Administration. *Safety Belt Usage by Commercial Motor Vehicle Drivers
> (SBUCMVD) 2007 Survey, Final Report*. Washington, DC: Government
> Printing Office, 2008. http://www.fmcsa.dot.gov/safety-security
> /safety-belt/exec-summary-2007.htm.

| **CHICAGO** ELECTRONIC SOURCES | Entries for Sources from an Online Database |

Sources from an Online Database

Many articles and other materials published in print and electronically are
also archived and available online through free or subscription databases.

34. A Scholarly Journal Article

Endnote

> 34. Monroe Billington, "Freedom to Serve: The President's Committee
> on Equality of Treatment and Opportunity in the Armed Forces, 1949–1950,"
> *Journal of Negro History* 51, no. 4 (1966): 264, http://www.jstor.org
> /stable/2716101.

Use a DOI, a number that applies to an article in all of the media in which
it may be published, rather than a URL if one is available. If you use a URL,
cite the shorter, more stable form that will take you to the article's location
in a database.

Bibliography

> Billington, Monroe. "Freedom to Serve: The President's Committee on
> Equality of Treatment and Opportunity in the Armed Forces,
> 1949–1950," *Journal of Negro History* 51, no. 4 (1966): 262–74.
> http://www.jstor.org/stable/2716101.

If there is no stable URL, include the name of the database and put any identifying database number in parentheses: **(ERIC).** If the article or document does not have a date of publication or revision, include an access date.

CHICAGO ELECTRONIC SOURCES Entries for Sources from Internet Sites

Internet-Specific Sources

35. A Web Site or Home Page

Endnote

> 35. David Perdue, "Dickens's Journalistic Career," David Perdue's Charles Dickens Page, accessed October 25, 2010, http://www.fidnet .com/~dap1955/dickens.

Titles of Web sites are in regular type (roman). Titles of pages or sections on a site are in quotation marks. If there is no date of publication, give an access date. Web site content is not usually listed in a bibliography.

36. An Email

Endnote

> 36. Meg Halverson, "Scuba Report," email message to author, April 2, 2010.

Email messages can also be mentioned in the text; they are not listed in the bibliography.

37. A Listserv Posting

Include the name of the list, the date of the individual posting, and the URL for the archive.

Endnote

> 37. Dave Shirlaw to Underwater Archeology discussion list, September 6, 2010, http://lists.asu.edu/archives/sub-arch.html.

Listserv postings are not listed in the bibliography.

23b   Chicago Humanities Manuscript Guidelines

CHECKLIST
Typing Your Paper

When you type your paper, use the student paper in **23c** as your model.

❑ On the title page, type the full title of your paper in capitals. Also include your name, the course title, and the date.

continued

Typing Your Paper *(continued)*

❑ Double-space all text in your paper. Single-space block quotations, table titles, figure captions, footnotes, endnotes, and bibliography entries. Double-space between footnotes, endnotes, and bibliography entries.

❑ Leave a one-inch margin at the top, at the bottom, and on both sides of the page.

❑ Indent the first line of each paragraph one-half inch. Set off a long prose block quotation (five or more lines) from the text by indenting the quotation one-half inch from the left-hand margin. Do not use quotation marks. Double-space before and after the block quotation.

❑ Number all pages consecutively at the top of the page (centered or flush right) or centered at the bottom. Page numbers should appear at a consistent distance (at least three-fourths of an inch) from the top margin. Do not number the title page; the first full page of the paper is page 1.

❑ Use superscript numbers to indicate in-text citations. Type superscript numbers at the end of cited material (quotations, paraphrases, or summaries). Place the note number at the end of a sentence or clause (with no intervening space). The number follows any punctuation mark except a dash, which it precedes.

See 23a

❑ Citations should follow Chicago humanities documentation style.

CHECKLIST
Using Visuals

According to *The Chicago Manual of Style*, there are two types of visuals: **tables** and **figures** (or **illustrations**), including charts, graphs, photographs, maps, and diagrams.

Tables

❑ Give each **table** a label and a consecutive arabic number (**Table 1, Table 2**) followed by a period.

❑ Give each table a concise descriptive title in noun form without a period. Place the title after the table number.

❑ Place both the label and the title flush left above the table.

❑ Place source information flush left below the table, introduced by the word **Source** or **Sources**. Otherwise style the source as a complete footnote.

Source: David E. Fisher and Marshall Jon Fisher, *Tube: The Invention of Television* (Washington, DC: Counterpoint Press, 1996), 185.

If you do not cite this source elsewhere in your paper, do not list it in your bibliography.

Figures

❑ Give each **figure** a label, a consecutive arabic number, and a caption.

❑ Place the label, the number, and a period flush left below the figure. Then, leave a space and add the caption.

❑ Place source information (credit line) at the end of the caption after a period.

Figure 1. Television and its influence on young children. Photograph from ABC Photos.

CHECKLIST

Preparing the Chicago-Style Endnotes Page

When typing your endnotes page, follow these guidelines:

❏ Begin the endnotes on a new page after the last page of the text of the paper and preceding the bibliography.

❏ Type the title **NOTES** entirely in capitals and center it one inch from the top of the page. Then double-space and type the first note.

❏ Number the page on which the endnotes appear as the next page of the paper.

❏ Type and number notes in the order in which they appear in the paper, beginning with number 1. Type the note number on (not above) the line, followed by a period and one space.

❏ Indent the first line of each note one-half inch; type subsequent lines flush with the left-hand margin.

❏ Single-space lines within a note. Double-space between notes.

❏ Break DOIs and URLs after a colon or double slashes, before punctuation marks (period, single slash, comma, hyphen, and so on), or before or after the symbols = and &.

CHECKLIST

Preparing the Chicago-Style Bibliography

When typing your bibliography, follow these guidelines:

❏ Begin entries on a separate page after the endnotes.

❏ Type the title **BIBLIOGRAPHY** entirely in capitals, and center it one inch from the top of the page. Then double-space and type the first entry.

❏ List entries alphabetically according to the author's last name.

❏ Type the first line of each entry flush with the left-hand margin. Indent subsequent lines one-half inch.

❏ Single-space within an entry; double-space between entries.

23c Model Chicago Humanities Research Paper (Excerpts)

The following pages are from a student paper, "The Flu of 1918 and the Potential for Future Pandemics," written for a history course. It uses Chicago humanities documentation and has a title page, notes page, and bibliography. The Web citations in this student paper do not have DOIs, so URLs have been provided instead.

Title page is
not numbered

Title (all capitals)
centered

THE FLU OF 1918 AND THE POTENTIAL FOR
FUTURE PANDEMICS

Name
Course title
Date

Rita Lin
American History 301
May 3, 2011

1"

3/4"
1

Title if required by instructor (centered)

The Flu of 1918 and the Potential for

Future Pandemics

1/2" ⟶   In November 2002, a mysterious new illness surfaced in

China. By May 2003, what became known as SARS (Severe Acute

Respiratory Syndrome) had been transported by air travelers

to Europe, South America, South Africa, Australia, and North

America, and the worldwide death toll had grown to 250.[1] By June

2003, there were more than 8,200 suspected cases of SARS in 30

countries and 750 deaths related to the outbreak, including 30 in

Toronto. Just when SARS appeared to be waning in Asia, a second

outbreak in Toronto, the hardest hit of all cities outside of Asia,

reminded everyone that SARS remained a deadly threat.[2] As SARS

continued to claim more victims and expand its reach, fears of a

new pandemic spread throughout the world.

Double-space the text of the paper

Introduction

Superscript numbers refer to endnotes

1"   1"

The belief that a pandemic could occur in the future is not

a far-fetched idea. During the twentieth century, there were

three, and the most deadly one, in 1918, had several significant

similarities to the SARS outbreak. As David Brown points out, the

1918 influenza pandemic is in many ways a mirror reflecting the

causes and symptoms, as well as the future potential, of SARS.

Both are caused by a virus, lead to respiratory illness, and spread

through casual contact and coughing. Outbreaks of both are often

traced to one individual, quarantine is the major weapon against

the spread of both, and both probably arose from mutated animal

viruses. Moreover, as Brown observes, the greatest fear regarding

SARS was that it would become so widespread that transmission

chains would be undetectable, and health officials would be

helpless to restrain outbreaks. Such was the case with the 1918

influenza, which also began mysteriously in China and was

transported around the globe (at that time by World War I

1"

2

military ships). By the time the flu lost its power in the spring of 1919, just one year later, it had killed more than 50 million people worldwide,[3] more than twice as many as those who died during the four and a half years of World War I. Thus, if SARS is a reflection of the potential for a future flu pandemic—and experts believe it is—the international community needs to acknowledge the danger, accelerate its research, and develop an extensive virus surveillance system.

Clearly, the 1918 flu was different from anything previously known to Americans. Among the peculiarities of the pandemic were its origin and cause. In the spring of 1918, the virus, in relatively mild form, mysteriously appeared on a Kansas military base. After apparently dying out, the flu returned to the United States in late August. At that point, the influenza was no ordinary flu; it "struck with incredible speed, often killing a victim within hours of contact[,] . . . so fast that such infections rarely had time to set in."[4] Unlike previous strains, the 1918 flu struck healthy young people.

The initial spring outbreak in the United States, confined primarily to military bases, was largely ignored by public officials and the press because the nation's attention was focused on the war overseas. As a result, little was done to prepare for the deadly fall and winter to come. During the

---

Thesis statement

History of 1918 pandemic

Brackets indicate that comma was added by student writer

1″

NOTES

r title
ouble-
before
ote

1. Nancy Shute, "SARS Hits Home," *U.S. News & World Report,* May 5, 2003, 42.

t ½″

2. "Canada Waits for SARS News as Asia Under Control," *Sydney Morning Herald on the Web,* June 2, 2003, http://www.smh.com.au.

Single-space within a note; double-space between notes

3. David Brown, "A Grim Reminder in SARS Fight: In 1918, Spanish Flu Swept the Globe, Killing Millions," MSNBC News Online, June 4, 2003, http://www.msnbc.com/news/921901.asp.

A long URL for an online newspaper article can be shortened after the first single slash

4. Doug Rekenthaler, "The Flu Pandemic of 1918: Is a Repeat Performance Likely?—Part 1 of 2," Disaster Relief: New Stories, February 22, 1999, http://www.disasterrelief.org/Disasters/990219Flu.

5. Lynette Iezzoni, *Influenza 1918: The Worst Epidemic in American History* (New York: TV Books, 1999), 40.

Endnotes listed in order in which they appear in the paper

6. "1918 Influenza Timeline," *Influenza 1918,* 1999, http://www.pbs.org/wgbh/amex/influenza/timeline/index.html.

7. Iezonni, *Influenza 1918,* 131–32.

Subsequent references to the same source include author's last name, shortened title, and page number(s)

s used for
sequent
ence to
me source
there are
tervening
ences

8. Brown, "Grim Reminder."

9. Iezonni, *Influenza 1918,* 88–89.

10. Ibid., 204.

13

BIBLIOGRAPHY

"1918 Influenza Timeline." *Influenza 1918,* 1999. http://
    www.pbs.org/wgbh/amex/influenza/timeline
    /index.html.

Billings, Molly. "The Influenza Pandemic of 1918." Human
    Virology at Stanford: Interesting Viral Web Pages, June
    1997. http://www.stanford.edu/group/virus/uda
    /index.html.

Brown, David. "A Grim Reminder in SARS Fight: In 1918,
    Spanish Flu Swept the Globe, Killing Millions." MSNBC
    News Online, June 4, 2003. http://www.msnbc.com
    /news/921901.asp.

"Canada Waits for SARS News as Asia Under Control." *Sydney
    Morning Herald on the Web,* June 2, 2003. http://www
    .smh.com.au/text.

Cooke, Robert. "Drugs vs. the Bug of 1918: Virus' Deadly
    Code Is Unlocked to Test Strategies to Fight It."
    Newsday, October 1, 2002.

Crosby, Alfred W., Jr. *America's Forgotten Pandemic: The
    Influenza of 1918.* New York: Cambridge University Press,
    1989.

Dandurant, Daren. "Virus Changes Can Make Flu a Slippery
    Foe to Combat." MSNBC News Online, January 17, 2003.
    http://www.msnbc.com/local/sco/m8052.asp.

Center title and double-space before first entry

First line of each entry is flush with the left-hand margin; subsequent lines are indented ½"

Single-space within entries; double-space between them

URLs are provided for Web citations that do not have DOIs

Entries are listed alphabetically according to the author's last name

Directory of CSE Reference List Entries

PRINT SOURCES: *Entries for Articles*

Articles in Scholarly Journals

Articles in Magazines and Newspapers

PRINT SOURCES: *Entries for Books*

Authors

Parts of Books

Professional and Technical Publications

ENTRIES FOR MISCELLANEOUS PRINT AND NONPRINT SOURCES

Films, Videotapes, Recordings, and Maps

ELECTRONIC SOURCES: *Entries for Sources from Internet Sites*

Internet-Specific Sources

CHAPTER 24

CSE and Other Documentation Styles

24a Using CSE Style

CSE style,* recommended by the Council of Science Editors (CSE), is used in biology, zoology, physiology, anatomy, and genetics. CSE style has two parts—*documentation in the text* and a *reference list.*

1 Documentation in the Text

CSE style permits either of two documentation formats: *citation-sequence format* and *name-year format.*

Citation-Sequence Format   The **citation-sequence format** calls for either **superscripts** (raised numbers) in the text of the paper (the preferred form) or numbers inserted parenthetically in the text of the paper.

One study[1] has demonstrated the effect of low dissolved oxygen.

These numbers refer to a list of references at the end of the paper. Entries are numbered in the order in which they appear in the text of the paper. For example, if **James** is mentioned first in the text, **James** will be number 1 in the reference list. When you refer to more than one source in a single note, the numbers are separated by a hyphen if they are in sequence and by a comma if they are not.

Some studies[2-3] dispute this claim.

Other studies[3,6] support these findings.

Note: The **citation-name** format is a variation of the citation-sequence format. In the citation-name format, the names in the reference list are listed in alphabetical order. The numbers assigned to the references are used as in-text references, regardless of the order in which they appear in the paper.

---

*CSE style follows the guidelines set in the style manual of the Council of Science Editors: *Scientific Style and Format: The CSE Manual for Authors, Editors, and Publishers,* 7th ed. New York: Rockefeller UP, 2006.

Name-Year Format   The **name-year format** calls for the author's name and the year of publication to be inserted parenthetically in the text. If the author's name is used to introduce the source material, only the date of publication is needed in the parenthetical citation.

A great deal of heat is often generated during this process (McGinness 2010).

According to McGinness (2010), a great deal of heat is often generated during this process.

When two or more works are cited in the same parentheses, the sources are arranged chronologically (from earliest to latest) and separated by semicolons.

Epidemics can be avoided by taking tissue cultures (Domb 2010) and by intervention with antibiotics (Baldwin and Rigby 2005; Martin and others 2006; Cording 2010).

Note: The citation **Baldwin and Rigby 2005** refers to a work by two authors; the citation **Martin and others 2006** refers to a work by three or more authors.

2 Reference List

The format of the reference list depends on the documentation format you use. If you use the **name-year** documentation format, your reference list will resemble the reference list for an **APA** paper (see **Chapter 22**). If you use the **citation-sequence** documentation style (as in the paper in **24c**), your sources will be listed by number, in the order in which they appear in your paper, on a **References** page. In either case, double-space within and between entries; type each number flush left, followed by a period and one space; and align the second and subsequent lines with the first letter of the author's last name.

CSE PRINT SOURCES Entries for Articles

List the author or authors by last name; after one space, list the initial or initials (unspaced) of the first and middle names (followed by a period); the title of the article (not in quotation marks, and with only the first word capitalized); the abbreviated name of the journal (with all major words capitalized, but not italicized or underlined); the year (followed by a semicolon); the volume number, the issue number (in parentheses), followed by a colon; and inclusive page numbers. No spaces separate the year, the volume number, and the page numbers.

Author's last name | Initial | Title of article (only first word capitalized) | Volume number

2. Davies P. How to build a time machine: it wouldn't be easy, but it might be possible. Sci Am. 2003;287(3):50–55.

Number of entry | Title of periodical (abbreviated) | Year of publication | Issue number (in parentheses) | Inclusive page numbers

Semicolon

Articles in Scholarly Journals

1. An Article in a Journal Paginated by Issue

1. Sarmiento JL, Gruber N. Sinks for anthropogenic carbon. Phy Today. 2002;55(8):30-36.

2. An Article in a Journal with Continuous Pagination

2. Brazil K, Krueger P. Patterns of family adaptation to childhood asthma. J Pediatr Nurs. 2002;17:167-173.

Note: Omit the month (and the day for weeklies) and issue number for journals with continuous pagination through an annual volume.

Articles in Magazines and Newspapers

3. A Magazine Article (Signed)

3. Nadis S. Using lasers to detect E.T. Astronomy. 2002 Sep:44-49.

Note: Month names longer than three letters are abbreviated by their first three letters.

4. A Magazine Article (Unsigned)

4. Brown dwarf glows with radio waves. Astronomy. 2001 Jun:28.

5. A Newspaper Article (Signed)

5. Husted B. Don't wiggle out of untangling computer wires. Atlanta Journal-Constitution. 2002 Jul 21;Sect Q:1 (col 1).

6. A Newspaper Article (Unsigned)

6. Scientists find gene tied to cancer risk. New York Times (Late Ed.). 2002 Apr 22;Sect A:18 (col 6).

CSE PRINT SOURCES Entries for Books

List the author or authors (last name first); the title (not underlined, and with only the first word capitalized); the place of publication; the full name of the publisher (followed by a semicolon); the year (followed by a period); and the total number of pages (including back matter, such as the index).

```
      Author's      Initials              Title (only first
      last name    (unspaced)           word capitalized)                    City and state
         |            |                        |                                  |
    1.  Abbott EA.  Flatland: a romance of many dimensions.  Boston (MA):

         |    Shambhala;  1999.  238 p.
         |        |         |      |
    Number    Publisher   Year of   Total number
    of entry            publication   of pages
              Semicolon
```

Authors

7. A Book with One Author

7. Hawking SW. A brief history of time: from the big bang to black holes. New York (NY): Bantam; 1995. 198 p.

Note: No comma follows the author's last name, and no period separates the unspaced initials of the first and middle names.

8. A Book with More Than One Author

8. Horner JR, Gorman J. Digging dinosaurs. New York (NY): Workman; 1988. 210 p.

9. An Edited Book

9. Goldfarb TD, editor. Taking sides: clashing views on controversial environmental issues. 2nd ed. Guilford (CT): Dushkin; 1987. 323 p.

Note: The publisher's state, province, or country can be added within parentheses to clarify the location. The two-letter postal service abbreviation can be used for the state or province.

10. An Organization as Author

10. National Institutes of Health (US). Human embryonic stem-cell derived neurons treat stroke in rats. Bethesda (MD): US Dept. of Health and Human Services; 2008. 92 p.

Parts of Books

11. A Chapter or Other Part of a Book with a Separate Title but with the Same Author

11. Asimov I. Exploring the earth and cosmos: the growth and future of human knowledge. New York (NY): Crown; 1984. Part III, The horizons of matter; p. 245-294.

12. **A Chapter or Other Part of a Book with a Different Author**

> 12. Gingerich O. Hints for beginning observers. In: Mallas JH, Kreimer E, editors. The Messier album: an observer's handbook. Cambridge (GB): Cambridge Univ Pr; 1978. p. 194-195.

Professional and Technical Publications

13. **Published Proceedings of a Conference**

> 13. Al-Sherbini A. New applications of lasers in photobiology and photochemistry. Modern Trends of Physics Research, 1st International Conference; 2004 May 12-14; Cairo, Egypt. Melville (NY): American Institute of Physics; 2005. 14 p.

14. **A Technical Report**

> 14. Forman, GL. Feature selection for text classification. 2007 Feb 12. Hewlett-Packard technical reports HPL-2007-16R1. 24 p. Available from www.hpl.hp.com/techreports/2007/HPL-2007-16R1.html

CSE ENTRIES FOR MISCELLANEOUS PRINT AND NONPRINT SOURCES

Films, Videotapes, Recordings, and Maps

15. **An Audiocassette**

> 15. Bronowski J. The ascent of man [audiocassette]. New York: Jeffrey Norton Pub; 1974. 1 audiocassette: 2-track, 55 min.

16. **A Film, Videotape, or DVD**

> 16. Stoneberger B, Clark R, editors. Women in science [videocassette]. American Society for Microbiology, producer. Madison (WI): Hawkhill; 1998. 1 videocassette: 42 min., sound, color, 1/2 in. Accompanied by: 1 guide.

17. **A Map**

A Sheet Map

> 17. Amazonia: a world resource at risk [ecological map]. Washington (DC): National Geographic Society; 2008. 1 sheet.

A Map in an Atlas

> 17. Central Africa [political map]. In: Hammond citation world atlas. Maplewood (NJ): Hammond; 2008. p. 114-115. Color, scale 1:13,800,000.

CSE ELECTRONIC SOURCES   Entries for Sources from Internet Sites

With Internet sources, include a description of the medium, the date of access, and the URL.

Author's last name | Initials (unspaced) | Title of article (only first word capitalized) | Title of periodical (abbreviated)

3. Sarra SA. The method of characteristics with applications to conservation laws. J Online Math and Its Apps [Internet]. 2003 [cited 2003 Aug 26];3. Available from: http://www.joma.org/vol3/articles/sarra/sarra.html

Number of entry | Year of publication | Date of access (abbreviated: in brackets) | Semicolon | Volume number | URL | Description of medium (in brackets)

Internet-Specific Sources

18. An Online Journal

18. Lasko P. The *Drosophila melanogaster* genome: translation factors and RNA binding proteins. J Cell Biol [Internet]. 2000 [cited 2008 Aug 15]; 150(2):F51-56. Available from: http://www.jcb.org/search.dtl

19. An Online Book

19. Bohm D. Causality and chance in modern physics [Internet]. Philadelphia: Univ of Pennsylvania Pr; c1999 [cited 2008 Aug 17]. Available from: http://www.netlibrary.com/ebook_info.asp? product_id517169

24b   CSE-Style Manuscript Guidelines

CHECKLIST

Typing Your Paper

When you type your paper, use the student paper in **24c** as your model.

❑ Do not include a title page. Type your name, the course, and the date flush left one inch from the top of the first page.

❑ If required, include an **abstract** (a 250-word summary of the paper) on a separate numbered page.

❑ Double-space throughout.

❑ Insert tables and figures in the body of the paper. Number tables and figures in separate sequences (**Table 1, Table 2; Fig. 1, Fig. 2;** and so on).

continued

See
24a

Typing Your Paper *(continued)*

❑ Number pages consecutively in the upper right-hand corner; include a shortened title before the number.

❑ When you cite source material in your paper, follow **CSE documentation style**.

CHECKLIST

Preparing the CSE Reference List

When typing your reference list, follow these guidelines:

❑ Begin the reference list on a new page after the last page of the paper, numbered as the next page.

❑ Center the title **References, Literature Cited,** or **References Cited** one inch from the top of the page.

❑ For citation-sequence format, list entries in the order in which they first appear in the paper—not alphabetically. For name-year format, list entries alphabetically.

❑ Number the entries consecutively; type the note numbers flush left on (not above) the line, followed by a period.

❑ Leave one space between the period and the first letter of the entry; align subsequent lines directly beneath the first letter of the author's last name.

❑ Double-space within and between entries.

24c   Model CSE-Style Research Paper (Excerpts)

The following pages are from a student paper that explores the dangers of global warming for humans and wildlife. The paper, which cites seven sources and includes a line graph, illustrates CSE citation-sequence format.

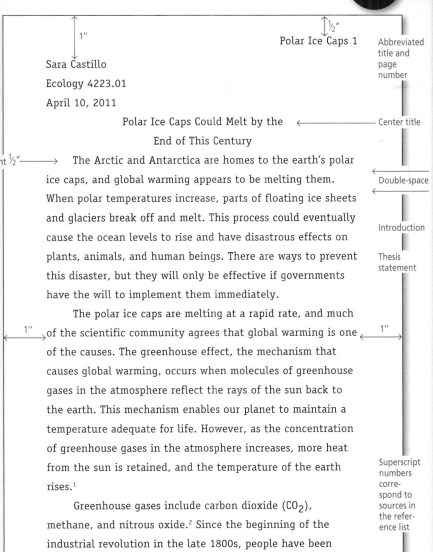

Abbreviated title and page number

Sara Castillo
Ecology 4223.01
April 10, 2011

Polar Ice Caps Could Melt by the ← Center title
End of This Century

The Arctic and Antarctica are homes to the earth's polar ice caps, and global warming appears to be melting them. When polar temperatures increase, parts of floating ice sheets and glaciers break off and melt. This process could eventually cause the ocean levels to rise and have disastrous effects on plants, animals, and human beings. There are ways to prevent this disaster, but they will only be effective if governments have the will to implement them immediately.

Double-space

Introduction

Thesis statement

The polar ice caps are melting at a rapid rate, and much of the scientific community agrees that global warming is one of the causes. The greenhouse effect, the mechanism that causes global warming, occurs when molecules of greenhouse gases in the atmosphere reflect the rays of the sun back to the earth. This mechanism enables our planet to maintain a temperature adequate for life. However, as the concentration of greenhouse gases in the atmosphere increases, more heat from the sun is retained, and the temperature of the earth rises.[1]

Superscript numbers correspond to sources in the reference list

Greenhouse gases include carbon dioxide (CO_2), methane, and nitrous oxide.[2] Since the beginning of the industrial revolution in the late 1800s, people have been burning fossil fuels that create CO_2.[3] This CO_2 has led to an increase in the greenhouse effect and has contributed to the global warming that is melting the polar ice caps. As Figure 1 shows, the surface temperature of the earth has

Figure 1 Introduced

Polar Ice Caps 2

increased by about 1 degree Celsius (1.8 degrees Fahrenheit) since the 1850s. Some scientists have predicted that temperatures will increase even further.

Figure placed close to where it is discussed

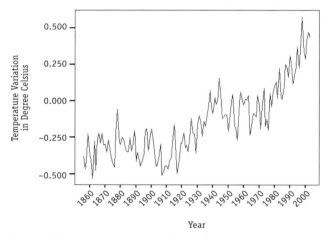

Label, caption, and full source information

Fig. 1. Global temperature variation from the average during the base period 1860-2000 (adapted from Climatic research unit: data: temperature 2003) [Internet]. [cited 2011 Mar 11]. Available from: http://www.cru.uea.ac.uk/cru/data/temperature.

It is easy to see the effects of global warming. For example, the Pine Island Glacier in Antarctica was depleted at a rate of 1.6 meters per year between 1992 and 1999. This type of melting is very likely to increase the fresh water that

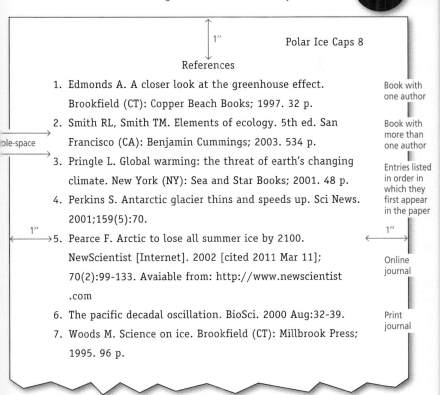

Polar Ice Caps 8

References

1. Edmonds A. A closer look at the greenhouse effect. Brookfield (CT): Copper Beach Books; 1997. 32 p.

   Book with one author

2. Smith RL, Smith TM. Elements of ecology. 5th ed. San Francisco (CA): Benjamin Cummings; 2003. 534 p.

   Book with more than one author

3. Pringle L. Global warming: the threat of earth's changing climate. New York (NY): Sea and Star Books; 2001. 48 p.

   Entries listed in order in which they first appear in the paper

4. Perkins S. Antarctic glacier thins and speeds up. Sci News. 2001;159(5):70.

5. Pearce F. Arctic to lose all summer ice by 2100. NewScientist [Internet]. 2002 [cited 2011 Mar 11]; 70(2):99-133. Avaiable from: http://www.newscientist .com

   Online journal

6. The pacific decadal oscillation. BioSci. 2000 Aug:32-39.

   Print journal

7. Woods M. Science on ice. Brookfield (CT): Millbrook Press; 1995. 96 p.

ble-space (1″, 1″ markers)

24d Using Other Documentation Styles

The following style manuals describe documentation formats and manuscript guidelines used in various fields.

CHEMISTRY

Coghill, Anne M., and Lorrin R. Garson, eds. *The ACS Style Guide: Effective Communication of Scientific Information.* 3rd ed. Washington: American Chemical Society, 2006. Print.

GEOLOGY

United States Geological Survey. *Suggestions to Authors of the Reports of the United States Geological Survey.* 7th ed. Washington: GPO, 1991. Print.

GOVERNMENT DOCUMENTS

Cheney, Debora. *The Complete Guide to Citing Government Information Resources: A Manual for Social Science & Business Research.* 3rd ed. Bethesda: Congressional Information Service, 2002. Print.

United States Government Printing Office. *Style Manual.* Washington: GPO, 2009. Print.

JOURNALISM

Christian, Darrell, Sally Jacobsen, and David Minthorn, eds. *The Associated Press Stylebook and Briefing on Media Law 2011.* 46th ed. New York: Basic, 2011. Print.

LAW

The Bluebook: A Uniform System of Citation. Comp. Editors of Columbia Law Review et al. 18th ed. Cambridge: Harvard Law Review Association, 2008. Print.

MATHEMATICS

American Mathematical Society. *AMS Author Handbook.* Providence: American Mathematical Society, 2008. Print.

MEDICINE

Iverson, Cheryl. *AMA Manual of Style: A Guide for Authors and Editors.* 10th ed. Oxford: Oxford UP, 2007. Print.

MUSIC

Holoman, D. Kern. *Writing about Music: A Style Sheet.* 2nd ed. Berkeley: U of California P, 2008. Print.

PHYSICS

American Institute of Physics. *AIP Style Manual.* 5th ed. Melville: American Institute of Physics, 2000. Print.

SCIENTIFIC AND TECHNICAL WRITING

Rubens, Philip, ed. *Science and Technical Writing: A Manual of Style.* 2nd ed. New York: Routledge, 2001. Print.

PART 7

Creating Documents in a Digital Age

Creating Documents in a Digital Age

❓ Frequently Asked Questions

Writing in a Digital Environment

In email, social-networking sites, computerized classroom environments, blogs, wikis, and chat rooms, electronic communication occurs daily on a wide variety of topics. Because of the nature of the Internet, online communication is somewhat different from print communication. In order to write effectively for an online audience, you should be aware of the demands of writing in an electronic environment.

25a Considering Audience and Purpose

The most obvious difference between electronic communication and print communication is the nature of the **audience.** Audiences for print documents are relatively passive: they read a discussion from beginning to end, form their own ideas about it, and then stop. Depending on the writing situation, however, audiences for electronic documents often respond differently. Although in some cases readers may be passive, in other cases they can be quite active, posting and emailing responses and directly communicating with the writer (sometimes in real time) as well as with one another.

The **purpose** of electronic communication may also be quite different from that of print communication. Unlike print documents, which appear as carefully crafted finished products in newspapers and magazines, electronic documents are frequently written in immediate response to other people's arguments or ideas. In fact, by including links to a writer's email address or to a blog, many online documents are works in progress, encouraging readers to respond—or, in the case of wikis, to add content. For this reason, in addition to trying to inform or persuade, the purpose of electronic documents may also be to support, refute, react, clarify, expand, or correct.

25b Writing in a Wired Classroom

Much of the writing you do in a wired classroom involves **collaboration,** a process in which more than one person contributes to the creation of a document. In some cases, students write a draft of a paper and then post it or distribute it electronically to members of a peer-editing group, who then

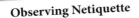

Observing Netiquette

Netiquette refers to the guidelines that responsible users of the Internet should follow when they write in cyberspace. When you communicate via the Internet, keep the following guidelines in mind:

- **Don't shout.** All-uppercase letters indicate that a person is SHOUTING.
- **Watch your tone.** Make sure you send the message you actually intend to send. What might seem humorous to you may seem disrespectful to someone else.
- **Be careful what you write.** Remember, once you hit *Send*, it is often too late to call the message back. Be sure to consider carefully what you have written.
- **Don't flame.** When you flame, you send an insulting electronic message. This tactic is not only immature, but also rude and annoying.
- **Make sure you use the correct electronic address.** Be certain that your message goes to the right person. Nothing is more embarrassing than sending an email to the wrong address.
- **Use your computer ethically and responsibly.** Don't use computer labs for personal communications or for entertainment. Not only is this a misuse of the facility but it also ties up equipment that others may be waiting to use.

make revision suggestions. Comments can be sent via email or they can be inserted into the document with *Microsoft Word*'s Comment tool or with Track Changes. In other cases, students meet in groups and jointly contribute to the prewriting, drafting, and revision and editing of an entire document.

Central to this type of instruction is communication between students and between instructors and students. With **synchronous communication,** all parties involved in the communication process are online at the same time and can be involved in a real-time conversation. Chatrooms, instant messaging, and texting are examples of synchronous communication. With **asynchronous communication,** there is a delay between the time a message is sent and the time it is received. Asynchronous exchanges occur with email, blogs, wikis, Web forums, and discussion forums.

Increasingly—both in distance-learning situations and in traditional classrooms—instructors are using the Internet as well as specific Web-based technology to teach writing. Some of the most popular tools that students use to create Web-based content in an electronic writing environment are discussed in the pages that follow.

① Using Email

Email enables you to exchange ideas with classmates, ask questions of your instructors, and communicate with the writing center or other campus services. You can insert email links in Web documents, and you can transfer files as email attachments from one computer to another. In many classes, writing assignments are submitted as email attachments.

CHECKLIST

Writing Emails

Although personal email tends to be extremely informal, email to classmates and instructors should be more formal. For academic and public writing, follow these guidelines:

❑ **Write in complete sentences.** Avoid the slang, imprecise diction, abbreviations, and emoticons that are commonplace in personal emails.

❑ **Include a subject line that clearly identifies your content.** If your subject line is vague, your email may be deleted without being read.

❑ **Make your email as short as possible.** Because most emails are read on the screen, long discussions are difficult to follow.

❑ **Use short paragraphs.** If your email message is more than five or six lines long, divide it into paragraphs, and leave extra space between paragraphs.

❑ **Do not use text slang or abbreviations.** These terms may be appropriate for your friends, but they are absolutely out of place in an email to an instructor.

❑ **Edit and proofread before you send your email.** Look carefully for typos and other errors that will undermine your credibility.

❑ **Check your routing list.** Be careful not to send your email to unintended recipients.

❑ **Respect people's privacy.** Don't forward an email unless you have the permission of the sender.

Close-Up EMAIL ADDRESSES

Avoid using an email address that is cute or witty or that contains puns or double entendres. Although it may be fine for your friends, this kind of address is not appropriate for the classroom or for a résumé or job application letter.

❷ Using Blogs

A **blog** (short for Web log) is like an online personal journal. Most blogs offer commentary, news, or personal reactions—usually presented in reverse chronological order, with the most recent entry first. Blogs can also function as online diaries, communicating the personal views of the author.

Some teachers of writing encourage students to create and maintain blogs that function as online writing journals. Blogs are not limited to text; they can contain photographs, videos, music, audio, and personal artwork as well as links to Web sites. Most course management systems (such as *Blackboard, Moodle,* and *Angel*) make it easy for instructors or students to create a blog and post comments. Although many blogs are open to everyone, some are password protected.

The following excerpt shows a post and two comments on a class blog for a first-year writing course. The student posted her draft on the course Web site and received comments from several students. These comments, along with advice in an email from her instructor, helped her to revise her paper.

Wednesday, September 28, 2011

The Omnivore's Dilemma **by Michael Pollan**

In an excerpt from his book *The Omnivore's Dilemma*, Michael Pollan discusses the drinking habits of nineteenth-century Americans and makes a connection between the cause of this "national drinking binge" and the factors behind our twenty-first-century unhealthy diets. In both cases, he blames the overproduction of grain by American farmers. He links nineteenth-century overproduction of corn and the current overproduction of grain with various social crises. Although there are certainly other causes of our current problems with obesity, particularly among young children, Pollan's analogy makes sense.

Posted by Julie at 7:14 PM

2 COMMENTS:

Alison said . . .
You did a good job of summarizing Pollan's main points in that part of the book. But I think you could give more details about the "various social crises" Pollan is writing about. I feel like I need to know what they are to understand why he's writing about them in the first place. Maybe use a quote here?

Jeremy said . . .
My response to Pollan was like yours, but at the end I gave more of an evaluation of Pollan's book, I think. Yours just ends with "Pollan's analogy makes sense," and I guess I want to know why you think it makes sense, and why it's important. I'm thinking you could just add another sentence that kind of sums things up—and explains your opinion of the book.

---

3 Using Wikis

Unlike a blog, which is created by an individual and does not allow visitors to edit the posted content, a **wiki** (Hawaiian for *fast*) is a Web site that allows users to add, remove, or change content. The best-known wiki is *Wikipedia*, the online encyclopedia.

In the writing classroom, wikis are used for collaborative writing. They allow students to engage in peer review and to add (or delete) content. Groups of students use wikis to plan projects and to compile class notes. Wiki sites also enable students to view the history of a revision and to compare the relative merits of various drafts of a paper. In research projects, wikis permit students to collaborate on developing research questions, to exchange hyperlinks, to share bibliographical information, to collaborate on drafts of their papers, and to get help with documentation.

> **CHECKLIST**
> ## Wiki Advice
>
> When working on a wiki, keep the following guidelines in mind:
>
> ❑ **Be constructive.** Make sure your suggestions are polite. Your purpose is to help other students, not to be sarcastic or rude.
>
> ❑ **Avoid slang and abbreviations.** Make sure you write in a way that is easy to understand.
>
> ❑ **Do not delete the work of others.** Don't delete other students' writing unless it is absolutely necessary.
>
> ❑ **Don't overedit.** Make sure your edits actually improve the text's content and style.
>
> ❑ **Keep the assignment in mind.** Make sure your edits reflect your assignment's purpose.
>
> ❑ **Proofread before you hit Enter.** Make sure your work is accurate, grammatical, and spelled correctly before you post it.

4 Using Listservs

Listservs (sometimes called **discussion lists**), electronic mailing lists to which users must subscribe, enable individuals to communicate with groups of people interested in particular topics. (Many schools, and even individual courses, have listservs.) Subscribers to a listserv send emails to a main email address, and these messages are routed to all members of the group. Listservs can be especially useful in composition classes, permitting students to post comments on reading assignments as well as to discuss other subjects with the entire class.

5 Using Newsgroups

Like listservs, **newsgroups** are discussion groups. Unlike listserv messages, which are sent as email, newsgroup messages are collected on the Usenet system, a global collection of news servers, where anyone who subscribes can access them. In a sense, newsgroups function as gigantic bulletin boards where users post messages that others read and respond to. Thus, newsgroups can provide specific information as well as suggestions about where to look for specific information.

Some composition instructors establish newsgroups for their classes. Students access the newsgroup to get messages from their classmates or to download papers and assignments. An advantage of newsgroups is that messages are posted and downloaded only when the need arises, so they don't take up space in students' email files.

6 Using Podcasts

Originally, the term **podcast** referred to material that could be downloaded to Apple's iPod. Now, however, it refers to any audio broadcast that has been converted to an MP3 or similar format for playback on the Internet. You can access a podcast with a computer, with an iPad, or with an MP3 playback device.

Podcasting is becoming increasingly common in college classrooms. On the most basic level, instructors podcast class lectures that students can access at their leisure. Instructors also use podcasts to present commentary on students' writing, to distribute supplementary material such as audio recordings or speeches, to record student presentations, or to communicate class information or news. Students may also be asked to analyze podcasts of political speeches, radio programs, or short stories from radio programs such as National Public Radio's *Selected Shorts*. Some instructors even ask students to make their own podcasts. For example, students can read their own essays and add sound clips or visual files.

7 Using *Twitter* and *Facebook*

Twitter is a social network that enables users to send messages called *tweets* to a list of followers. Tweets can be made public, thereby giving anyone the ability to view them, or they can be restricted to friends or members of a particular group. A number of businesses use *Twitter* to keep customers informed, and political candidates use *Twitter* to keep constituents updated.

Instructors also use *Twitter* as a tool to teach writing. Because tweets have a one-hundred-and-forty character limit, they force students to be concise. As a result, in some writing classes, instructors ask students to tweet their thesis statements to the class. This exercise encourages students to state the thesis in clear, precise language. In addition, instructors can use *Twitter* as an easy way to get in touch with students (*Don't forget. Class cancelled tomorrow.*) and to reinforce important course concepts (*Your arguments must be supported by evidence. Look out for logical fallacies.*).

Some instructors form *Facebook* groups and post links to Web sites, documents, and other links on the group pages. Students can ask questions about class assignments and discuss topics that interest them. Joining these groups is usually optional because some students have concerns about *Facebook*'s security.

CHAPTER **26**

Designing Effective Documents

Document design refers to the principles that help you determine how to design a piece of written work so that it communicates your ideas clearly and effectively. Although formatting conventions—for example, how tables and charts are constructed and how information is arranged on a title page— may differ from discipline to discipline, all well-designed documents share the same general characteristics: *an effective format, clear headings, useful lists,* and *helpful visuals.*

 26a Creating an Effective Visual Format

An effective document contains visual cues that help readers find, read, and interpret information on a page. For example, wide margins can give a page a balanced, uncluttered appearance; white space can break up a long discussion; and a distinctive type size and typeface can make a word or phrase stand out on a page.

1 Margins

Margins frame a page and keep it from looking overcrowded. Because long lines of text can overwhelm readers and make a document difficult to read, every page should have margins. Different disciplines have somewhat different specifications concerning margins. For example, MLA style requires a one-inch margin at the top, bottom, and sides of a paper. APA style calls for *at least* a one-inch margin on all sides of a paper. CSE style, however, does not specify a style for an undergraduate paper. Because conventions vary from discipline to discipline, before you type a paper for a course, you should be familiar with your instructor's formatting guidelines.

Except for documents such as flyers and brochures, where you might want to isolate blocks of text for emphasis, you should **justify** (uniformly align, except for paragraph indentations) the left-hand margin. You can either leave a ragged edge on the right, or you can justify your text so all the words are aligned evenly along the right margin.

2 White Space

White space is the area of a page that is intentionally left blank. Used effectively, white space can isolate material and thus focus a reader's attention on it. You can use white space around a block of text—a paragraph or a section, for example—or around visuals such as charts, graphs, and photographs. White space can eliminate clutter, break a discussion into manageable chunks, and help readers process information more easily.

Close-Up BORDERS, HORIZONTAL RULES, AND SHADING

Your word-processing program enables you to create borders, horizontal rules, and shaded areas of text. Border and shading options are usually found under the Format menu (or in the Formatting Palette). With these features, you can select line style, thickness, and color and adjust white space, boxed text, and the degree of shading. Keep in mind that these features should be used only when appropriate, so check with your instructor.

3 Color

Color (when used in moderation) can help to emphasize and clarify information while making it visually appealing. In addition to using color to emphasize information, you can use a color scheme to distinguish certain types of information. For example, titles can be one color and subheadings can be another, complementary color. (You can also use color to differentiate the segments of a chart or the bars of a graph.) Software applications, including *Microsoft Word* and *PowerPoint,* contain templates (such as the one shown in Figure 26.1) that make it easy for you to choose a color scheme of your own. Remember, however, that too many colors can confuse readers and detract from your visual emphasis.

4 Typeface and Type Size

Your computer gives you a wide variety of typefaces and type sizes (measured in **points**) from which to choose.

Typefaces are distinctively designed sets of letters, numbers, and punctuation marks. The typeface you choose should be suitable for your purpose and audience. In your academic writing, avoid fancy or elaborate typefaces—*script* or 𝔬𝔩𝔡 𝔈𝔫𝔤𝔩𝔦𝔰𝔥, for example—that call attention to themselves and distract readers. Instead, select a typeface that is simple and direct—Cambria, Times New Roman, or Arial, for example. In nonacademic documents—such as Web pages and flyers—decorative typefaces may be used to emphasize information or attract a reader's attention.

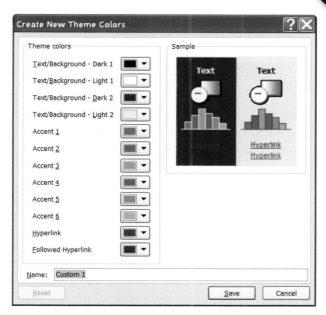

FIGURE 26.1 *Microsoft PowerPoint* color scheme menu. Copyright 2011, Microsoft Corporation. All Rights Reserved.

You also have a wide variety of **type sizes** available to you. For most of your academic papers, you will use 10- or 12-point type (headings will sometimes be larger). Documents such as advertisements, brochures, and Web pages, however, may require a variety of type sizes.

5 Line Spacing

Line spacing refers to the amount of space between the lines of a document. If the lines are too far apart, the text will seem to lack cohesion; if the lines are too close together, the text will appear crowded and be difficult to read. The type of writing you do determines the line spacing. For example, the paragraphs of business letters, memos, and some reports are usually single-spaced and separated by a double space, but the paragraphs of academic papers are usually double-spaced.

26b Using Headings

Used effectively, **headings** act as signals that help readers process information, and they also break up a text, making it inviting and easy to read. Different academic disciplines have different requirements concerning headings.

For this reason, you should consult the appropriate style manual (or your instructor) before inserting headings in a paper.

❶ Number of Headings

The number of headings you use depends on the document. A long, complicated document will need more headings than a shorter, less complicated one. Keep in mind that too few headings may not be of much use, but too many headings will make your document look like an outline.

❷ Phrasing

See
43a

Headings should be brief, informative, and to the point. They can be single words—**Summary** or **Introduction**, for example—or they can be phrases (always stated in <u>parallel</u> terms): **Traditional Family Patterns**, **Alternative Family Patterns, Modern Family Patterns**. Finally, headings can be questions (**How Do You Choose a Major?**) or statements (**Choose Your Major Carefully**).

❸ Indentation

Indenting is one way of distinguishing one level of heading from another. Keep in mind, however, that style guides for different disciplines provide different guidelines concerning the placement of headings. For example, the APA style guide makes the following recommendations: first-level headings should be centered, second-level headings should be justified left, and third-level headings should be indented one-half inch. Consult the appropriate style manual for guidelines on this issue.

❹ Typographical Emphasis

You can emphasize important words in headings (and further distinguish different levels) by using **boldface,** *italics*, or ALL CAPITAL LETTERS. Used in moderation, these distinctive typefaces make a text easier to read. Used excessively, however, they slow readers down.

❺ Consistency

Headings at the same level should have the same typeface, type size, spacing, and color. In addition, if one first-level heading is boldfaced and centered, all other first-level headings must be boldfaced and centered. Using consistent patterns reinforces the connection between content and ideas and makes a document easier to understand.

Note: Never separate a heading from the text that goes with it: if a heading is at the bottom of one page and the text that goes with it is on the next page, move the heading onto the next page along with the text.

Close-Up   SAMPLE HEADING FORMATS

Flush Left, Boldfaced, Uppercase and Lowercase
  Indented, Boldfaced, Uppercase and Lowercase
  Indented, italicized, lowercase; run into the text at the beginning of a paragraph; ends with a period.

                              Or

            Centered, Boldfaced, Uppercase and Lowercase
Flush Left, Underlined, Uppercase and Lowercase
  Indented, underlined, lowercase; run into the text at the beginning of a paragraph; ends with a period.

                              Or
              ALL CAPITAL LETTERS, CENTERED

26c   Constructing Lists

By breaking long discussions into a series of key ideas, a list makes information easier to understand. By isolating individual pieces of information and by providing visual cues (such as bullets or numbers), a list also directs readers to important information.

CHECKLIST
Constructing Effective Lists

When constructing lists, you should follow these guidelines:

❏ **Indent each item.** Each item in a list should be indented so that it stands out from the text around it.

❏ **Set off items with bullets or numbers.** Use **bullets** when items are not organized according to any particular sequence (the members of a club, for example). Use **numbers** when you want to indicate that items are organized according to a sequence (the steps in a process, for example).

❏ **Introduce a list with a complete sentence.** Do not simply drop a list into a document; introduce it with a complete sentence (followed by a colon) that tells readers what to look for in the list.

❏ **Use parallel structure.** Lists are easiest to read when all items are parallel and about the same length.

A decrease in several factors can cause high unemployment:
• consumer spending
• factory orders
• factory output

continued

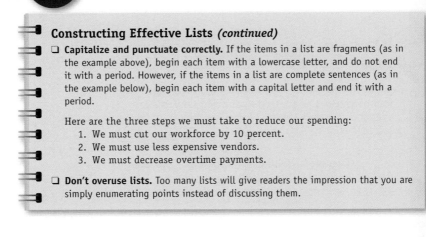

Constructing Effective Lists *(continued)*

❑ **Capitalize and punctuate correctly.** If the items in a list are fragments (as in the example above), begin each item with a lowercase letter, and do not end it with a period. However, if the items in a list are complete sentences (as in the example below), begin each item with a capital letter and end it with a period.

Here are the three steps we must take to reduce our spending:
1. We must cut our workforce by 10 percent.
2. We must use less expensive vendors.
3. We must decrease overtime payments.

❑ **Don't overuse lists.** Too many lists will give readers the impression that you are simply enumerating points instead of discussing them.

Figure 26.2 shows a page from a student's report for an introduction to cultural anthropology course that incorporates some of the effective design elements discussed in **26a–c**. Notice that the use of different typefaces and type sizes contributes to the document's overall readability.

FIGURE 26.2 A well-designed page from a student's report. Created by Karen Mauk.

26d **Using Visuals**

Visuals, such as tables, graphs, diagrams, and photographs, can help you convey complex ideas that are difficult to communicate with words. They can also help you attract readers' attention.

Note: Use a visual in the text only if you plan to discuss it in your paper (otherwise, place the visual in an appendix).

1 **Tables**

Tables present data in a condensed, visual format—arranged in rows and columns. Tables may contain numerical data, text, or a combination of the two. When you plan your table, make sure you include only the data that you will need; discard information that is too detailed or difficult to understand. Keep in mind that tables interrupt the flow of your discussion, so include only those that are necessary to support your conclusions. (The table in Figure 26.3 reports the student writer's original research and therefore needs no documentation.)

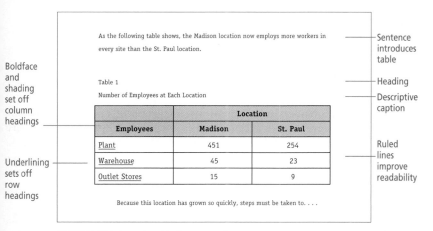

As the following table shows, the Madison location now employs more workers in every site than the St. Paul location. ——— Sentence introduces table

Boldface and shading set off column headings

Table 1 ——— Heading

Number of Employees at Each Location ——— Descriptive caption

Employees	Location	
	Madison	St. Paul
Plant	451	254
Warehouse	45	23
Outlet Stores	15	9

Underlining sets off row headings

Ruled lines improve readability

Because this location has grown so quickly, steps must be taken to. . . .

FIGURE 26.3 Sample table from a student paper.

2 **Graphs**

Like tables, **graphs** present data in visual form. Whereas tables may present specific numerical data, graphs convey the general pattern or trend that the data suggest. Because graphs tend to be more general (and therefore less accurate) than tables, they are frequently accompanied by tables. Figure 26.4 is an example of a bar graph showing data from a source.

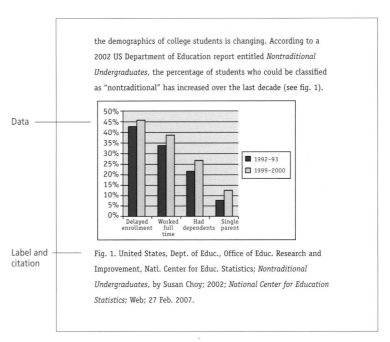

Data

the demographics of college students is changing. According to a 2002 US Department of Education report entitled *Nontraditional Undergraduates*, the percentage of students who could be classified as "nontraditional" has increased over the last decade (see fig. 1).

Label and citation

Fig. 1. United States, Dept. of Educ., Office of Educ. Research and Improvement, Natl. Center for Educ. Statistics; *Nontraditional Undergraduates*, by Susan Choy; 2002; *National Center for Education Statistics*; Web; 27 Feb. 2007.

FIGURE 26.4 Sample graph from a student paper. © US Department of Education.

❸ Diagrams

A **diagram** calls readers' attention to specific details of a mechanism or object. Diagrams are often used in scientific and technical writing to clarify concepts that are difficult to explain in words. Figure 26.5, which illustrates the sections of an orchestra, serves a similar purpose in a music education paper.

❹ Photographs

Photographs enable you to show exactly what something or someone looks like—an animal in its natural habitat, a painting, or an actor in costume, for example. Although it is easy to paste photographs directly into a text, you should do so only when they provide necessary explanation or support for your points. The photograph of a wooded trail in Figure 26.6 illustrates the student writer's description.

The sections of an orchestra are arranged precisely to allow for a powerful and cohesive performance. Fig. 1 illustrates the placement of individual sections of an orchestra.

Label, descriptive caption, and citation

Fig. 1. The sections of an orchestra; *The Lyric Opera of Waco: Education Outreach;* Lyric Opera of Waco, 23 Aug. 2002; Web; 11 Nov. 2009.

FIGURE 26.5 Sample diagram from a student paper. Diagram © Lyric Opera of Waco.

Photo sized and placed appropriately within text with consistent white space above and below

travelers are well advised to be prepared, to always carry water, and to dress for the conditions. Loose fitting, lightweight wicking material covering all exposed skin is necessary in summer, and layers of warm clothing are needed for cold-weather outings. Hats and sunscreen are always a good idea no matter what the temperature, although most of the trails are quite shady with huge oak trees. Fig. 1 shows a shady portion of the trail.

Reference to photo provides context

Fig. 1. Greenbelt Trail in springtime (author photo).

Label and descriptive caption

FIGURE 26.6 Sample photograph from a student paper.

CHECKLIST

Using Visuals

When using visuals in your papers, follow these guidelines:

❑ Use a visual only when it contributes something important to the discussion, not for embellishment.

❑ Introduce each visual with a complete sentence.

❑ Follow each visual with a discussion of its significance.

❑ Leave wide margins around each visual.

❑ Place the visual as close as possible to the section of your paper in which it is discussed.

❑ Label each visual appropriately.

❑ Document each visual borrowed from a source.

CHAPTER **27**

Creating a Writing Portfolio

A **writing portfolio,** a collection of coursework in print or electronic form, offers a unique opportunity for you to present your intellectual track record, showing where you've been and how you've developed as a writer. Increasingly, colleges have been using portfolios as a way to assess individual students' performance—and sometimes to see if the student body as a whole is meeting university standards.

The purpose of a writing portfolio is to demonstrate a writer's improvement and achievements. Portfolios allow writers to collect a body of writing in one place and to organize and present it in an effective, attractive format, giving the instructor a view of a student's writing that focuses more on the complete body of work than on individual assignments. While compiling individual items (sometimes called **artifacts**) to include in their portfolios, students reflect on their work and measure their progress; as they do so, they may improve their ability to evaluate their own work.

There are two kinds of portfolios:

1. **Growth** or **process portfolios** are designed to show a writer's improvement over time. They may include multiple essay drafts with instructor comments (and sometimes peer reviewers' comments as well) in addition to other work completed in and out of class for each assignment.
2. **Best-works** or **presentation portfolios** are designed to highlight a writer's notable achievements. They will contain only finished products, such as the final drafts of essays or reports.

Portfolios may be assembled in print or electronic form. A **print portfolio** collects and presents hard copy in a file folder. In contrast, an **electronic portfolio** compiles material in electronic files stored on a USB flash drive, a rewritable CD or DVD, or a Web site. Some portfolios combine print and electronic formats—for example, posting finished material on a Web site and collecting hard copies of early essay drafts with handwritten instructor comments in a folder.

27a Assembling a Print Portfolio

Before you begin assembling artifacts for a print portfolio, make sure you understand what items your instructor expects you to include.

353

See
27c

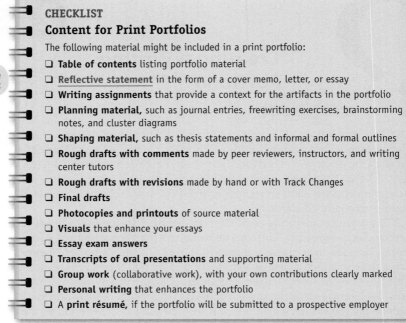

CHECKLIST

Content for Print Portfolios

The following material might be included in a print portfolio:

❏ **Table of contents** listing portfolio material

❏ <u>Reflective statement</u> in the form of a cover memo, letter, or essay

❏ **Writing assignments** that provide a context for the artifacts in the portfolio

❏ **Planning material,** such as journal entries, freewriting exercises, brainstorming notes, and cluster diagrams

❏ **Shaping material,** such as thesis statements and informal and formal outlines

❏ **Rough drafts with comments** made by peer reviewers, instructors, and writing center tutors

❏ **Rough drafts with revisions** made by hand or with Track Changes

❏ **Final drafts**

❏ **Photocopies and printouts** of source material

❏ **Visuals** that enhance your essays

❏ **Essay exam answers**

❏ **Transcripts of oral presentations** and supporting material

❏ **Group work** (collaborative work), with your own contributions clearly marked

❏ **Personal writing** that enhances the portfolio

❏ A **print résumé,** if the portfolio will be submitted to a prospective employer

Once you are sure you understand your instructor's requirements, you can begin to assemble your print portfolio, using the following checklist as a guide.

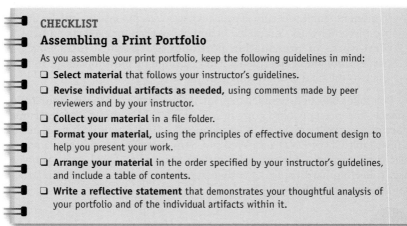

CHECKLIST

Assembling a Print Portfolio

As you assemble your print portfolio, keep the following guidelines in mind:

❏ **Select material** that follows your instructor's guidelines.

❏ **Revise individual artifacts as needed,** using comments made by peer reviewers and by your instructor.

❏ **Collect your material** in a file folder.

❏ **Format your material,** using the principles of effective document design to help you present your work.

❏ **Arrange your material** in the order specified by your instructor's guidelines, and include a table of contents.

❏ **Write a reflective statement** that demonstrates your thoughtful analysis of your portfolio and of the individual artifacts within it.

Figure 27.1 shows the contents page for a student's print portfolio. Notice how an effective design emphasizes important elements and distinguishes them from one another.

highlights
, student's
he, and
s dem-
trated by
tfolio

English Composition I Portfolio

by

Samantha Mahoney

Drafting and Revising | Thinking Critically |

Identifying an Audience

Color-coded
type can be used
to emphasize
elements and
distinguish skill
categories

Contents

eted list
ntifies
tfolio's
tents

- Reflective Statement
- "Moments of Silence" (Relationship Essay)
- "Winter Meal" (Observational Descriptive Essay)
- "Pass the Brussels Sprouts" (Research Project)

ructor

rse

e submitted

Professor Russell

English 101, Section 046

4 October 2011

FIGURE 27.1 Table of contents for student's print portfolio. © Cengage Learning 2013.

27b   Assembling an Electronic Portfolio

As with a print portfolio, the material you include in an electronic portfolio depends on individual course requirements. An electronic format allows for a wide range of possible content, including multimedia content—for example, video or audio clips, *PowerPoint* presentations, and Web pages.

Many academic disciplines are moving toward electronic portfolios because when posted on the Internet, they are immediately accessible to peers, instructors, and prospective employers. However, not all material lends itself to an electronic format. You may need to supplement your electronic portfolio with print documents if they cannot be easily scanned.

See 27c

CHECKLIST
Content for Electronic Portfolios

The following material might be included in an electronic portfolio:

- ❏ **Table of contents or home page with internal hyperlinks** to portfolio material
- ❏ **Reflective statement** in the form of a cover memo, letter, or essay, with internal hyperlinks to portfolio content
- ❏ **Writing assignments** that form the basis for portfolio content
- ❏ **Planning material,** such as electronic journal and blog entries
- ❏ **Shaping material,** such as thesis statements and informal and formal outlines
- ❏ **Rough drafts with revisions** made with Track Changes
- ❏ **Scanned rough drafts with comments** made by peer reviewers, instructors, and writing center tutors
- ❏ **Final drafts**
- ❏ **External hyperlinks** to online source material and other Web sites that support the portfolio
- ❏ **Visuals** that enhance your documents
- ❏ **Audio and video clips of oral presentations**
- ❏ *PowerPoint* **slides**
- ❏ **Group work** (collaborative work), with your own contributions clearly marked
- ❏ An **electronic résumé,** if the portfolio will be submitted to a prospective employer

---

Once you are sure you understand your instructor's requirements, you can assemble your electronic portfolio, using the following checklist as a guide.

CHECKLIST

Assembling an Electronic Portfolio

As you assemble your electronic portfolio, keep the following guidelines in mind:

❏ **Select material** that corresponds to your instructor's guidelines.

❏ **Revise your material,** using comments made by peer reviewers and by your instructor.

❏ **Compile your material** in electronic files and save your files on a storage device or post them to a Web site.

❏ **Format your material,** using principles of effective Web design to help you present your work.

❏ **Arrange your material** in the order specified by your instructor's guidelines, and include a home page.

❏ **Write a reflective statement** that demonstrates your thoughtful analysis of your portfolio and of the individual artifacts within it.

❏ **Collect additional materials** as hard copy in a folder (if necessary).

Close-Up   STORING FILES FOR ELECTRONIC PORTFOLIOS

Storage Device	Benefit	Limitation
USB flash drive	Files can be resaved; compact and easy to transport	High storage capacity flash drives can be expensive; can be easy to lose
Recordable CD (CD+/–R)	Relatively inexpensive	Files cannot be resaved
Recordable DVD (DVD+/–R)	Holds more content than CD+/–R	Files cannot be resaved; more expensive than CD+/–R
Rewritable CD (CD +/–RW)	Files can be resaved	Holds less content than DVD+/–RW; more expensive than CD+/–R
Rewritable DVD (DVD+/–RW)	Files can be resaved; holds more content than CD+/–RW	More expensive than CD+/–R
Web site	Files can be edited offline with Web authoring software and uploaded	Files must be password protected for privacy

Close-Up FREE VERSUS PROPRIETARY ELECTRONIC PORTFOLIO TOOLS

Electronic portfolio tools available through free or **open-source** software, such as *Drupal, Sakai,* and *uPortal,* allow users to edit the software's source code and customize their online portfolio experience. Because open-source software is free, users are granted unlimited access.

Proprietary or **closed-source** software, such as *WebCT* and *Blackboard,* restricts users from editing its code but may still allow various customization options. Proprietary software requires a paid subscription that expires unless renewed. If you consider using an electronic portfolio tool, be sure to find out what its restrictions are before using it to assemble your portfolio.

Figure 27.2 shows the home page for a student's electronic writing portfolio. Notice how effective Web design elements highlight and distinguish key information on the page.

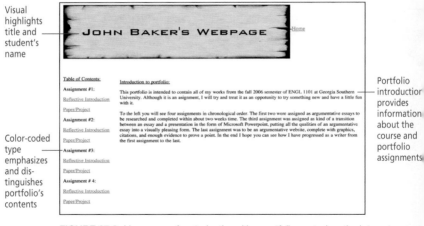

FIGURE 27.2 Home page for student's writing portfolio posted on the Internet. © John Baker.

27c Writing a Reflective Statement

Instructors usually require students to introduce their portfolios with a **reflective statement**—a memo, letter, or essay in which students honestly assess their writing improvement and achievements over a period of time.

Reflective statements allow students to see themselves as writers and to discover both their strengths and the areas in which there is still room for improvement. Keep in mind that a reflective statement is not merely a summary of your completed work; it is an opportunity for you to look closely and analytically at your writing and thus to gain insights about your development as a writer.

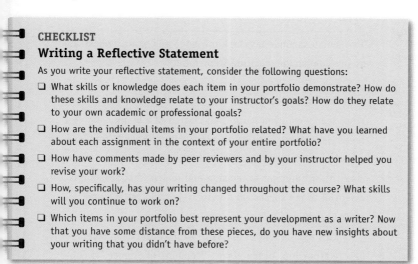

CHECKLIST

Writing a Reflective Statement

As you write your reflective statement, consider the following questions:

❑ What skills or knowledge does each item in your portfolio demonstrate? How do these skills and knowledge relate to your instructor's goals? How do they relate to your own academic or professional goals?

❑ How are the individual items in your portfolio related? What have you learned about each assignment in the context of your entire portfolio?

❑ How have comments made by peer reviewers and by your instructor helped you revise your work?

❑ How, specifically, has your writing changed throughout the course? What skills will you continue to work on?

❑ Which items in your portfolio best represent your development as a writer? Now that you have some distance from these pieces, do you have new insights about your writing that you didn't have before?

Following is an excerpt from the reflective statement for a student's print portfolio. Notice how both content and design highlight the achievements and improvement demonstrated by the student's writing portfolio.

Mahoney 1

To: Professor Russell

From: Samantha Mahoney

Subject: English Composition I Portfolio

Date: October 4, 2011

This memo summarizes the knowledge and skills demostrated by my English Composition I Portfolio.

Drafting and Revising

What scares me even more than staring at a blank computer screen is working hard on an essay only to have it returned covered in red ink. The relationship essay assignment made me confront my fear of revision and realize that revision is essential to my success as a writer—both in college and after I graduate.

This assignment asked us to explore the deep layers of a relationship. In my essay, "Moments of Silence," I wrote about the relationship I have with my hair and what it says about the relationships I have with my mother, my history, and my identity. While the topic was personal and interesting to me, I was unsure how to present it to my readers so that it would interest them. I ended up writing my first draft in a standard five-paragraph format, stating my main idea in a thesis statement and then discussing supporting points in the body paragraphs.

However, comments I received from peers and from you during our one-on-one conferences made me realize that my structure and general approach to my topic needed work. One peer reviewer told me that my essay's traditional organization made him feel distanced from a story that should have been both personal and unique. I worked

Margin annotations:

Opening component

Purpose statement

Color-coded headings can be used to emphasize and distinguish skill categories

Body of memo describes each assignment, how each essay responds to the assignment, and what the writer learned

Explanation of how peer and instructor feedback helped student writer to revise

Mahoney 2

through another draft before realizing that my essay needed to show my readers why this particular relationship is so important to me. At that point, I changed the entire structure of the essay into a personal narrative to better convey the emotional impact of the relationship I was describing.

This assignment showed me that it is not enough to have a compelling topic; I also need to present that topic to readers in a compelling way. As I realized again and again throughout the semester, considering my audience and incorporating suggestions from my readers will help me to achieve my purpose for writing. This assignment made me see early in the semester how important revision is to my development as a college writer and (as I explain later) as an aspiring journalist.

> Discussion of how revision relates to course goals as well as to student writer's academic and professional goals

27d Evaluating Writing Portfolios

Evaluation criteria for portfolios may differ from discipline to discipline, but all effective writing portfolios should be *comprehensive, well-organized, attractively presented,* and *consistent with your instructor's style and format guidelines.*

Comprehensive   A **comprehensive** portfolio includes a varied collection of coursework and demonstrates a writer's ability to respond to various writing situations. Be sure to include all the material requested by your instructor.

Well-Organized   A **well-organized** portfolio follows a consistent, logical organization that smoothly guides readers through a writer's work.

Portfolio content may be organized in various ways. For example, portfolios may be arranged chronologically, or they may be arranged by assignment, format, skill, level of improvement, or applicability to a student's major. Regardless of the method you use, be sure to label each item in your portfolio with a title, your name, your instructor's name, the course number, the date it was submitted, and any other information your instructor requires. To show the portfolio's content and organization at a glance, include a table of contents for print portfolios (refer back to Figure 27.1 on page 355) and a home page for electronic portfolios (refer back to Figure 27.2 on page 358).

Attractively Presented   An **attractively presented** portfolio presents a writer's work in the best possible light. You should use the principles of effective document design or Web design to enhance the readability and accessibility of your work. Remember, however, that design elements should never be superfluous or obtrusive; rather, they should always identify and emphasize important information on a page.

Consistent with Your Instructor's Style and Format Guidelines   A portfolio that is consistent with your instructor's style and format guidelines fulfills expectations established by the instructor and by his or her academic discipline. Carefully follow the documentation style and format guidelines your instructor requires for each assignment.

Close-Up   PORTFOLIOS IN OTHER DISCIPLINES

Portfolios are not limited to writing courses; in fact, instructors in disciplines other than writing often require portfolios that collect and assess students' work. For example, a math portfolio might indicate a student's progress during a particular unit of study or over an entire semester, and a Web design portfolio might demonstrate mastery of a particular set of skills.

CHAPTER **28**

Writing Essay Exams

See
Ch. 8

To write an essay exam (or even a paragraph-length response to an exam question), you must do more than memorize facts; you must see the relationships among them. In other words, you must **think critically** about your subject.

Be sure you know beforehand the scope and format of the exam. How much of your text and class notes will be covered—the entire semester's work or only the material presented since the last exam? Will you have to answer every question, or will you be able to choose among alternatives? Will the exam be composed entirely of fill-in, multiple-choice, or true/false questions, or will it call for sentence-, paragraph-, or essay-length answers? Will the exam test your ability to recall specific facts, or will it require you to demonstrate your understanding of the course material by drawing conclusions?

Different kinds of exams require different strategies. When you prepare for a short-answer exam, you may memorize facts without analyzing their relationship to one another or their relationship to a body of knowledge as a whole. When you prepare for an essay exam, however, you must do more than remember bits of information; you must also make connections among ideas.

When you are sure you know what to expect, see if you can anticipate the essay questions your instructor might ask. Try out likely questions on classmates in a **study group,** and see whether you can do some collaborative brainstorming to outline answers to possible questions. (If you have time, you might even practice answering one or two in writing.)

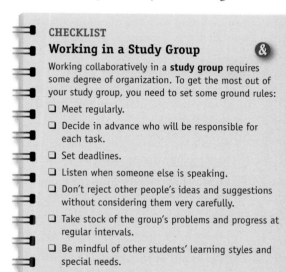

CHECKLIST

Working in a Study Group &

Working collaboratively in a **study group** requires some degree of organization. To get the most out of your study group, you need to set some ground rules:

❑ Meet regularly.

❑ Decide in advance who will be responsible for each task.

❑ Set deadlines.

❑ Listen when someone else is speaking.

❑ Don't reject other people's ideas and suggestions without considering them very carefully.

❑ Take stock of the group's problems and progress at regular intervals.

❑ Be mindful of other students' learning styles and special needs.

28a Planning an Essay Exam Answer

Because you are under time pressure during an exam, you may be tempted to skip the planning and revision stages of the writing process. However, if you write in a frenzy and hand in your exam without a second glance, you are likely to produce a disorganized or even incoherent answer. With careful planning and editing, you can write an answer that demonstrates your understanding of the material.

1 Read through the Entire Exam

Before you begin to write, read the questions carefully to determine your priorities and your strategy. First, be sure that your copy of the test is complete and that you understand exactly what each question requires. If you need clarification, ask your instructor or proctor for help. Then, plan carefully, deciding how much time you should devote to answering each question. Often, the point value of each question or the number of questions on the exam indicates how much time you should spend on each answer. If an essay question is worth fifty out of one hundred points, for example, you should spend at least half (and perhaps more) of your time planning, writing, and proofreading your answer.

Next, decide where to start. Responding first to questions whose answers you are sure of is usually a good strategy. This tactic ensures that you will not become bogged down in a question that baffles you, left with too little time to write a strong answer to a question that you understand well. Moreover, starting with the questions that you are sure of can help build your confidence.

❓② Read Each Question Carefully

To write an effective answer, you need to understand the question. As you read any essay question, you may find it helpful to underline key words and important terms.

Sociology: <u>Distinguish</u> among <u>Social Darwinism</u>, <u>instinct theory</u>, and <u>sociobiology</u>, giving <u>examples</u> of each.

Music: <u>Explain how</u> Milton <u>Babbitt</u> used the <u>computer</u> to expand Schoenberg's <u>twelve-tone</u> method.

Philosophy: <u>Define existentialism</u> and <u>identify three</u> influential existentialist <u>works</u>, explaining <u>why</u> they are important.

Look carefully at the wording of each question. If the question calls for a comparison and contrast of two styles of management, an analysis of one style, no matter how comprehensive, will not be acceptable; if the question asks for causes and effects, a discussion of causes alone will not do.

Close-Up   KEY WORDS IN EXAM QUESTIONS

Pay careful attention to the words used in exam questions:

- explain
- compare
- contrast
- trace
- evaluate
- discuss

- clarify
- relate
- justify
- analyze
- interpret
- describe

- classify
- identify
- illustrate
- define
- support
- summarize

The wording of the exam question suggests what you should emphasize. For instance, an American history instructor would expect very different responses to the following two questions:

- Give a detailed explanation of the major <u>causes</u> of the Great Depression, noting briefly some of the effects of the economic collapse on the United States.
- Give a detailed summary of the <u>effects</u> of the Great Depression on the United States, briefly discussing the major causes of the economic collapse.

Although these two questions look alike, the first calls for an essay that stresses *causes*, whereas the second calls for one that stresses *effects*.

❸ Brainstorm to Find Ideas

Once you think you understand the question, you need to find something to say. Begin by brainstorming, quickly listing all the relevant ideas you can remember. Then, identify the most important points on your list, and delete the others. A quick review of the exam question and your supporting ideas should lead you toward a workable thesis for your essay answer.

28b   Shaping an Essay Exam Answer

Like an essay, an effective exam answer has a **thesis-and-support** structure.

See 5a–c

❶ Stating a Thesis

Often, you can rephrase the exam question as a **thesis statement.** For example, the American history exam question "Give a detailed summary of the effects of the Great Depression on the United States, briefly discussing the major causes of the economic collapse" suggests the following thesis statement:

Effective Thesis Statement: The Great Depression, caused by the American government's economic policies, had major political, economic, and social effects on the United States.

This effective thesis statement addresses all aspects of the question but highlights only relevant concerns.

The following thesis statements are not effective:

Vague Thesis Statement: The Great Depression, caused largely by profligate spending patterns, had a number of very important results.

Incomplete Thesis Statement: The Great Depression caused major upheaval in the United States.

Irrelevant Thesis Statement: The Great Depression, caused largely by America's poor response to the 1929 stock market crash, had more important consequences than World War II did.

2 Constructing an Informal Outline

Because time is limited, you should plan your answer before you write it. Therefore, once you have decided on a suitable thesis, you should make an **informal outline** that lists your major points. Once you have completed your outline, check it against the exam question to make certain it covers everything the question calls for—and *only* what the question calls for.

See
5d

28c Writing and Revising an Essay Exam Answer

Referring to your outline, you can now begin to draft your answer. Don't bother crafting an elaborate or unusual **introduction;** your time is precious, and so is your reader's. A simple statement of your thesis that summarizes your answer is your best introductory strategy: this approach is efficient, and it reminds you to address the question directly.

To develop the **body** of the essay, follow your outline point by point, using clear topic sentences and transitions to indicate your progression and to help your instructor see that you are answering the question in full. Such signals, along with **parallel** sentence structure and repeated key words, make your answer easy to follow.

See
43a

The most effective **conclusion** for an essay examination is a clear, simple restatement of the thesis or a summary of the essay's main points.

Although essay answers should be complete and detailed, they should not contain irrelevant material. Every unnecessary fact or opinion increases your chance of error, so don't repeat yourself or volunteer unrequested information, and don't express your own feelings or opinions unless you are asked to do so. In addition, be sure to support all your general statements with specific examples.

Finally, be sure to leave enough time to revise what you have written. If you remember something you want to add, you can insert a few additional words with a caret (∧). Neatly insert a longer addition at the end of your answer, box it, and label it so your instructor will know where it belongs.

In the following excerpt from an essay exam answer, notice how the student restates the question in her thesis statement and keeps the question in focus by repeating key words like *cause, effect, result,* and *impact.*

ESL TIP

Because of time pressure, it is difficult to write in-class essay exam answers that are as polished as your out-of-class writing. Even so, you should do your best to convey your ideas as clearly as you can, but keep in mind that instructors are usually more concerned with the accuracy of the content of your answers than with your writing style. Therefore, instead of wasting time searching for the "perfect" words or phrases, use words and grammatical constructions that are familiar to you. You can use any remaining time to check your grammar and mechanics. Finally, don't waste time recopying your work unless what you have written is illegible.

Effective Essay Exam Answer

Question: Give a detailed summary of the effects of the Great Depression on the United States, briefly discussing the major causes of the economic collapse.

The Great Depression, caused by the American government's economic policies, had major political, economic, and social effects on the United States.

Introduction—thesis statement rephrases exam question

The Depression was precipitated by the stock market crash of October 1929, but its actual causes were more subtle: they lay in the US government's economic policies. First, personal income was not well distributed. Although production rose during the 1920s, the farmers and other workers got too little of the profits; instead, a disproportionate amount of income went to the richest 5 percent of the population. The tax policies at this time made inequalities in income even worse. A good deal of income also went into development of new manufacturing plants. This expansion stimulated the economy but encouraged the production of more goods than consumers could purchase. Finally, during the economic boom of the 1920s, the government did not attempt to limit speculation or impose regulations on the securities market; it also did little to help build up farmers' buying power. Even after the crash began, the government made mistakes: instead of trying to address the country's deflationary economy, the government focused on keeping the budget balanced and making sure the United States adhered to the gold standard.

Policies leading to Depression (¶ 2 summarizes causes)

The Depression, devastating to millions of individuals, had a tremendous impact on the nation as a whole. Its political, economic, and social consequences were great.

Transition from causes to effects

Between October 1929 and Roosevelt's inauguration on March 4, 1932, the economic situation grew worse. Businesses were going bankrupt, banks were failing, and stock prices were falling. Farm prices fell drastically, and hungry farmers were forced to burn their corn to heat their homes. There was massive unemployment, with millions of workers jobless and humiliated, losing skills and self-respect. President Hoover's Reconstruction

Early effects of the Depression

Finance Corporation made loans available to banks, railroads, and businesses, but Hoover thought state and local funds (not the federal government) should finance public works programs and relief. Confidence in the president declined as the country's economic situation worsened.

One important effect: Roosevelt's emergency measures

One result of the Depression was the election of Franklin Delano Roosevelt. By the time of his inauguration, most American banks had closed, thirteen million workers were unemployed, and millions of farmers were threatened by foreclosure. Roosevelt's response was immediate: two days after he took office, he closed all the remaining banks and took steps to support the stronger ones with loans and to prevent the weaker ones from reopening. During the first hundred days of his administration, he kept Congress in special session. Under his leadership, Congress enacted emergency measures designed to provide "Relief, Recovery, and Reform."

CHAPTER **29**

Writing for the Public

Some of the writing you do—such as diaries and journals—is strictly private, written just for yourself. Other writing—such as research papers and essay exams—is directed at an academic audience. At times, you may also be called upon to do **public writing,** producing documents directed to individuals and groups in the community outside your school.

In a composition course, a work-study job, a service-learning course, a co-op placement, or an internship (and, later, in the workplace), you may be required to write letters, proposals, flyers, brochures, media releases, and newsletters as well as Web pages, **blog posts,** and **email messages** directed at a community beyond the classroom.

See 25b 1–2

See Pt. 3

Many courses in various academic **disciplines** also include public-writing components. Depending on the discipline, you might be assigned to produce a variety of documents—for example, an op-ed piece for a criminal justice or political science course, a brochure for a public health course, book or film reviews for a literature class, or popular "translations" of scientific or technical material for a science or engineering course.

Through public writing, you learn more about how to identify an audience and accommodate its needs as well as how to write for a variety of purposes. You also have an opportunity to practice the principles of good <u>document design.</u> And, of course, the skills you develop in public writing projects can help you succeed in the workplace. For example, you can develop rhetorical skills you might use in writing business reports, memos, and proposals or in developing a marketing campaign. More generally, working on public-writing projects can help you learn to write concise prose, to work as a member of a team, and to communicate with nonexpert audiences in business-to-business contexts.

See Ch. 26

The following sections discuss *media releases, proposals, brochures,* and *flyers.* These documents are typical of the kinds of writing students can create for the public.

29a Writing Media Releases

One common kind of public writing is the **media release,** a document designed to provide information about a project or event to media outlets (newspapers, magazines, online publications, and so on). This information can be used to help publications develop articles informing their readers about the subject of the media release.

The media release that follows was written by a student in an advanced composition course. It was sent to various local media outlets to advertise an upcoming conference on her university's campus. Note that the media release includes an attention-getting headline set in boldface and large type and a standard heading that provides contact information. (Sometimes a media release is accompanied by a cover letter. **See 30a** for information on business letter format.)

Sample Media Release

For Immediate Release:

Contact:

Carol Hulse

Instructor of English at the University of West Florida

(850) 474-2933

<u>chulse@uwf.edu</u>

Linda Moore
Instructor of English at the University of West Florida
(850) 857-6074
lmoore@uwf.edu

HIGH SCHOOL ARTICULATION CONFERENCE TO BE HELD AT UWF ON MARCH 8, 2011
UWF English Department Will Host Event for Escambia and Santa Rosa High Schools

University of West Florida—On March 8, 2011, a high school articulation conference will be held for high school teachers in Escambia and Santa Rosa County from 8:00 a.m. to 3:00 p.m. The UWF English Department and students of composition are sponsoring this event, which will be held in Building 51. Students, teachers, and administrators are all invited to attend. The purpose of the conference is to establish better communication with local high schools in order to improve high school graduates' preparation for college-level coursework.

This year's keynote speaker will be Dr. David Jolliffe, the former Advanced Placement Exam Chief Reader and current Brown Chair in English Literacy at the University of Arkansas. Other speakers will include Dr. Peggy Jolly, Professor and Director of Freshman English and Developmental Studies at the University of Alabama at Birmingham; Bruce Swain, Chairperson of Communication Arts at UWF; and the winner of the "Call for Papers" abstract contest. The main topic of the conference will be "The Severity of Plagiarism."

A tour of the UWF Writing Lab will be available from 11:00 a.m. to 12:00 p.m., and lunch will be provided. Please contact Carol Hulse or Linda Moore for more information.

The UWF English Department and students of composition are sponsoring this event in order to promote better college readiness and success.

###

29b Writing Proposals

In public writing, **proposals** are often written to identify a specific problem in a community and propose a detailed, concrete plan for solving it.

After reading about the widespread problem of decreased literacy levels in the United States, students in an advanced composition course were asked to work in teams to design a new program, campaign, or service to improve literacy in their community. The following proposal outlines one team's idea, a campus book drive. The purpose of the proposal (directed at the university's student government association) was to appeal for funding to support the project. Note that the proposal includes internal headings to identify various sections and help readers locate information. (See p. 374 for the brochure the student team designed to promote the book drive.)

Sample Proposal

To: April Jardine, University of West Florida Student Government
        Association President

From: Christian Cabral, Justin Ellis, Sara Holcomb, Sarah Neuland,
        Carl Shouppe (composition students)

Date: September 29, 2011

Subject: Proposal for Campus Book Drive

In our English Composition II class, we have been studying the problem of illiteracy in the United States. Our research has shown us that there is a great need to encourage reading, especially in young children. Many families would like to have books for their children but do not have the time or money to acquire reading materials. Because our campus is a part of a larger community, we believe that the University of West Florida has the responsibility to help such families. To do our part to increase literacy levels in the United States, we believe we must begin locally, increasing our community's literacy rates first. Therefore, we propose that a community book drive be held on campus during the month of November. We will need financial support as we plan, advertise, and implement this book drive, and we hope SGA will consider funding this important project.

Background and Rationale

Illiteracy is one of the great plagues of the twenty-first century. According to the article "Grim Illiteracy Statistics Indicate Americans Have a Reading Problem" published on the *Education Portal* Web site, 42 million American adults cannot read. In fact, as our society has become more and more technologically advanced, America's young people have been reading less. The online *Chronicle of Higher Education* article "Literary Reading Is Declining Faster than Before, Arts Endowment's New Report Says" describes "a steady drop, over two decades, in the percentage of Americans who read books of any sort. . . ." Many children do not own books, and many parents cannot afford to purchase books for their children. The book drive we propose can be a starting point for getting books into children's hands.

We are appealing to the SGA on behalf of our fellow students, requesting your financial assistance in support of our project. Our goal is to help children in our community whose families cannot afford to purchase books—particularly those children who live in foster homes and shelters.

Plans

To help spread awareness about our book drive, we plan to begin by creating a brochure for mass distribution. (We will also use other means to spread the word about the event, including posters, banners, flyers, and media releases to be sent to the *Pensacola News Journal,* the *Voyager,* and *Argus*.) The purpose of the brochure will be to publicize the book drive and explain its rationale to students, faculty, and staff on the University of West Florida campus. According to the *National Center for Family Literacy* Web site, "Children participating in family literacy programs demonstrated greater gains than children in child-focused programs." Our book drive can create an opportunity for families to read together, and the brochure—distributed on and around the University of West Florida campus—can spread awareness about the project and encourage members of the University community to donate books.

To publicize our project, we plan to appeal to the university community to design and produce flyers and posters, which we will distribute to local churches and shopping malls as well as throughout our campus. Distributing flyers and posters in high-volume areas will enable us to gather more books from wider sources—not only from college students but from members of the larger community as well.

Of course, advertising costs money. For example, we will need at least one thousand sheets of paper for flyers as well as poster board and paint.

We would also like to set up drop boxes on campus—and, if possible, off campus as well—where people can donate books. In addition, we will need help recruiting volunteers to help design, produce, and distribute flyers, banners, and posters on campus and to assist in other areas if needed—for example, to sort the donated books by age and subject. Finally, we will need a room in which to meet as a group to set up, organize, collect, and sort the books we receive.

Conclusion and Recommendations

As the organization ProLiteracy Worldwide states in the report *The State of Adult Literacy 2006*, "there are 771 million illiterate adults in the world . . ." (3). Many of them are Americans. As ProLiteracy Worldwide points out, "If today's children are to become the adult readers of tomorrow, we must treat the acquisition of literacy skills as a neverending process" (13).

We know that the literacy problem cannot be solved overnight, but our group is committed to doing what it can. We ask that you, the president of SGA, approve our proposal and grant us the resources we need to support our book drive. A tentative budget and timetable are attached. Thank you for taking the time to consider our project.

29c Designing Brochures

A **brochure** is a short pamphlet or booklet that provides information about a service, program, or event.

The following student brochure, directed at the campus community (students, faculty, and staff) was designed to promote a book drive on a university campus in support of the school's efforts to fight illiteracy in the community.

? *Sample Brochure*

The following people are coordinating this project:

Sara Holcomb
Christian Cabral
Justin Ellis
Carl Shouppe
Sarah Neuland

For more information, please contact

Student Government Association
University of West Florida
11000 University Parkway
Commons Bldg. 22, Room 227
Pensacola, FL 32514
Phone: (850) 474-2393
Fax: (850) 474-2390
www.uwf.edu/sga/

November 7-21

Front and back cover of brochure. © Cengage Learning 2013.

Why have a book drive?

- To promote the importance of literacy throughout our community
- To provide books for people who cannot afford to buy them
- To supply books to residents of shelters for homeless families
- To encourage families to read together
- To improve literacy for future generations of children

Why should you help to promote literacy?

- 771 million people in the world are illiterate
- In the US alone, 42 million people cannot read
- Nonreaders lack the skills they need to succeed in the workplace

How can you help make this book drive successful?

- Look for bright green boxes around campus, and donate new or gently used books for children and adults
- Volunteer to help sort through and distribute the books that are collected
- SPREAD THE WORD!

Inside pages of brochure. © Cengage Learning 2013.

29d Designing Flyers

A **flyer** is a one-page document that uses text and graphics to advertise an upcoming event. (**See 26a** for information on creating an effective visual format.)

Students in a composition course created the flyer below to promote a benefit concert on their campus.

Sample Flyer

Mayland Community College

Benefit Concert

Featuring six local bands and appetizers donated by the State Street Grill

Art Building, Main Campus   **March 21ˢᵗ – 7pm**   **$10**

Proceeds from this event go to the Herter-O'Neal Scholarship fund sponsored by the Young Professionals student association.

Created by Karen Mauk.

CHAPTER **30**

Writing for the Workplace

Employers value good writing skills. To make sure that job applicants can communicate effectively, some businesses even include a writing assessment as part of the hiring process. They know that a good part of each workday is spent writing. In fact, the higher up people go in a company, the more they write. Poorly written memos, letters, and reports can cost businesses millions of dollars each year. Because good writing skills are so important in the business world, the writing skills you learn in the academic environment can give you a competitive advantage in the workplace.

30a Writing Business Letters

Business letters should be brief and to the point, with important information placed early in the letter. Be concise, avoid digressions, and try to sound as natural as possible.

The first paragraph of your letter should introduce your subject and mention any pertinent previous correspondence. The body of your letter should present the information readers need to understand your points. (If your ideas are complicated, present your points in a bulleted or numbered **list**.) Your conclusion should reinforce your message.

See
26c

Single-space within paragraphs, and double-space between paragraphs. (Note that paragraphs in business letters are not indented.) Proofread carefully to make sure there are no errors in spelling or punctuation. Most often, business letters use **block format,** with all parts of the letter aligned with the left-hand margin.

30b Writing Letters of Application

A **letter of application** (also called a **cover letter**) summarizes your qualifications for a specific job. Letters of application (print or electronic) should be short and focused. Your primary objective in writing this letter is to obtain an interview.

Begin your letter of application by identifying the job you are applying for and stating where you heard about it—in a newspaper, in a professional journal, on a Web site, or from your school's job placement service, for example. Be sure to include the date of the advertisement and the exact title of the position. End your introduction with a statement that expresses your confidence in your ability to do the job.

Sample Letter of Application

246 Hillside Drive
Urbana, IL 61801
Kr237@metropolis.105.com
(217) 283-3017

March 21, 2011

Mr. Maurice Snyder, Personnel Director
Guilford, Fox, and Morris
22 Hamilton Street
Urbana, IL 61822

Dear Mr. Snyder:

My college advisor, Dr. Raymond Walsh, has told me that you are interested in hiring a summer accounting intern. I believe that my academic background and my work experience qualify me for this position.

I am presently a junior accounting major at the University of Illinois. During the past year, I have taken courses in taxation, trusts, and business law. I am also proficient in *PeachTree Complete* and *QuickBooks Pro*. Last spring, I gained practical accounting experience by working in our department's tax clinic.

After I graduate, I hope to get a master's degree in taxation and then return to the Urbana area. I believe that my experience in taxation as well as my familiarity with the local business community would enable me to contribute to your firm.

I have enclosed a résumé for your examination. I will be available for an interview any time after midterm examinations, which end March 25. I look forward to hearing from you.

Sincerely,

Sandra Kraft

Sandra Kraft

Enc: Résumé

In the body of your letter of application, provide the specific information that will convince readers of the strength of your qualifications—for example, relevant courses you have taken and pertinent job experience. Be sure to address any specific points mentioned in the advertisement. Above all, emphasize your strengths, and explain how they relate to the specific job for which you are applying.

Conclude by saying that you have enclosed your résumé and that you are available for an interview, noting any dates on which you will not be available. Be sure to include both your phone number and your email address in your letter.

30c Writing Follow-Up Emails

After you have been interviewed, send a **follow-up email** to the person (or persons) who interviewed you. First, thank your interviewer for taking the time to see you. Then, briefly summarize your qualifications and reinforce your interest in the position. Because many applicants do not write follow-up emails, this kind of message can have a positive effect on the recipient.

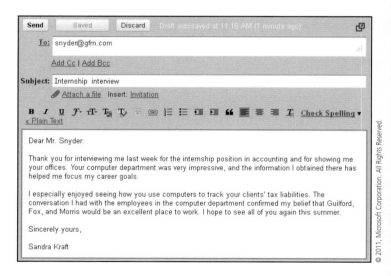

30d Designing Print Résumés

A **résumé** lists relevant information about your education, your job experience, your goals, and your personal interests.

There is no single correct format for a résumé. You will most likely 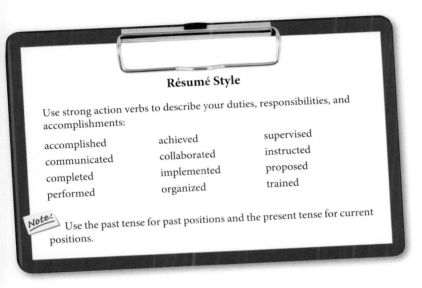 arrange your résumé in **chronological order** (see page 380), listing your education and work experience in sequence (beginning with the most recent). Whatever a résumé's arrangement, it should be brief—one page is usually sufficient for an undergraduate—easy to read, clear and emphatic, logically organized, and free of errors.

Résumé Style

Use strong action verbs to describe your duties, responsibilities, and accomplishments:

accomplished	achieved	supervised
communicated	collaborated	instructed
completed	implemented	proposed
performed	organized	trained

Note: Use the past tense for past positions and the present tense for current positions.

Close-Up RÉSUMÉ TEMPLATES

Microsoft Word contains **résumé templates,** preformatted documents that help you design a résumé. Keep in mind, however, that many employers and recruiters will dismiss résumés that closely follow one of these standardized formats. In their view, if a candidate does not take the time to put together an original résumé, why should they take the time to read it?

These templates can give you ideas about what your résumé should look like, but you should not simply plug information into them. Take the time to create your own résumé, one that communicates your initiative and leads a prospective employer to conclude that you are a strong candidate for the job.

Sample Résumé: Chronological Order

	SCHOOL	HOME
	3812 Hamilton St. Apt. 18	110 Ascot Ct.
KAREN L. OLSON	Philadelphia, PA 19104	Harmony, PA 16037
	215-382-0831	412-452-2944
	olsont@dunm.ocs.drexel.edu	

EDUCATION

DREXEL UNIVERSITY, Philadelphia, PA 19104
Bachelor of Science in Graphic Design
Anticipated Graduation: June 2012
Cumulative Grade Point Average: 3.2 on a 4.0 scale

COMPUTER SKILLS AND COURSEWORK

HARDWARE
Familiar with both Macintosh and PC systems

SOFTWARE
Adobe Illustrator, Photoshop, and *Type Align; QuarkXPress 8; CorelDRAW; Adobe InDesign CS4*

COURSES
Corporate Identity, Environmental Graphics, Typography, Photography, Painting and Printmaking, Sculpture, Computer Imaging, Art History

EMPLOYMENT EXPERIENCE

THE TRIANGLE, Drexel University, Philadelphia, PA 19104
January 2009–present
Graphics Editor. Design all display advertisements submitted to Drexel's student newspaper.

UNISYS CORPORATION, Blue Bell, PA 19124
June–September 2009, Cooperative Education
Graphic Designer. Designed interior pages as well as covers for target marketing brochures. Created various logos and spot art designed for use on interoffice memos and departmental publications.

CHARMING SHOPPES, INC, Bensalem, PA 19020
June–December 2008, Cooperative Education
Graphic Designer/Fashion Illustrator. Created graphics for future placement on garments. Did some textile designing. Drew flat illustrations of garments to scale in computer. Prepared presentation boards.

DESIGN AND IMAGING STUDIO, Drexel University, Philadelphia, PA 19104
October 2007–June 2008
Monitor. Supervised computer activity in studio. Answered telephone. Assisted other graphic design students in using computer programs.

ACTIVITIES AND AWARDS

The Triangle, Graphics Editor: 2009–present
Kappa Omicron Nu Honor Society, vice president: 2009–present
Graphics Group, vice president: 2008–present
Dean's List: spring 2008, fall and winter 2009

REFERENCES AND PORTFOLIO

Available upon request.

30e Designing Electronic Résumés

The majority of résumés are still submitted on paper, but electronic résumés—both scannable and Web-based—are gaining in popularity.

1 Scannable Résumés

Many employers request scannable résumés that they can store in a database for future reference. When preparing such a résumé, keep in mind that scanners will not pick up columns, bullets, or italics and that shaded or colored paper will make your résumé difficult to scan.

Whereas in a print résumé you use specific action verbs (**edited**) to describe your accomplishments, in a scannable résumé you also use key nouns (**editor**) that can be entered into a company database. These words will help employers find your résumé when they carry out a keyword search for applicants with certain skills. To facilitate a keyword search, applicants often include a Skills section on their résumé. For example, if you wanted to emphasize your computer skills, you would include keywords such as *WordPerfect, FileMaker Pro, PowerPoint*, and *C++*.

> **ESL TIP**
>
> In some countries, job applicants list information about their age and marital status in their job application materials. However, in the United States, this is usually not done.

Sample Résumé: Scannable

Deborah Keller
2000 Clover Lane
Fort Worth, TX 76107

Phone: (817) 735-9120
Email: kell5@aol.com

Employment Objective: Entry-level position in an organization that will enable me to use my academic knowledge and the skills that I learned in my work experience.

Education:

University of Texas at Arlington, Bachelor of Science in Civil Engineering, June 2011. Major: Structural Engineering. Graduated Magna Cum Laude. Overall GPA: 3.754 on a 4.0 base.

Scholastic Honors and Awards:

Member of Phi Eta Sigma First-Year Academic Honor Society, Chi Epsilon Civil Engineering Academic Society, Tau Beta Pi Engineering Academic Society, Golden Key National Honor Society.

Jack Woolf Memorial Scholarship for Outstanding Academic Performance.

Grant from the Society of Women Engineers.

Cooperative Employment Experience:

Johnson County Electric Cooperative, Clebume, TX, Jan. 2011 to June 2011. Junior Engineer in Plant Dept. of Maintenance and Construction Division. Inspected and supervised in-plant construction. Devised solutions to construction problems. Estimated costs of materials for small construction projects. Presented historical data relating to the function of the department.

Dallas-Fort Worth International Airport, Tarrant County, TX, Dec. 2009 to June 2010. Assistant Engineer. Supervised and inspected airfield paving, drainage, and utility projects as well as terminal building renovations. Performed on-site and laboratory soil tests. Prepared concrete samples for load testing.

Dallas-Fort Worth International Airport, Tarrant County, TX, Jan. 2009 to June 2009. Draftsperson in Design Office. Prepared contract drawings and updated base plans as well as designed and estimated costs for small construction projects.

Skills:

Organizational and leadership skills. Written and oral communication skills, C++, IBM, Macintosh, DOS, Windows XP and Windows 7, Mac OS 10.5.5, Word, Excel, FileMakerPro, PowerPoint, WordPerfect, and Internet client software. Computer model development. Technical editor.

2 Web-Based Résumés

It is becoming common to have a version of your résumé posted on a Web site such as *Monster.com* or *CareerBuilder.com*. Usually, a Web-based résumé is an alternative to a print résumé that you have mailed or a scannable version that you have submitted to a database or as an email attachment. Figure 30.1 shows a Web-based version of a student's résumé.

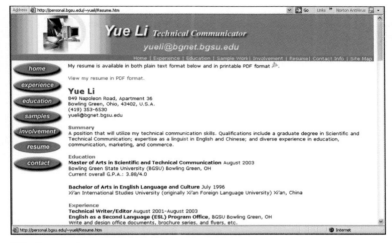

FIGURE 30.1 Sample student Web-based résumé.

30f Writing Memos

Memos communicate information within an organization. Begin your memo with a purpose statement, followed by a background section. In the body of your memo, support your main point. If your memo is short, use bulleted or numbered lists to emphasize information. If it is more than two or three paragraphs, use headings to designate individual sections. End your memo by stating your conclusions and recommendations.

Sample Memo

Opening component

TO: Ina Ellen, Senior Counselor
FROM: Kim Williams, Student Tutor Supervisor
SUBJECT: Construction of a Tutoring Center
DATE: November 10, 2011

Purpose statement

This memo proposes the establishment of a tutoring center in the Office of Student Affairs.

BACKGROUND

Under the present system, tutors must work with students at a number of facilities scattered across the university campus. As a result, tutors waste a lot of time running from one facility to another and are often late for appointments.

Body

NEW FACILITY

I propose that we establish a tutoring facility adjacent to the Office of Student Affairs. The two empty classrooms next to the office, presently used for storage of office furniture, would be ideal for this use. We could furnish these offices with the desks and file cabinets already stored in these rooms.

BENEFITS

The benefits of this facility would be the centralizing of the tutoring services and the proximity of the facility to the Office of Student Affairs. The tutoring facility could also use the secretarial services of the Office of Student Affairs.

RECOMMENDATIONS

Conclusion

To implement this project we would need to do the following:

1. Clean up and paint rooms 331 and 333
2. Use folding partitions to divide each room into five single-desk offices
3. Use stored office equipment to furnish the center

I am certain these changes would do much to improve the tutoring service. I look forward to discussing this matter with you in more detail.

30g Using Email and Voice Mail

1 Using Email

In many workplaces, virtually all internal (and many external) communications are transmitted as email. Although personal email tends to be informal, business email should observe the conventions of standard written communication. In addition, email should follow certain guidelines that can help you communicate effectively in an electronic environment. (See **25b1** for a list of those guidelines.)

2 Using Voice Mail

Like email, voice mail can present challenges. The following tips can help you deliver a voice-mail message clearly and effectively.

CHECKLIST

Using Voice Mail

❑ **Organize your message before you deliver it.** Before you call, take the time to think about what want to say. Long, meandering messages will frustrate listeners.

❑ **Begin your message by identifying yourself.** State your name and affiliation as well as the date and time of your call.

❑ **State the subject of your message first.** Then, fill in the details.

❑ **Speak slowly.** Many experts advise people to speak more slowly than they would in normal conversation.

❑ **Speak clearly.** Enunciate your words so that a listener will understand your message the first time.

❑ **Give your phone number twice.** No one wants to replay a long voice-mail message just to get a phone number.

CHAPTER 3

Making Oral Presentations

At school and on the job, you may be called on to make **oral presentations.** Although many people are uncomfortable about giving oral presentations, the guidelines that follow can make the experience easier and less stressful.

31a Getting Started

Just as with writing an essay, the preparation stage of an oral presentation is as important as the speech itself. The time you spend on this stage of the process will make your task easier later on.

Identify Your Topic The first thing you should do is identify the topic of your speech. Sometimes you are given a topic; at other times, you have the option of choosing your own. Once you have a topic, you will be able to decide how much information, as well as what kind of information, you will need.

Consider Your Audience The easiest way to determine what kind of information you will need is to consider the nature of your audience. Is your audience made up of experts or of people who know little about your topic? How much background information will you have to provide? Can you use technical terms, or should you avoid them? Do you think your audience will be interested in your topic, or will you have to create interest? What preconceptions about your topic will the members of your audience bring with them?

> **ESL TIP**
> When making oral presentations, some ESL students choose topics related to their cultural backgrounds or home countries. This is a good idea because they are often able to provide insightful information on these topics that is new to their instructor and classmates. If you choose such a topic, try to determine beforehand how much background your audience has by speaking with your instructor and classmates.

Consider Your Purpose Your speech should have a specific purpose that you can sum up concisely. To help you zero in on your purpose, ask yourself what you are trying to accomplish with your presentation. It is a good idea to write out this purpose and to keep it in front of you as you plan your speech.

<u>Purpose:</u> to convince an audience that college athletes should be paid a salary

Consider Your Constraints How much time do you have for your presentation? (Obviously, a ten-minute presentation requires more information and preparation than a three-minute presentation.) Do you already know enough about your topic, or will you have to do research?

Close-Up GROUP PRESENTATIONS

Whether you are participating in a panel discussion or are part of a team making a long speech, you should be aware that group presentations require a great deal of coordination. Before you begin to plan your speech, you should take these steps:

- Choose a leader who will coordinate the team's efforts.
- Determine who is responsible for each part of the presentation.
- Determine who will prepare and display visuals.
- Agree on a schedule for both work and rehearsal.
- Agree on acceptable team behavior—for example, how to dress and how to behave during the presentation.

31b Planning Your Speech

In the planning phase, you develop a thesis; then, you decide what specific points you will discuss and divide your speech into a few manageable sections.

Develop a Thesis Statement Before you plan your speech, you need to develop a **thesis statement** that clearly and concisely communicates your main idea to your audience. If you know a lot about your topic, you can develop a thesis on your own. If you do not know a lot, you will have to gather information before you can decide on a thesis.

See 5b

Decide on Your Points Once you have developed a thesis, you can decide what points you will discuss. Unlike readers, who can read and reread a passage until they understand it, listeners must understand information the first time they hear it. For this reason, effective speeches should focus on just a few points that are clear and easy to follow.

Gather Support You cannot expect your listeners to simply accept what you say. You must supply details, facts, and examples that will convince them that what you are saying is both accurate and reasonable. You can gather this supporting material on the Web, in the library, or from your own experience.

Outline the Individual Parts of Your Speech   Every speech has a beginning, a middle, and an end.

- The **introduction** should introduce your subject, engage your audience's interest, and state your thesis.
- The **body,** or middle section, of your speech should present (one at a time) the points that support your thesis. It should also include the support that will clarify your points and convince listeners that your thesis is reasonable.
- The **conclusion** should bring your speech to an end and reinforce your thesis.

Note: Be sure to plan your introduction and your conclusion carefully. Because these sections are what your audience hears first and last, they play a large part in determining the impression your speech makes. Don't make the mistake of thinking that you can make up an introduction or conclusion as you deliver your speech.

31c   Preparing Your Presentation Notes

Most people use some form of presentation notes when they give a speech. Each system of notes has advantages and disadvantages.

Full Text   Some people like to type out the full text of their speech and refer to it during their presentation. If the type is large enough, and if you triple-space, this strategy can be useful. The main disadvantage of using the full text of your speech is that it is easy to lose your place and become disoriented; another is that you may find yourself simply reading your speech.

Index Cards   Some people write key points on index cards. Cards are portable, so they can be flipped through easily. They are also small, so they can be placed inconspicuously on a podium or a table. With some practice, you can learn to use note cards effectively. You have to be careful, however, not to become so dependent on the cards that you lose eye contact with your audience or begin fidgeting with the cards as you speak.

Outlines   Some people like to refer to an outline when they give a speech. As they speak, they can glance down at the outline to get their bearings or to remind themselves of a point they have to make. Because an outline does not contain the full text of a speech, the temptation to read is eliminated. However, if for some reason you draw a blank, an outline gives you very little to fall back on.

31d Preparing Visual Aids

1 Using Visuals

Visual aids, such as overhead transparencies or posters, can reinforce important information and make your speech easier to understand. For a short speech, a visual aid may be no more than a few key terms, definitions, or names written on the board. For a longer, more complicated presentation you might need charts, graphs, diagrams, photographs, or objects.

If you are using equipment, such as an overhead projector, make sure you know how to operate it—and have a contingency plan just in case the equipment does not work (for example, have printouts that you can distribute if the need arises). If possible, visit the room in which you will be giving your speech ahead of time, and see whether it has the equipment you need (and whether the equipment works).

2 Using Presentation Software

Microsoft PowerPoint, the most widely used presentation software package, enables you to organize an oral presentation and prepare professional-looking slides. Effective slides are open and easy to read, and they reinforce important information (see Figure 31.1). Ineffective slides have the opposite effect and can undercut an otherwise effective presentation (see Figure 31.2 on page 390).

PowerPoint's more advanced features enable you to create multimedia presentations that combine images, video, audio, and animation. You can also use the Insert menu to insert various items—for example, clip art, word art, and image files you have created with a digital camera or scanner—

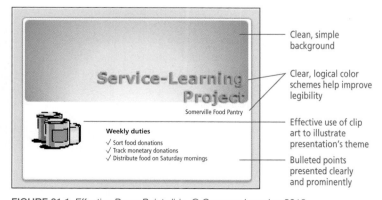

FIGURE 31.1 Effective *PowerPoint* slide. © Cengage Learning 2013.

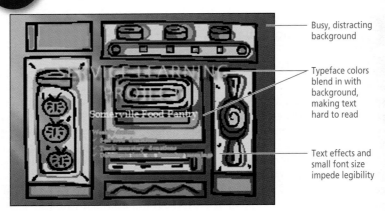

Busy, distracting background

Typeface colors blend in with background, making text hard to read

Text effects and small font size impede legibility

FIGURE 31.2 Ineffective *PowerPoint* slide. © Cengage Learning 2013.

into your slide templates (see Figure 31.3). You can even import charts and tables from *Microsoft Word* and *Excel* and download images from Internet sites directly into your slide templates.

FIGURE 31.3 *Microsoft PowerPoint* Insert menu. Copyright 2011, Microsoft Corporation. All Rights Reserved.

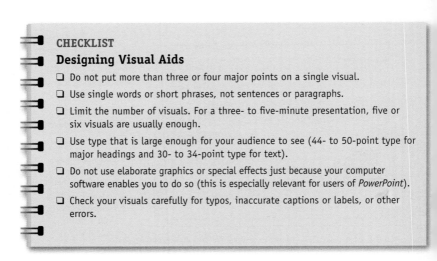

CHECKLIST

Designing Visual Aids

❑ Do not put more than three or four major points on a single visual.

❑ Use single words or short phrases, not sentences or paragraphs.

❑ Limit the number of visuals. For a three- to five-minute presentation, five or six visuals are usually enough.

❑ Use type that is large enough for your audience to see (44- to 50-point type for major headings and 30- to 34-point type for text).

❑ Do not use elaborate graphics or special effects just because your computer software enables you to do so (this is especially relevant for users of *PowerPoint*).

❑ Check your visuals carefully for typos, inaccurate captions or labels, or other errors.

3 Using *YouTube*

Because *YouTube* provides access to millions of videos, it is an excellent resource for oral presentations. You can find videos on almost any subject—for example, how to change the oil in a car, how to create a Web page, or even how to land a plane. You can also find videos showing current events, speeches, and television news shows. Figure 31.4 shows the *YouTube* home page.

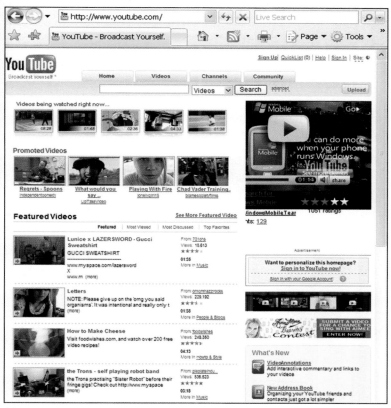

FIGURE 31.4 *YouTube* home page. © YouTube/Google, Inc.

PowerPoint 2010 enables users to insert a video link directly into their presentations. You can also download a *YouTube* link onto your computer and access it during your presentation. (Keep in mind that it is a good idea to have a backup plan in case a computer problem prevents you from using videos in your presentation.)

During your speech, you should show only the part of the video that is necessary to illustrate your point. Long videos that include irrelevant material will cause listeners to lose interest. Before you begin a video, introduce it, tell listeners why you are showing it to them, and identify the source. During the video, point out important sections and explain how various elements illustrate your point. Don't just stand silently and watch.

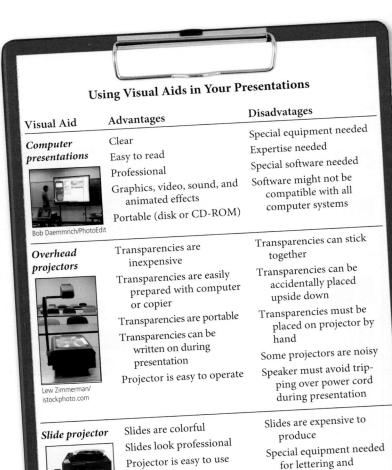

Using Visual Aids in Your Presentations

Visual Aid	Advantages	Disadvatages
Computer presentations Bob Daemmrich/PhotoEdit	Clear Easy to read Professional Graphics, video, sound, and animated effects Portable (disk or CD-ROM)	Special equipment needed Expertise needed Special software needed Software might not be compatible with all computer systems
Overhead projectors Lew Zimmerman/istockphoto.com	Transparencies are inexpensive Transparencies are easily prepared with computer or copier Transparencies are portable Transparencies can be written on during presentation Projector is easy to operate	Transparencies can stick together Transparencies can be accidentally placed upside down Transparencies must be placed on projector by hand Some projectors are noisy Speaker must avoid tripping over power cord during presentation
Slide projector Andy Crawford/Dorling Kindersley/Getty Images	Slides are colorful Slides look professional Projector is easy to use Order of slides can be rearranged during presentation Portable (slide carousel)	Slides are expensive to produce Special equipment needed for lettering and graphics Dark room needed for presentation Slides can jam in projector

Visual Aid	Advantages	Disadvatages
Posters or flip charts Matjaz Boncina/ istockphoto.com	Low-tech and personal Good for small-group presentations Portable	May not be large enough to be seen in some rooms Artistic ability needed May be expensive if prepared professionally Must be secured to an easel
Chalkboards or whiteboards Jeffrey Coolidge/Stone/ Getty Images	Available in most rooms Easy to use Easy to erase or change information during presentation	Difficult to draw complicated graphics Handwriting must be legible Must catch errors while writing Cannot face audience when writing or drawing Very informal

31e Rehearsing Your Speech

Practice your speech often—at least five times—and make sure you practice with your visuals. Do not try to memorize your entire speech, but be sure you know it well enough so you can move from point to point without constantly looking at your notes. Finally, time yourself. Make certain your three-minute speech actually takes three minutes to deliver.

31f Delivering Your Speech

The most important part of your speech is your delivery. Keep in mind that a certain amount of nervousness is normal, so try not to focus on it too much. Channel the nervous energy into your speech, and let it work for you. While you are waiting to begin, take some deep breaths. Once you get to the front of the room, don't start right away; wait until your audience settles down.

CHECKLIST
Delivering Your Speech

As you deliver your speech, keep in mind the following tips on body language, eye contact, and pacing:

❑ Make sure your visuals are positioned properly.

❑ Make sure your equipment is operating properly.

❑ Position yourself effectively.

❑ Stand straight.

❑ Speak slowly and clearly.

❑ Maintain eye contact with the audience.

❑ Use natural gestures.

❑ Face the audience at all times.

❑ Do not just show or read visuals to your audience. Tell your audience more than they can see or read for themselves.

❑ Do not block your visuals.

❑ If you forget something, don't let your audience know. Work the information in later.

❑ Leave time for questions.

❑ Distribute any handouts before or after the speech, not during it.

31g Answering Audience Questions

Most speeches you give will end with audience members asking you questions, and this question-and-answer session is as much a part of your presentation as your prepared remarks are. The impression you make here will play a large part in how they judge your speech. For this reason, when you prepare your speech, you should take time to anticipate audience questions.

As you review your presentation notes, think of the most obvious questions listeners could ask—and the most difficult or perplexing questions listeners could ask. Then, write down and rehearse your answers. If necessary, prepare a note card with any specific information—statistics or facts—that you will need. A bit of preparation at this stage will pay off later.

Once the question-and-answer part of your presentation begins, keep the following guidelines in mind:

- **Control the situation.** Try to call on people in the order in which they raise their hands. Don't let audience members ask questions at will.
- **Listen carefully.** Give your questioners your full attention, and don't interrupt them. Wait until they are finished asking their questions before you begin your answer.

- **Repeat questions.** By repeating questions, you make sure that everyone can hear them. You also give yourself time to put together an answer.
- **Answer questions concisely.** Keep your answers concise, direct, and focused. If a question is complicated and will require a long answer, summarize your response, and ask the questioner to see you after the presentation.
- **Be polite.** Don't indicate that you think a question is silly or misguided. Answer all questions respectfully.
- **Don't fake an answer.** If you don't know the answer to a question, say so. Then, tell the person that you will research the answer and email it to him or her.

Revising Common Sentence Errors

Revising Common Sentence Errors

? Frequently Asked Questions

CHAPTER 32

Revising Fragments

32a Recognizing Fragments

A **fragment** is an incomplete sentence—a phrase or clause that is punctu-
ated as if it were a complete sentence. A sentence may be incomplete for any
of the following reasons:

- **It lacks a subject.**

  Many astrophysicists now believe that galaxies are distributed in
  clusters. <u>And even form supercluster complexes.</u>

- **It lacks a verb.**

  Every generation has its defining events. <u>Usually the events with the
  most news coverage.</u>

- **It lacks both a subject and a verb.**

  Researchers are engaged in a variety of studies. <u>Suggesting a link
  between alcoholism and heredity.</u> (*Suggesting* is a **verbal,** which cannot
  serve as a sentence's main verb.)

- **It is a <u>dependent clause.</u>**

  See
  46c1

  Bishop Desmond Tutu was awarded the 1984 Nobel Peace Prize.
  <u>Because he fought to end apartheid.</u>

  The pH meter and the spectrophotometer are two scientific
  instruments. <u>That changed the chemistry laboratory dramatically.</u>

Note: A sentence cannot consist of a single clause that begins with a subordinating conjunction (such as *because*) or a relative pronoun (such as *that*);
moreover, unless it is a question, a sentence cannot consist of a single clause
beginning with *when, where, who, which, what, why*, or *how*.

GRAMMAR CHECKER Identifying Fragments

Your grammar checker will be able to help you identify many (although not all)
fragments. As you type, they will be underlined in green, and you will be

(continued)

GRAMMAR CHECKER   Identifying Fragments *(continued)*

prompted to revise them. However, not every word group identified as a fragment will actually be a fragment. You, not your grammar checker, will have to make the final decision about whether or not a sentence is grammatically complete—and decide how to correct it.

Spelling and Grammar: English (U.S.)

Fragment:

Present and past, town and country, familiar and foreign.

Suggestions:

Fragment (consider revising)

32b   Correcting Fragments

To correct a fragment, use one of these two strategies:

● Attach the fragment to an adjacent independent clause that contains the missing words.
● Supply the missing subject or verb (or both).

1 Attach the Fragment to an Independent Clause

In most cases, the simplest way to correct a fragment is by attaching it to an adjacent **independent clause** that contains the missing words.

President Lyndon Johnson did not seek reelection/ ~~For~~ *for* a number of reasons. (prepositional phrase fragment)

Students sometimes take a leave of absence/ ~~To~~ *to* decide on definite career goals. (verbal phrase fragment)

The pilot changed course/ ~~Realizing~~ *, realizing* that the weather was worsening. (verbal phrase fragment)

Brian was the star forward of the Blue Devils/ ~~The~~ *, the* team with the most wins. (appositive fragment)

Fairy tales are full of damsels in distress/ ~~Such~~ *, such* as Rapunzel. (appositive fragment)

                                          , and
People with dyslexia have trouble reading/~~And~~ may also find it difficult
to write. (part of compound predicate)

                                      , and
They took only a compass and a canteen/~~And~~ some trail mix. (part of
compound object)

                              although
Property taxes rose sharply/~~Although~~ city services declined. (dependent
clause fragment)

                          , which
The battery is dead/~~Which~~ means the car won't start. (dependent
clause fragment)

Note: Another way to correct a dependent clause fragment like the last two
examples above is to simply delete the subordinating conjunction or relative pronoun.

                          City
Property taxes rose sharply. ~~Although city~~ services declined. (subordinating conjunction *although* deleted)

                          This
The battery is dead. ~~Which~~ means the car won't start. (relative pronoun
which replaced by *this*, a word that can serve as the sentence's subject)

However, simply deleting the subordinating conjunction or relative pronoun is usually the least desirable way to revise because it is likely to create
two choppy sentences and obscure the connection between them.

Close-Up LISTS

When a fragment takes the form of a list, add a colon to connect the list to
the independent clause that introduces it.

See
26c

                                                        :
Tourists often outnumber residents in four European cities/~~Venice~~, Florence,
Canterbury, and Bath.

2 Supply the Missing Subject or Verb

Another way to correct a fragment is to add the missing words (a subject or
a verb or both) that are needed to make the fragment a sentence.

It was divided
In 1948, India became independent. ~~Divided~~ into the nations of India and Pakistan. (verbal phrase fragment)

It reminds
A familiar trademark can increase a product's sales. ~~Reminding~~ shoppers that the product has a longstanding reputation. (verbal phrase fragment)

See 7b2

Close-Up FRAGMENTS INTRODUCED BY TRANSITIONS

Many fragments are word groups that are introduced by **transitional words and phrases,** such as *also, finally, in addition,* and *now,* but are missing subjects and verbs. To correct such a fragment, add the missing subject and verb.

he found
Finally, a new home for the family.

we need
In addition, three new keyboards for the computer lab.

32c Using Fragments Intentionally

Fragments are often used in speech and in personal email and other informal writing—as well as in journalism, political slogans, creative writing, and advertising (see Figure 32.1). In professional and academic writing, however, sentence fragments are generally not acceptable.

Close-Up USING FRAGMENTS INTENTIONALLY

It is permissable to use fragments in the following special situations:

- In lists
- In captions that accompany visuals
- In topic outlines
- In quoted dialogue
- In *PowerPoint* presentations
- In titles and subtitles of papers and reports

FIGURE 32.1 Intentional fragments used in advertising. Images courtesy of The Advertising Archives.

CHAPTER **33**

Revising Run-Ons

33a Recognizing Comma Splices and Fused Sentences

A **run-on** is an error created when two independent clauses are joined incorrectly.

A **comma splice** is a run-on that occurs when two independent clauses are joined by just a comma. A **fused sentence** is a run-on that occurs when two independent clauses are joined with no punctuation.

Comma Splice: Charles Dickens created the character of Mr. Micawber, he also created Uriah Heep.

Fused Sentence: Charles Dickens created the character of Mr. Micawber he also created Uriah Heep.

GRAMMAR CHECKER Revising Comma Splices

Your grammar checker will highlight comma splices and prompt you to revise them.

Your grammar checker may also highlight fused sentences, but it may identify them simply as long sentences that need editing. Moreover, it will not offer suggestions for revising fused sentences.

> **Spelling and Grammar: English (U.S.)**
>
> Comma Use:
>
> I went to the mall, she went to the beach.
>
> Suggestions:
>
> Comma Use (consider revising)

33b Correcting Comma Splices and Fused Sentences

To correct a comma splice or fused sentence, use one of the following strategies:

1. Add a period between the clauses.
2. Add a semicolon between the clauses.
3. Add an appropriate coordinating conjunction.
4. Subordinate one clause to the other, creating a complex sentence.

1 Add a Period

You can correct a comma splice or fused sentence by adding a period between the independent clauses, creating two separate sentences. This is a good strategy to use when the clauses are long or when they are not closely related.

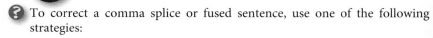

In 1894 Frenchman Alfred Dreyfus was falsely convicted of
     . His
treason/~~his~~ struggle for justice made his case famous.

Close-Up COMMA SPLICES AND FUSED SENTENCES

Do not use a comma to punctuate an interrupted quotation that consists of two complete sentences; this creates a comma splice. Instead, use a period.

     ."In
"This is a good course," Eric said/~~"in~~ fact, I wish I'd taken it sooner."

2 Add a Semicolon

You can correct a comma splice or fused sentence by adding a **semicolon** between two closely related clauses that convey parallel or contrasting information. The result will be a **compound sentence.**

See 47a

> Before World War II, very few Europeans had access to a university education/however, this situation changed dramatically after the war.

Note: When you use a **transitional word or phrase** (such as *however, therefore,* or *for example*) to connect two independent clauses, the transitional element must be preceded by a semicolon and followed by a comma. If you use a comma alone, you create a comma splice. If you omit punctuation entirely, you create a fused sentence.

See 7b2

3 Add a Coordinating Conjunction

You can use a coordinating conjunction (*and, or, but, nor, for, so, yet*) to join two closely related clauses of equal importance into one **compound sentence.** The coordinating conjunction you choose indicates the relationship between the clauses: addition (*and*), contrast (*but, yet*), causality (*for, so*), or a choice of alternatives (*or, nor*). Be sure to add a comma before the coordinating conjunction.

> Elias Howe invented the sewing machine, *and* Julia Ward Howe was a poet and social reformer.

4 Create a Complex Sentence

When the ideas in two independent clauses are not of equal importance, you can use an appropriate subordinating conjunction or a relative pronoun to join the clauses into one **complex sentence,** placing the less important idea in the dependent clause.

> Stravinsky's ballet *The Rite of Spring* shocked Parisians in 1913/ *because* its rhythms seemed erotic.

> Lady Mary Wortley Montagu *, who* had suffered from smallpox herself' ~~she~~ helped spread the practice of inoculation.

CHAPTER 34

Revising Agreement Errors

ESL
58a1

Agreement is the correspondence between words in number, gender, and person. Subjects and verbs <u>agree</u> in **number** (singular or plural) and **person** (first, second, or third); pronouns and their antecedents agree in number, person, and **gender** (masculine, feminine, or neuter).

34a Making Subjects and Verbs Agree

Singular subjects take singular verbs, and plural subjects take plural verbs.

Singular: <u>Hydrogen peroxide</u> <u>is</u> an unstable compound.

Plural: <u>Characters</u> <u>are</u> not well developed in O. Henry's short stories.

ESL
58a2

Present tense verbs, except *be* and *have,* add *-s* or *-es* when the subject is third-person singular. (Third-person singular subjects include nouns; the personal pronouns *he, she, it,* and *one;* and many **indefinite pronouns,** such as *everyone* and *anyone.*)

The <u>president</u> <u>has</u> the power to veto congressional legislation.

<u>She</u> frequently <u>cites</u> statistics to support her points.

In every group <u>somebody</u> <u>emerges</u> as a natural leader.

Present tense verbs do not add *-s* or *-es* when the subject is a plural noun, a first-person or second-person pronoun (*I, we, you*), or a third-person plural pronoun (*they*).

<u>Experts</u> <u>recommend</u> that dieters avoid processed meat.

At this stratum, <u>we</u> <u>see</u> rocks dating back ten million years.

<u>They</u> <u>say</u> that some wealthy people default on their student loans.

In the following situations, making subjects and verbs agree can be challenging for writers.

1 When Words Come between Subject and Verb

If a modifying phrase comes between subject and verb, the verb should agree with the subject, not with the last word in the modifying phrase.

The <u>sound</u> of the drumbeats <u>builds</u> in intensity in Eugene O'Neill's play *The Emperor Jones.*

The <u>games</u> won by the intramural team <u>are</u> few and far between.

<u>Communication</u> among family members <u>is</u> strained.

Note: This rule also applies to phrases introduced by *along with, as well as, in addition to, including,* and *together: Heavy <u>rain</u>, along with high winds, <u>causes</u> hazardous driving conditions.*

2 When Compound Subjects Are Joined by *And*

Compound subjects joined by *and* usually take plural verbs.

<u>Air bags and antilock brakes</u> <u>are</u> standard on all new models.

There are, however, two exceptions to this rule:

- Compound subjects joined by *and* that stand for a single idea or person are treated as a unit and take singular verbs.

  <u>Rhythm and blues</u> <u>is</u> a forerunner of rock and roll.

- When *each* or *every* precedes a compound subject joined by *and,* the subject takes a singular verb.

  <u>Every desk and file cabinet</u> <u>was</u> searched.

3 When Compound Subjects Are Joined by *Or*

Compound subjects joined by *or* (or by *either . . . or* or *neither . . . nor*) may take either a singular or a plural verb.

If both subjects are singular, use a singular verb; if both subjects are plural, use a plural verb. If one subject is singular and the other is plural, the verb agrees with the subject that is nearer to it.

<u>Either radiation treatments or chemotherapy</u> <u>is</u> combined with surgery for the most effective results. (Singular verb agrees with *chemotherapy.*)

<u>Either chemotherapy or radiation treatments</u> <u>are</u> combined with surgery for effective results. (Plural verb agrees with *treatments.*)

4 When Indefinite Pronouns Serve as Subjects

Most <u>**indefinite pronouns**</u>—*another, anyone, everyone, one, each, either, neither, anything, everything, something, nothing, nobody,* and *somebody*—are singular and take singular verbs.

ESL
58c3

<u>Anyone</u> <u>is</u> welcome to apply for this grant.

Some indefinite pronouns—*both, many, few, several, others*—are always plural and take plural verbs.

Several of the articles <u>are</u> useful.

A few indefinite pronouns—*some, all, any, more, most,* and *none*—can be singular or plural, depending on the noun they refer to.

<u>Some</u> of this trouble <u>is</u> to be expected. (*Some* refers to *trouble.*)

<u>Some</u> of the spectators <u>are</u> getting restless. (*Some* refers to *spectators.*)

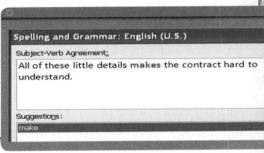

GRAMMAR CHECKER   Subject-Verb Agreement

Your grammar checker will highlight and offer revision suggestions for many subject-verb agreement errors, including errors in sentences that have indefinite pronoun subjects.

Spelling and Grammar: English (U.S.)

Subject-Verb Agreement:

All of these little details makes the contract hard to understand.

Suggestions:

make

Copyright 2011, Microsoft Corporation. All Rights Reserved.

5 **When Collective Nouns Serve as Subjects**

A **collective noun** names a group of persons or things—for instance, *navy, union, association, band.* When it refers to the group as a unit (as it usually does), a collective noun takes a singular verb; when it refers to the individuals or items that make up the group, it takes a plural verb.

To many people, the royal <u>family</u> <u>symbolizes</u> Great Britain. (The family, as a unit, is the symbol.)

The <u>family</u> all <u>eat</u> at different times. (Each family member eats separately.)

Note: If a plural verb sounds awkward with a collective noun, reword the sentence: *Family members* all <u>eat</u> *at different times.*

ESL TIP

In British English, which you may have learned if you took ESL classes outside the United States, collective nouns tend to take plural verbs more often than they do in American English: *Management* <u>are</u> *considering giving workers a bonus.*

Phrases that name fixed amounts—*three-quarters, twenty dollars, the majority*—are treated like collective nouns. When the amount denotes a unit, it takes a singular verb; when it denotes part of the whole, it takes a plural verb.

<u>Three-quarters</u> of his usual salary <u>is</u> not enough to live on.

Three-quarters of the patients improve after treatment.

Note: *The number* is always singular, and *a number* is always plural: *The number of voters has declined. A number of students have missed preregistration.*

6 When Singular Subjects Have Plural Forms

A singular subject takes a singular verb, even if the form of the subject is plural.

Statistics deals with the collection and analysis of data.

When such a word has a plural meaning, however, use a plural verb.

The statistics prove him wrong.

Note: Some nouns retain their Latin plural forms, which do not look like English plural forms. Be particularly careful to use the correct verbs with such words: *criterion is, criteria are; medium is, media are; bacterium is, bacteria are.*

7 When Subject-Verb Order Is Inverted

Even when **word order** is inverted and the verb comes before the subject (as it does in questions and in sentences beginning with *there is* or *there are*), the subject and verb must agree.

Is either answer correct?

There are currently thirteen circuit courts of appeals in the federal system.

ESL 58f

8 With Linking Verbs

A **linking verb** should agree with its subject, not with the subject complement.

The problem was termites.

Termites were the problem.

See 39a

9 With Relative Pronouns

When you use a **relative pronoun** (*who, which, that,* and so on) to introduce a dependent clause, the verb in that clause agrees with the pronoun's **antecedent,** the word to which the pronoun refers.

The farmer is among the ones who suffer during a grain embargo.

The farmer is the only one who suffers during a grain embargo.

34b Making Pronouns and Antecedents Agree

A pronoun must agree with its **antecedent**—the word or word group to which the pronoun refers.

Singular pronouns—such as *he, him, she, her, it, me, myself,* and *oneself*—should refer to singular antecedents. Plural pronouns—such as *we, us, they, them,* and *their*—should refer to plural antecedents.

In the following special situations, pronoun-antecedent agreement can present challenges for writers.

1 With Compound Antecedents

In most cases, use a plural pronoun to refer to a **compound antecedent** (two or more antecedents connected by *and* or *or*).

Mormonism and Christian Science were similar in their beginnings.

However, this general rule has several exceptions:

- If a compound antecedent denotes a single unit—one person or thing or idea—use a singular pronoun to refer to the compound antecedent.

In 1904, the husband and father brought his family to America.

- Use a singular pronoun when a compound antecedent is preceded by *each* or *every.*

Every programming language and software package has its limitations.

- Use a singular pronoun to refer to two or more singular antecedents linked by *or* or *nor.*

Neither Thoreau nor Whitman lived to see his work read widely.

- When one part of a compound antecedent is singular and one part is plural, the pronoun agrees in person and number with the antecedent that is nearer to it.

Neither the boy nor his parents had fastened their seat belts.

2 With Collective Noun Antecedents

If the meaning of a collective noun antecedent is singular (as it will be in most cases), use a singular pronoun. If the meaning is plural, use a plural pronoun.

The teachers' union announced its plan to strike. (The members act as a unit.)

The team ran onto the field and took their positions. (Each member acts individually.)

3 With Indefinite Pronoun Antecedents

Most **indefinite pronouns**—*each, either, neither, one, anyone,* and the like—are singular and are used with singular pronouns.

ESL
58c3

Neither of the men had his proposal ready by the deadline.

Each of these neighborhoods has its own traditions and values.

Close-Up PRONOUN-ANTECEDENT AGREEMENT

In speech and in informal writing, many people use the plural pronouns *they* or *their* with singular indefinite pronouns that refer to people, such as *someone, everyone,* and *nobody.*

Everyone can present their own viewpoint.

In college writing, however, do not use a plural pronoun with a singular indefinite pronoun subject. Instead, you can use both masculine and feminine pronouns.

Everyone can present his or her own viewpoint.

Or, you can make the sentence's subject plural.

All participants can present their own viewpoints.

The use of *his* alone to refer to a singular indefinite pronoun (*Everyone can present his own viewpoint*) is considered **sexist language**.

See
44f2

GRAMMAR CHECKER   Pronoun-Antecedent Agreement

Your grammar checker will highlight and offer revision suggestions for many pronoun-antecedent agreement errors. In general, you should accept those suggestions.

Spelling and Grammar: English (U.S.)
Pronoun Use:
Everybody should take responsibility for their actions.
Suggestions:
his or her

CHAPTER **35**

Revising Awkward or Confusing Sentences

The most common causes of awkward or confusing sentences are *unwarranted shifts, mixed constructions, faulty predication,* and *illogical comparisons.*

35a   Revising Unwarranted Shifts

1 Shifts in Tense

See 37b

ESL 58a2

Verb **tense** in a sentence (or in a group of related sentences) should not shift without a good reason—to indicate a change of time, for example. Unwarranted shifts in tense can be confusing.

I registered for the advanced philosophy seminar because I wanted

a challenge. However, by the first week I ~~start~~ *started* having trouble under-

standing the reading. (unwarranted shift from past to present)

Jack Kerouac's novel *On the Road* follows a group of friends
drive
who ~~drove~~ across the United States in the 1950s. (unwarranted shift
from present to past)

See 12b

Note: Discussions of **literary works** generally use present tense.

2 Shifts in Voice

Unwarranted shifts from active to passive **voice** (or from passive to active)
can be confusing. In the following sentence, for instance, the shift from active (*wrote*) to passive (*was written*) makes it unclear who wrote *The Great
Gatsby*.

See 37d

ESL 58a6

he *wrote*
F. Scott Fitzgerald wrote *This Side of Paradise,* and later *The Great*

Gatsby ~~was written.~~

Note: Sometimes a shift from active to passive voice within a sentence may
be necessary to give the sentence proper emphasis: *Even though consumers
protested, the sales tax was increased.* (To say *the legislature increased the
sales tax* would draw the sentence's emphasis away from *consumers*.)

3 Shifts in Mood

Unwarranted shifts in **mood** can also create awkward sentences.

See 37c

be
Next, heat the mixture in a test tube, and ~~you should make~~ sure it does
not boil. (unwarranted shift from imperative to indicative)

4 Shifts in Person and Number

Person indicates who is speaking (first person—*I, we*), who is spoken to
(second person—*you*), and who is spoken about (third person—*he, she, it,
one,* and *they*). Most unwarranted shifts in a sentence occur between second
and third person.

ESL 58a

you look
When ~~one looks~~ for a car loan, you compare the interest rates of several
banks. (unwarranted shift from third to second person)

Number indicates one (singular—*novel, it*) or more than one (plural—
novels, they, them). Singular pronouns should refer to singular **antecedents**
and plural pronouns to plural antecedents.

See 38c

ESL 58c1

he or she
If a student does not study regularly, ~~they~~ will have a difficult time
passing this class. (unwarranted shift from singular to plural)

5 Shifts from Direct to Indirect Discourse

Direct discourse reports the exact words of a speaker or writer. It is always enclosed in quotation marks and is often accompanied by an identifying tag (*he says, she said*).

Indirect discourse summarizes the words of a speaker or writer. No quotation marks are used, and the reported words are often introduced with the word *that* or, in the case of questions, with *who, what, why, whether, how,* or *if.*

Direct Discourse: My instructor said, "I want your paper by this Friday."

Indirect Discourse: My instructor said that he wanted my paper by this Friday.

Unwarranted shifts between indirect and direct discourse are often confusing.

During the trial, John Brown repeatedly defended his actions and said
that ~~I am~~ *he was* not guilty. (shift from indirect to direct discourse)

"Are you   *?"*
My mother asked, ~~was I~~ ever going to get a job/ (neither indirect nor direct discourse)

35b Revising Mixed Constructions

A **mixed construction** is an error created when a dependent clause, prepositional phrase, or independent clause is incorrectly used as the subject of a sentence.

Because she studies every day, ~~explains why~~ she gets good grades. (dependent clause used as subject)

you can
By calling for information, ~~is the way to~~ learn more about the benefits of ROTC. (prepositional phrase used as subject)

Being
~~He was~~ late ~~was what~~ made him miss the first act. (independent clause used as subject)

35c Revising Faulty Predication

Faulty predication occurs when a sentence's predicate does not logically complete its subject.

1 Incorrect Use of *Be*

Faulty predication is especially common in sentences that contain a **linking verb**—a form of the verb *be*, for example—and a subject complement.

> *caused*
> Mounting costs and decreasing revenues ~~were~~ the downfall of the hospital.

This sentence incorrectly states that mounting costs and decreasing revenues were the downfall of the hospital when, in fact, they were the reasons for its downfall.

2 *Is When* or *Is Where*

Faulty predication also occurs when a one-sentence definition includes the construction *is where* or *is when*. (In a definition, *is* must be preceded and followed by a noun or noun phrase.)

> *the construction of*
> Taxidermy is ~~where you construct~~ a lifelike representation of an animal from its preserved skin.

3 *The Reason . . . Is Because*

Finally, faulty predication occurs when the phrase *the reason is* precedes *because*. In this situation, *because* (which means "for the reason that") is redundant and should be deleted.

> *that*
> The reason we drive is ~~because~~ we are afraid to fly.

GRAMMAR CHECKER   Revising Faulty Predication

Your grammar checker will highlight certain instances of faulty predication and offer suggestions for revision, but it will miss many unwarranted shifts, mixed constructions, and incomplete or illogical constructions, so you will need to proofread carefully for these errors.

35d Revising Incomplete or Illogical Comparisons

A comparison tells how two things are alike or unlike. When you make a comparison, be sure it is **complete** (that it specifies the two items that are being compared) and **logical** (that it equates two comparable items).

> *than Nina's*
> My chemistry course is harder. (What two things are being compared?)

> *dog's*
> A pig's intelligence is greater than a ~~dog~~. (illogically compares "a pig's intelligence" to "a dog")

CHAPTER **36**

Revising Misplaced and Dangling Modifiers

A **modifier** is a word, phrase, or clause that describes, limits, or qualifies another word or word group in a sentence. A modifier should be placed close to the word it modifies.

> Wendy watched the storm, <u>fierce and threatening</u>. *(fierce and threatening* modifies *storm)*

Faulty modification is the awkward or confusing placement of modifiers or the modification of nonexistent words.

36a Revising Misplaced Modifiers

❓ A **misplaced modifier** is a word or word group whose placement suggests that it modifies one word when it is intended to modify another.

> *Wendy watched the storm, fierce*
> ~~Fierce~~ and threatening, ~~Wendy watched the storm,~~ (The storm, not Wendy, was fierce and threatening.)

> *The lawyer argued that the defendant, with*
> ~~With~~ an IQ of just 52, ~~the lawyer argued that the defendant~~ should not get the death penalty. (The defendant, not the lawyer, had an IQ of 52.)

❶ Place Modifying Words Precisely

Limiting modifiers—such as *almost, only, even, hardly, merely, nearly, exactly, scarcely, simply,* and *just*—should immediately precede the words they modify. A different placement will change the meaning of the sentence.

> Nick *just* set up camp at the edge of town. (He did it just now.)
>
> *Just* Nick set up camp at the edge of town. (He did it alone.)
>
> Nick set up camp *just* at the edge of town. (His camp was precisely at the edge.)

When a limiting modifier is placed so that it is not clear whether it modifies the word before it or the word after it, it is called a **squinting modifier.**

The life that everyone thought would fulfill her totally bored her.

To correct a squinting modifier, place the modifier so that it is clear which word it modifies.

The life that everyone thought would <u>totally</u> fulfill her bored her.
(Everyone expected her to be totally fulfilled.)

The life that everyone thought would fulfill her bored her <u>totally</u>.
(She was totally bored.)

❷ Relocate Misplaced Phrases

Placing a modifying phrase incorrectly can change the meaning of a sentence or create an unclear or confusing (or even unintentionally humorous) construction.

To avoid ambiguity, place phrases as close as possible to the words they modify.

● Place **verbal phrase** modifiers directly before or directly after the words or word groups they modify.

Roller-skating along the shore,
Jane watched the boats ~~roller skating along the shore.~~

● Place **prepositional phrase** modifiers immediately after the words they modify.

with no arms
Venus de Milo is a statue created by a famous artist ~~with no arms.~~

❸ Relocate Misplaced Dependent Clauses

A dependent clause that serves as a modifier must be clearly related to the word it modifies.

● An **adjective clause** appears immediately *after* the word it modifies.

During the Civil War, Lincoln was the president <u>who governed the United States</u>.

● An **adverb clause** can appear in any of several positions, as long as its relationship to the word or word group it modifies is clear.

<u>When Lincoln was president</u>, the Civil War raged.

The Civil War raged <u>when Lincoln was president</u>.

36b Revising Intrusive Modifiers

An **intrusive modifier** awkwardly interrupts a sentence, making it difficult to understand.

● Revise when a long modifier comes between an auxiliary verb and the main verb.

Without
^She had, ~~without~~ giving it a second thought or considering the
                    she had
consequences,^planned to reenlist.

● Revise when a modifier creates an awkward **split infinitive**—that is, when a modifier comes between ("splits") the word *to* and the base form of the verb.

            beat his previous record
He hoped to^in a matter of months, if not days,/~~beat his previous record.~~

Note: A split infinitive is acceptable when the intervening modifier is short, especially if the alternative would be awkward or ambiguous: *She expected to almost beat her previous record.*

GRAMMAR CHECKER   Revising Faulty Modification

Your grammar checker will identify some modification problems, including certain awkward **split infinitives**. However, the grammar checker will not offer revision suggestions. You will have to revise awkward split infinitives on your own, as illustrated in **36b**.

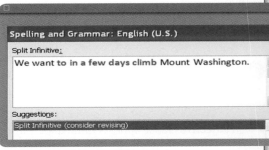

Spelling and Grammar: English (U.S.)

Split Infinitive:

We want to in a few days climb Mount Washington.

Suggestions:

Split Infinitive (consider revising)

Copyright 2011, Microsoft Corporation. All Rights Reserved.

36c Revising Dangling Modifiers

A **dangling modifier** is a word or phrase that cannot logically modify any word in the sentence.

Dangling: Using this drug, many undesirable side effects are experienced. (Who is using this drug?)

• One way to correct this dangling modifier is to **create a new subject** by adding a word or word group that *using this drug* can logically modify.

Revised: Using this drug, patients experience many undesirable side effects.

• Another way to correct the dangling modifier is to **create a dependent clause.**

Revised: When patients use this drug, they experience many undesirable side effects.

Close-Up DANGLING MODIFIERS AND THE PASSIVE VOICE

Most sentences that include dangling modifiers are in the passive voice. Changing the passive voice to active voice often corrects the dangling modifier.

See
37d

ESL
58a6

Writing Grammatical Sentences

Sentences

Writing Grammatical Sentences

❓ Frequently Asked Questions

CHAPTER 37

Using Verbs

37a Understanding Verb Forms

Every verb has four **principal parts:** a **base form** (the present tense form of the verb used with *I*), a **present participle** (the *-ing* form of the verb), a **past tense form,** and a **past participle.**

Note: The verb *be* is so irregular that it is the one exception to this definition; its base form is *be.*

1 Regular Verbs

A **regular verb** forms both its past tense and its past participle by adding *-d* or *-ed* to the base form of the verb.

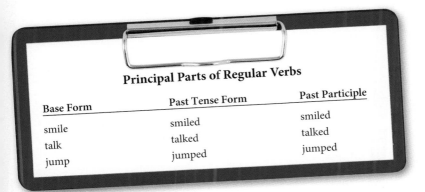

Principal Parts of Regular Verbs

Base Form	Past Tense Form	Past Participle
smile	smiled	smiled
talk	talked	talked
jump	jumped	jumped

2 Irregular Verbs

Irregular verbs do not follow the pattern discussed above. The chart that follows lists the principal parts of the most frequently used irregular verbs.

Frequently Used Irregular Verbs

Base Form	Past Tense Form	Past Participle
arise	arose	arisen
awake	awoke, awaked	awoke, awaked
be	was/were	been
beat	beat	beaten
begin	began	begun
bend	bent	bent
bet	bet, betted	bet
bite	bit	bitten
blow	blew	blown
break	broke	broken
bring	brought	brought
build	built	built
burst	burst	burst
buy	bought	bought
catch	caught	caught
choose	chose	chosen
cling	clung	clung
come	came	come
cost	cost	cost
deal	dealt	dealt
dig	dug	dug
dive	dived, dove	dived
do	did	done
drag	dragged	dragged
draw	drew	drawn
drink	drank	drunk
drive	drove	driven
eat	ate	eaten
fall	fell	fallen
fight	fought	fought
find	found	found
fly	flew	flown
forget	forgot	forgotten, forgot

Base Form	Past Tense Form	Past Participle
freeze	froze	frozen
get	got	gotten
give	gave	given
go	went	gone
grow	grew	grown
hang (execute)	hanged	hanged
hang (suspend)	hung	hung
have	had	had
hear	heard	heard
keep	kept	kept
know	knew	known
lay	laid	laid
lead	led	led
lend	lent	lent
let	let	let
lie (recline)	lay	lain
lie (tell an untruth)	lied	lied
make	made	made
prove	proved	proved, proven
read	read	read
ride	rode	ridden
ring	rang	rung
rise	rose	risen
run	ran	run
say	said	said
see	saw	seen
set (place)	set	set
shake	shook	shaken
shrink	shrank, shrunk	shrunk, shrunken
sing	sang	sung
sink	sank	sunk
sit	sat	sat
sneak	sneaked, snuck	sneaked, snuck
speak	spoke	spoken
speed	sped, speeded	sped, speeded
spin	spun	spun
spring	sprang	sprung

(continued)

Frequently Used Irregular Verbs *(continued)*

Base Form	Past Tense Form	Past Participle
stand	stood	stood
steal	stole	stolen
strike	struck	struck, stricken
swear	swore	sworn
swim	swam	swum
swing	swung	swung
take	took	taken
teach	taught	taught
throw	threw	thrown
wake	woke, waked	waked, woken
wear	wore	worn
wring	wrung	wrung
write	wrote	written

GRAMMAR CHECKER   Using Correct Verb Forms

Your grammar checker will highlight incorrect verb forms in your writing and offer revision suggestions.

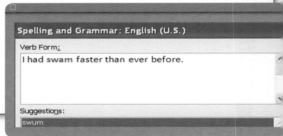

Spelling and Grammar: English (U.S.)

Verb Form:

I had swam faster than ever before.

Suggestions:

swum

Copyright 2011, Microsoft Corporation. All Rights Reserved.

Close-Up   *LIE/LAY* AND *SIT/SET*

Lie means "to recline" and does not take an object ("He likes to *lie* on the floor"); *lay* means "to place" or "to put" and does take an object ("He wants to *lay* a rug on the floor").

Base Form	Past Tense Form	Past Participle
lie	lay	lain
lay	laid	laid

Sit means "to assume a seated position" and does not take an object ("She wants to *sit* on the table"); *set* means "to place" or "to put" and usually takes an object ("She wants to *set* a vase on the table").

Base Form	Past Tense Form	Past Participle
sit	sat	sat
set	set	set

Understanding Tense

<u>Tense</u> is the form a verb takes to indicate when an action occurred or when a condition existed.

ESL
58a2

English Verb Tenses

Simple Tenses
Present (I *finish*, she or he *finishes*)
Past (I *finished*)
Future (I *will finish*)

Perfect Tenses
Present perfect (I *have finished*, she or he *has finished*)
Past perfect (I *had finished*)
Future perfect (I *will have finished*)

Progressive Tenses
Present progressive (I *am finishing*, she or he *is finishing*)
Past progressive (I *was finishing*)
Future progressive (I *will be finishing*)
Present perfect progressive (I *have been finishing*)
Past perfect progressive (I *had been finishing*)
Future perfect progressive (I *will have been finishing*)

 Using the Simple Tenses

The **simple tenses** include *present*, *past*, and *future*.

- The **present tense** usually indicates an action that is taking place at the time it is expressed. It can also indicate an action that occurs regularly.

I see your point. (an action taking place when it is expressed)

We wear wool in the winter. (an action that occurs regularly)

Close-Up SPECIAL USES OF THE PRESENT TENSE

The present tense has four special uses.

To Indicate Future Time: The grades arrive next Thursday.

To State a Generally Held Belief: Studying pays off.

To State a Scientific Truth: An object at rest tends to stay at rest.

To Discuss a Literary Work: *Family Installments* tells the story of a Puerto Rican family.

- The **past tense** indicates that an action has already taken place.

  John Glenn orbited the earth three times on February 20, 1962. (an action completed in the past)

  As a young man, Mark Twain traveled through the Southwest. (an action that occurred once or many times in the past but did not extend into the present)

- The **future tense** indicates that an action will or is likely to take place.

  Halley's Comet will reappear in 2061. (a future action that will definitely occur)

  The increase in oil prices will probably continue. (a future action that is likely to occur)

2 Using the Perfect Tenses

The **perfect tenses** designate actions that were or will be completed before other actions or conditions. The perfect tenses are formed with the appropriate tense form of the auxiliary verb *have* plus the past participle.

- The **present perfect** tense can indicate two types of continuing action beginning in the past.

  Dr. Kim has finished studying the effects of BHA on rats. (an action that began in the past and is finished at the present time)

  My mother has invested her money wisely. (an action that began in the past and extends into the present)

- The **past perfect** tense indicates an action occurring before a certain time in the past.

  By 1946, engineers <u>had built</u> the first electronic digital computer.

- The **future perfect** tense indicates that an action will be finished by a certain future time.

  By Tuesday, the transit authority <u>will have run out</u> of money.

Close-Up   *COULD HAVE, SHOULD HAVE,* AND *WOULD HAVE*

Do not use the preposition *of* after *would, should, could,* and *might.* Use the auxiliary verb *have* after these words.

      have
I should ̭of̭ left for class earlier.

---

❸ Using the Progressive Tenses

The **progressive tenses** express continuing action. They are formed with the appropriate tense of the verb *be* plus the present participle.

- The **present progressive** tense indicates that something is happening at the time it is expressed.

  The volcano <u>is erupting</u>, and lava <u>is flowing</u> toward the town.

- The **past progressive** tense indicates two kinds of past action.

  Roderick Usher's actions <u>were becoming</u> increasingly bizarre. (a continuing action in the past)

  The French revolutionary Marat was stabbed to death while he <u>was bathing</u>. (an action occurring at the same time in the past as another action)

- The **future progressive** tense indicates a continuing action in the future.

  The treasury secretary <u>will be monitoring</u> the money supply regularly.

- The **present perfect progressive** tense indicates action continuing from the past into the present and possibly into the future.

  Rescuers <u>have been working</u> around the clock.

- The **past perfect progressive** tense indicates that a past action went on until another one occurred.

Before President Kennedy was assassinated, he <u>had been working</u> on civil rights legislation.

- The **future perfect progressive** tense indicates that an action will continue until a certain future time.

By eleven o'clock we <u>will have been driving</u> for seven hours.

4 Using Verb Tenses in a Sentence

Within a sentence, you may need to use different tenses to indicate that actions are taking place at different times. By choosing tenses that accurately express these times, you enable readers to follow the sequence of actions.

- *When a **verb** appears in a dependent clause, its tense depends on the tense of the main verb in the independent clause.* When the main verb in the independent clause is in the past tense, the verb in the dependent clause is usually in the past or past perfect tense. When the main verb in the independent clause is in the past perfect tense, the verb in the dependent clause is usually in the past tense. (When the main verb in the independent clause is in any tense except the past or past perfect, the verb in the dependent clause may be in any tense needed for meaning.)

Main Verb	Verb in Dependent Clause
George Hepplewhite <u>was</u> (past) an English cabinetmaker	who <u>designed</u> (past) distinctive chair backs.
The battle <u>had ended</u> (past perfect)	by the time reinforcements <u>arrived</u>. (past)

- *When an **infinitive** appears in a verbal phrase, the tense it expresses depends on the tense of the sentence's main verb.* The ***present infinitive*** (the *to* form of the verb) indicates an action happening at the same time as or later than the main verb. The ***perfect infinitive*** (*to have* plus the past participle) indicates action happening earlier than the main verb.

Main Verb	Infinitive
I <u>went</u>	<u>to see</u> the Rangers play last week. (Present infinitive indicates that the going and seeing occurred at the same time.)
I <u>want</u>	<u>to see</u> the Rangers play tomorrow. (Present infinitive indicates that wanting occurs in the present and seeing will occur in the future.)
I would <u>like</u>	<u>to have seen</u> the Rangers play. (Perfect infinitive indicates that liking occurs in the present and seeing would have occurred in the past.)

- *When a **participle** appears in a verbal phrase, its tense depends on the tense of the sentence's main verb.* The *present participle* indicates action happening at the same time as the action of the main verb. The *past participle* or the *present perfect participle* indicates action occurring before the action of the main verb.

Participle	Main Verb
Addressing the 1896 Democratic Convention,	William Jennings Bryan <u>delivered</u> his Cross of Gold speech. (The addressing and the delivery occurred at the same time.)
Having written her term paper,	Camille <u>studied</u> for her history final. (The writing occurred before the studying.)

37c Understanding Mood

Mood is the form a verb takes to indicate whether a writer is making a statement or asking a question (*indicative mood*), giving a command (*imperative mood*), or expressing a wish or a contrary-to-fact statement (*subjunctive mood*).

- The **indicative** mood expresses an opinion, states a fact, or asks a question: *Jackie Robinson <u>had</u> a great impact on professional baseball.* (The indicative is the mood used in most English sentences.)

- The **imperative** mood is used in commands and direct requests. Usually, the imperative includes only the base form of the verb without a subject: <u>Use</u> *a dictionary.*

- The **subjunctive** mood was common in the past, but it now is used less and less often, and usually only in formal contexts.

1 Forming the Subjunctive Mood

The **present subjunctive** uses the base form of the verb, regardless of the subject. The **past subjunctive** has the same form as the past tense of the verb. (The auxiliary verb *be*, however, takes the form *were* regardless of the number or person of the subject.)

Dr. Gorman suggested that I <u>study</u> the Cambrian Period. (present subjunctive)

I wish I <u>were</u> going to Europe. (past subjunctive)

2 Using the Subjunctive Mood

The present subjunctive is used in *that* clauses after words such as *ask, suggest, require, recommend,* and *demand.*

The report recommended that juveniles <u>be</u> given mandatory counseling.

Captain Ahab insisted that his crew <u>hunt</u> the white whale.

The past subjunctive is used in **conditional statements** (statements beginning with *if* that are contrary to fact, including statements that express a wish).

If John <u>were</u> here, he could see Marsha. (John is not here.)

The father acted as if he <u>were</u> having the baby. (The father couldn't be having the baby.)

I wish I <u>were</u> more organized. (expresses a wish)

Note: In many situations, the subjunctive mood can sound stiff or formal. Alternative expressions can often eliminate the need for subjunctive constructions.

The group asked ~~that~~ the city council ^{to} ban smoking in public places.

37d Understanding Voice

Voice is the form a verb takes to indicate whether its subject acts or is acted upon.

When the subject of a verb does something—that is, acts—the verb is in the **active voice.** When the subject of a verb receives the action—that is, is acted upon—the verb is in the **passive voice.**

Active Voice: Hart Crane <u>wrote</u> *The Bridge.*

Passive Voice: *The Bridge* <u>was written</u> by Hart Crane.

Close-Up VOICE

Whenever possible, use active constructions in your college writing. Because the active voice emphasizes the person or thing performing an action, it is usually briefer, clearer, and more emphatic than the passive voice.

Some situations, however, require use of the passive voice. For example, you should use passive constructions when the actor is unknown or unimportant or when the recipient of an action should logically receive the emphasis.

DDT <u>was found</u> in soil samples. (Passive voice emphasizes the discovery of DDT; who found it is not important.)

Grits <u>are eaten</u> throughout the South. (Passive voice emphasizes the fact that grits are eaten, not who eats them.)

1 Changing Verbs from Passive to Active Voice

You can change a verb from passive to active voice by making the subject of the passive verb the object of the active verb. The person or thing performing the action then becomes the subject of the new sentence.

Passive: The novel *Frankenstein* <u>was written</u> by Mary Shelley.

Active: Mary Shelley <u>wrote</u> the novel *Frankenstein*.

If a passive verb has no object, you must supply one that will become the subject of the active verb.

Passive: Baby elephants are taught to avoid humans. (By whom are baby elephants taught?)

Active: <u>Adult elephants</u> teach baby elephants to avoid humans.

2 Changing Verbs from Active to Passive Voice

You can change a verb from active to passive voice by making the object of the active verb the subject of the passive verb. The person or thing performing the action then becomes the object of the passive verb.

Active: Sir James Murray <u>compiled</u> *The Oxford English Dictionary.*

Passive: *The Oxford English Dictionary* <u>was compiled</u> by Sir James Murray.

Remember that an active verb must have an object or else it cannot be put into the passive voice. If an active verb has no object, supply one. This object will become the subject of the passive sentence.

Active: Jacques Cousteau invented.
Cousteau invented __?__ .

Passive: __?__ was invented by Jacques Cousteau.
The scuba was invented by Jacques Cousteau.

CHAPTER 38

Using Nouns and Pronouns

38a Understanding Case

Case is the form a noun or pronoun takes to indicate its function in a sentence. **Nouns** change form only in the possessive case: the *cat's* eyes, *Molly's* book. **Pronouns**, however, have three cases: *subjective, objective,* and *possessive.*

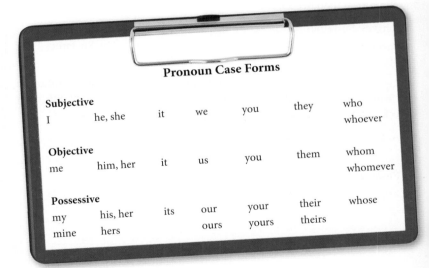

Pronoun Case Forms

Subjective

I   he, she   it   we   you   they   who
whoever

Objective

me   him, her   it   us   you   them   whom
whomever

Possessive

my   his, her   its   our   your   their   whose
mine   hers   ours   yours   theirs

1 Subjective Case

A pronoun takes the **subjective case** in the following situations.

Subject of a Verb: I bought a new cell phone.

Subject Complement: It was <u>he</u> who volunteered at the shelter.

2 Objective Case

A pronoun takes the **objective case** in the following situations.

Direct Object: The boss asked Adam and <u>me</u> to work late.

Indirect Object: The plumber's bill gave <u>them</u> quite a shock.

Object of a Preposition: Between <u>us</u>, we own ten shares of stock.

Close-Up   *I* VERSUS *ME*

I is not always more appropriate than *me*. In the following example, *me* is correct.

Just between you and <u>me</u> [not *I*], I think we're going to have a quiz.
(*Me* is the object of the preposition *between*.)

---

3 Possessive Case

A pronoun takes the **possessive case** when it indicates ownership (*our* car, *your* book). The possessive case is also used before a **gerund.**

Napoleon gave <u>his</u> approval to <u>their</u> ruling Naples. (*His* indicates ownership; *ruling* is a gerund.)

38b   Determining Pronoun Case in Special Situations

1 In Comparisons with *Than* or *As*

When a comparison ends with a pronoun, the pronoun's function in the sentence determines your choice of pronoun case. If the pronoun functions as a subject, use the subjective case; if it functions as an object, use the objective case. You can determine the function of the pronoun by completing the comparison.

Darcy likes John more than <u>I</u>. (. . . *more than <u>I</u> like John:* <u>I</u> is the subject.)

Darcy likes John more than <u>me</u>. (. . . *more than she likes <u>me</u>:* <u>me</u> is the object.)

2 With *Who* and *Whom*

The case of the pronouns *who* and *whom* depends on their function *within their own clause.* When a pronoun serves as the subject of its clause, use *who* or *whoever*; when it functions as an object, use *whom* or *whomever*.

The Salvation Army gives food and shelter to <u>whoever</u> is in need. (*Whoever* is the subject of the dependent clause *whoever is in need.*)

I wonder <u>whom</u> jazz musician Miles Davis influenced. (*Whom* is the object of *influenced* in the dependent clause *whom jazz musician Miles Davis influenced.*)

Close-Up PRONOUN CASE IN QUESTIONS

To determine whether to use the subjective case (*who*) or the objective case (*whom*) in a question, use a personal pronoun to answer the question. If the pronoun in your answer is the subject, use *who;* if the pronoun is the object, use *whom*.

<u>Who</u> wrote *The Age of Innocence*? <u>She</u> wrote it. (subject)

<u>Whom</u> do you support for mayor? I support <u>her</u>. (object)

---

❸ With Appositives

ESL
58c4

An **appositive** is a noun or noun phrase that identifies or renames an adjacent noun or pronoun. The case of a pronoun in an appositive depends on the function of the word the appositive identifies or renames.

Two Motown recording artists, <u>he</u> and Smokey Robinson, had contracts with Motown Records. (*Artists* is the subject of the sentence, so the pronoun in the appositive *he and Smokey Robinson* takes the subjective case.)

We heard two Motown recording artists, Smokey Robinson and <u>him</u>. (*Artists* is the object of the verb *heard*, so the pronoun in the appositive *Smokey Robinson and him* takes the objective case.)

❹ With *We* and *Us* before a Noun

When a first-person plural pronoun directly precedes a noun, the case of the pronoun depends on how the noun functions in the sentence.

<u>We</u> women must stick together. (*Women* is the subject of the sentence, so the pronoun *we* must be in the subjective case.)

Teachers make learning easy for <u>us</u> students. (*Students* is the object of the preposition *for*, so the pronoun *us* must be in the objective case.)

38c Revising Pronoun Reference Errors

An **antecedent** is the word or word group to which a pronoun refers. The connection between a pronoun and its antecedent should always be clear. If the **pronoun reference** is not clear, revise the sentence.

ESL
58c1

1 Ambiguous Antecedent

Sometimes it is not clear to which antecedent a pronoun—for example, *this, that, which,* or *it*—refers. In such cases, eliminate the ambiguity by substituting a noun for the pronoun.

The accountant took out his calculator and added up the list of
numbers. Then, he put ~~it~~ *the calculator* into his briefcase. (The pronoun *it* can refer either to *calculator* or to *list of numbers.*)

2 Remote Antecedent

If a pronoun is far from its antecedent, readers will have difficulty making a connection between them. To eliminate this problem, replace the pronoun with a noun.

During the mid-1800s, many Czechs began to immigrate to America.

By 1860, about 23,000 had left their country; by 1900, 13,000 Czechs
were coming to ~~its~~ *America's* shores each year.

3 Nonexistent Antecedent

Sometimes a pronoun—for example, *this*—refers to an antecedent that does not exist. In such cases, add the missing antecedent.

Some one-celled organisms contain chlorophyll yet are considered
animals. This ~~*paradox*~~ illustrates the difficulty of classifying single-celled

organisms. (Exactly what does *this* refer to?)

Note: Expressions such as "*It* says in the paper" and "*He* said on the news," which refer to unidentified antecedents, are not acceptable in college writing. When you revise, substitute an appropriate noun for the unclear pronoun: "The <u>article</u> in the paper says . . ." and "In his commentary, <u>Keith Olberman</u> observes. . . ."

❓ **④** *Who,* *Which,* and *That*

In general, *who* refers to people or to animals that have names. *Which* and *that* refer to things or to unnamed animals. When referring to an antecedent, be sure to choose the appropriate pronoun (*who, which,* or *that*).

> David Henry Hwang, <u>who</u> wrote the Tony Award-winning play *M. Butterfly*, also wrote *Chinglish*.

> The spotted owl, <u>which</u> lives in old-growth forests, is in danger of extinction.

> Houses <u>that</u> are built today are usually more energy efficient than those built years ago.

Never use *that* to refer to a person.

> who
> The man ~~that~~ holds the world record for eating hot dogs is my neighbor.
>   ^

Note: Be sure to use *which* in <u>**nonrestrictive clauses**</u>, which are always set off with commas, and to use *that* in <u>**restrictive clauses**</u>, which are not set off with commas.

See 46d1

C H A P T E R **39**

Using Adjectives and Adverbs

❓ **Adjectives** modify nouns and pronouns. **Adverbs** modify verbs, adjectives, or other adverbs—or entire phrases, clauses, or sentences.

The function of a word, not its form, determines whether it is an adjective or an adverb. Although many adverbs (such as *immediately* and *hopelessly*) end in *-ly*, others (such as *almost* and *very*) do not. Moreover, some words that end in *-ly* (such as *lively*) are adjectives.

ESL TIP

For information on correct placement of adjectives and adverbs in a sentence, **see 58d1**. For information on correct order of adjectives in a series, **see 58d2**.

39a Using Adjectives

Be sure to use an **adjective,** not an adverb, as a subject complement. A **subject complement** is a word that follows a linking verb and modifies the sentence's subject, not its verb. A **linking verb** does not show physical or emotional action. *Seem, appear, believe, become, grow, turn, remain, prove, look, sound, smell, taste, feel,* and the forms of the verb *be* are or can be used as linking verbs.

> Michelle seemed <u>brave</u>. (*Seemed* shows no action and is therefore a linking verb. Because *brave* is a subject complement that modifies the noun *Michelle*, it takes the adjective form.)

> Michelle smiled <u>bravely</u>. (*Smiled* shows action, so it is not a linking verb. *Bravely* modifies *smiled*, so it takes the adverb form.)

Note: Sometimes the same verb can function as either a linking verb or an action verb: *He remained <u>stubborn</u>.* (He was still stubborn.) *He remained <u>stubbornly</u>.* (He remained, in a stubborn manner.)

39b Using Adverbs

Be sure to use an **adverb,** not an adjective, to modify verbs, adjectives, or other adverbs—or entire phrases, clauses, or sentences.

Most students did ~~great~~ on the midterm. *[very well]*

My friends dress a lot more conservative than I do. *[ly]*

Close-Up USING ADJECTIVES AND ADVERBS

In informal speech, adjective forms such as *good, bad, sure, real, slow, quick,* and *loud* are often used to modify verbs, adjectives, and adverbs. Avoid these informal modifiers in college writing.

The program ran ~~real good~~ the first time we tried it, but the new *[really well]* system performed ~~bad~~. *[badly]*

39c Using Comparative and Superlative Forms

Most adjectives and adverbs have **comparative** and **superlative** forms.

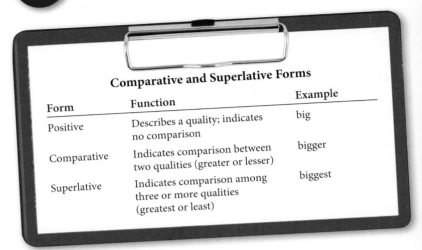

Comparative and Superlative Forms

Form	Function	Example
Positive	Describes a quality; indicates no comparison	big
Comparative	Indicates comparison between two qualities (greater or lesser)	bigger
Superlative	Indicates comparison among three or more qualities (greatest or least)	biggest

1 Regular Comparative Forms

To form the comparative, all one-syllable adjectives and many two-syllable adjectives (particularly those that end in *-y*, *-ly*, *-le*, *-er*, and *-ow*) add *-er*: slow<u>er</u>, funn<u>ier</u>. (Note that a final *y* becomes *i* before *-er* is added.)

Other two-syllable adjectives and all long adjectives form the comparative with *more*: <u>more</u> famous, <u>more</u> incredible.

Adverbs ending in *-ly* also form the comparative with *more*: <u>more</u> slowly. Other adverbs use the *-er* ending to form the comparative: soon<u>er</u>.

All adjectives and adverbs form the comparative with *less*: <u>less</u> lovely, <u>less</u> slowly.

2 Regular Superlative Forms

Adjectives that form the comparative with *-er* add *-est* to form the superlative: nic<u>est</u>, funni<u>est</u>. Adjectives that indicate the comparative with *more* use *most* to indicate the superlative: <u>most</u> famous, <u>most</u> challenging.

The majority of adverbs use *most* to indicate the superlative: <u>most</u> quickly. Others use the *-est* ending: soon<u>est</u>.

All adjectives and adverbs form the superlative with *least*: <u>least</u> interesting, <u>least</u> willingly.

Close-Up   USING COMPARATIVES AND SUPERLATIVES

- Never use both *more* and *-er* to form the comparative or both *most* and *-est* to form the superlative.

Nothing could have been ~~more~~ easier.

Jack is the ~~most~~ meanest person in town.

- Never use the superlative when comparing only two things.

  older
  Stacy is the ~~oldest~~ of the two sisters.

- Never use the comparative when comparing more than two things.

  earliest
  We chose the ~~earlier~~ of the four appointments.

3 Irregular Comparatives and Superlatives

Some adjectives and adverbs have irregular comparative and superlative forms.

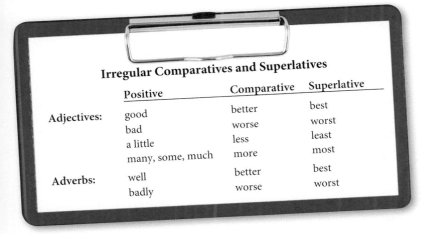

Irregular Comparatives and Superlatives

	Positive	Comparative	Superlative
Adjectives:	good	better	best
	bad	worse	worst
	a little	less	least
	many, some, much	more	most
Adverbs:	well	better	best
	badly	worse	worst

39d Avoiding Illogical Comparatives and Superlatives

Many adjectives—for example, _perfect, unique, excellent, impossible, parallel, empty, fatal_ and _dead_—are **absolutes** and therefore have no comparative or superlative forms.

_an_
I read ~~the most~~ excellent story.

_a_
I saw ~~the most~~ unique vase in the museum.

These words can, however, be modified by words that suggest approaching the absolute state—*nearly* or *almost,* for example.

He revised until his draft was <u>almost perfect</u>.

Note: Some adverbs, particularly those indicating time, place, and degree (*almost, very, here, immediately*), do not have comparative or superlative forms.

PART 11

Improving Sentence Style

Improving Sentence Style

❓ Frequently Asked Questions

CHAPTER 40

Writing Varied Sentences

Varied sentences can make your writing livelier and more interesting. This strategy can also help you emphasize the most important ideas in your sentences.

40a Using Compound and Complex Sentences

Paragraphs that mix simple, compound, and complex sentences are more varied—and therefore more interesting—than those that do not.

1 Compound Sentences

A **compound sentence** consists of two or more independent clauses joined with *coordinating conjunctions, transitional words and phrases, correlative conjunctions, semicolons,* or *colons.*

Coordinating Conjunctions

The pianist made some mistakes, <u>but</u> the concert was a success.

 Use a comma before a coordinating conjunction—*and, or, nor, but, for, so,* and *yet*—that joins two **independent clauses**.

See B3.2

Transitional Words and Phrases

Exercise can help lower blood pressure; <u>however</u>, those with high blood pressure should still limit salt intake.

The saxophone does not belong to the brass family; <u>in fact</u>, it is a member of the woodwind family.

 Use a semicolon—not a comma—before a transitional word or phrase that joins two independent clauses. Frequently used **transitional words and phrases** include conjunctive adverbs like *consequently, finally, still,* and *thus* as well as expressions like *for example, in fact,* and *for instance.*

See 7b2

Correlative Conjunctions

Diana <u>not only</u> passed the exam, <u>but</u> she <u>also</u> received the highest grade in the class.

<u>Either</u> he left his coat in his locker, <u>or</u> he left it on the bus.

Semicolons

Alaska is the largest state; Rhode Island is the smallest.

Colons

He got his orders: he was to leave for Afghanistan on Sunday.

Close-Up   USING COMPOUND SENTENCES

When you join independent clauses to create compound sentences, you help readers to see the relationships between your ideas. Compound sentences can indicate the following relationships:

- Addition (*and, in addition, not only . . . but also*)
- Contrast (*but, however*)
- Causal relationships (*so, therefore, consequently*)
- Alternatives (*or, either . . . or*)

---

② Complex Sentences

A **complex sentence** consists of one independent clause and at least one dependent clause.

A **dependent clause** cannot stand alone; it must be combined with an independent clause to form a sentence. In a complex sentence, a **subordinating conjunction** or **relative pronoun** links the independent and dependent clauses and indicates the relationship between them.

> dependent clause   independent clause
> [<u>After</u> the town was evacuated], [the hurricane began].

> independent clause   dependent clause
> [Officials watched the storm] [<u>that</u> threatened the town].

Sometimes a dependent clause may be embedded within an independent clause.

> dependent clause
> Town officials, [<u>who</u> were very concerned], watched the storm.

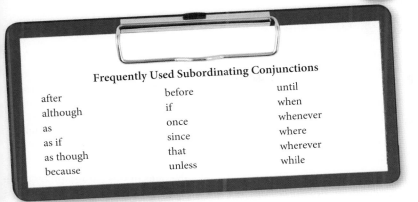

Frequently Used Subordinating Conjunctions

after	before	until
although	if	when
as	once	whenever
as if	since	where
as though	that	wherever
because	unless	while

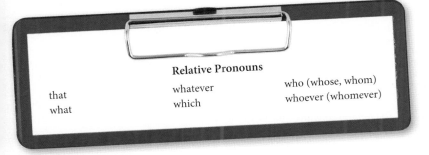

Relative Pronouns

that	whatever	who (whose, whom)
what	which	whoever (whomever)

Close-Up   USING COMPLEX SENTENCES

When you join clauses to create complex sentences, you help readers to see the relationships between your ideas. Complex sentences can indicate the following relationships:

- Time relationships (*before, after, until, when, since*)
- Contrast (*however, although*)
- Causal relationships (*therefore, because, so that*)
- Conditional relationships (*if, unless*)
- Location (*where, wherever*)
- Identity (*who, which, that*)

40b Combining Choppy Simple Sentences

Strings of short simple sentences can be tedious—and sometimes hard to follow, as the paragraph below illustrates.

> John Peter Zenger was a newspaper editor. He waged and won an important battle for freedom of the press in America. He criticized the policies of the British governor. He was charged with criminal libel as a result. Zenger's lawyers were disbarred by the governor. Andrew Hamilton defended him. Hamilton convinced the jury that Zenger's criticisms were true. Therefore, the statements were not libelous.

You can revise choppy sentences like the ones in this paragraph by using *coordination*, *subordination*, or *embedding* to combine them with adjacent sentences.

1 Using Coordination

Coordination pairs similar elements—words, phrases, or clauses—giving equal weight to each.

Two choppy sentences linked with *and*, creating a compound sentence
> John Peter Zenger was a newspaper editor. He waged and won an important battle for freedom of the press in America. He criticized the policies of the British governor, and he was charged with criminal libel as a result. Zenger's lawyers were disbarred by the governor. Andrew Hamilton defended him. Hamilton convinced the jury that Zenger's criticisms were true. Therefore, the statements were not libelous.

2 Using Subordination

Subordination places the more important idea in an independent clause and the less important idea in a dependent clause.

Complex sentence

Complex sentence
> John Peter Zenger was a newspaper editor who waged and won an important battle for freedom of the press in America. He criticized the policies of the British governor, and he was charged with criminal libel as a result. When Zenger's lawyers were disbarred by the governor, Andrew Hamilton defended him. Hamilton convinced the jury that Zenger's criticisms were true. Therefore, the statements were not libelous.

3 Using Embedding

Embedding is the working of additional words and phrases into sentences.

The sentence *Hamilton convinced the jury.* . . . becomes the phrase *convincing the jury*
> John Peter Zenger was a newspaper editor who waged and won an important battle for freedom of the press in America. He criticized the policies of the British governor, and he was charged with criminal libel as a result. When Zenger's lawyers were disbarred by the governor, Andrew Hamilton defended him, convincing the jury that Zenger's criticisms were true. Therefore, the statements were not libelous.

This final revision of the original paragraph's choppy sentences is interesting and readable because it is composed of varied and logically linked sentences. (The short, simple sentence at the end has been retained for emphasis.)

40c Breaking Up Strings of Compound Sentences

When you write, try to avoid creating an unbroken series of compound sentences. A string of compound sentences can be extremely monotonous; moreover, if you connect clauses only with coordinating conjunctions, you may find it difficult to indicate exactly how ideas are related and which idea is most important.

All Compound Sentences: A volcano that is erupting is considered *active,* but one that may erupt is designated *dormant,* and one that has not erupted for a long time is called *extinct.* Most active volcanoes are located in "The Ring of Fire," a belt that circles the Pacific Ocean, and they can be extremely destructive. Italy's Vesuvius erupted in AD 79, and it destroyed the town of Pompeii. In 1883, Krakatoa, located between the Indonesian islands of Java and Sumatra, erupted, and it caused a tidal wave, and more than 36,000 people were killed. Martinique's Mont Pelée erupted in 1902, and its hot gas and ash killed 30,000 people, and this completely wiped out the town of St. Pierre.

Varied Sentences: A volcano that is erupting is considered *active.* (simple sentence) One that may erupt is designated *dormant,* and one that has not erupted for a long time is called *extinct.* (compound sentence) Most active volcanoes are located in "The Ring of Fire," a belt that circles the Pacific Ocean. (simple sentence with modifier) Active volcanoes can be extremely destructive. (simple sentence) Erupting in AD 79, Italy's Vesuvius destroyed the town of Pompeii. (simple sentence with modifier) When Krakatoa, located between the Indonesian islands of Java and Sumatra, erupted in 1883, it caused a tidal wave that killed 36,000 people. (complex sentence with modifier) The eruption of Martinique's Mont Pelée in 1902 produced hot gas and ash that killed 30,000 people, completely wiping out the town of St. Pierre. (complex sentence with modifier)

40d Varying Sentence Openings

 Rather than beginning every sentence with the subject (*I* or *It*, for example), try beginning with a modifying *word, phrase,* or *clause.*

Words

<u>Proud</u> and <u>relieved</u>, Henry's parents watched him receive his diploma. (adjectives)

<u>Hungrily</u>, he devoured his lunch. (adverb)

Phrases

<u>For better or for worse</u>, credit cards are now widely available to college students. (prepositional phrase)

<u>Located on the west coast of Great Britain</u>, Wales is part of the United Kingdom. (participial phrase)

<u>The scope of his artistic interests widening</u>, Picasso designed ballet sets and illustrated books. (absolute phrase)

Clauses

<u>After Woodrow Wilson was incapacitated by a stroke</u>, his wife Edith unofficially performed many presidential duties. (adverb clause)

GRAMMAR CHECKER Coordinating Conjunctions and Fragments

If you begin a sentence with a coordinating conjunction, use your grammar checker to make sure that it is a complete sentence and not a fragment. If the grammar checker identifies a word group as a fragment, you will need to revise it, following the guidelines in **32b**.

> **Spelling and Grammar: English (U.S.)**
>
> Fragment:
>
> **And then the speaker.**
>
> Suggestions:
>
> Fragment (consider revising)

Copyright 2011, Microsoft Corporation. All Rights Reserved.

Writing Emphatic Sentences

In speaking, we emphasize certain ideas and deemphasize others with into-
nation and gestures; in writing, we convey **emphasis**—the relative importance of ideas—through the selection and arrangement of words.

41a Conveying Emphasis through Word Order

Because readers tend to focus on the beginning and end of a sentence, you
should place the most important information there.

1 Beginning with Important Ideas

Placing key ideas at the beginning of a sentence stresses their importance.
The unedited version of the following sentence emphasizes the study, not
those who conducted it or those who participated in it. Editing shifts this
focus and puts the emphasis on the researcher, not on the study.

~~In a landmark study of alcoholism,~~ Dr. George Vaillant of Harvard
, in a landmark study of alcoholism,
followed two hundred Harvard graduates and four hundred inner-

city, working-class men from the Boston area.

Close-Up *THERE IS* AND *THERE ARE*

Beginning a sentence with an empty phrase such as *there is* or *there are*
generally weakens the sentence.

MIT places
~~There is~~ heavy emphasis ~~placed~~ on the development of computational

skills *at MIT.*

Situations that call for straightforward presentations—reports, memos,
technical papers, business correspondence, and the like—require sentences
that present vital information first and qualifiers later.

451

Treating cancer with interferon has been the subject of a good deal of **research.** (emphasizes the treatment, not the research)

Dividends will be paid if the stockholders agree. (emphasizes the dividends, not the stockholders)

2 Ending with Important Ideas

Placing key elements at the end of a sentence is another way to convey their importance.

Using a Colon or a Dash   A colon or a dash can emphasize an important word or phrase by isolating it at the end of a sentence.

Beth had always dreamed of owning one special car : a 1953 Corvette.

The elderly need a good deal of special attention—but they do not always get that attention.

Close-Up   PLACING TRANSITIONAL WORDS AND PHRASES

When they are placed at the end of a sentence, conjunctive adverbs or other transitional expressions lose their power to indicate the relationship between ideas. Placed earlier in the sentence, transitional words and phrases can link ideas and add emphasis.

however,
Smokers do have rights;ˬthey should not try to impose their habit on

others ˬ however.

Using Climactic Word Order   **Climactic word order,** the arrangement of a series of items from the least to the most important, places emphasis on the last item in the series.

Binge drinking can lead to vandalism, car accidents, and even death. (*Death* is the most serious consequence.)

3 Experimenting with Word Order

ESL 58f In English sentences, the most common **word order** is subject-verb-object (or subject-verb-complement). When you depart from this expected word order, you call attention to the word, phrase, or clause you have relocated.

More modest and less inventive than Turner's paintings are John Constable's landscapes.

Here the writer calls special attention to the modifying phrase *more modest and less inventive than Turner's paintings* by inverting word order, placing the complement and the verb before the subject (*John Constable's landscapes*).

41b Conveying Emphasis through Sentence Structure

As you write, try to construct sentences that emphasize more important ideas and deemphasize less important ones.

1 Using Cumulative Sentences

A **cumulative sentence** begins with an independent clause, followed by the additional words, phrases, or clauses that expand or develop it.

> She holds me in strong arms, arms that have chopped cotton, dismembered trees, scattered corn for chickens, cradled infants, shaken the daylights out of half-grown upstart teenagers. (Rebecca Hill, *Blue Rise*)

Because it presents its main idea first, a cumulative sentence tends to be clear and straightforward. (Most English sentences are cumulative.)

2 Using Periodic Sentences

A periodic sentence moves from supporting details, expressed in modifying phrases and dependent clauses, to the sentence's key idea, which is placed in the independent clause at the end of the sentence.

> Unlike World Wars I and II, which ended decisively with the unconditional surrender of US enemies, the war in Vietnam did not have a clear-cut resolution.

 In some periodic sentences, the modifying phrase or dependent clause comes between the subject and predicate: *Columbus, after several discouraging and unsuccessful voyages, finally reached America.*

41c Conveying Emphasis through Parallelism and Balance

See
43a

By reinforcing the similarity between grammatical elements, **parallelism** can help you emphasize information.

> We seek an individual <u>who is</u> a self-starter, <u>who owns</u> a car, and <u>who is</u> willing to work evenings. (classified advertisement)

> <u>Do not pass</u> go; <u>do not collect</u> $200. (instructions)

> The Faust legend is central <u>in</u> Benét's *The Devil and Daniel Webster,* <u>in</u> Goethe's *Faust,* and <u>in</u> Marlowe's *Dr. Faustus.* (exam answer)

A **balanced sentence** is neatly divided between two parallel structures—for example, two independent clauses in a compound sentence. The symmetrical structure of a balanced sentence adds emphasis by highlighting similarities or differences between the ideas in the two clauses.

> In the 1950s, the electronic miracle was the television, but in the 1980s, the electronic miracle was the computer.

> Alive, the elephant was worth at least a hundred pounds; dead, he would only be worth the value of his tusks, five pounds, possibly. (George Orwell, "Shooting an Elephant")

41d Conveying Emphasis through Repetition

See 42b

<u>Unnecessary repetition</u> makes sentences dull and monotonous as well as wordy.

> He had a good arm and <u>also</u> could field well, and he was <u>also</u> a fast runner.

Effective repetition, however, can emphasize key words or ideas.

> They decided <u>to begin</u> again: <u>to begin</u> hoping, <u>to begin</u> trying to change, <u>to begin</u> working toward a goal.

> During those years when I was just learning to speak, my mother and father addressed me only <u>in Spanish; in Spanish</u> I learned to reply. (Richard Rodriguez, *Aria: Memoir of a Bilingual Childhood*)

Aria: Memoir of a Bilingual Childhood by Richard Rodriguez. Copyright © 1980 by Richard Rodriguez. Originally appeared in *The American Scholar.* Reprinted by permission of Georges Borchardt, Inc., on behalf of the author.

41e Conveying Emphasis through Active Voice

See 37d

ESL 58a6

The <u>active voice</u> is generally more emphatic than the <u>passive voice</u>.

Passive: The prediction that oil prices will rise is being made by economists.

Active: Economists are predicting that oil prices will rise.

Notice that the passive voice sentence above does not draw readers' attention to who is performing the action. In a passive voice sentence, the subject is the recipient of the action, so the actor fades into the background (*by economists*)—or may even be omitted entirely (*the prediction . . . is being made*). In contrast, active voice places the emphasis where it belongs: on the actor or actors (*Economists*).

Sometimes, of course, you *want* to stress the action rather than the actor; if this is the case, use the passive voice.

Passive: The West was explored by Lewis and Clark. (stresses the exploration of the West, not who explored it)

Active: Lewis and Clark explored the West. (stresses the contribution of the explorers)

GRAMMAR CHECKER   Avoiding Passive Voice

Your grammar checker will highlight passive voice constructions in your writing and offer revision suggestions.

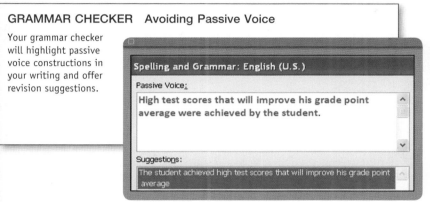

Spelling and Grammar: English (U.S.)

Passive Voice:

High test scores that will improve his grade point average were achieved by the student.

Suggestions:

The student achieved high test scores that will improve his grade point average

Note: Passive voice is also used when the identity of the person performing the action is irrelevant or unknown (*The course was canceled*). For this reason, the passive voice is frequently used in scientific and technical writing: *The beaker was filled with a saline solution.*

GRAMMAR CHECKER   Using Passive Voice

Sometimes the clearest way to express your ideas is by using passive verbs. Here, the use of passive voice in the example sentence is necessary for clarity. The grammar checker's suggestion is awkward—and incorrect.

Spelling and Grammar: English (U.S.)

Passive Voice:

The spreadsheet is sorted by number.

Suggestions:

Number sorts the spreadsheet

Writing Concise Sentences

A sentence is not concise simply because it is short; a concise sentence contains only the words necessary to make its point.

Close-Up   TEXT MESSAGES

If you send texts, which are limited to 140 characters, you have already learned how to be concise. In text messages, you omit articles and other nonessential words, and you use nonstandard spellings (*nite*) and shorthand (*ru home?*). This kind of language is not acceptable in college writing. In college writing, you need to find other strategies (such as those discussed in this chapter) to make your writing concise.

42a   Eliminating Wordiness

A good way to find out which words are essential in a sentence is to underline the key words. Look carefully at the remaining words so you can see which are unnecessary and then eliminate wordiness by deleting them.

> It seems to me that it does not make sense to allow any <u>bail</u> to be <u>granted</u> to <u>anyone</u> who has ever been <u>convicted</u> of a <u>violent</u> <u>crime</u>.

The underlining shows you immediately that none of the words in the long introductory phrase are essential. The following revision includes just the words necessary to convey the key ideas:

> Bail should not be granted to anyone who has ever been convicted of a violent crime.

Whenever possible, delete nonessential words—*deadwood, utility words,* and *circumlocution*—from your writing.

1 Eliminate Deadwood

The term **deadwood** refers to unnecessary phrases that take up space and add nothing to meaning.

> *Many*
> ~~There were many~~ factors ~~that~~ influenced his decision to become a priest.

> The two plots are ~~both~~ similar in ~~the way~~ that they trace the characters' increasing rage.

> Shoppers ~~who are~~ looking for bargains often go to outlets.

> *an exhausting*
> They played a racquetball game ~~that was exhausting~~.

> *This*
> ~~In this~~ article ~~it~~ discusses lead poisoning.

> *is*
> The most tragic character in *Hamlet* ~~would have to be~~ Ophelia.

Deadwood also includes unnecessary statements of opinion, such as *I feel, it seems to me,* and *in my opinion.*

> *The*
> ~~I think the~~ characters seem undeveloped.

> *This*
> ~~As far as I'm concerned, this~~ course should not be required.

2 Eliminate Utility Words

Utility words act as filler and contribute nothing to the meaning of a sentence. Utility words include nouns with imprecise meanings (*factor, situation, type, aspect,* and so on); adjectives so general that they are almost meaningless (*good, bad, important*); and common adverbs denoting degree (*basically, actually, quite, very, definitely*). Often you can just delete the utility word; if you cannot, replace it with a more precise word.

> *Registration*
> ~~The registration situation~~ was disorganized.

> *an*
> The scholarship ~~basically~~ offered Fran ~~a good~~ opportunity to study Spanish.

> It was ~~actually~~ a worthwhile book, but I didn't ~~really~~ finish it.

3 Avoid Circumlocution

Circumlocution is taking a roundabout way to say something (using ten words when five will do). Instead of complicated constructions, use concise, specific words and phrases that come right to the point.

The
~~It is not unlikely that the~~ trend toward lower consumer spending
probably
will continue.

while
Joe was in the army ~~during the same time that~~ I was in college.

Close-Up   REVISING WORDY PHRASES

A wordy phrase can almost always be replaced by a more concise, more direct term.

Wordy	Concise
at the present time	now
at this point in time	now
for the purpose of	for
due to the fact that	because
on account of the fact that	because
until such time as	until
in the event that	if
by means of	by
in the vicinity of	near
have the ability to	be able to

42b   Eliminating Unnecessary Repetition

See 41d

Repetition can make your writing more **emphatic**, but unnecessary repetition and **redundant** word groups (repeated words or phrases that say the same thing, such as *intentionally choose, reunite together,* and *unanticipated surprise*) can obscure your meaning. Correct unnecessary repetition by using one of the following strategies.

❶ Delete Redundancy

People's clothing ~~attire~~ can reveal a good deal about their personalities.

These stories hint at ~~a suggestion of~~ the supernatural.

GRAMMAR CHECKER Deleting Redundancy

Your grammar checker will highlight some redundant expressions and offer suggestions for revision.

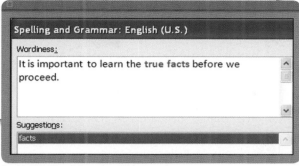

Spelling and Grammar: English (U.S.)

Wordiness:

It is important to learn the true facts before we proceed.

Suggestions:

facts

2 Substitute a Pronoun

Fictional detective Miss Marple solved many crimes. *The Murder at the Vicarage* was one of ~~Miss Marple's~~ *her* most challenging cases.

3 Create an Appositive

Red Barber , ~~was~~ a sportscaster / ~~He~~ was known for his colorful expressions.

4 Create a Compound

John F. Kennedy was the youngest man ever elected president / *and* ~~He was~~ the first Catholic to hold this office.

5 Create a Complex Sentence

Americans value freedom of speech / *, which* ~~Freedom of speech~~ is guaranteed by the First Amendment.

42c Tightening Rambling Sentences

The combination of nonessential words, unnecessary repetition, and complicated syntax creates **rambling sentences**. Revising such sentences frequently requires extensive editing.

1 **Eliminate Excessive Coordination**

When you string a series of clauses together with coordinating conjunctions, you create a rambling, unfocused compound sentence. To revise such sentences, first identify the main idea, and then add the supporting details.

> **Wordy:** Puerto Rico is a large island and it is very mountainous, and it has steep slopes, and they fall to gentle plains along the coast.
>
> **Concise:** A large island, Puerto Rico is very mountainous, with steep slopes falling to gentle plains along the coast. (Puerto Rico's mountainous terrain is the sentence's main idea.)

2 **Eliminate Adjective Clauses**

See
B3.2

A series of **adjective clauses** is also likely to produce a rambling sentence. To revise, substitute concise modifying words or phrases for the adjective clauses.

> **Wordy:** *Moby-Dick*, which is a novel about a white whale, was written by Herman Melville, who was friendly with Nathaniel Hawthorne, who urged him to revise the first draft.
>
> **Concise:** *Moby-Dick*, a novel about a white whale, was written by Herman Melville, who revised the first draft at the urging of his friend Nathaniel Hawthorne.

3 **Eliminate Passive Constructions**

See
37d

Unnecessary use of the **passive voice** can also create a rambling sentence. Correct this problem by changing passive to active voice.

ESL
58a6

~~Water rights are being fought for in court by~~ Indian tribes like

are fighting in court for water rights.

the Papago in Arizona and the Pyramid Lake Paiute in Nevada/˄

4 **Eliminate Wordy Prepositional Phrases**

See
B3.1

When you revise, substitute adjectives or adverbs for wordy **prepositional phrases**.

dangerous   *exciting.*
The trip was ˄~~one of danger~~ but also ˄~~one of excitement.~~

confidently   *authoritatively.*
He spoke ˄~~in a confident manner~~ and ˄~~with a lot of authority.~~

5 **Eliminate Wordy Noun Constructions**

See
B3.1

Substitute strong verbs for wordy **noun phrases**.

decided
We have ‸made the decision to postpone the meeting until the
appear
appearance of all the board members‸.

CHAPTER **43**

Using Parallelism

Parallelism—the use of matching words, phrases, or clauses to express
equivalent ideas—adds unity, balance, and force to your writing. Effective
parallelism can help you write clearer sentences, but **faulty parallelism** can
create awkward sentences that obscure your meaning and confuse readers.

See
43b

43a Using Parallelism Effectively

Parallelism highlights the correspondence between *items in a series, paired
items,* and elements in *lists and outlines.*

1 With Items in a Series

Eat, drink, and be merry.

Baby food consumption, toy production, and school construction are
likely to decline as the US population ages.

Three factors influenced his decision to seek new employment:
his desire to relocate, his need for greater responsibility, and his
dissatisfaction with his current job.

 For information on punctuating items in a series, **see 46b** and **47b.**

2 With Paired Items

The thank-you note was short but sweet.

Roosevelt represented the United States, and Churchill represented
Great Britain.

Ask not what your country can do for you; ask what you can do for your country. (John F. Kennedy)

Paired elements linked by **correlative conjunctions** (such as *not only/but also, both/and, either/or, neither/nor,* and *whether/or*) should always be parallel.

The design team paid close attention not only to color but also to texture.

Either repeat physics or take calculus.

Parallelism also highlights the contrast between paired elements linked by *than* or *as.*

Richard Wright and James Baldwin chose to live in Paris rather than to remain in the United States.

Success is as much a matter of hard work as a matter of luck.

3 In Lists and Outlines

See 26c

Elements in a **list** should be parallel.

The Irish potato famine had four major causes:
1. The establishment of the landlord-tenant system
2. The failure of the potato crop
3. The reluctance of England to offer adequate financial assistance
4. The passage of the Corn Laws

See 15h

Elements in an **outline** should also be parallel.

43b Revising Faulty Parallelism

Faulty parallelism occurs when elements that have the same function in a sentence are not presented in parallel terms.

Many people in developing countries suffer because the countries
                                        sufficient
lack sufficient housing, sufficient food, and ̧their health-care

facilities ̧are also insufficient.

To correct faulty parallelism, match nouns with nouns, verbs with verbs, and phrases or clauses with similarly constructed phrases or clauses.

Popular exercises for men and women include yoga, weight
lifting
 ̧lifters, and jogging.

                                        having
I look forward to hearing from you and to ̧have an opportunity
to tell you more about myself.

Close-Up   REPEATING KEY WORDS

Although the use of similar grammatical structures may sometimes be enough to convey parallelism, sentences are often clearer if certain key words (for example, prepositions that introduce items in a series) are also parallel. In the following sentence, repeating the preposition *by* makes it clear that *not* applies only to the first phrase.

Computerization has helped industry by not allowing labor costs to
                    by   *by*
skyrocket,ᴧincreasing the speed of production, andᴧimproving efficiency.

GRAMMAR CHECKER   Revising Faulty Parallelism

Grammar checkers are not very useful for identifying faulty parallelism. Although your grammar checker may highlight some nonparallel constructions, it may miss others.

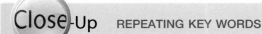

CHAPTER **44**

Choosing Words

44a   Using a Dictionary

Every writer should use a dictionary (electronic or print) to check the spelling, meaning, and usage of unfamiliar words. The most widely used dictionary is the one-volume **desk dictionary** or **college dictionary.**

To fit a lot of information into a small space, dictionaries use a system of symbols, abbreviations, and typefaces (see Figure 44.1 on page 464). Consult the preface of your dictionary to determine how its system operates.

44b   Choosing an Appropriate Level of Diction

Diction, which comes from the Latin word for *say,* refers to the choice and use of words. Different audiences and situations call for different levels of diction.

Entry word   Pronunciation guide   Usage labels

cou•ple (kŭp′əl) *n.* **1.** Two items of the same kind; a pair. **2.** Something that joins or connects two things together; a link. **3.** *(used with a sing. or pl. verb)* **a.** Two people united, as by betrothal or marriage. **b.** Two people together. **4.** *Informal* A few; several: *a couple of days.* **5.** *Physics* A pair of forces of equal magnitude acting in parallel but opposite directions, capable of causing rotation but not translation. ❖ *v.* **-pled, -pling, -ples** —*tr.* **1.** To link together; connect: *coupled her refusal with an explanation.* **2a.** To join as spouses; marry. **b.** To join in sexual union. **3.** *Electricity* To link (two circuits or currents) as by magnetic induction. —*intr.* **1.** To form pairs; join. **2.** To unite sexually; copulate. **3.** To join chemically. ❖ *adj. Informal* Two or few: *"Every couple years the urge strikes, to . . . haul off to a new site"* (Garrison Keillor). [Middle English, from Old French, from Latin *cōpula,* bond, pair.]

Grammatical functions

Part-of-speech labels

Meaning

Quotation

Etymology (word history)

Usage Note When used to refer to two people who function socially as a unit, as in *a married couple,* the word *couple* may take either a singular or a plural verb, depending on whether the members are considered individually or collectively: *The couple were married last week. Only one couple was left on the dance floor.* When a pronoun follows, *they* and *their* are more common than *it* and *its: The couple decided to spend their* (less commonly *its*) *vacation in Florida.* Using a singular verb and a plural pronoun, as in *The couple wants their children to go to college,* is widely considered to be incorrect. Care should be taken that the verb and pronoun agree in number: *The couple want their children to go to college.* • Although the phrase *a couple of* has been well established in English since before the Renaissance, modern critics have sometimes maintained that *a couple of* is too inexact to be appropriate in formal writing. But the inexactitude of *a couple of* may serve a useful purpose, suggesting that the writer is indifferent to the precise number of items involved. Thus the sentence *She lives only a couple of miles away* implies not only that the distance is short but that its exact measure is unimportant. This usage should be considered unobjectionable on all levels of style. • The *of* in the phrase *a couple of* is often dropped in speech, but this omission is usually considered a mistake, especially in formal contexts. Three-fourths of the Usage Panel finds the sentence *I read a couple books over vacation* to be unacceptable; however, another 20% of the Panel finds the sentence to be acceptable in informal speech and writing.

Usage note

FIGURE 44.1 Entry from *The American Heritage Dictionary of the English Language.* Copyright © 2010 by Houghton Mifflin Harcourt Publishing Company. Reproduced by permission from *The American Heritage Dictionary of the English Language,* Fourth Edition.

❶ Formal Diction

Formal diction is grammatically correct and uses words familiar to an educated audience. A writer who uses formal diction often maintains emotional distance from the audience by using the impersonal *one* rather than the more personal *I* and *you.* In addition, the tone of the writing—as determined by word choice, sentence structure, and choice of subject—is dignified and objective.

❷ Informal Diction

Informal diction is the language that people use in conversation and in personal emails. You should use informal diction in your college writing only to reproduce speech or dialect or to give a paper a conversational tone.

Colloquial Diction **Colloquial diction** is the language of everyday speech. Contractions—*isn't, I'm*—are typical colloquialisms, as are **clipped forms**—*phone* for *telephone, TV* for *television, dorm* for *dormitory.* Other colloquialisms include placeholders like *kind of* and utility words like *nice* for *acceptable, funny* for *odd,* and *great* for almost anything. Colloquial English also includes expressions like *get across* for *communicate, come up with* for *find,* and *check out* for *investigate.*

> **ESL TIP**
> Some of the spoken expressions you learn from other students or from television are not appropriate for use in college writing. When you hear new expressions, pay attention to the contexts in which they are used.

Slang **Slang,** language that calls attention to itself, is used to establish or reinforce identity within a group—urban teenagers, rock musicians, or computer users, for example. One characteristic of slang vocabulary is that it is usually relatively short-lived, coming into existence and fading out much more quickly than other words do. Because slang terms can emerge and disappear so quickly, no dictionary—even a dictionary of slang—can list all or even most of the slang terms currently in use.

In personal email and instant messages, writers commonly use **emoticons**—typed characters, such as :-) or ;-), that indicate emotions or feelings—and **Internet slang,** (or **text shorthand**), such as BTW (by the way) or 2 Day. Although these typographical devices are common in informal electronic communication, they are always inappropriate in academic essays or emails to professors or supervisors.

Regionalisms **Regionalisms** are words, expressions, and idiomatic forms that are used in particular geographical areas but may not be understood by a general audience. In eastern Tennessee, for example, a paper bag is a *poke,* and empty soda bottles are *dope bottles.* And New Yorkers stand *on line* for a movie, whereas people in most other parts of the country stand *in line.*

Nonstandard Diction **Nonstandard diction** refers to words and expressions not generally considered a part of standard English—words like *ain't, nohow, anywheres, nowheres, hisself,* and *theirselves.*

No absolute rules distinguish standard from nonstandard usage. In fact, some linguists reject the idea of nonstandard usage altogether, arguing that this designation relegates both the language and those who use it to second-class status.

Note: Remember, colloquial expressions, slang, regionalisms, and nonstandard diction are almost always inappropriate in your college writing.

3 College Writing

The level of diction appropriate for college writing depends on your assignment and your audience. A personal-experience essay calls for a somewhat informal style, but a research paper, an exam, or a report requires a more formal level of diction. Most college writing falls somewhere between formal and informal English, using a conversational tone but maintaining grammatical correctness and using a specialized vocabulary when the situation requires it. (This is the level of diction that is used in this book.)

Close-Up   EMAILS TO INSTRUCTORS

Different instructors have different opinions about how students should address them. Unless you are told otherwise, however, think of emails to your instructors as business communications. Avoid highly informal salutations, such as "Hi prof"; instead, use a more formal salutation, such as "Dr. Sweeny."

44c   Choosing the Right Word

Choosing the right word to use in a particular context is very important. If you use the wrong word—or even *almost* the right one—you run the risk of misrepresenting your ideas.

1 Denotation and Connotation

A word's **denotation** is its basic dictionary meaning, what it stands for without any emotional associations. A word's **connotations** are the emotional, social, and political associations it has in addition to its denotative meaning.

Word	Denotation	Connotation
politician	someone who holds a political office	opportunist; wheeler-dealer

Selecting a word with the appropriate connotation can be challenging. For example, the word *skinny* has negative connotations, whereas *thin* is neutral, and *slender* is positive. And words and expressions like *mentally ill, insane, neurotic, crazy, psychopathic,* and *emotionally disturbed,* although similar in meaning, have different emotional, social, and political connotations that affect the way people respond. If you use terms without considering their connotations, you run the risk of undercutting your credibility, to say nothing of confusing and possibly angering your readers.

Close-Up   USING A THESAURUS

Synonyms are words that have similar meanings, such as *well* and *healthy*. **Antonyms** are words that have opposite meanings, such as *courage* and *cowardice*.

When you consult a **thesaurus,** a list of synonyms and antonyms, remember that no two words have exactly the same meanings. Use synonyms carefully, checking your dictionary to make sure the connotation of the synonym is close to that of the original word.

2 Euphemisms

A **euphemism** is a mild or polite term used in place of a blunt or harsh term to describe something unpleasant or embarrassing. College writing is no place for euphemisms. Say what you mean—*pregnant*, not *expecting; died,* not *passed away*; and *strike*, not *work stoppage.*

3 Specific and General Words

Specific words refer to particular persons, items, or events; **general** words denote entire classes or groups. *Queen Elizabeth II*, for example, is more specific than *monarch; jeans* is more specific than *clothing;* and *hybrid* is more specific than *vehicle.* You can use general words to describe entire classes of items, but you should use specific words to clarify such generalizations.

Take particular care to avoid general words such as *nice, great,* and *terrific* that say nothing and could be used in almost any sentence. These utility words convey only enthusiasm, not precise meanings. Replace them with more specific words.

See 42a2

4 Abstract and Concrete Words

Abstract words—*beauty, truth, justice,* and so on—refer to ideas, qualities, or conditions that cannot be perceived by the senses. **Concrete** words name things that readers can see, hear, taste, smell, or touch. As with general and specific words, whether a word is abstract or concrete is relative. The more concrete your words and phrases, the more vivid the image you evoke in the reader's mind.

44d   Using Figures of Speech

Writers often use **figures of speech** (such as *similes* and *metaphors*) to go beyond the literal meanings of words. By doing so, they make their writing more vivid or emphatic.

Commonly Used Figures of Speech

A **simile** is a comparison between two unlike things on the basis of a shared quality. A simile is introduced by *like* or *as*.

> Like travelers with exotic destinations on their minds, the graduates were remarkably forgetful. (Maya Angelou, *I Know Why the Caged Bird Sings*)

A **metaphor** also compares two dissimilar things, but instead of saying that one thing is like another, it equates them.

> Perhaps it is easy for those who have never felt the stings and darts of segregation to say, "Wait." (Martin Luther King Jr., "Letter from Birmingham Jail")

An **analogy** explains an unfamiliar item or concept by comparing it to a more familiar one.

> According to Robert Frost, writing free verse is like playing tennis without a net.

Personification gives an idea or inanimate object human attributes, feelings, or powers.

> Truth strikes us from behind, and in the dark, as well as from before in broad daylight. (Henry David Thoreau, *Journals*)

A **hyperbole** (or overstatement) is an intentional exaggeration for emphasis. For example, Jonathan Swift uses hyperbole in his essay "A Modest Proposal" when he suggests that eating Irish babies would help the English solve their food shortage.

Understatement intentionally makes something seem less important than it actually is.

> According to Mao Tse-tung, a revolution is not a tea party.

44e Avoiding Inappropriate Language

① Jargon

Jargon, the specialized or technical vocabulary of a trade, a profession, or an academic discipline, is useful for communicating in the field for which it was developed. Outside that field, however, it is often imprecise and confusing. For example, business executives may want departments to *interface* effectively, and sociologists may identify the need for *perspectivistic thinking* to achieve organizational goals. If they are addressing other professionals in their respective fields, these terms can facilitate communication. If, however, they are addressing a general audience, these terms will be confusing.

❷ Neologisms

Neologisms are newly coined words that are not part of standard English. New situations call for new words, however, and frequently a neologism will become an accepted part of the language—*app, locavore, phishing, blog,* and *outsource,* for example. Other coined words are never fully accepted—for example, the neologisms created when the suffix -*wise* is added to existing words, creating nonstandard words like *weatherwise, sportswise, timewise,* and *productwise.*

❸ Pretentious Diction

Good writing is clear and direct, not pompous or flowery. Revise to eliminate **pretentious diction,** inappropriately elevated and wordy language.

asleep   *thought*   *hiking*
As I fell ~~into slumber~~, I ~~cogitated~~ about my day ~~ambling~~ through ~~the splendor of~~ the Appalachian Mountains.

Frequently, pretentious diction is formal diction used in a relatively informal situation. In such a context, it is out of place. For every pretentious word, there is a clear and direct alternative.

Pretentious	Clear	Pretentious	Clear
ascertain	discover	reside	live
commence	start	terminate	end
implement	carry out	utilize	use
minuscule	small	individual	person

❹ Clichés

Clichés are expressions that have been used so often that their power has been drained away. At one time, expressions such as "hit the nail on the head" or "pass the buck" might have called up vivid images in a reader's mind, but because of overuse, they have become clichés—pat, meaningless phrases.

back in the day
the bottom line
it is what it is
face the music
game plan
give 110 percent
smoking gun
a level playing field
a perfect storm
wake up and smell the coffee
old school
what goes around comes around

Writers sometimes resort to clichés when they run out of ideas. To capture your readers' attention, you should take the time to think of original expressions.

44f   Avoiding Offensive Language

Because the language we use not only expresses our ideas but also shapes our thinking, you should avoid using words that insult or degrade others.

1   Stereotypes

Race and Ethnicity   When referring to any racial, ethnic, or religious group, use words with neutral connotations or words that the group itself uses in formal speech or writing—for example, *African American, Latino* or *Latina, Native American, Chinese American,* and so on.

 Note: It is acceptable to use *black* in second references to *African Americans.*

Age   Avoid potentially offensive labels relating to age. Many older people like to call themselves *senior citizens* or *seniors,* and these terms are commonly used by the media and the government.

Class   Do not demean certain jobs because they are low paying or praise others because they have impressive titles. Similarly, do not use words—*hick, cracker, redneck,* or *trailer trash,* for example—that denigrate people based on their social class.

Physical Disability   Use respectful language when referring to people with physical or mental disabilities. Refer to a person's disability only when it is important to the discussion. Also, avoid outdated terms such as *retarded,* and *crippled.* Instead use terms such as *mentally challenged* and *physically disabled.*

Sexual Orientation Always use neutral terms (such as *gay, lesbian,* and *transgendered*), but do not mention a person's sexual orientation unless it is relevant to your discussion.

2 Sexist Language

Avoid **sexist language** that promotes and reinforces gender stereotypes. 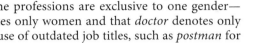 Sexist language entails much more than the use of derogatory words, however. Assuming that some professions are exclusive to one gender— for instance, that *nurse* denotes only women and that *doctor* denotes only men—is also sexist. So is the use of outdated job titles, such as *postman* for *letter carrier, fireman* for *firefighter,* and *stewardess* for *flight attendant.*

Eliminating Sexist Language

For every sexist usage, there is a nonsexist alternative.

Sexist Usage	Possible Revisions
Mankind	People, human beings
Man's accomplishments	Human accomplishments
Man-made	Synthetic
Female engineer/lawyer/ accountant, and so on; model	Engineer/lawyer/accountant and so on; model
Policeman/woman	Police officer
Salesman/woman/girl	Salesperson, sales representative
Businessman/woman	Businessperson, executive
<u>Everyone</u> should complete <u>his</u> application by Tuesday.	<u>Everyone</u> should complete <u>his or her</u> application by Tuesday. <u>All students</u> should complete <u>their</u> applications by Tuesday.

Note: When trying to avoid sexist use of *he* and *him* in your writing, be careful not to use the plural pronoun *they* or *their* to refer to a singular antecedent.

Drivers
~~Any driver~~ caught speeding should have their driving privileges suspended.

Sexist language occurs when a writer fails to apply the same terminology to both men and women. For example, refer to two scientists with PhDs not as Dr. Sagan and Mrs. Yallow, but as Dr. Sagan and Dr. Yallow. Refer to two writers as James and Wharton, or Henry James and Edith Wharton, not James and Mrs. Wharton.

In your writing, always use *women*—not *girls, gals,* or *ladies*—when referring to adult females. Use *Ms.* as the form of address when a woman's marital status is unknown or irrelevant (for example, in business correspondence). Finally, avoid using the generic *he* or *him* when your subject could be either male or female. Use the third-person plural (*they*) or the phrase *he or she* (not *he/she*).

Sexist: Before boarding, each passenger should make certain that <u>he</u> has <u>his</u> ticket.

Revised: Before boarding, <u>passengers</u> should make certain that they have <u>their</u> tickets.

Revised: Before boarding, each <u>passenger</u> should make certain that <u>he or she</u> has a ticket.

Note: Remember not to use words to refer to a woman that you would not use to describe a man. For example, do not describe a woman as *pushy* if you would not use the same term to describe a man.

Close-Up ABBREVIATIONS WITHOUT PERIODS

Abbreviations composed of all capital letters do not usually require periods unless they stand for initials of people's names (E. B. White).

>   NYPD   FDNY   NFL   TMZ

Familiar abbreviations of names of corporations or government agencies and abbreviations of scientific and technical terms do not require periods.

>   IBM   CD-ROM   DNA   EPA   HBO

Acronyms—new words formed from the initial letters or first few letters of a series of words—do not include periods.

>   modem   op-ed   scuba   radar
>   OSHA   AIDS   NAFTA   C-SPAN

Clipped forms (commonly accepted shortened forms of words, such as *gym, dorm, math,* and *fax*) do not use periods.
Postal abbreviations do not include periods.

>   TX   CA   MS   PA   FL   NY

3 Marking Divisions in Dramatic, Poetic, and Biblical References

Use periods to separate act, scene, and line numbers in plays; book and line numbers in long poems; and chapter and verse numbers in biblical references. (Do not space between the periods and the elements they separate.)

Dramatic Reference: *Hamlet* 2.2.1–5

Poetic Reference: *Paradise Lost* 7.163–67

Biblical Reference: Judges 4.14

Note: In **MLA parenthetical references**, titles of literary and biblical works are often abbreviated: **(*Ham.* 2.2.1-5)**; **(Judg. 4.14)**.

See 21a1

4 Marking Divisions in Electronic Addresses

Periods, along with other punctuation marks (such as slashes and colons), are also used in electronic addresses (URLs).

>   http://academic.cengage.com

Note: When you type a URL, do not end it with a period or add spaces after periods within the address.

45b Using Question Marks

1 Marking the End of a Direct Question

Use a question mark to signal the end of a direct question.

Who was at the door?

2 Marking Questionable Dates and Numbers

Use a question mark in parentheses to indicate uncertainty about a date or number.

Aristophanes, the Greek playwright, was born in 448 (?) BC and died in 380 (?) BC.

3 Editing Misused Question Marks

Use a period, not a question mark, with an **indirect question** (a question that is not quoted directly).

The personnel officer asked whether he knew how to type?.

Do not use a question mark to convey sarcasm. Instead, suggest your attitude through your choice of words.

          not very
I refused his generous (?) offer.

Do not use question marks along with other punctuation marks (except for closing quotation marks).

"Can it be true?/" he asked.

Note: Never use more than one question mark to end a sentence.

45c Using Exclamation Points

Use an exclamation point to signal the end of an emotional or emphatic statement, an emphatic interjection, or a forceful command.

Remember the *Maine*!

"No! Don't leave!" he cried.

Note: Except for recording dialogue, exclamation points are almost never appropriate in college writing. Even in informal writing, use exclamation points sparingly—and never use two or more in a row.

CHAPTER 46

Using Commas

46a Setting Off Independent Clauses

Use a comma when you form a compound sentence by linking two independent clauses with a **coordinating conjunction** or a pair of **correlative conjunctions.**

The House approved the bill, but the Senate rejected it.

Either the hard drive is full, or the modem is too slow.

Note: You may omit the comma if the two independent clauses are very short: *Love it or leave it.*

46b Setting Off Items in a Series

1 Coordinate Elements

Use commas between items in a series of three or more **coordinate elements** (words, phrases, or clauses joined by a coordinating conjunction).

Chipmunk, *raccoon*, and *Mugwump* are Native American words.

You may pay by check, with a credit card, or in cash.

Brazilians speak Portuguese, Colombians speak Spanish, and Haitians speak French and Creole.

Note: To avoid ambiguity, always use a comma before the *and* (or other coordinating conjunction) that separates the last two items in a series of three or more items: *He was inspired by his parents, the Dalai Lama, and Mother Teresa.*

Do not use a comma to introduce or to close a series.

Three important criteria are/ fat content, salt content, and taste.

The provinces Quebec, Ontario, and Alberta/are in Canada.

See
47b
Note: If phrases or clauses in a **series** already contain commas, separate the items with semicolons.

2 Coordinate Adjectives

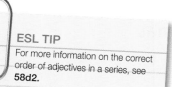

ESL TIP

For more information on the correct order of adjectives in a series, see **58d2**.

Use a comma between items in a series of two or more **coordinate adjectives**—adjectives that modify the same word or word group—unless they are joined by a conjunction.

> She brushed her <u>long</u>, <u>shining</u> hair.

> The baby was <u>tired</u> and <u>cranky</u> and <u>wet</u>. (no commas required)

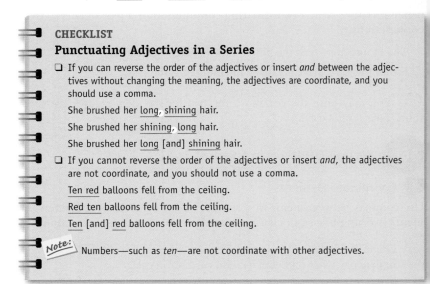

CHECKLIST
Punctuating Adjectives in a Series

❑ If you can reverse the order of the adjectives or insert *and* between the adjectives without changing the meaning, the adjectives are coordinate, and you should use a comma.

She brushed her <u>long</u>, <u>shining</u> hair.

She brushed her <u>shining</u>, <u>long</u> hair.

She brushed her <u>long</u> [and] <u>shining</u> hair.

❑ If you cannot reverse the order of the adjectives or insert *and*, the adjectives are not coordinate, and you should not use a comma.

<u>Ten red</u> balloons fell from the ceiling.

<u>Red ten</u> balloons fell from the ceiling.

<u>Ten</u> [and] <u>red</u> balloons fell from the ceiling.

Note: Numbers—such as *ten*—are not coordinate with other adjectives.

46c Setting Off Introductory Elements

1 Dependent Clauses

An introductory **dependent clause** is generally set off from the rest of the sentence by a comma.

> <u>Although the CIA used to call undercover agents *penetration agents*,</u> they now routinely refer to them as *moles*.

> <u>When war came to Baghdad,</u> many victims were children.

If the dependent clause is short and designates time, you may omit the comma—provided the sentence will be clear without it.

<u>When I exercise</u> I drink plenty of water.

Note: Do not use a comma to set off a dependent clause at the *end* of a sentence: *I drink plenty of water, when I exercise.*

❷ Verbal and Prepositional Phrases

An introductory **verbal phrase** is generally set off by a comma.

<u>Thinking that this might be his last chance</u>, Peary struggled toward the North Pole. (participial phrase)

<u>To write well</u>, one must read a lot. (infinitive phrase)

However, a verbal phrase that serves as a subject is *not* set off by a comma.

<u>Laughing out loud</u> can release tension. (gerund phrase)

<u>To know him</u> is to love him. (infinitive phrase)

An introductory **prepositional phrase** is also usually set off by a comma.

<u>During the Depression</u>, movie attendance rose.

However, if an introductory prepositional phrase is short and no ambiguity is possible, you may omit the comma.

<u>After lunch</u> I took a four-hour nap.

❸ Transitional Words and Phrases

When a **transitional word or phrase** begins a sentence, it is usually set off with a comma.

<u>However</u>, any plan that is enacted must be fair.

<u>In other words</u>, we cannot act hastily.

46d Setting Off Nonessential Material

Sometimes words, phrases, or clauses *contribute* to the meaning of a sentence but are not *essential* for conveying the sentence's main point. Use commas to set off such **nonessential** material whether it appears at the beginning, in the middle, or at the end of a sentence.

1 Nonrestrictive Modifiers

Use commas to set off **nonrestrictive modifiers,** which supply information that is not essential to the meaning of the words they modify. (Do *not* use commas to set off **restrictive modifiers,** which supply information that *is* essential to the meaning of the words they modify.)

> **Nonrestrictive** (commas required): Actors, who have inflated egos, are often insecure. (*All* actors—not just those with inflated egos—are insecure.)

> **Restrictive** (no commas): Actors who have inflated egos are often insecure. (Only those actors with inflated egos—not all actors—are insecure.)

In the following examples, commas set off only nonrestrictive modifiers—those that supply nonessential information. Commas do not set off restrictive modifiers, which supply essential information.

Adjective Clauses

> **Nonrestrictive:** He ran for the bus, which was late as usual.

> **Restrictive:** He ran for the bus that was pulling away from the bus stop.

Prepositional Phrases

> **Nonrestrictive:** The clerk, with a nod, dismissed me.

> **Restrictive:** The man with the gun demanded their money.

Verbal Phrases

> **Nonrestrictive:** The marathoner, running his fastest, beat his previous record.

> **Restrictive:** The candidates running for mayor have agreed to a debate.

Appositives

> **Nonrestrictive:** *Citizen Kane,* Orson Welles's first film, made him famous.

> **Restrictive**: The film *Citizen Kane* made Orson Welles famous.

CHECKLIST
Restrictive and Nonrestrictive Modifiers

To determine whether a modifier is restrictive or nonrestrictive, ask yourself these questions:

❑ Is the modifier essential to the meaning of the word it modifies (*The man with the gun*, not just any man)? If so, it is restrictive.

- ❏ Is the modifier introduced by *that* (*something that most people fear*)? If so, it is restrictive. *That* cannot introduce a nonrestrictive clause.
- ❏ Can you delete the relative pronoun without causing ambiguity or confusion (*something [that] most people fear*)? If so, the clause is restrictive.
- ❏ Is the appositive more specific than the noun that precedes it (*the film* Citizen Kane)? If so, it is restrictive.

Close-Up   USING COMMAS WITH *THAT* AND *WHICH*

- *That* introduces only restrictive clauses, which are not set off by commas.

  I bought a used car that cost $2,000.

- *Which* generally introduces only nonrestrictive clauses, which are set off by commas.

  The used car I bought, which cost $2,000, broke down after a week.

GRAMMAR CHECKER   *That* or *Which*

Your grammar checker may label *which* as an error when it introduces a restrictive clause. It will prompt you to add commas (using *which* to introduce a nonrestrictive clause) or to change *which* to *that*. Carefully consider the meaning of your sentence, and revise accordingly.

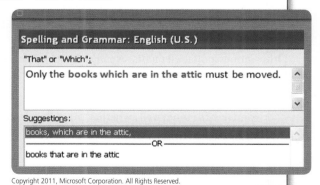

Spelling and Grammar: English (U.S.)

"That" or "Which":

Only the books which are in the attic must be moved.

Suggestions:

books, which are in the attic,

———————OR———————

books that are in the attic

Copyright 2011, Microsoft Corporation. All Rights Reserved.

➋ Transitional Words and Phrases

Transitional words and phrases—which include conjunctive adverbs such as *however, therefore, thus,* and *nevertheless* as well as expressions such as *for example* and *on the other hand*—qualify, clarify, and make connections. However, they are not essential to a sentence's meaning. For this reason, they are always set off by commas when they interrupt a clause or when they begin or end a sentence.

The Outward Bound program, for example, is extremely safe.

In fact, Outward Bound has an excellent reputation.

Other programs are not so safe, however.

Note: When a transitional word or phrase joins two independent clauses, it must be preceded by a semicolon and followed by a comma: *Laughter is the best medicine; of course, penicillin also comes in handy sometimes.*

3 Contradictory Phrases

A phrase that expresses a **contradiction** is usually set off by commas.

This medicine is taken after meals, never on an empty stomach.

Mark McGwire, not Sammy Sosa, was the first to break Roger Maris's home run record.

4 Absolute Phrases

An **absolute phrase,** which includes a noun or pronoun and a participle and modifies an entire independent clause, is always set off by a comma from the clause it modifies.

His fear increasing, he waited to enter the haunted house.

Many soldiers were lost in Southeast Asia, their bodies never recovered.

5 Miscellaneous Nonessential Elements

Other nonessential elements usually set off by commas include tag questions, names in direct address, mild interjections, and *yes* and *no*.

This is your first day on the job, isn't it?

I wonder, Mr.Honeywell, whether Mr. Albright deserves a raise.

Well, it's about time.

Yes, that's what I thought.

46e Using Commas in Other Conventional Contexts

1 With Direct Quotations

In most cases, use commas to set off a direct quotation from the **identifying tag**—the phrase that identifies the speaker (*he said, she answered,* and so on).

Emerson said, "I greet you at the beginning of a great career."

"I greet you at the beginning of a great career," Emerson said.

"I greet you," Emerson said, "at the beginning of a great career."

When the identifying tag comes between two complete sentences, however, the tag is introduced by a comma but followed by a period.

"Winning isn't everything," Coach Vince Lombardi once said. "It's the only thing."

If the first sentence of an interrupted quotation ends with a question mark or an exclamation point, do not use commas.

"Should we hold the front page?" she asked. "It's a slow news day."

"Hold the front page!" he cried. "There's breaking news!"

2 With Titles or Degrees Following a Name

Hamlet, Prince of Denmark, is Shakespeare's most famous character.

Michael Crichton, MD, wrote *Jurassic Park*.

3 In Addresses and Dates

When a date or an address falls within a sentence, use a comma after the last element.

On August 30, 1983, the space shuttle *Challenger* exploded.

Do not use a comma to separate the street number from the street or the state name from the ZIP code.

Her address is 600 West End Avenue, New York, NY 10024.

Note: When only the month and year are given, do not use a comma to separate the month from the year: *August 1983*.

46f Using Commas to Prevent Misreading

In some cases, you need a comma to avoid ambiguity. For example, consider the following sentence.

Those who can, sprint the final lap.

Without the comma, *can* appears to be an auxiliary verb ("Those who <u>can</u> <u>sprint</u>. . . ."), and the sentence seems incomplete. The comma tells readers to pause, thereby preventing confusion.

Also use a comma to acknowledge the omission of a repeated word, usually a verb, and to separate words repeated consecutively.

Pam carried the box; Tim, the suitcase.

Everything bad that could have happened, happened.

46g Editing Misused Commas

Do not use commas in the following situations.

1 To Join Two Independent Clauses

A comma alone cannot join two independent clauses; it must be followed by a coordinating conjunction. Using just a comma to connect two independent clauses creates a **comma splice.**

but
The season was unusually cool,⁁the orange crop was not seriously harmed.

2 To Set Off Restrictive Modifiers

Commas are not used to set off restrictive modifiers. (Commas are only used to set off nonrestrictive modifiers.)

The film⁄ *Malcolm X*⁄ was directed by Spike Lee.

They planned a picnic⁄ in the park.

3 Between Inseparable Grammatical Constructions

Do not place a comma between grammatical elements that cannot be logically separated: a subject and its predicate, a verb and its complement or direct object, a preposition and its object, or an adjective and the word or phrase it modifies.

A woman with dark red hair⁄ opened the door. (comma incorrectly placed between subject and predicate)

Louis Braille developed⁄ an alphabet of raised dots for the blind. (comma incorrectly placed between verb and object)

They relaxed somewhat during⁄ the last part of the obstacle course. (comma incorrectly placed between preposition and object)

Wind-dispersed weeds include the well-known and plentiful⁄ dandelions, milkweed, and thistle. (comma incorrectly placed between adjective and words it modifies)

4 **Between a Verb and an Indirect Quotation**
   or Indirect Question

Do not use a comma between a verb and an indirect quotation or between a
verb and an indirect question.

General Douglas MacArthur vowed/ that he would return. (comma
incorrectly placed between verb and indirect quotation)

The landlord asked/ if we would sign a two-year lease. (comma incorrectly placed between verb and indirect question)

5 **In Compounds That Are Not Composed of**
   Independent Clauses

Do not use a comma before a coordinating conjunction, such as *and* or ❓
but, when it joins two elements of a compound subject, predicate, object,
or complement.

During the 1400s plagues/ and pestilence were common. (compound
subject)

Many women thirty-five and older are returning to college/ and tend to
be good students. (compound predicate)

Mattel has marketed a lab coat/ and an astronaut suit for its Barbie doll.
(compound object)

People buy bottled water because it is pure/ and fashionable. (compound complement)

6 **Before a Dependent Clause at the End of a Sentence**

Do not use a comma before a dependent clause that falls at the end of a
sentence.

Jane Addams founded Hull House/ because she wanted to help
Chicago's poor.

CHAPTER 4

Using Semicolons

A **semicolon** is used only between items of equal grammatical rank: two independent clauses, two phrases, and so on.

47a Separating Independent Clauses

Use a semicolon between closely related independent clauses that convey parallel or contrasting information but are not joined by a coordinating conjunction.

> Paul Revere's *The Boston Massacre* is traditional American protest art; Edward Hicks's paintings are socially conscious art with a religious strain.

Note: Using only a comma or no punctuation at all between independent clauses creates a **run-on.**

Use a semicolon before a transitional word or phrase that joins two independent clauses (the transitional element is followed by a comma).

> Thomas Jefferson brought two hundred vanilla beans and a recipe for vanilla ice cream back from France; <u>thus</u>, he gave America its all-time favorite ice cream flavor.

47b Separating Items in a Series

Use semicolons between items in a series when one or more of these items include commas.

> Three papers are posted on the bulletin board outside the building: a description of the exams; a list of appeal procedures for students who fail; and an employment ad from an automobile factory, addressed specifically to candidates whose appeals are turned down. (Andrea Lee, *Russian Journal*)

> Laramie, Wyoming; Wyoming, Delaware; and Delaware, Ohio, were three of the places they visited.

47c Editing Misused Semicolons

Do not use semicolons in the following situations.

1 Between a Phrase and a Clause

Use a comma, not a semicolon, between a phrase and a clause.

Increasing rapidly, computer crime poses a challenge for business and government.

2 Between a Dependent and an Independent Clause

Use a comma, not a semicolon, between a dependent and an independent clause.

Because drugs can now suppress the body's immune reaction, fewer organ transplants are rejected.

3 To Introduce a List

Use a colon, not a semicolon, to introduce a **list**.

Many people maintain a profile on one of three popular social

networking sites: *MySpace, Facebook,* or *Friendster.*

See
26c

Note: Always introduce a list with a complete sentence followed by a **colon**.

See
50a

4 To Introduce a Quotation

Do not use a semicolon to introduce **quoted speech or writing**.

See
49a

Marie Antoinette may not have said, "Let them eat cake."

Using Apostrophes

Use an apostrophe to form the possessive case, to indicate omissions in contractions, and to form certain plurals.

48a Forming the Possessive Case

The possessive case indicates ownership. In English, the possessive case of nouns and indefinite pronouns is indicated either with a phrase that includes the word *of* (the hands *of* the clock) or with an apostrophe and, in most cases, an *s* (the clock's hands).

1 Singular Nouns and Indefinite Pronouns

To form the possessive case of **singular nouns** and **indefinite pronouns,** add -'s.

> "The Monk's Tale" is one of Chaucer's *Canterbury Tales.*

> When we would arrive was anyone's guess.

2 Singular Nouns Ending in -s

To form the possessive case of **singular nouns that end in** -s, add -'s in most cases.

> Reading Henry James's *The Ambassadors* was not Maris's idea of fun.

> The class's time was changed to 8 a.m.

Note: With some singular nouns that end in -s, pronouncing the possessive ending as a separate syllable can sound awkward. In such cases, it is acceptable to use just an apostrophe: *Crispus Attucks' death, Aristophanes' Lysistrata, Achilles' left heel.*

3 Plural Nouns

To form the possessive case of **regular plural nouns** (those that end in -s or -es), add only an apostrophe.

> Laid-off employees received two weeks' severance pay and three months' medical benefits.

The Lopezes' three children are triplets.

To form the possessive case of nouns that have **irregular plurals**, add -'s.

The Children's Hour is a play by Lillian Hellman.

4 Compound Nouns or Groups of Words

To form the possessive case of **compound nouns** (nouns formed from two or more words) or of word groups, add -'s to the last word.

The President accepted the Secretary of State's resignation.

This is someone else's responsibility.

5 Two or More Items

To indicate **individual ownership** of two or more items, add -'s to each item.

Ernest Hemingway's and Gertrude Stein's writing styles have some similarities.

To indicate **joint ownership,** add -'s only to the last item.

We studied Lewis and Clark's expedition.

48b Indicating Omissions in Contractions

1 Omitted Letters

Apostrophes replace omitted letters in **contractions** that combine a pronoun and a verb (*he + will = he'll*) or the elements of a verb phrase (*do + not = don't*).

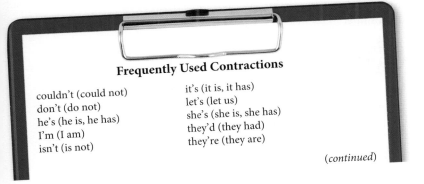

Frequently Used Contractions

couldn't (could not)
don't (do not)
he's (he is, he has)
I'm (I am)
isn't (is not)

it's (it is, it has)
let's (let us)
she's (she is, she has)
they'd (they had)
they're (they are)

(continued)

Frequently Used Contractions (*continued*)

we'd (we would)
we'll (we will)
we're (we are)
we've (we have)

who's (who is, who has)
won't (will not)
wouldn't (would not)
you'd (you would)

Note: Contractions are very informal. Do not use contractions in college writing unless you are quoting a text that includes them.

Close-Up USING APOSTROPHES

Be careful not to confuse contractions (which always include apostrophes) with the possessive forms of personal pronouns (which never include apostrophes).

Contractions	Possessive Forms
Who's on first?	Whose book is this?
They're playing our song.	Their team is winning.
It's raining.	Its paws were muddy.
You're a real pal.	Your résumé is impressive.

2 Omitted Numbers

In informal writing, an apostrophe may also be used to represent the century in a year: Class of '03, the '60s. In college writing, however, write out the number in full: 2003, 1960s.

48c Forming Plurals

In a few special situations, add -'s to form plurals.

Plurals of Letters
The Italian language has no *j*'s, *k*'s, or *w*'s.

Plurals of Words Referred to as Words
The supervisor would accept no *if*'s, *and*'s, or *but*'s.

Note: Elements spoken of as themselves (letters, numerals, or words) are set in italic type; the plural ending, however, is not.

Note: Apostrophes are not used in plurals of abbreviations (including acronyms) or numbers.

DVDs   PACs   1960s

48d Editing Misused Apostrophes

Do not use apostrophes with plural nouns that are not possessive.

The Thompson's are not at home.

Down vest's are very warm.

The Philadelphia 76er's have had good years and bad.

Do not use apostrophes to form the possessive case of personal pronouns.

This ticket must be your's or her's.

The next turn is their's.

Her doll had lost it's right eye.

The next great moment in history is our's.

Note: Be careful not to confuse the possessive forms of personal pronouns with contractions.

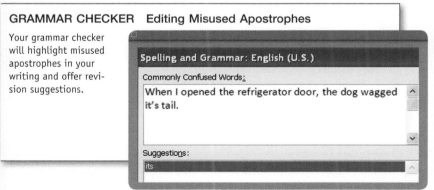

GRAMMAR CHECKER   Editing Misused Apostrophes

Your grammar checker will highlight misused apostrophes in your writing and offer revision suggestions.

Spelling and Grammar: English (U.S.)

Commonly Confused Words:

When I opened the refrigerator door, the dog wagged it's tail.

Suggestions:

its

CHAPTER 49

Using Quotation Marks

Use quotation marks to set off brief passages of quoted speech or writing, to set off titles, and to set off words used in special ways. Do not use quotation marks when quoting long passages of prose or poetry.

49a Setting Off Quoted Speech or Writing

When you quote a word, phrase, or brief passage of someone's speech or writing, enclose the quoted material in a pair of quotation marks.

> Gloria Steinem observed, "We are becoming the men we once hoped to marry."

> Galsworthy writes that Aunt Juley is "prostrated by the blow" (329). (Note that in this example from a student paper, the end punctuation follows the parenthetical documentation.)

Close-Up USING QUOTATION MARKS WITH DIALOGUE

When you record **dialogue** (conversation between two or more people), enclose the quoted words in quotation marks. Begin a new paragraph each time a new speaker is introduced.

When you are quoting several paragraphs of dialogue by one speaker, begin each new paragraph with quotation marks. However, use closing quotation marks only at the end of the *entire quoted passage*, not at the end of each paragraph.

Special rules govern the punctuation of a quotation when it is used with an **identifying tag,** a phrase (*such as he said*) that identifies the speaker or writer. Punctuation guidelines for various situations involving identifying tags are outlined below.

1 Identifying Tag in the Middle of a Quoted Passage

Use a pair of commas to set off an identifying tag that interrupts a quoted passage.

"In the future," <u>pop artist Andy Warhol once said,</u> "everyone will be world famous for fifteen minutes."

If the identifying tag follows a completed sentence but the quoted passage continues, use a period after the tag. Begin the new sentence with a capital letter, and enclose it in quotation marks.

"Be careful," <u>Erin warned.</u> "Reptiles can be tricky."

2 Identifying Tag at the Beginning of a Quoted Passage

Use a comma after an identifying tag that introduces quoted speech or writing.

<u>The Raven repeated,</u> "Nevermore."

Use a colon instead of a comma before a quotation if the identifying tag is a complete sentence.

<u>She gave her final answer:</u> "No."

GRAMMAR CHECKER Checking Punctuation with Quotation Marks

Your grammar checker will often highlight missing punctuation in sentences containing quotation marks and offer suggestions for revision. In most cases, you should accept the grammar checker's suggestion.

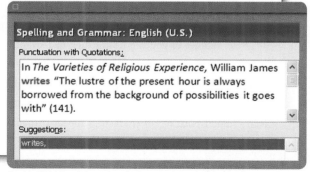

3 Identifying Tag at the End of a Quoted Passage

Use a comma to set off a quotation from an identifying tag that follows it.

"Be careful out there," the sergeant warned.

If the quotation ends with a question mark or an exclamation point, use that punctuation mark instead of the comma. (In this situation, the identifying tag begins with a lowercase letter even though it follows end punctuation.)

"Is Ankara the capital of Turkey?" <u>she asked</u>.

"Oh, boy!" <u>he cried</u>.

Note: A comma or period at the end of a quotation is always placed *before* the quotation marks. For information on placement of other punctuation marks with quotation marks, **see 49e.**

49b Setting Off Long Prose Passages and Poetry

1 Long Prose Passages

Do not enclose a **long prose passage** (a passage of more than four lines) in quotation marks. Instead, set it off by indenting the entire passage one inch from the left-hand margin. Treat the quoted passage like regular text: double-space above and below it, and double-space between lines within it. Introduce the passage with a colon, and place parenthetical documentation one space *after* the end punctuation.

> The following portrait of Aunt Juley illustrates several of the devices Galsworthy uses throughout *The Forsyte Saga*, such as a journalistic detachment that is almost cruel in its scrutiny, a subtle sense of the grotesque, and an ironic stance:
>
>> Aunt Juley stayed in her room, prostrated by the blow. Her face, discoloured by tears, was divided into compartments by the little ridges of pouting flesh which had swollen with emotion. . . . At fixed intervals she went to her drawer, and took from beneath the lavender bags a fresh pocket-handkerchief. Her warm heart could not bear the thought that Ann was lying there so cold. (329)
>
> Many similar portraits of characters appear throughout the novel.

Close-Up QUOTING LONG PROSE PASSAGES

When you quote a long prose passage that is a single paragraph, do not indent the first line. When quoting two or more paragraphs, however, indent the first line of each paragraph (including the first) an additional one-quarter inch. If the first sentence of the quoted passage does not

> begin a paragraph in the source, do not indent it—but do indent the first line of each subsequent paragraph. If the passage you are quoting includes material set in quotation marks, reproduce those quotation marks.

APA guidelines differ from those summarized here, which conform to MLA style.

See 22b

2 Poetry

Treat one line of poetry like a short prose passage: enclose it in quotation marks, and run it into the text.

> One of John Donne's best-known poems begins with the line, "Go and catch
> a falling star."

If you quote two or three lines of poetry, separate the lines with **slashes,** and run the quotation into the text. (Leave one space before and one space after the slash.)

> Alexander Pope writes, "True Ease in Writing comes from Art, not
> Chance, / As those move easiest who have learned to dance."

If you quote more than three lines of poetry, set them off like a **long prose passage.** (For special emphasis, you may set off fewer lines in this manner.) Be sure to reproduce punctuation, spelling, capitalization, and indentation of the quoted lines *exactly* as they appear in the poem.

See 49b1

> Wilfred Owen, a poet who was killed in action in World War I,
> expressed the horrors of war with vivid imagery:
>
>> Bent double, like old beggars under sacks.
>> Knock-kneed, coughing like hags, we cursed through sludge.
>> Till on the haunting flares we turned our backs
>> And towards our distant rest began to trudge.

49c Setting Off Titles

Titles of short works and titles of parts of long works are enclosed in quotation marks. Other titles are italicized.

Titles Requiring Quotation Marks

Articles in Magazines, Newspapers, and Professional Journals
"Why Johnny Can't Write"

Essays, Short Stories, Short Poems, and Songs
"Fenimore Cooper's Literary Offenses"
"Flying Home"
"The Road Not Taken"
"The Star-Spangled Banner"

Chapters or Sections of Books
"Miss Sharp Begins to Make Friends" (Chapter 10 of *Vanity Fair*)

Episodes of Radio or Television Series
"Lucy Goes to the Hospital" (*I Love Lucy*)

49d Setting Off Words Used in Special Ways

Enclose a word used in a special or unusual way in quotation marks. (If you use *so-called* before an unusual usage, do not use quotation marks as well.)

It was clear that adults approved of children who were "readers," but it was not at all clear why this was so. (Annie Dillard)

Also enclose a **coinage**—an invented word—in quotation marks.

After the twins were born, the minivan became a "babymobile."

49e Using Quotation Marks with Other Punctuation

At the end of a quotation, punctuation is sometimes placed before the quotation marks and sometimes placed after the quotation marks.

● Place a comma or period *before* the quotation marks at the end of a quotation.

Many, like the poet Robert Frost, think about "the road not taken," but not many have taken "the one less traveled by."

- Place a semicolon or colon *after* the quotation marks at the end of a quotation.

  Students who do not pass the test receive "certificates of completion"; those who pass are awarded diplomas.

  Taxpayers were pleased with the first of the candidate's promised "sweeping new reforms": a balanced budget.

- If a question mark, exclamation point, or dash is part of the quotation, place the punctuation mark *before* the quotation marks.

  "Who's there?" she demanded.

  "Stop!" he cried.

  "Should we leave now, or—" Vicki paused, unable to continue.

- If a question mark, exclamation point, or dash is *not* part of the quotation, place the punctuation mark *after* the quotation marks.

  Did you finish reading "The Black Cat"?

  Whatever you do, don't yell "Uncle"!

  The first story—Updike's "*A&P*"—provoked discussion.

Close-Up   QUOTATIONS WITHIN QUOTATIONS   ?

Use *single* quotation marks to enclose a quotation within a quotation.

> Claire noted, "Liberace always said, 'I cried all the way to the bank.'"

Also use single quotation marks within a quotation to indicate a title that would normally be enclosed in double quotation marks.

> I think what she said was, "Play it, Sam. Play 'As Time Goes By.'"

Use *double* quotation marks around quotations or titles within a <u>long prose passage</u>.

See 49b1

49f   Editing Misused Quotation Marks

Do not use quotation marks in the following situations.

❶ To Set Off Indirect Quotations

Do not use quotation marks to set off **indirect quotations** (someone else's written or spoken words that are not quoted exactly).

Freud wondered ⸜what women wanted.⸝

❷ To Set Off Slang or Technical Terms

Do not use quotation marks to set off slang or technical terms. (Note that slang is not appropriate in college writing.)

Dawn is ⸜into⸝ running.

⸜Biofeedback⸝ is sometimes used to treat migraine headaches.

Close-Up   TITLES OF YOUR OWN PAPERS

Do not use quotation marks (or italics) to set off the titles of your own papers.

CHAPTER **50**

Using Other Punctuation Marks

50a   Using Colons

The **colon** is a strong punctuation mark that points readers ahead to the material that follows it. When a colon introduces a list or series, explanatory material, or a quotation, *it must be preceded by a complete sentence.*

❶ Introducing Lists or Series

Use colons to set off lists or series, including those introduced by phrases like *the following* or *as follows.*

Waiting tables requires three skillls: memory, speed, and balance.

2 Introducing Explanatory Material

Use a colon to introduce material that explains, exemplifies, or summarizes. Frequently, such material is presented as an **appositive,** a word group that identifies or renames an adjacent noun or pronoun.

Painter Diego Rivera was well known for a controversial mural: the one commissioned for Rockefeller Center in the 1930s.

She had one dream: to play professional basketball.

Close-Up   USING COLONS

When a complete sentence follows a colon, the sentence may begin with either a capital or a lowercase letter. However, if the sentence is a quotation, the first word is always capitalized (unless it was not capitalized in the source).

3 Introducing Quotations

When you quote a long prose passage, always introduce it with a colon. Also use a colon before a short quotation when it is introduced by a complete sentence.

See 49b1

With dignity, Bartleby repeated the familiar words: "I prefer not to."

Colons are also used in the following situations:

● **To Separate Titles from Subtitles**

Family Installments: Memories of Growing Up Hispanic

● **To Separate Minutes from Hours**

6:15 a.m.

● **After Salutations in Business Letters**

Dear Dr. Evans:

● **To Separate Place of Publication from Name of Publisher in an MLA works-cited list**

See 21a2

Boston: Wadsworth, 2006.

❹ Editing Misused Colons

Do not use colons after *namely, for example, such as,* or *that is.*

> The Eye Institute treats patients with a wide variety of conditions, such as⫶ myopia, glaucoma, and cataracts.

Do not place colons between verbs and their objects or complements or between prepositions and their objects.

> James Michener wrote⫶ *Hawaii, Centennial, Space,* and *Poland.*

> Hitler's armies marched through⫶ the Netherlands, Belgium, and France.

50b Using Dashes

❶ Setting Off Nonessential Material

Like commas, **dashes** can set off nonessential material. Unlike commas, however, dashes call attention to the material they set off. Indicate a dash with two unspaced hyphens (which your word-processing program will automatically convert to a dash).

For emphasis, you may use dashes to set off explanations, qualifications, examples, definitions, and appositives.

> Neither of the boys—both nine-year-olds—had any history of violence.

> Too many parents learn the dangers of swimming pools the hard way—after a toddler has drowned.

❷ Introducing a Summary

Use a dash to introduce a statement that summarizes a list or series before it.

> "Study hard," "Respect your elders," "Don't talk with your mouth full"—Sharon had often heard her parents say these things.

❸ Indicating an Interruption

In dialogue, a dash may indicate a hesitation or an unfinished thought.

> "I think—no, I know—this is the worst day of my life," Julie sighed.

❹ Editing Overused Dashes

Too many dashes can make your writing seem disorganized and out of control, so be careful not to overuse them.

> Registration was a nightmare⸻ ^. Most^ of the courses I wanted to take—geology and conversational Spanish, for instance—met at inconvenient times⸻or were closed by the time I tried to sign up for them.

50c Using Parentheses

1 Setting Off Nonessential Material

Use **parentheses** to enclose material that expands, clarifies, illustrates, or supplements.

In some European countries (notably Sweden and France), high-quality day care is offered at little or no cost to parents.

When a complete sentence enclosed in parentheses falls within another sentence, it should not begin with a capital letter or end with a period.

The area is so cold (temperatures average in the low twenties) that it is virtually uninhabitable.

However, if the parenthetical sentence does *not* fall within another sentence, it must begin with a capital letter and end with appropriate punctuation.

The region is very cold. (Temperatures average in the low twenties.)

2 Using Parentheses in Other Situations

Use parentheses around letters and numbers that identify points on a list, dates, cross-references, and documentation.

All reports must include the following components: (1) an opening summary, (2) a background statement, and (3) a list of conclusions.

Russia defeated Sweden in the Great Northern War (1700–1721).

Other scholars also make this point (see p. 54).

One critic has called the novel "puerile" (Arvin 72).

Note: Never use a comma before an opening parenthesis. A comma may follow the closing parenthesis, however.

50d Using Brackets

1 Setting Off Comments within Quotations

Brackets within quotations tell readers that the enclosed words are yours and not those of your source. You can bracket an explanation, a clarification, a correction, or an opinion.

"Even at Princeton he [F. Scott Fitzgerald] felt like an outsider."

If a quotation contains an error, indicate that the error is not yours by following the error with the Latin word *sic* ("thus") in brackets.

"The octopuss [sic] is a cephalopod mollusk with eight arms."

Note: Use brackets to indicate changes that you make in order to fit a quotation smoothly into your sentence.

2 Replacing Parentheses within Parentheses

When one set of parentheses falls within another, use brackets in place of the inner set.

In her classic study of American education (*The Troubled Crusade* [New York: Basic, 1963]), Diane Ravitch addresses issues like educational reforms and campus unrest.

50e Using Slashes

1 Separating One Option from Another

The either/or fallacy is a common error in logic.

Writer/director M. Night Shyamalan spoke at the film festival.

In this situation, there is no space before or after the slash.

2 Separating Lines of Poetry Run into the Text

The poet James Schevill writes, "I study my defects / And learn how to perfect them."

In this situation, leave one space before and one space after the slash.

50f Using Ellipses

Use ellipses in the following situations.

1 Indicating an Omission in Quoted Prose

Use an **ellipsis**—three *spaced* periods—to indicate that you have omitted words from a prose quotation. (Note that an ellipsis in the middle of a quoted passage can indicate the omission of a word, a sentence or two, or even a whole paragraph or more.) When deleting material from a quotation, be very careful not to change the meaning of the original passage.

Original: "When I was a young man, being anxious to distinguish myself, I was perpetually starting new propositions." (Samuel Johnson)

With Omission: "When I was a young man, . . . I was perpetually starting new propositions."

Note that when you delete words immediately after an internal punctuation mark (such as the comma in the above example), you retain the punctuation mark before the ellipsis.

When you delete material at the end of a sentence, place the ellipsis after the sentence's period or other end punctuation.

According to humorist Dave Barry, "from outer space Europe appears to be shaped like a large ketchup stain. . . . " (period followed by ellipsis)

 Note: Never begin a quoted passage with an ellipsis.

When you delete material between sentences, place the ellipsis after any punctuation that appeared in the original passage.

Deletion from Middle of One Sentence to End of Another According to Donald Hall, "Everywhere one meets the idea that reading is an activity desirable in itself. . . . People surround the idea of reading with piety and do not take into account the purpose of reading." (period followed by ellipsis)

Deletion from Middle of One Sentence to Middle of Another "When I was a young man, . . . I found that generally what was new was false." (Samuel Johnson) (comma followed by ellipsis)

 Note: If a quoted passage already contains an ellipsis, MLA recommends that you enclose any ellipses of your own in brackets to distinguish them from those that appear in the original quotation.

Close-Up   USING ELLIPSES

If a quotation ending with an ellipsis is followed by parenthetical documentation, the final punctuation *follows* the documentation.

As Jarman argues, "Compromise was impossible . . ." (161).

2 Indicating an Omission in Quoted Poetry

Use an ellipsis when you omit a word or phrase from a line of poetry. When you omit one or more lines of poetry, use a line of spaced periods. (The

length may be equal either to the line above it or to the missing line—but it
should not be longer than the longest line of the poem.)

Original:

Stitch! Stitch! Stitch!
In poverty, hunger, and dirt,
And still with a voice of dolorous pitch,
Would that its tone could reach the Rich,
She sang this "Song of the Shirt!"

(Thomas Hood)

With Omission:

Stitch! Stitch! Stitch!
In poverty, hunger, and dirt,
. . . .
She sang this "Song of the Shirt!"

Understanding Spelling and Mechanics

PART 13

Understanding Spelling and Mechanics

? Frequently Asked Questions

CHAPTER 51

Improving Spelling

Like most students, you probably use a spell checker when you write and revise your papers, but this does not eliminate your need to know how to spell. For one thing, a spell checker will only check words that are in its dictionary. In addition, a spell checker will not tell you if you have confused *principal* for *principle,* and it will not catch typos such as *form* for *from* or *its* for *it's.* For these reasons, you still have to be a competent speller.

51a Understanding Spelling and Pronunciation

Because pronunciation in English often provides few clues to spelling, you must memorize the spellings of many words and use a dictionary and a spell checker regularly.

1 Vowels in Unstressed Positions

Many unstressed vowels sound exactly alike. For instance, it is hard to tell from pronunciation alone that the *i* in *terrible* is not an *a*. In addition, the unstressed vowels *a, e,* and *i* are impossible to distinguish in the suffixes *-able* and *-ible, -ance* and *-ence,* and *-ant* and *-ent.*

comfort<u>able</u>	brilli<u>ance</u>	serv<u>ant</u>
compat<u>ible</u>	excell<u>ence</u>	independ<u>ent</u>

2 Silent Letters

Some English words contain silent letters, such as the *b* in *climb* and the *t* in *mortgage.*

ai<u>s</u>le	depo<u>t</u>	<u>p</u>neumonia
clim<u>b</u>	kni<u>gh</u>t	sil<u>h</u>ouette
condem<u>n</u>	mor<u>t</u>gage	so<u>v</u>ereign

3 Words That Are Often Pronounced Carelessly

Words like the following are often misspelled because they are pronounced carelessly in everyday speech. Consequently, people tend to leave out, add, or transpose letters when they spell them.

candidate	library	recognize
environment	lightning	specific
February	nuclear	supposed to
government	perform	surprise
hundred	quantity	used to

4 American and British Spellings

Some words are spelled one way in the United States and another way in Great Britain.

American	**British**
color	colour
defense	defence
judgment	judgement
theater	theatre
toward	towards
traveled	travelled

5 Homophones

Homophones are words—such as *accept* and *except*—that are pronounced alike but spelled differently.

accept	to receive
except	other than
affect	to have an influence on (*verb*)
effect	result (*noun*); to cause (*verb*)
its	possessive of *it*
it's	contraction of *it is*
principal	most important (*adjective*); head of a school (*noun*)
principle	a basic truth; rule of conduct

For a full list of these and other homophones, along with their meanings and sentences illustrating their use, see **Appendix C, Glossary of Usage**.

Close-Up   ONE WORD OR TWO?

Some words may be written as one word or two, depending on their meaning.

any way vs. anyway
The early pioneers made the trip west *any way* they could.
It began to rain, but the game continued *anyway*.

every day vs. *everyday*
Every day brings new opportunities.
John thought of his birthday as an *everyday* event.

Other words are frequently misspelled because people are not sure whether they are one word or two.

One Word	Two Words
already	a lot
cannot	all right
classroom	even though
overweight	no one

Consult a dictionary if you have any doubts about whether a word is written as one word or two.

51b Learning Spelling Rules

Knowing a few reliable rules can help you overcome problems caused by the inconsistency between pronunciation and spelling.

1 The *ie/ei* Combinations

Use *i* before *e* except after *c* or when pronounced *ay*, as in *neighbor*.

i before *e*: belief, chief, niece, friend

ei after *c*: ceiling, deceit, receive

ei pronounced *ay*: weigh, freight, eight

Exceptions: *either, neither, foreign, leisure, weird,* and *seize.* In addition, if the *ie* combination is not pronounced as a unit, the rule does not apply: *atheist, science.*

2 Doubling Final Consonants

The only words that double their consonants before a suffix that begins with a vowel (*-ed* or *-ing*) are those that pass the following three tests:

1. They have one syllable or are stressed on the last syllable.
2. They contain only one vowel in the last syllable.
3. They end in a single consonant.

The word *tap* satisfies all three conditions: it has only one syllable, it contains only one vowel (*a*), and it ends in a single consonant (*p*). Therefore, the final consonant doubles before a suffix beginning with a vowel (*tapped, tapping*).

The word *relent*, however, meets only two of the three conditions: it is stressed on the last syllable, and it has one vowel in the last syllable, but it does not end in a single consonant. Therefore, its final consonant is not doubled (*relented, relenting*).

3 Prefixes

The addition of a prefix never affects the spelling of the root (*mis + spell = misspell*). Some prefixes can cause spelling problems, however, because they are pronounced alike although they are not spelled alike: *ante-/anti-, en-/in-, per-/pre-,* and *de-/di-*.

antebellum	antiaircraft
encircle	integrate
perceive	prescribe
deduct	direct

4 Silent e before a Suffix

When a suffix that begins with a consonant is added to a word ending in a silent *e*, the *e* is generally kept: *hope/hopeful; lame/lamely; bore/boredom*. **Exceptions:** *argument, truly, ninth, judgment,* and *acknowledgment*.

When a suffix that begins with a vowel is added to a word ending in a silent *e*, the *e* is generally dropped: *hope/hoping; trace/traced; grieve/grievance; love/lovable*. **Exceptions:** *changeable, noticeable,* and *courageous*.

5 *y* before a Suffix

When a word ends in a consonant plus *y*, the *y* generally changes to an *i* when a suffix is added (*beauty + ful = beautiful*). The *y* is kept, however, when the suffix -*ing* is added (*tally + ing = tallying*) and in some one-syllable words (*dry + ness = dryness*).

When a word ends in a vowel plus *y*, the *y* is kept (*joy + ful = joyful; employ + er = employer*). **Exception:** *day + ly = daily*.

6 *seed* Endings

Endings with the sound *seed* are nearly always spelled *cede*, as in *precede, intercede, concede,* and so on. **Exceptions:** *supersede, exceed, proceed,* and *succeed*.

7 *-able, -ible*

If the root of a word is itself a word, the suffix -*able* is most commonly used. If the root of a word is not a word, the suffix -*ible* is most often used.

agreeable	compatible
comfortable	incredible
dryable	plausible

8 Plurals

Most nouns form plurals by adding *-s: savage/savages, tortilla/tortillas, boat/boats.* There are, however, a number of exceptions.

Words Ending in -f or -fe   Some words ending in *-f* or *-fe* form plurals by changing the *f* to *v* and adding *-es* or *-s: life/lives, self/selves.* Others add just *-s: belief/beliefs, safe/safes.* Words ending in *-ff* take *-s* to form plurals: *tariff/tariffs.*

Words Ending in -y   Most words that end in a consonant followed by *y* form plurals by changing the *y* to *i* and adding *-es: baby/babies.* **Exceptions:** proper nouns such as *Kennedys* (never *Kennedies*).

Words that end in a vowel followed by a *y* form plurals by adding *-s: monkey/monkeys.*

Words Ending in -o   Words that end in a vowel followed by *o* form the plural by adding *-s: radio/radios, stereo/stereos, zoo/zoos.* Most words that end in a consonant followed by *o* add *-es* to form the plural: *tomato/tomatoes, hero/heroes.* **Exceptions:** *silo/silos, piano/pianos, memo/memos, soprano/sopranos.*

Words Ending in -s, -ss, -sh, -ch, -x, and -z   These words form plurals by adding *-es: Jones/Joneses, mass/masses, rash/rashes, lunch/lunches, box/boxes, buzz/buzzes.* **Exceptions:** Some one-syllable words that end in *-s* or *-z* double their final consonants when forming plurals: *quiz/quizzes.*

Compound Nouns   **Compound nouns**—nouns formed from two or more words—usually form the plural with the last word in the compound construction: *welfare state/welfare states; snowball/snowballs.* However, compound nouns whose first element is more important than the others form the plural with the first element: *sister-in-law/sisters-in-law, attorney general/attorneys general, hole in one/holes in one.*

Foreign Plurals   Some words, especially those borrowed from Latin or Greek, keep their foreign plurals.

Singular	Plural
criterion	criteria
datum	data
larva	larvae
medium	media
memorandum	memoranda
stimulus	stimuli

CHAPTER 5

Knowing When to Capitalize

Close-Up REVISING CAPITALIZATION ERRORS

In *Microsoft Word*, the AutoCorrect tool will automatically capitalize certain words—such as the first word of a sentence or the days of the week. You can also designate additional words to be automatically capitalized for you as you type. To do this, select AutoCorrect from the Tools menu, and type in the words you want to capitalize. Be sure to proofread your documents after using the AutoCorrect tool, though, since it may introduce capitalization errors into your writing.

52a Capitalizing the First Word of a Sentence

Capitalize the first word of a sentence, including a sentence of quoted speech or writing.

As Shakespeare wrote, "Who steals my purse steals trash."

Do not capitalize a sentence set off within another sentence by dashes or parentheses.

Finding the store closed—it was a holiday—they went home.

The candidates are Frank Lester and Jane Lester (they are not related).

Close-Up USING CAPITAL LETTERS IN POETRY

Remember that the first word of a line of poetry is generally capitalized. If the poet uses a lowercase letter to begin a line, however, follow that style when you quote the line.

52b Capitalizing Proper Nouns

Proper nouns—the names of specific persons, places, animals, or things—are capitalized, and so are adjectives formed from proper nouns.

1 Specific People's Names

Always capitalize people's names: Olympia Snowe, Barack Obama.

Capitalize a title when it precedes a person's name (Senator Olympia Snowe) or is used instead of the name (Dad). Do not capitalize titles that *follow* names (Olympia Snowe, the senator from Maine) or those that refer to the general position, not the particular person who holds it (a stay-at-home dad).

> **ESL TIP**
> Do not capitalize a word simply because you want to emphasize its importance. If you are not sure whether a noun should be capitalized, look it up in a dictionary.

You may, however, capitalize titles that indicate very high-ranking positions even when they are used alone or when they follow a name: the Pope; Barack Obama, President of the United States. Never capitalize a title denoting a family relationship when it follows an article or a possessive pronoun (an uncle, his mom).

Capitalize titles that represent academic degrees or abbreviations of those degrees even when they follow a name: Dr. Sanjay Gupta; Sanjay Gupta, MD.

2 Names of Particular Structures, Special Events, Monuments, and So On

the *Titanic*	the World Series
the Brooklyn Bridge	Mount Rushmore

3 Places and Geographical Regions

Saturn	the Straits of Magellan
Budapest	the Western Hemisphere
Lake Erie	Kings County

Capitalize *north, east, south,* and *west* when they denote particular geographical regions, but not when they designate directions.

There are more tornadoes in Kansas than in the East. (*East* refers to a specific region.)

Turn west at Broad Street and continue north to Market. (*West* and *north* refer to directions, not specific regions.)

4 **Days of the Week, Months, and Holidays**

Saturday	Diwali
January	Cinco de Mayo

5 **Historical Periods, Documents, and Names of Legal Cases**

the Reformation	the Treaty of Versailles
the Battle of Gettysburg	*Brown v. Board of Education*

Note: Names of court cases are italicized in the text of your papers but not in works-cited entries.

6 **Philosophic, Literary, and Artistic Movements**

Naturalism	Dadaism
Romanticism	Expressionism

7 **Races, Ethnic Groups, Nationalities, and Languages**

African American	Korean
Latino/Latina	Farsi

Note: When the words *black* and *white* refer to races, they have tradition-ally not been capitalized. Current opinion is divided on whether or not to capitalize *black*.

8 **Religions and Their Followers; Sacred Books and Figures**

Jews	the Talmud	Buddha
Islam	God	the Bible

9 **Specific Organizations**

the New York Yankees	the American Bar Association
the Democratic Party	the Anti-Defamation League

10 **Businesses, Government Agencies, and Other Institutions**

General Electric
the Environmental Protection Agency
Lincoln High School
the University of Maryland

11 **Brand Names and Words Formed from Them**

Coke   Astroturf   Rollerblades   Post-it   Velcro

Note: In general, use generic references, not brand names, in college writing—*photocopy*, not *Xerox*, for example. These generic names are not capitalized.

12 Specific Academic Courses

Sociology 201   English 101

Note: Do not capitalize a general subject area (sociology, zoology) unless it is the name of a language (French).

13 Adjectives Formed from Proper Nouns

Keynesian economics   Elizabethan era
Freudian slip   Shakespearean sonnet

Note: When words derived from proper nouns have lost their specialized meanings, do not capitalize them: *china bowl, french fries.*

GRAMMAR CHECKER   Checking Proper Nouns

Your spell checker may not recognize many of the proper nouns you use in your documents, particularly those that have irregular capitalization, such as *Leonardo da Vinci,* and therefore will identify these nouns as spelling errors. It may also fail to recognize certain discipline-specific proper nouns.

To solve this problem, click Ignore once to instruct the spell checker to ignore the word one time and Ignore All to instruct the spell checker to ignore all uses of the word in your document.

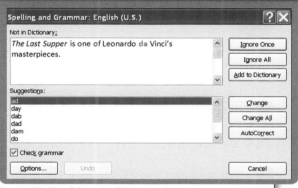

Copyright 2011, Microsoft Corporation. All Rights Reserved.

52c   Capitalizing Important Words in Titles

In general, capitalize all words in titles with the exception of articles (*a, an,* and *the*), prepositions, coordinating conjunctions, and the *to* in infinitives. If an article, preposition, or coordinating conjunction is the *first* or *last* word in the title or subtitle, however, do capitalize it.

"Dover Beach"   On the Waterfront
The Declaration of Independence   *Madame Curie: A Biography*
Across the River and into the Trees   "What Friends Are For"

52d Capitalizing the Pronoun *I*, the Interjection *O*, and Other Single Letters in Special Constructions

Always capitalize the pronoun *I* even if it is part of a contraction (*I'm, I'll, I've*).

Always capitalize the interjection *O*.

Give us peace in our time, O Lord.

However, do not capitalize the interjection *oh* unless it begins a sentence.

Note: Many other single letters are capitalized in certain usages: *an A in history, vitamin B, C major.* Check a dictionary to determine whether or not to use a capital letter.

52e Editing Misused Capitals

Do not use capital letters for emphasis or as an attention-getting strategy. If you are not certain whether a word should be capitalized, consult your dictionary.

1 Seasons

Do not capitalize the names of the seasons—summer, fall, winter, spring—unless they are personified, as in *Old Man Winter.*

2 Centuries and Loosely Defined Historical Periods

Do not capitalize the names of centuries or of general historical periods.

seventeenth-century poetry
the automobile age

Do, however, capitalize the names of specific historical, anthropological, and geological periods.

the Renaissance   Iron Age   Paleozoic Era

3 Diseases and Other Medical Terms

Do not capitalize names of diseases or medical tests or conditions unless a proper noun is part of the name or unless the disease is an **acronym.**

smallpox	Apgar test	AIDS
Lyme disease	mumps	SIDS

CHAPTER 53

Using Italics

53a   Setting Off Titles and Names

Use italics for the categories of titles and names listed in the box below. All other titles are set off with quotation marks.

Titles and Names Set in Italics

Books: *Twilight, Harry Potter and the Deathly Hallows*

Newspapers: the *Washington Post*, the *Philadelphia Inquirer* (According to MLA style, the word *the* is not italicized in titles of newspapers.)

Magazines and Journals: *Rolling Stone, Scientific American*

Online Magazines and Journals: *salon.com, theonion.com*

Web Sites or Home Pages: *urbanlegends.com, movie-mistakes.com*

Pamphlets: *Common Sense*

Films: *Citizen Kane, Avatar*

Television Programs: *Glee, American Idol, The Biggest Loser*

Radio Programs: *All Things Considered, A Prairie Home Companion*

Long Poems: *John Brown's Body, The Faerie Queen*

Plays: *Macbeth, A Raisin in the Sun*

Long Musical Works: *Rigoletto, Eroica*

Software Programs: *Microsoft Word, PowerPoint*

Search Engines and Web Browsers: *Google, Internet Explorer, Safari*

Databases: *Academic Search Premier, Expanded Academic ASAP Plus*

Paintings and Sculpture: *Guernica, Pietà*

Ships: *Lusitania*, U.S.S. *Saratoga* (S.S. and U.S.S. are not italicized.)

Trains: *City of New Orleans*, the *Orient Express*

Aircraft: the *Hindenburg, Enola Gay* (Only particular aircraft, not makes or types such as Piper Cub or Boeing 757, are italicized.)

Spacecraft: *Challenger, Enterprise*

Names of sacred books, such as the Bible and the Qur'an, and well-known documents, such as the Constitution and the Declaration of Independence, are neither italicized nor placed within quotation marks.

53b Setting Off Foreign Words and Phrases

Italics are often used to set off foreign words and phrases that have not become part of the English language.

> *"C'est la vie,"* Madeleine said when she saw the long line for the concert.

> *Spirochaeta plicatilis* is a corkscrew-like bacterium.

If you are not sure if a foreign word has been assimilated into English, consult a dictionary.

53c Setting Off Elements Spoken of as Themselves and Terms Being Defined

Use italics to set off letters, numerals, and words that refer to the letters, numerals, and words themselves.

> Is that a *p* or a *g*?

> I forget the exact address, but I know it has a *3* in it.

> Does *through* rhyme with *cough*?

Also use italics to set off words and phrases that you go on to define.

> A *closet drama* is a play meant to be read, not performed.

 When you quote a dictionary definition, put the word you are defining in italics and the definition itself in quotation marks.

> To *infer* means "to draw a conclusion"; to *imply* means "to suggest."

53d Using Italics for Emphasis

 Italics can occasionally be used for emphasis.

> Initially, poetry might be defined as a kind of language that says *more* and says it *more intensely* than does ordinary language. (Lawrence Perrine, *Sound and Sense*)

> However, overuse of italics is distracting. Instead of italicizing, try to indicate emphasis through word choice and sentence structure.

CHAPTER 54

Using Hyphens

Hyphens have two conventional uses: to break a word at the end of a line and to link words in certain compounds.

54a Breaking a Word at the End of a Line

A computer never breaks a word at the end of a line; if the full word will not fit, it is automatically brought down to the next line. Sometimes, however, you may want to break a word with a hyphen—for example, to fill in space at the end of a line.

When you break a word at the end of a line, divide it only between syllables, consulting a dictionary if necessary. Never divide a word at the end of a page, and never hyphenate a one-syllable word. In addition, never leave a single letter at the end of a line or carry only one or two letters to the next line.

If you divide a **compound word** at the end of a line, put the hyphen between the elements of the compound (*snow-mobile,* not *snowmo-bile*).

See
54b

 Close-Up DIVIDING ELECTRONIC ADDRESSES (URLS)

Never insert a hyphen to divide an electronic address (URL) at the end of a line. (Readers might think the hyphen is part of the address.) MLA style recommends that you break the URL after a slash. If this is not possible, break it in a logical place—after a period, for example—or avoid the problem altogether by moving the entire URL to the next line.

54b Dividing Compound Words

A **compound word** is composed of two or more words. Some familiar compound words are always hyphenated: *no-hitter, helter-skelter.* Other compounds are written as one word (*peacetime, fireplace*) or as two separate words (*labor relations, bunk bed*). Many formerly hyphenated compound nouns (for example, *daycare* and *healthcare*) are now often written as one word. Consult a dictionary to determine whether a particular compound requires a hyphen.

GRAMMAR CHECKER Hyphenating Compound Words

Your grammar checker will highlight certain compound words with incorrect or missing hyphenation and offer suggestions for revision. In most cases, you should follow the grammar checker's suggestion.

Spelling and Grammar: English (U.S.)

Compound Words:

Self reliance is a concept Emerson explores in his famous essay with the same name.

Suggestions:

Self-reliance

Hyphens are generally used in the following compounds.

❶ In Compound Adjectives

A **compound adjective** is made up of two or more words that function together as an adjective.

● When a compound adjective *precedes* the noun it modifies, use hyphens to join its elements.

The research team tried to use <u>nineteenth-century</u> technology to design a <u>space-age</u> project.

● When a compound adjective *follows* the noun it modifies, do not use hyphens to join its elements.

The three government-operated programs were run smoothly, but the one that was not <u>government operated</u> was short of funds.

Note: A compound adjective formed with an adverb ending in *-ly* is not hyphenated even when it precedes the noun: *Many <u>upwardly mobile</u> families are on tight budgets.*

Use **suspended hyphens**—hyphens followed by a space or by appropriate punctuation and a space—in a series of compounds that modify the same word.

Graduates of two- and four-year colleges were eligible for the grants.

The exam called for sentence-, paragraph-, and essay-length answers.

2 With Certain Prefixes or Suffixes

Use a hyphen between a prefix and a proper noun or proper adjective.

mid-July   pre-Columbian

Use a hyphen to connect the prefixes *all-*, *ex-*, *half-*, *quarter-*, *quasi-*, and *self-* and the suffix *-elect* to a noun.

ex-senator   self-centered
quarter-moon   president-elect

Note: The words *selfhood*, *selfish*, and *selfless* do not include hyphens because in these cases, *self* is the root, not a prefix.

3 In Compound Numerals and Fractions

Hyphenate compounds that represent numbers below one hundred (even if they are part of a larger number).

the twenty-first century
three hundred sixty-five days

Also hyphenate the written form of a fraction when it modifies a noun.

a two-thirds share of the business

4 For Clarity

Hyphenate to prevent readers from misreading one word for another.

In order to reform criminals, we must re-form our ideas about prisons.

Hyphenate to avoid certain hard-to-read combinations, such as two *i*'s (*semi-illiterate*) or more than two of the same consonant (*skill-less*).

In most cases, hyphenate between a capital initial and a word when the two combine to form a compound: *A-frame*, *T-shirt*, *D-day*.

5 In Coined Compounds

A **coined compound,** one that uses a new combination of words as a unit, requires hyphens.

He looked up with a who-do-you-think-you-are expression.

CHAPTER 55

Using Abbreviations

Generally speaking, **abbreviations** are not appropriate in college writing except in tables, charts, and works-cited lists. Some abbreviations are acceptable in scientific, technical, or business writing, or only in a particular academic <u>discipline</u>. If you have questions about the appropriateness of a particular abbreviation, check the style manual of the field for which you are writing.

See
Pt. 3

Close-Up   ABBREVIATIONS IN ELECTRONIC
COMMUNICATIONS

Like emoticons, which are popular in personal email and instant messages, shorthand abbreviations and symbols—such as GR8 (great) and 2NITE (tonight)—are common in text messages. Although acceptable in informal electronic communication, such abbreviations are not appropriate in college writing or in business communications.

55a   Abbreviating Titles

Titles before and after proper names are usually abbreviated.

Mr. Homer Simpson	Rep. Carolyn McCarthy
Henry Kissinger, PhD	Dr. Martin Luther King, Jr.

Do not, however, use an abbreviated title without a name.

doctor
The ~~Dr.~~ diagnosed hepatitis.

55b   Abbreviating Organization Names and Technical Terms

Well-known businesses and government, social, and civic organizations are frequently referred to by capitalized initials. These abbreviations fall into two categories: those in which the initials are pronounced as separate units (EPA, MTV) and **acronyms,** in which the initials are pronounced as words (UNICEF, NATO).

To save space, you may also use accepted abbreviations for complex technical terms that are not well known, but be sure to spell out the full term the first time you mention it, followed by the abbreviation in parentheses.

> Citrus farmers have been using ethylene dibromide (EDB), a chemical pesticide, for more than twenty years. Now, however, EDB has contaminated water supplies.

Close-Up   ABBREVIATIONS IN MLA DOCUMENTATION

<u>MLA documentation style</u> requires abbreviations of publishers' company names—for example, **Columbia UP** for *Columbia University Press*—in the works-cited list. Do not, however, use such abbreviations in the text of your paper.

See
21a

MLA style permits the use of abbreviations that designate parts of written works (**ch. 3, sec. 7**)—but only in the works-cited list and parenthetical documentation.

Finally, MLA recommends abbreviating literary works and books of the Bible in parenthetical references: *Oth.* (*Othello*), **Exod.** (Exodus). These words should not be abbreviated in the text of your paper.

55c   Abbreviating Dates, Times of Day, and Temperatures

Dates, times of day, and temperatures are often abbreviated.

50 BC (*BC* follows the date)	AD 432 (*AD* precedes the date)
3:03 p.m.	180° F (Fahrenheit)

Always capitalize *BC* and *AD*. (The alternatives *BCE*, for "before the Common Era," and *CE*, for "Common Era," are also capitalized.) Use lowercase letters for *a.m.* and *p.m.*, but use these abbreviations only when they are accompanied by numbers.

morning.

I'll see you in the ̠a̶.̶m̶.̶

Note: Avoid the abbreviation *no.* (written either *no.* or *No.*), except in technical writing, and then use it only before a specific number: *The unidentified substance was labeled <u>no.</u> 52.*

55d Editing Misused Abbreviations

In college writing, the following are not abbreviated.

❶ Names of Days, Months, or Holidays

Do not abbreviate days of the week, months, or holidays.

On ~~Sat., Dec.~~ *Saturday, December* 23, I started my ~~Xmas~~ *Christmas* shopping.

❷ Names of Streets and Places

In general, do not abbreviate names of streets and places.

He lives on Riverside ~~Dr.~~ *Drive* in ~~NYC.~~ *New York City.*

Exceptions: The abbreviation *US* is often acceptable (*US Coast Guard*), as is *DC* in *Washington, DC*. Also permissible are *Mt.* before the name of a mountain (*Mt. Etna*) and *St.* in a place name (*St. Albans*).

❸ Names of Academic Subjects

Do not abbreviate names of academic subjects.

~~Psych.~~ *Psychology* and English ~~lit.~~ *literature* are required courses.

❹ Names of Businesses

Write company names exactly as the firms themselves write them: *AT&T*, *Charles Schwab & Co., Inc.* Abbreviations for *company*, *corporation*, and the like are used only along with a company name.

The ~~corp.~~ *corporation* merged with a ~~co.~~ *company* in Ohio.

❺ Latin Expressions

Abbreviations of the common Latin phrases *i.e.* ("that is"), *e.g.* ("for example"), and *etc.* ("and so forth") are not appropriate in college writing.

Other musicians (~~e.g.~~ *for example,* Bruce Springsteen) have also been influenced by Bob Dylan.

Poe wrote "The Raven," "Annabel Lee," ~~etc.~~ *and other poems.*

6 Units of Measurement

In technical and business writing, some units of measurement are abbreviated when they are preceded by a numeral.

The hurricane had winds of more than 35 mph.

One new hybrid car gets over 50 mpg.

MLA style, however, requirses that you write out units of measurement and spell out words such as *inches, feet, years, miles, pints, quarts,* and *gallons.*

7 Symbols

The symbols +, =, and # are acceptable in technical and scientific writing but not in nontechnical college writing. The symbols % and $ are acceptable only when used with **numerals** (15%, $15,000), not with spelled-out numbers.

See
56b4, 7

CHAPTER **56**

Using Numbers

Convention determines when to use a **numeral** (22) and when to spell out a number (twenty-two). Numerals are commonly used in scientific and technical writing and in journalism, but they are used less often in the humanities.

Note: The guidelines in this chapter are based on the *MLA Handbook for Writers of Research Papers,* 7th ed. (2009). APA style, however, requires that all numbers below ten be spelled out if they do not represent specific measurements and that numbers ten and above be expressed in numerals.

56a Spelled-Out Numbers versus Numerals

Unless a number falls into one of the categories listed in **56b,** spell it out if you can do so *in one or two words.*

The Hawaiian alphabet has only <u>twelve</u> letters.

Class size stabilized at <u>twenty-eight</u> students.

The subsidies are expected to total about <u>two</u> million dollars.

Numbers *more than two words* long are expressed in figures.

The dietitian prepared <u>125</u> sample menus.

The developer of the community purchased <u>300,000</u> doorknobs and <u>153,000</u> faucets.

Never begin a sentence with a numeral. If necessary, reword the sentence.

~~250 students are currently enrolled~~ in World History 106.

Current enrollment is 250 students.

Note: When one number immediately precedes another in a sentence, spell out the first, and use a numeral for the second: *five 3-quart containers.*

GRAMMAR CHECKER Spelled-Out Numbers versus Numerals

Your grammar checker will often highlight numerals in your writing and suggest that you spell them out. Before making a change, be sure that the number does not fall into one of the categories listed in **56b.**

Spelling and Grammar: English (U.S.)

Spell Out Number:

This essay by Walter Benjamin focuses on 2 groups of people: the victors and the vanquished.

Suggestions:

two

56b Conventional Uses of Numerals

1 Addresses

1920 Walnut Street, Philadelphia, PA 19103

2 Dates

January 15, 1929   1914–1919

3 Exact Times

9:16   10 a.m. (or 10:00 a.m.)

Exceptions: Spell out times of day when they are used with *o'clock:* <u>eleven</u> *o'clock,* not *11 o'clock.* Also spell out times expressed as round numbers: *They were in bed by* <u>ten</u>*.*

4 Exact Sums of Money

$25.11 $6,752.00

Note: Always use a numeral (not a spelled-out number) with a $ symbol. You may spell out a round sum of money if you use sums infrequently in your paper, provided you can do so in two or three words: *five dollars; two thousand dollars.*

5 Divisions of Written Works

Use arabic (not roman) numerals for chapter and volume numbers; for acts, scenes, and lines of plays; for chapters and verses of the Bible; and for line numbers of long poems.

6 Measurements before an Abbreviation or Symbol

12"   55 mph
32°   15 cc

7 Percentages and Decimals

80%   3.14

Note: You may spell out a percentage (*eighty percent*) if you use percentages infrequently in your paper, provided the percentage can be expressed in two or three words. However, always use a numeral (not a spelled-out number) with a % symbol.

8 Ratios, Scores, and Statistics

In a paper that follows **APA** style, use numerals for numbers presented as a comparison.

See Ch. 22

Children preferred Fun Flakes over Graino by a ratio of 20 to 1.

The Orioles defeated the Phillies 6–0.

The median age of the voters was 42; the mean age was 40.

9 Identification Numbers

Route 66   Track 8   Channel 12

When writing out large numbers, insert a comma every three digits from the right, beginning after the third digit.

3,000   25,000   6,751,098

Do not, however, use commas in four-digit page and line numbers, addresses, or year numbers.

page 1202   3741 Laurel Ave.   1968

P A R T **14**

Resources for Bilingual and ESL Writers

Resources for Bilingual and ESL Writers

❓ Frequently Asked Questions

CHAPTER 57

Adjusting to the US Classroom

If you went to school outside of the United States, you may not be familiar with the way writing is taught in US composition classes.

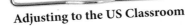

Adjusting to the US Classroom

Here are some aspects of US classrooms that may be unfamiliar to you:

- **Punctuality** Students are expected to be in their seats and ready to begin class at the scheduled time. If you are late repeatedly, your grade may be lowered.
- **Student–Instructor Relationships** The relationship between students and instructors may be more casual or friendly than you are used to. However, instructors still expect students to abide by the rules they set.
- **Class Discussion** Instructors typically expect students to volunteer ideas in class and may even enjoy it when students disagree with their opinions (as long as the students can make good arguments for their positions). Rather than being a sign of disrespect, this is usually considered to be evidence of interest and involvement in the topic under discussion.

57a Understanding the Writing Process

Typically, US composition instructors teach writing as a **process**. This process usually includes the following components:

See
Chs. 4–6

- **Planning and shaping your writing** Your instructor will probably help you get ideas for your writing by assigning relevant readings, conducting class discussions, and asking you to keep a journal or engage in **freewriting** and **brainstorming**.

See
4e

- **Writing multiple drafts** After you write your paper for the first time, you will probably get feedback from your instructor or your classmates so that you can **revise** (improve) your paper before receiving a grade on it.

Instructors expect students to use the suggestions they receive to make significant improvements to their papers. (For more information on the drafting process, **see Chapter 6.**)

- **Looking at sample papers** Your instructor may provide the class with sample papers of the type that he or she has assigned. Such samples can help you understand how to complete the assigned paper. Sometimes the samples are strong papers that can serve as good examples of what to do. However, most samples will have both strengths and weaknesses, so be sure you understand your instructor's opinion of the samples he or she provides.

See 6c2

- **Engaging in** peer review (sometimes called peer editing) Your instructor may ask the class to work in small groups or in pairs to exchange ideas about an assigned paper. You will be expected to provide other students with feedback on the strengths and weaknesses of their papers. Afterward, you should think carefully about your classmates' comments about your paper and make changes to improve it.

- **Attending conferences** Your instructor may schedule one or more appointments with you to discuss your writing and may ask you to bring a draft of the paper you are working on. Your instructor may also be available to help you with your paper without an appointment during his or her office hours. In addition, many educational institutions have **writing centers** where tutors help students get started on their papers or improve their drafts. When you meet with your instructor or writing center tutor, bring a list of specific questions about your paper, and be sure to make careful notes about what you discuss. You can refer to these notes when you revise your paper.

Close-Up USING YOUR NATIVE LANGUAGE

Depending on your language background and skills, you may find it helpful to use your native language in some stages of your writing.

When you are making notes about the content of your paper, you may be able to generate more ideas and record them more quickly if you do some of the work in your native language. Additionally, when you are drafting your paper and cannot think of a particular word in English, it may be better simply to write the word in your native language (and come back to it later) so you do not lose your train of thought.

However, if you use another language a great deal as you draft your writing and then try to translate your work into English, the English may sound awkward or be hard for readers to understand. The best strategy when you draft your papers is to write in English as much as you can, using the vocabulary and structures that you already know.

57b Understanding English Language Basics

Getting used to writing and editing your work in English will be easier if you understand a few basic principles:

- **In English, words may change their form according to their function.** For example, <u>verbs</u> change form to communicate whether an action is taking place in the past, present, or future. ESL 58a
- **In English, context is extremely important to understanding function.** In the following sentences, for instance, the very same words can perform different functions according to their relationships to other words.

    > Juan and I are taking a <u>walk</u>. (*Walk* is a noun, a direct object of the verb *taking*, with an article, *a*, attached to it.)

    > If you <u>walk</u> instead of driving, you will help conserve the Earth's resources. (*Walk* is a verb, the predicate of the subject *you*.)

- **Spelling in English is not always phonetic and sometimes may seem illogical.** <u>Spelling</u> in English may be related more to the history of the word and to its origins in other languages than to the way the word is pronounced. Therefore, learning to spell correctly is often a matter of memorization, not sounding out the word phonetically. For example, "ough" is pronounced differently in *tough*, *though*, and *thought*. See Ch. 51
- **<u>Word order</u> is extremely important in English sentences.** In English sentences, word order may indicate which word is the subject of the sentence and which is the object, whether the sentence is a question or a statement, and so on. ESL 58f

57c Learning to Edit Your Work

<u>Editing</u> your papers involves focusing on grammar, spelling, punctuation, and mechanics. The approach you take to editing for grammar errors should depend on your strengths and weaknesses in English. See 6d1

If you learned English mostly by speaking it, if you have strong oral skills, and if you instinctively make correct judgments about English, the best approach for you may be reading your paper aloud and listening for mistakes, correcting them by deciding what sounds right. You may even find that as you read aloud, you automatically correct your written mistakes. (Be sure to transfer those corrections to your paper.) In addition to proofreading your paper from beginning to end, you might find it helpful to start from the end of the paper, reading and proofreading sentence by sentence. This strategy can keep you from being distracted by your ideas, allowing you to focus on grammar alone.

If you learned English mostly by reading, studying grammar rules, and/ or translating between your native language and English, you may not feel that you have good instincts about what sounds right in English. If this is the case, you should take a different approach to editing your papers. First, identify the errors you make most frequently by looking at earlier papers your instructor has marked or by asking your instructor for help. Once you have identified your most common errors, read through your paper, checking each sentence for these errors. Try to apply the grammar and mechanics rules you already know, or check the relevant grammar explanations in **Chapter 58** for help.

After you check your paper for grammar errors, you should check again to make sure that you have used proper punctuation, capitalization, and spelling. If you have difficulty with spelling, you can use a spell checker to help you, but remember that spell checkers cannot catch every error. After you have made grammar and mechanics corrections on your own, you can seek outside help in identifying errors you might have missed. You should also keep a notebook with a list of your most frequent grammatical errors and review it often.

CHAPTER **58**

Grammar and Style for ESL Writers

For ESL writers (as for many native English writers), grammar can be a persistent problem. Grammatical knowledge in a second language usually develops slowly, with time and practice, and much about English is idiomatic and not subject to easy-to-learn rules. This chapter is designed to provide you with the tools you will need to address some of the most common grammatical problems ESL writers face.

58a Using Verbs

❓ **1** Subject-Verb Agreement

See A3 English **verbs** change their form according to person, number, and tense. The verb in a sentence must **agree** with the subject in both person and number. **Person** refers to *who* or *what* is performing the action of the verb (for example, *I, you,* or someone else), and **number** refers to *how many* people or things are performing the action (one or more than one).

See 34a

In English, the rules for **subject-verb agreement** are very important. Unless you use the correct person and number in the verbs in your sentences, you will confuse your English-speaking audience by communicating meanings you do not intend.

Close-Up SUBJECT-VERB AGREEMENT

Follow these basic guidelines when selecting verbs for your sentences:

- If the subject consists of only one noun or pronoun, use a singular verb.

  He is at the park.

- If the subject consists of two or more nouns or pronouns connected with the word *and,* use a plural verb.

  Bob and Carol are at the park.

- If the subject contains both a singular and a plural noun or pronoun connected with the word *or,* the verb should agree with the noun that is nearer to it.

  Bob or the boys are at the park.

  The boys or Bob is at the park.

Note: Don't be confused by phrases that come between the subject and the verb. The verb should agree with the subject of the sentence, not with a noun that appears within an intervening phrase.

The woman with all of the children is at the park.

The coach, as well as the players, is nervous.

For information on subject-verb agreement with **indefinite pronouns,** such as *each, everyone,* and *nobody,* see **34a4.**

2 Verb Tense

See 37b

Tense refers to *when* the action of the verb takes place. One problem that many nonnative speakers of English have with English verb tenses results from the large number of **irregular verbs** in English. For example, the first-person singular present tense of *be* is not "I be" but "I am," and the past tense is not "I beed" but "I was."

See 37a2

Note: ESL writers whose first language is Chinese, Japanese, Korean, Russian, Thai, or Vietnamese are especially likely to have difficulty with verb tenses.

Close-Up CHOOSING THE SIMPLEST VERB FORMS

Some nonnative English speakers use verb forms that are more complicated than they need to be. They may do this because their native language
uses more complicated verb forms than English does or because they
"overcorrect" their verbs into complicated forms. Specifically, nonnative
speakers tend to use progressive and perfect verb forms instead of simple
verb forms. To communicate your ideas clearly to an English-speaking
audience, choose the simplest possible verb form.

3 Auxiliary Verbs

The **auxiliary verbs** (also known as **helping verbs**) *be, have*, and *do* are used
to create some present, past, and future forms of verbs in English: "Julio is
taking a vacation"; "I have been tired lately"; "He does not need a license."
The auxiliary verbs *be, have*, and *do* change form to reflect the time frame of
the action or situation and to agree with the subject.

Note: ESL writers whose first language is Arabic, Chinese, Creole, Haitian,
or Russian are likely to have more difficulty with auxiliary verbs because
their first language sometimes omits the *be* verb.

Close-Up AUXILIARY VERBS

Only auxiliary verbs, not the verbs they "help," change form to indicate
person, number, and tense.

Present: We have to eat.

Past: We had to eat. (*not* "We had to ate.")

Modal auxiliaries (such as *can* and *should*) do not change form to indicate
tense, person, or number.

See
A3

4 Negative Verbs

The meaning of a verb may be made negative in English in a variety of ways,
chiefly by adding the words *not* or *does not* to the verb (is, is *not*; can ski,
can't ski; drives a car, *does not* drive a car).

Close-Up   CORRECTING DOUBLE NEGATIVES

A **double negative** occurs when the meaning of a verb is made negative not just once but twice in a single sentence.

any   *has*

Henry doesn't have ~~no~~ friends. (*or* Henry ~~doesn't have~~ no friends.)

I looked for articles in the library, but there weren't ~~none~~. (*or* I looked for

any

articles in the library, but there weren't ~~none~~.)

Note: ESL writers whose first language is Spanish may tend to use double negatives.

5 Phrasal Verbs

Many verbs in English are composed of two or more words that are combined to create a new idiomatic expression—for example, *check up on, run for, turn into,* and *wait on.* These verbs are called **phrasal verbs.** It is important to become familiar with phrasal verbs and their definitions so you will recognize these verbs as phrasal verbs (instead of as verbs that are followed by prepositions).

Separable Phrasal Verbs   Often, the words that make up a phrasal verb can be separated from each other by a direct object. In these **separable phrasal verbs,** the object can come either before or after the preposition. For example, "Ellen turned down the job offer" and "Ellen turned the job offer down" are both correct. However, when the object is a pronoun, the pronoun must come before the preposition. Therefore, "Ellen turned it down" is correct, but "Ellen turned down it" is incorrect.

Close-Up   SEPARABLE PHRASAL VERBS

Verb	Definition
call off	cancel
carry on	continue
cheer up	make happy

(continued)

SEPARABLE PHRASAL VERBS *(continued)*

Verb	Definition
clean out	clean the inside of
cut down	reduce
figure out	solve
fill in	substitute
find out	discover
give back	return something
give up	stop doing something or stop trying
leave out	omit
pass on	transmit
put away	place something in its proper place
put back	place something in its original place
put off	postpone
start over	start again
talk over	discuss
throw away/out	discard
touch up	repair

Inseparable Phrasal Verbs   Some phrasal verbs—such as *look into, make up for,* and *break into*—consist of words that can never be separated. With these **inseparable phrasal verbs,** you do not have a choice about where to place the object; the object must always directly follow the preposition. For example, "<u>Anna</u> <u><u>cared for</u></u> her niece" is correct, but "<u>Anna</u> <u><u>cared</u></u> her niece <u><u>for</u></u>" is incorrect.

 Close-Up   INSEPARABLE PHRASAL VERBS

Verb	Definition
come down with	develop an illness
come up with	produce
do away with	abolish
fall behind in	lag
get along with	be congenial with
get away with	avoid punishment
keep up with	maintain the same achievement or speed
look up to	admire

Verb	Definition
make up for	compensate
put up with	tolerate
run into	meet by chance
see to	arrange
show up	arrive
stand by	wait or remain loyal to
stand up for	support
watch out for	beware of or protect

6 Voice

See 37d

Verbs may be in either active or passive <u>voice</u>. When the subject of a sentence performs the action of the verb, the verb is in **active voice.** When the action of the verb is performed on the subject, the verb is in **passive voice.**

<u>Karla and Miguel</u> <u>purchased</u> the tickets. (active voice)

<u>The tickets</u> <u>were purchased</u> by Karla and Miguel. (passive voice)

<u>The tickets</u> <u>were purchased</u>. (passive voice)

Because your writing will usually be clearer and more concise if you use the active voice, you should use the passive voice only when you have a good reason to do so.

When deciding whether to use the passive or active voice, you need to consider what you want to focus on. In the first example above, the focus is on Karla and Miguel. However, the second and third examples above, which use the passive voice, put the focus on the fact that the tickets *were purchased* rather than on *who* purchased them.

Note: ESL writers whose first language is Creole, Japanese, Korean, Russian, Thai, or Vietnamese encounter unique challenges with voice when writing in English.

7 Transitive and Intransitive Verbs

Many nonnative English speakers find it difficult to decide whether or not a verb needs an object and in what order direct and indirect objects should appear in a sentence. Learning the difference between transitive verbs and intransitive verbs can help you with such problems.

A **transitive verb** is a verb that has a direct object: "<u>My father</u> <u>asked</u> a question" (subject + verb + direct object). In this example, *asked* is a transitive verb; it needs an object to complete its meaning.

An **intransitive verb** is a verb that does not take an object: "<u>The doctor</u> <u>smiled</u>" (subject + verb). In this example, *smiled* is an intransitive verb; it does not need an object to complete its meaning.

A transitive verb may be followed by a direct object or by both an indirect object and a direct object. (An indirect object answers the question "To whom?" or "For whom?") The indirect object may come before or after the direct object. If the indirect object follows the direct object, the preposition *to* or *for* must precede the indirect object.

> <small>s   v   do</small>
> Keith <u>wrote</u> a letter. (subject + verb + direct object)

> <small>s   v   io   do</small>
> Keith <u>wrote</u> his friend a letter. (subject + verb + indirect object + direct object)

> <small>s   v   do   io</small>
> Keith <u>wrote</u> a letter to his friend. (subject + verb + direct object + to/for + indirect object)

Some verbs in English look similar and have similar meanings, except that one is transitive and the other is intransitive. For example, *lie* is intransitive, *lay* is transitive; *sit* is intransitive, *set* is transitive; *rise* is intransitive, *raise* is transitive. Knowing whether a verb is transitive or intransitive will help you with troublesome verb pairs like these and will help you place words in the correct order. (See the **Glossary of Usage** for more on these verb pairs.)

<small>See 37d</small>

Note: It is also important to know whether a verb is transitive or intransitive because only transitive verbs can be used in the <u>passive voice.</u> To determine whether a verb is transitive or intransitive—that is, to determine whether or not it needs an object—consult the example phrases in a dictionary.

⑧ Infinitives and Gerunds

In English, two verb forms may be used as nouns: **infinitives,** which always begin with *to* (as in *to work, to sleep, to eat*), and **gerunds,** which always end in *-ing*, (as in *working, sleeping, eating*).

> <u>To bite into this steak</u> <u>requires</u> better teeth than mine. (infinitive used as a noun)

> <u>Cooking</u> <u>is</u> one of my favorite hobbies. (gerund used as a noun)

Sometimes the gerund and the infinitive form of the same verb can be used interchangeably. For example, "He continued *to sleep*" and "He continued *sleeping*" convey the same meaning. However, this is not always the case. Saying, "Marco and Lisa stopped *to eat* at Julio's Café" is not the same as saying, "Marco and Lisa stopped *eating* at Julio's Café." In this example, the meaning of the sentence changes depending on whether a gerund or infinitive is used.

Note: ESL writers whose first language is Arabic, Chinese, Farsi, French, Greek, Korean, Portuguese, Spanish, or Vietnamese may have difficulty with gerunds.

9 Participles

In English, verb forms called **present participles** and **past participles** are frequently used as adjectives. Present participles end in *-ing*, as in *working, sleeping,* and *eating,* and past participles usually end in *-ed, -t,* or *-en,* as in *worked, slept,* and *eaten.*

> She had a <u>burning</u> desire to be president. (present participle used as an adjective)

> Some people think raw fish is healthier than <u>cooked</u> fish. (past participle used as an adjective)

A **participial phrase** is a group of words consisting of the participle plus the noun phrase that functions as the object or complement of the action being expressed by the participle. To avoid confusion, the participial phrase must be placed as close as possible to the noun it modifies.

> <u>Having visited San Francisco last week</u>, Jim and Lynn showed us pictures from their vacation. (The participial phrase is used as an adjective that modifies *Jim and Lynn*.)

10 Verbs Formed from Nouns

In English, nouns can sometimes be used as verbs, with no change in form (other than the addition of an *-s* for agreement with third-person singular subjects or the addition of past tense endings). For example, the nouns *chair, book, frame,* and *father* can all be used as verbs.

> She <u>chairs</u> a committee on neighborhood safety.

> We <u>booked</u> a flight to New York for next week.

> I will <u>frame</u> my daughter's diploma after she graduates.

> He <u>fathered</u> seventeen children.

58b Using Nouns

<u>Nouns</u> name things: people, animals, objects, places, feelings, ideas. If a noun names one thing, it is singular; if a noun names more than one thing, it is plural.

See A1

1 Recognizing Noncount Nouns

Some English nouns do not have a plural form. These are called **noncount nouns** because what they name cannot be counted.

Note: ESL writers whose first language is Chinese or Japanese are likely to have trouble with noncount nouns.

Close-Up   NONCOUNT NOUNS

The following commonly used nouns are noncount nouns. These words have no plural forms. Therefore, you should never add -s to them.

advice	homework
clothing	information
education	knowledge
equipment	luggage
evidence	merchandise
furniture	revenge

---

2 Using Articles with Nouns

English has two kinds of **articles**, *indefinite* and *definite.*

Use an **indefinite article** (*a* or *an*) with a noun when readers are not familiar with the noun you are naming—when you are introducing the noun for the first time, for example. To say, "James entered *a* building," signals to the audience that you are introducing the idea of the building for the first time. The building is indefinite, or not specific, until it has been identified.

The indefinite article *a* is used when the word following it (which may be a noun or an adjective) begins with a consonant or with a consonant sound: *a tree, a onetime offer.* The indefinite article *an* is used if the word following it begins with a vowel (*a, e, i, o,* or *u*) or with a vowel sound: *an apple, an honor.*

Use the **definite article** (*the*) when the noun you are naming has already been introduced, when the noun is already familiar to readers, or when the noun to which you refer is specific. To say, "James entered *the* building," signals to readers that you are referring to the same building you mentioned earlier. The building has now become specific and may be referred to by the definite article.

Note: ESL writers whose first language is Chinese, Farsi, Japanese, Russian, or Swahili will have difficulty with articles.

Close-Up   USING ARTICLES WITH NOUNS

There are two exceptions to the rules governing the use of articles with nouns:

1. **Plural** nouns do not require indefinite articles: "I love horses," not "I love a horses." (However, plural nouns do require definite articles if you have already introduced the noun or if you are referring to a specific noun: "I love the horses in the national park near my house.")

2. **Noncount nouns** may not require articles: "Love conquers all," not "A love conquers all" or "The love conquers all."

3 Using Other Determiners with Nouns

Determiners are words that function as adjectives to limit or qualify the meaning of nouns. In addition to articles, **demonstrative pronouns, possessive nouns and pronouns, numbers** (both **cardinal** and **ordinal**), and other words indicating number and order can function in this way.

Close-Up   USING OTHER DETERMINERS WITH NOUNS

- **Demonstrative pronouns** (*this, that, these, those*) communicate the following:

  1. the relative nearness or farness of the noun from the speaker's position (*this* and *these* for things that are *near*, *that* and *those* for things that are *far*): *this* book on my desk, *that* book on your desk; *these* shoes on my feet, *those* shoes in my closet.

  2. the number of things indicated (*this* and *that* for *singular* nouns, *these* and *those* for *plural* nouns): *this* (or *that*) flower in the vase, *these* (or *those*) flowers in the garden.

- **Possessive nouns and possessive pronouns** (*Ashraf's, his, their*) show who or what the noun belongs to: *Maria's* courage, *everybody's* fears, the *country's* natural resources, *my* personality, *our* groceries.
- **Cardinal** numbers (*three, fifty, a thousand*) indicate how many of the noun you mean: *seven* continents. **Ordinal** numbers (*first, tenth, thirtieth*) indicate in what order the noun appears among other items: *third* planet.

(continued)

> **USING OTHER DETERMINERS WITH NOUNS** *(continued)*
>
> - Words other than numbers may indicate **amount** (*many, few*) and **order** (*next, last*) and function in the same ways as cardinal and ordinal numbers: *few* opportunities, *last* chance.

58c Using Pronouns

See
A2

Any English noun may be replaced by a <u>**pronoun**</u>. Pronouns enable you to avoid repeating a noun over and over. For example, *doctor* may be replaced by *he* or *she*, *books* by *them*, and *computer* by *it*.

❶ Pronoun Reference

See
38c

<u>**Pronoun reference**</u> is very important in English sentences, where the noun the pronoun replaces (the **antecedent**) must be easily identified. In general, you should place the pronoun as close as possible to the noun it replaces so the noun to which the pronoun refers is clear. If this is impossible, use the noun itself instead of replacing it with a pronoun.

Unclear: When Tara met Emily, she was nervous. (Does *she* refer to Tara or to Emily?)

Clear: When Tara met Emily, <u>Tara</u> was nervous.

Unclear: Stefano and Victor love his DVD collection. (Whose DVD collection—Stefano's, Victor's, or someone else's?)

Clear: Stefano and Victor love <u>Emilio's</u> DVD collection.

Note: ESL writers whose first language is Spanish or Thai will likely have difficulty with pronoun reference.

❷ Pronoun Placement

Never use a pronoun immediately after the noun it replaces. For example, do not say, "Most of my classmates they are smart"; instead, say, "Most of my classmates are smart."

The only exception to this rule occurs with an **intensive pronoun,** which ends in *-self* and emphasizes the preceding noun or pronoun: *Marta <u>herself</u> was eager to hear the results.*

❸ Indefinite Pronouns

Unlike **personal pronouns** (*I, you, he, she, it, we, they, me, him, her, us, them,* and so on), **indefinite pronouns** do not refer to a particular person, place, or thing. Therefore, an indefinite pronoun does not require an antecedent. **Indefinite pronoun subjects** (*anybody, nobody, each, either,* *someone, something, all, some*), like personal pronouns, must <u>agree</u> in number with the sentence's verb.

See 34a

       has
Nobody ˄have failed the exam. (*Nobody* is a singular subject and requires a singular verb.)

④ Appositives

Appositives are nouns or noun phrases that identify or rename an adjacent noun or pronoun. An appositive usually follows the noun it explains or modifies but can sometimes precede it.

> My parents, Mary and John, live in Louisiana. (*Mary and John* identifies *parents*.)

Note: The <u>case</u> of a pronoun in an appositive depends on the case of the word it identifies.

See 38a

If an appositive is *not* essential to the meaning of the sentence, use commas to set off the appositive from the rest of the sentence. If an appositive *is* essential to the meaning of the sentence, do not use commas.

> His aunt Trang is in the hospital. (*Trang* is necessary to the meaning of the sentence because it identifies which aunt is in the hospital.)

> Akta's car, a 1997 Jeep, broke down last night, so she had to walk home. (*a 1997 Jeep* is not essential to the meaning of the sentence.)

⑤ Pronouns and Gender

A pronoun must agree in **gender** with the noun to which it refers.

> My sister sold <u>her</u> old car.

> Your uncle is walking <u>his</u> dog.

Keep in mind that in English, most nonhuman nouns are referred to as *it* because they do not have grammatical gender. However, exceptions are sometimes made for pets, ships, and countries. Pets are often referred to as *he* or *she*, depending on their sex, and ships and countries are sometimes referred to as *she*.

Note: ESL writers whose first language is Bengali, Farsi, Gujarati, or Thai are likely to have problems with pronouns and gender.

58d   Using Adjectives and Adverbs

<u>Adjectives and adverbs</u> are words that **modify** (describe, limit, or qualify) other words.

See Ch. 39, A4–5

1 Position of Adjectives and Adverbs

Adjectives in English usually appear *before* the nouns they modify. A native speaker of English would not say, "Cars *red and black* are involved in more accidents than *cars blue or green*" but would say instead, "*Red and black* cars are involved in more accidents than *blue or green* cars."

However, adjectives may appear *after* linking verbs ("The name seemed *familiar*"), *after* direct objects ("The coach was *tired* but *happy*"), and *after* indefinite pronouns ("Anything *sad* makes me cry").

Adverbs may appear before or after the verbs they describe, but they should be placed as close to the verb as possible: not "I *told* John that I couldn't meet him for lunch *politely*," but "I *politely* told John that I couldn't meet him for lunch" or "I *told* John *politely* that I couldn't meet him for lunch." When an adverb describes an adjective or another adverb, it usually comes *before* that adjective or adverb: "The essay has *basically* sound logic"; "You must express yourself *absolutely* clearly."

Never place an adverb between the verb and the direct object.

Incorrect: Rolf drank *quickly* the water.

Correct: Rolf drank the water *quickly* (or, Rolf *quickly* drank the water).

Incorrect: Suong took *quietly* the test.

Correct: Suong *quietly* took the test (or, Suong took the test *quietly*).

Note: ESL writers whose first language is Creole, French, or Haitian are likely to have problems with adverbs.

2 Order of Adjectives

A single noun may be modified by more than one adjective, perhaps even by a whole list of adjectives. Given a list of three or four adjectives, most native speakers would arrange them in a sentence in the same order. If, for example, shoes are to be described as *green* and *big*, numbering *two*, and of the type worn for playing *tennis*, a native speaker would say "two big green tennis shoes." Generally, the adjectives that are most important in completing the meaning of the noun are placed closest to the noun.

❷ Close-Up ORDER OF ADJECTIVES

1. Articles (*a, the*), demonstratives (*this, those*), and possessives (*his, our, Maria's, everybody's*)
2. Amounts (*one, five, many, few*), order (*first, next, last*)
3. Personal opinions (*nice, ugly, crowded, pitiful*)

4. Sizes and shapes (*small, tall, straight, crooked*)
5. Age (*young, old, modern, ancient*)
6. Colors (*black, white, red, blue, dark, light*)
7. Nouns functioning as adjectives to form a unit with the noun (*soccer* ball, *cardboard* box, *history* class)

58e Using Prepositions

In English, <u>**prepositions**</u> (such as *to, from, at, with, among, between*) give meaning to nouns by linking them with other words and other parts of the sentence. Prepositions convey various kinds of information:

See A6

- Relations to **time** (*at* nine o'clock, *in* five minutes, *for* a month)
- Relations of **place** (*in* the classroom, *at* the library, *beside* the chair) and **direction** (*to* the market, *onto* the stage, *toward* the freeway)
- Relations of **association** (go *with* someone, the tip *of* the iceberg)
- Relations of **purpose** (working *for* money, dieting *to* lose weight)

1 Commonly Used Prepositional Phrases

In English, the use of prepositions is often **idiomatic**—that is, governed by grammatical rules. In many cases, therefore, learners of English as a second language need to memorize which prepositions are used in which phrases.

In English, some prepositions that relate to time have specific uses with certain nouns, such as days, months, and seasons:

- *On* is used with days and specific dates: *on* Monday, *on* September 13, 1977.
- *In* is used with months, seasons, and years: *in* November, *in* the spring, *in* 1999.
- *In* is also used when referring to some parts of the day: *in* the morning, *in* the afternoon, *in* the evening.
- *At* is used to refer to other parts of the day: *at* noon, *at* night, *at* seven o'clock.

Close-Up DIFFICULT PREPOSITIONAL PHRASES

The following phrases (accompanied by their correct prepositions) sometimes cause difficulties for ESL writers:

according *to*	appeal *to*	*at* least
apologize *to*	different *from*	*at* most

(continued)

DIFFICULT PREPOSITIONAL PHRASES *(continued)*

refer *to*	similar *to*	subscribe *to*
relevant *to*		

② **Commonly Confused Prepositions**

The prepositions *to, in, on, into,* and *onto* are very similar to one another and are therefore easily confused.

Close-Up　USING COMMON PREPOSITIONS

When deciding whether to use *to, in, on, into,* or *onto,* follow these guidelines:

- *To* is the basic preposition of direction. It indicates movement toward a physical place: "She went *to* the restaurant"; "He went *to* the meeting." *To* is also used to form the infinitive of a verb: "He wanted *to deposit* his paycheck before noon"; "Irene offered *to drive* Maria to the baseball game."

- *In* indicates that something is within the boundaries of a particular space or period of time: "My son is *in* the garden"; "I like to ski *in* the winter"; "The map is *in* the car."

- *On* indicates position above or the state of being supported by something: "The toys are *on* the porch"; "The baby sat *on* my lap"; "The book is *on* top of the magazine."

- *Into* indicates movement to the inside or interior of something: "She walked *into* the room"; "I threw the stone *into* the lake"; "He put the photos *into* the box." Although *into* and *in* are sometimes interchangeable, note that usage depends on whether the subject is stationary or moving. *Into* usually indicates movement, as in "I jumped *into* the water." *In* usually indicates a stationary position relative to the object of the preposition, as in "Mary is swimming *in* the water."

- *Onto* indicates movement to a position on top of something: "The cat jumped *onto* the chair"; "Crumbs are falling *onto* the floor." Both *on* and *onto* can be used to indicate a position on top of something (and therefore they can sometimes be used interchangeably), but *onto* specifies that the subject is moving to a place from a different place or from an outside position.

Close-Up PREPOSITIONS IN IDIOMATIC EXPRESSIONS

Common Nonnative Speaker Usage	Native Speaker Usage
according *with*	according *to*
apologize *at*	apologize *to*
appeal *at*	appeal *to*
believe *at*	believe *in*
different *to*	different *from*
for least, *for* most	*at* least, *at* most
refer *at*	refer *to*
relevant *with*	relevant *to*
similar *with*	similar *to*
subscribe *with*	subscribe *to*

58f Understanding Word Order

In English, word order is extremely important, contributing a good deal to the meaning of a sentence.

1 Standard Word Order

Like Chinese, English is an "SVO" language, or one in which the most typical sentence pattern is "subject-verb-object." (Arabic, by contrast, is an example of a "VSO" language.)

2 Word Order in Questions

Word order in questions can be particularly troublesome for speakers of languages other than English, partly because there are so many different ways to form questions in English.

Close-Up WORD ORDER IN QUESTIONS

1. To **create a yes/no question** from a statement whose verb is a form of *be* (*am, is, are, was, were*), move the verb so it precedes the subject.

   Rasheem <u>is</u> in his laboratory.

   <u>Is</u> Rasheem in his laboratory?

(continued)

WORD ORDER IN QUESTIONS *(continued)*

When the statement is *not* a form of *be*, change the verb to include a form of *do* as a helping verb, and then move that helping verb so it precedes the subject.

Rasheem <u>researched</u> the depletion of the ozone level.

<u>Did</u> Rasheem <u>research</u> the depletion of the ozone level?

2. To **create a yes/no question** from a statement that includes one or more helping verbs, move the first helping verb so it precedes the subject.

Rasheem <u>is researching</u> the depletion of the ozone layer.

<u>Is</u> Rasheem <u>researching</u> the depletion of the ozone layer?

3. To **create a question asking for information,** replace the information being asked for with an interrogative word (*who, what, where, why, when, how*) at the beginning of the question, and invert the order of the subject and verb as with a yes/no question.

Rasheem <u>is</u> in his laboratory.

Where <u>is</u> Rasheem?

Rasheem <u>is researching</u> the depletion of the ozone layer.

What <u>is</u> Rasheem <u>researching</u>?

Rasheem <u>researched</u> the depletion of the ozone level.

What <u>did</u> Rasheem <u>research</u>?

If the interrogative word is the subject of the question, however, do *not* invert the subject and verb.

<u>Who is researching</u> the depletion of the ozone level?

4. You can also form a question by adding a **tag question** (such as *won't he?* or *didn't I?*) to the end of a statement. If the verb of the main statement is *positive*, then the verb of the tag question is *negative*; if the verb of the main statement is *negative*, then the verb of the tag question is *positive*.

Rasheem <u>is</u> researching the depletion of the ozone layer, <u>isn't</u> he?

Rasheem <u>doesn't</u> intend to write his dissertation about the depletion of the ozone layer, <u>does</u> he?

❸ Word Order in Imperative Sentences

Imperative sentences state commands. It is common for the subject of an imperative sentence to be left out because the word *you* is understood to be the subject: "Go to school"; "Eat your dinner." Therefore, the word order pattern in an imperative sentence is usually "verb-object," or "VO."

58g Distinguishing Commonly Confused Words

A number of word pairs in English have similar meanings. These word pairs can be confusing to nonnative English speakers because the ways in which the expressions are used in sentences are different although their meanings may be similar. (For additional examples of commonly confused words, see the **Glossary of Usage.**)

NO AND NOT

No is an adjective; *not* is an adverb. Therefore, use *no* with nouns, and use *not* with verbs, adjectives, and other adverbs.

> She has <u>no</u> desire to go to the football game.

> Sergio's sisters are <u>not</u> friendly.

TOO AND VERY

Too is an intensifier. It is used to add emphasis in a sentence and to indicate excess.

> It is <u>too</u> cold outside to go swimming.

Very is also an intensifier. It means greatly or intensely, but not to excess.

> It was <u>very</u> cold outside, but not cold enough to keep us from playing in the backyard.

EVEN, EVEN IF, AND EVEN THOUGH

As an adverb, *even* is used to intensify or indicate surprise.

> Greta felt <u>even</u> worse than she looked.

> <u>Even</u> my little brother knows how to figure that out!

Even if is used in a sentence where there is a condition that may or may not occur.

> <u>Even if</u> it rains tomorrow, I'm going to the park.

Even though is similar in meaning to *although*.

> <u>Even though</u> Christopher is a very fast runner, he did not make the national track team.

A FEW/A LITTLE AND FEW/LITTLE

A few and *a little* mean not much, but some or enough. *A few* is used with count nouns. *A little* is used with noncount nouns.

We have a few screws remaining from the project.

There is a little bit of paint left in the can.

Few and *little* mean a small number—there are some, but perhaps not as much as one would like.

Few singers are as talented as Kelly.

I have little hope that this situation will change.

MUCH AND MANY

Both *much* and *many* mean "a great quantity" or "to a great degree." Use *much* to modify noncount nouns: *much experience*; *much money*. Use *many* to modify count nouns: *many people*; *many incidents*.

MOST OF, MOST, AND THE MOST

Most and *most of* have similar meanings. *Most of* means "nearly all of something." Use *most of* when the noun that follows is a specific plural noun. When you use *most of*, be sure to use the definite article *the* before the noun.

Most of the children had cookies for dessert.

Most is used for more general observations and means "nearly all."

Most houses in the United States have electricity.

The most is used for comparing more than two of something.

Thomas has the most jellybeans.

Pedro is the most experienced of the engineers.

SOME AND ANY

Some denotes an unspecified amount or quantity that may be part of a larger amount. It can modify both count and noncount nouns: *somewater*; *some melons*. *Any* indicates an unspecified amount, which may be none, some, or all. It can modify both count and noncount nouns: *any person*; *any luggage*.

Parts of Speech

The eight basic **parts of speech**—the building blocks for all English sentences—are *nouns, pronouns, verbs, adjectives, adverbs, prepositions, conjunctions,* and *interjections.* How a word is classified depends on its function in a sentence.

A1 Nouns

Nouns name people, animals, places, things, ideas, actions, or qualities.

ESL
58b

A **common noun** names any of a class of people, places, or things: *artist, judge, building, event, city.*

A **proper noun,** always capitalized, refers to a particular person, place, or thing: *Mary Cassatt, Crimean War.*

A **count noun** names something that can be counted: *five dogs, two dozen grapes.*

A **noncount noun** names a quantity that is not countable: *time, dust, work, gold.* Noncount nouns generally have only a singular form.

A **collective noun** designates a group thought of as a unit: *committee, class, family.* Collective nouns are generally singular unless the members of the group are referred to as individuals.

An **abstract noun** refers to an intangible idea or quality: *love, hate, justice, anger, fear, prejudice.*

A2 Pronouns

Pronouns are words used in place of nouns or other pronouns. The word for which a pronoun stands is its **antecedent.**

ESL
58c

If you use a quotation in your paper, you must document it.

 Note: Although different types of pronouns may have exactly the same form, they are distinguished from one another by their function in a sentence.

A **personal pronoun** stands for a person or thing: *I, me, we, us, my, mine, our, ours, you, your, yours, he, she, it, its, him, his, her, hers, they, them, their, theirs.*

The firm made Debbie an offer, and she couldn't refuse it.

An **indefinite pronoun** does not refer to any particular person or thing, and so it does not require an antecedent. Indefinite pronouns include *another, any, each, few, many, some, nothing, one, anyone, everyone, everybody, everything, someone, something, either,* and *neither.*

Many are called, but few are chosen.

A **reflexive pronoun** ends with *-self* and refers to a recipient of the action that is the same as the actor: *myself, yourself, himself, herself, itself, oneself, themselves, ourselves, yourselves.*

They found themselves in downtown Pittsburgh.

An **intensive pronoun** emphasizes a noun or pronoun that directly precedes it. Intensive pronouns have the same form as reflexive pronouns.

Darrow himself was sure his client was innocent.

A **relative pronoun** introduces an adjective or noun clause in a sentence. Relative pronouns include *which, who, whom, that, what, whose, whatever, whoever, whomever,* and *whichever.*

Gandhi was the man who led India to independence. (introduces adjective clause)

Whatever happens will be a surprise. (introduces noun clause)

An **interrogative pronoun** introduces a question. Interrogative pronouns include *who, which, what, whom, whose, whoever, whatever,* and *whichever.*

Who is next?

A **demonstrative pronoun** points to a particular thing or group of things. *This, that, these,* and *those* are demonstrative pronouns.

This is one of Shakespeare's early plays.

A **reciprocal pronoun** denotes a mutual relationship. The reciprocal pronouns are *each other* and *one another. Each other* indicates a relationship between two individuals; *one another* denotes a relationship among more than two.

Cathy and I respect each other despite our differences.

Many of our friends do not respect one another.

A3 Verbs

A **verb** may express either action or a state of being.

ESL 58a

He <u>ran</u> for the train. (physical action)

He <u>thought</u> about taking the bus. (mental action)

Jen <u>became</u> ill after dinner. (state of being)

Verbs can be classified into two groups: *main verbs* and *auxiliary verbs.*

Main Verbs **Main verbs** carry most of the meaning in a sentence or clause. Some main verbs are action verbs.

Emily Dickinson <u>wrote</u> poetry.

He <u>wanted</u> a new laptop.

Other main verbs are linking verbs. A **linking verb** does not show any physical or emotional action. Its function is to link the subject to a **subject complement,** a word or phrase that renames or describes the subject. Linking verbs include *be, become,* and *seem* and verbs that describe sensations— *look, appear, feel, taste, smell,* and so on.

Carbon disulfide <u>smells</u> bad.

Auxiliary Verbs **Auxiliary verbs** (also called **helping verbs**), such as *be* and *have,* combine with main verbs to form **verb phrases.** Auxiliary verbs indicate tense, voice, or mood.

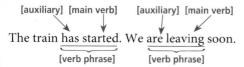

[auxiliary] [main verb]   [auxiliary] [main verb]

The train has started. We are leaving soon.

[verb phrase]   [verb phrase]

Certain auxiliary verbs, known as **modal auxiliaries,** indicate necessity, possibility, willingness, obligation, or ability.

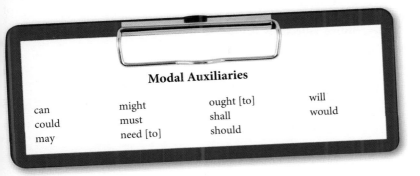

Modal Auxiliaries

can	might	ought [to]	will
could	must	shall	would
may	need [to]	should	

Verbals **Verbals,** such as *known* or *running* or *to go,* are verb forms that act as adjectives, adverbs, or nouns. A verbal can never serve as a sentence's main verb unless it is used with one or more auxiliary verbs (*He is running*). Verbals include *participles, infinitives,* and *gerunds.*

Participles Virtually every verb has a **present participle,** which ends in -*ing* (*loving, learning*), and a **past participle,** which usually ends in -*d* or -*ed* (*agreed, learned*). Some verbs have irregular past participles (*gone, begun, written*). Participles may function in a sentence as adjectives or as nouns.

> Twenty brands of <u>running</u> shoes were on display. (Present participle serves as adjective modifying *shoes.*)

> The <u>wounded</u> were given emergency first aid. (Past participle serves as subject.)

Infinitives An **infinitive** is made up of *to* and the base form of the verb (*to defeat*). An infinitive may function as an adjective, as an adverb, or as a noun.

> Ann Arbor was clearly the place <u>to be</u>. (Infinitive serves as adjective modifying *place.*)

> Carla went outside <u>to think</u>. (Infinitive serves as adverb modifying *went.*)

> <u>To win</u> was everything. (Infinitive serves as subject.)

Gerunds **Gerunds,** which like present participles end in -*ing*, always function as nouns.

> <u>Seeing</u> is <u>believing</u>. (Gerunds serve as subject and subject complement.)

> Andrew loves <u>skiing</u>. (Gerund is direct object of verb *loves.*)

A4 Adjectives

ESL
58d

<u>Adjectives</u> describe, limit, qualify, or in some other way modify nouns or pronouns.

Descriptive adjectives name a quality of the noun or pronoun they modify.

> After the game, they were <u>exhausted</u>.

> They ordered a <u>chocolate</u> soda and a <u>butterscotch</u> sundae.

When articles, pronouns, numbers, and the like function as adjectives, limiting or qualifying nouns or pronouns, they are referred to as **determiners.**

A5 Adverbs

ESL
58d1

Adverbs describe the action of verbs or modify adjectives or other adverbs (or complete phrases, clauses, or sentences). They answer the questions "How?" "Why?" "Where?" "When?" "Under what conditions?" and "To what extent?"

> He walked <u>rather hesitantly</u> toward the front of the room. (walked *how?*)

> Let's meet <u>tomorrow</u> for coffee. (meet *when?*)

Adverbs that modify adjectives or other adverbs limit or qualify the words they modify.

> He pitched an <u>almost</u> perfect game yesterday.

Interrogative Adverbs   The **interrogative adverbs** (*how, when, why,* and *where*) introduce questions.

> <u>Why</u> did the compound darken?

Conjunctive Adverbs   **Conjunctive adverbs** act as transitional words, joining and relating independent clauses.

Frequently Used Conjunctive Adverbs

accordingly	furthermore	meanwhile	similarly
also	hence	moreover	still
anyway	however	nevertheless	then
besides	incidentally	next	thereafter
certainly	indeed	nonetheless	therefore
consequently	instead	now	thus
finally	likewise	otherwise	undoubtedly

A6 Prepositions

ESL
58e

A **preposition** introduces a noun or pronoun (or a phrase or clause functioning in the sentence as a noun), linking it to other words in the sentence. The word or word group that the preposition introduces is its **object.**

```
          prep   obj        prep   obj
```
They received a postcard <u>from</u> Bobby telling <u>about</u> his trip.

Frequently Used Prepositions

about	beneath	inside	since
above	beside	into	through
across	between	like	throughout
after	beyond	near	to
against	by	of	toward
along	concerning	off	under
among	despite	on	underneath
around	down	onto	until
as	during	out	up
at	except	outside	upon
before	for	over	with
behind	from	past	within
below	in	regarding	without

A7　Conjunctions

Conjunctions connect words, phrases, clauses, or sentences.

Coordinating Conjunctions　Coordinating conjunctions (*and, or, but, nor, for, so, yet*) connect words, phrases, or clauses of equal weight.

Should I order chicken <u>or</u> fish? (*Or* links two nouns.)

Thoreau wrote *Walden* in 1854, <u>and</u> he died in 1862. (*And* links two independent clauses.)

Correlative Conjunctions　Always used in pairs, **correlative conjunctions** also link items of equal weight.

<u>Both</u> Hancock <u>and</u> Jefferson signed the Declaration of Independence. (Correlative conjunctions link nouns.)

<u>Either</u> I will renew my lease, <u>or</u> I will move. (Correlative conjunctions link independent clauses.)

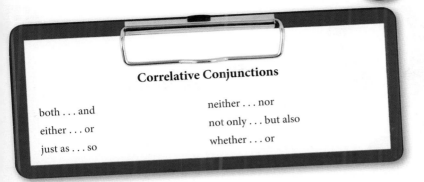

Correlative Conjunctions

both . . . and

either . . . or

just as . . . so

neither . . . nor

not only . . . but also

whether . . . or

Subordinating Conjunctions   Words such as *since, because,* and *although* are **subordinating conjunctions.** They introduce adverb clauses and thus connect the sentence's independent (main) clause to a dependent (subordinate) clause to form a complex sentence.

<u>Although</u> people may feel healthy, they can still have medical problems.

It is best to diagram your garden <u>before</u> you start to plant.

A8   Interjections

Interjections are words used as exclamations to express emotion: *Oh! Ouch! Wow! Alas! Hey!* They may be set off in a sentence by commas, or (for greater emphasis) they may be followed by an exclamation point.

APPENDIX **B**

Sentence Review

B1 Basic Sentence Elements

A **sentence** is an independent grammatical unit that contains a <u>subject</u> and a <u>predicate</u> (a verb or verb phrase) and expresses a complete thought.

<u>The quick brown fox</u> <u>jumped over the lazy dog</u>.

<u>It</u> <u>came from outer space</u>.

A **simple subject** is a noun or pronoun (*fox, it*) that tells who or what the sentence is about. A **simple predicate** is a verb or verb phrase (*jumped, came*) that tells or asks something about the subject. The **complete subject** of a sentence includes the simple subject plus all its modifiers (*the quick brown fox*). The **complete predicate** includes the verb or verb phrase and all the words associated with it—such as modifiers, objects, and complements (*jumped over the lazy dog, came from outer space*).

B2 Basic Sentence Patterns

A **simple sentence** consists of at least one subject and one predicate. Simple sentences conform to one of five patterns.

Subject + Intransitive Verb (s + v)

<u>The price of gold</u> <u>rose</u>.
     s   v

<u>Stock prices</u> <u>may fall</u>.
   s   v

In the sentences above, the verbs *rose* and *may fall* are **intransitive**—that is, they do not need an object to complete their meaning.

Subject + Transitive Verb + Direct Object (s + v + do)

<u>Van Gogh</u> <u>created</u> *The Starry Night*.
  s   v   do

<u>Caroline</u> <u>saved</u> Jake.
  s   v   do

In the preceding sentences, the verbs *created* and *saved* are **transitive**—they require an object to complete their meaning. In each case, a **direct object** indicates where the verb's action is directed and who or what is affected by it.

Subject + Transitive Verb + Direct Object + Object Complement (s + v + do + oc)

This pattern includes an object complement that describes or renames the direct object.

   s v   do oc
I found the exam easy. (Object complement *easy* describes direct object *exam.*)

    s   v   do   oc
The class elected Bridget treasurer. (Object complement *treasurer* renames direct object *Bridget.*)

Subject + Linking Verb + Subject Complement (s + v + sc)

    s   v   sc
The injection was painless.

     s   v   sc
David Cameron became prime minister.

In the sentences above, a **linking verb** (*was, became*) connects a subject to a **subject complement** (*painless, prime minister*), a word or phrase that describes or renames the subject. In the first sentence, the complement is a **predicate adjective** that describes the subject; in the second, the complement is a **predicate nominative** that renames the subject. The linking verb is like an equals sign, equating the subject with its complement (*David Cameron = prime minister*).

See
A3

Subject + Transitive Verb + Indirect Object + Direct Object (s + v + io + do)

The **indirect object** tells to whom or for whom the verb's action was done.

    s   v   io   do
Cyrano wrote Roxanne a poem. (Cyrano wrote a poem for Roxanne.)

   s   v   io do
Hester gave Pearl a kiss. (Hester gave a kiss to Pearl.)

B3   Phrases and Clauses

1 Phrases

A **phrase** is a group of related words that lacks a subject or predicate or both and functions as a single part of speech. It cannot stand alone as a sentence.

See
A6

See
A3

- A **verb phrase** consists of a **main verb** and all its auxiliary verbs. (Time *is flying*.) A **noun phrase** includes a noun or pronoun plus all related modifiers. (I'll climb *the highest mountain*.)
- A **prepositional phrase** consists of a <u>preposition</u>, its object, and any modifiers of that object.

  They discussed the ethical implications <u>of the animal studies</u>.

  He was last seen heading <u>into the sunset</u>.

- A **verbal phrase** consists of a <u>verbal</u> and its related objects, modifiers, or complements. A verbal phrase may be a **participial phrase,** a **gerund phrase,** or an **infinitive phrase.**

  <u>Encouraged by the voter turnout</u>, the candidate predicted a victory. (participial phrase)

  <u>Taking it easy</u> always makes sense. (gerund phrase)

  The jury recessed <u>to evaluate the evidence</u>. (infinitive phrase)

- An **absolute phrase** usually consists of a noun and a participle, accompanied by modifiers. It modifies an entire independent clause rather than a particular word or phrase.

  <u>Their toes tapping</u>, they watched the auditions.

2 Clauses

A **clause** is a group of related words that includes a subject and a predicate. An **independent** (main) **clause** may stand alone as a sentence, but a **dependent** (subordinate) **clause** cannot. It must always be joined to an independent clause to form a complex sentence.

[Lucretia Mott was an abolitionist]. [She was also a pioneer for women's rights]. (two independent clauses)

[Lucretia Mott was an abolitionist] [who was also a pioneer for women's rights]. (independent clause, dependent clause)

[Although Lucretia Mott was known for her support of women's rights], [she was also a prominent abolitionist]. (dependent clause, independent clause)

Dependent clauses may be *adjective, adverb,* or *noun* clauses.

- **Adjective clauses,** sometimes called **relative clauses,** modify nouns or pronouns and always follow the nouns or pronouns they modify. They are introduced by relative pronouns—*that, what, which, who,* and so forth—or by the adverbs *where* and *when.*

  Celeste's grandparents, <u>who were born in Romania</u>, speak little English. (Adjective clause modifies the noun *grandparents*.)

The Pulitzer Prizes are prestigious awards <u>that are presented for excellence in journalism</u>. (Adjective clause modifies the noun *awards*.)

Sophie's Choice is a novel set in Brooklyn, <u>where the narrator lives in a pink house</u>. (Adjective clause modifies the noun *Brooklyn*.)

- **Adverb clauses** modify verbs, adjectives, adverbs, entire phrases, or independent clauses. They are always introduced by subordinating conjunctions.

Mark will go <u>wherever there's a party</u>. (Adverb clause modifies *will go*, telling *where* Mark will go.)

<u>Because 75 percent of its exports are fish products</u>, Iceland's economy is heavily dependent on the fishing industry. (Adverb clause modifies independent clause, telling *why* the fishing industry is so important.)

- **Noun clauses** function as subjects, objects, or complements. A noun clause may be introduced by a relative pronoun or by *whether, when, where, why,* or *how.*

<u>What you see</u> is <u>what you get</u>. (Noun clauses are subject and subject complement.)

They wondered <u>why it was so quiet</u>. (Noun clause is direct object.)

To <u>whom it may concern</u>: (Noun clause is object of preposition.)

B4 Types of Sentences

1 Simple, Compound, Complex, and Compound-Complex Sentences

A **simple sentence** is a single independent clause. A simple sentence may consist of just a subject and a predicate.

<u>Jessica</u> <u>fell</u>.

Or, a simple sentence can be expanded with different kinds of modifying words and phrases.

<u>Jessica</u> <u>fell</u> hopelessly in love with the very mysterious Henry Goodyear.

A **compound sentence** consists of two or more simple sentences (independent clauses) linked by a coordinating conjunction (preceded by a comma), by a semicolon (alone or with a transitional word or phrase), by correlative conjunctions, or by a colon.

independent clause   independent clause

[The moon rose in the sky], <u>and</u> [the stars shone brightly].

independent clause

[José wanted to spend a quiet afternoon fishing and reading]; <u>however</u>,
independent clause
[his friends surprised him with a new set of plans].

A **complex sentence** consists of an independent clause along with one or more dependent clauses.

independent clause   dependent clause

[It was hard for us to believe] [that anyone could be so cruel].

dependent clause

[Because the program had been so poorly attended in the past],
independent clause   dependent clause
[the committee wondered] [whether it should be funded this year].

A **compound-complex sentence** is a compound sentence—made up of at least two independent clauses—that also includes at least one dependent clause.

dependent clause   independent

[Because driving a cab can be so dangerous], [my mother always
clause   dependent clause   independent
worried] [when my father had to work late], and [she could rarely
clause
sleep more than a few minutes at a time].

2 Declarative, Interrogative, Imperative, and Exclamatory Sentences

Sentences can also be classified according to their function.

Declarative sentences, the most common type, make statements: *World War II ended in 1945.*

Interrogative sentences pose questions, usually by inverting standard subject-verb order (often with an interrogative word) or adding a form of *do: Is Maggie at home? Where is Maggie? Does Maggie live here?*

Imperative sentences express commands or requests, using the second-person singular of the verb and generally omitting the pronoun subject *you: Go to your room. Please believe me. Stop that.*

Exclamatory sentences express strong emotion and end with an exclamation point: *The genocide in Darfur must stop now!*

C

Glossary of Usage

This glossary of usage lists words and phrases that writers often find troublesome and explains how they are used.

a, an Use *a* before words that begin with consonants and words with initial vowels that sound like consonants: *a* person, *a* historical document, *a* one-horse carriage, *a* uniform. Use *an* before words that begin with vowels and words that begin with a silent *h*: *an* artist, *an* honest person.

For a list of commonly confused words that present particular challenges for ESL writers, **see 58g.**

accept, except *Accept* is a verb that means "to receive"; *except* as a preposition or conjunction means "other than" and as a verb means "to leave out": The auditors will *accept* all your claims *except* the last two. Some businesses are *excepted* from the regulation.

advice, advise *Advice* is a noun meaning "opinion or information offered"; *advise* is a verb that means "to offer advice to": The broker *advised* her client to take his attorney's *advice*.

affect, effect *Affect* is a verb meaning "to influence"; *effect* can be a verb or a noun—as a verb it means "to bring about," and as a noun it means "result": We know how the drug *affects* patients immediately, but little is known of its long-term *effects*. The arbitrator tried to *effect* a settlement between the parties.

all ready, already *All ready* means "completely prepared"; *already* means "by or before this or that time": I was *all ready* to help, but it was *already* too late.

all right, alright Although the use of *alright* is increasing, current usage calls for *all right*.

allusion, illusion An *allusion* is a reference or hint; an *illusion* is something that is not what it seems: The poem makes an *allusion* to the Pandora myth. The shadow created an optical *illusion*.

a lot *A lot* is always two words.

among, between *Among* refers to groups of more than two things; *between* refers to just two things: The three parties agreed *among* themselves to settle the case. There will be a brief intermission *between* the two acts. (Note that *amongst* is British, not American, usage.)

amount, number   *Amount* refers to a quantity that cannot be counted; *number* refers to things that can be counted: Even a small *amount* of caffeine can be harmful. Seeing their commander fall, a large *number* of troops ran to his aid.

an, a   See **a, an.**

and/or   In business or technical writing, use *and/or* when either or both of the items it connects can apply. In college writing, however, avoid the use of *and/or.*

as . . . as . . .   In such constructions, *as* signals a comparison; therefore, you must always use the second *as:* John Steinbeck's *East of Eden* is *as* long *as* his *The Grapes of Wrath.*

as, like   *As* can be used as a conjunction (to introduce a complete clause) or as a preposition; *like* should be used as a preposition only: In *The Scarlet Letter,* Hawthorne uses imagery *as* (not *like*) he does in his other works. After classes, Fred works *as* a manager of a fast food restaurant. Writers *like* Carl Sandburg appear once in a generation.

at, to   Many people use the prepositions *at* and *to* after *where* in conversation: *Where* are you working *at*? *Where* are you going *to*? This usage is redundant and should not appear in college writing.

awhile, a while   *Awhile* is an adverb; *a while,* which consists of an article and a noun, is used as the object of a preposition: Before we continue, we will rest *awhile* (modifies the verb *rest*). Before we continue, we will rest for *a while* (object of the preposition *for*).

bad, badly   *Bad* is an adjective, and *badly* is an adverb: Some members of the school board thought that *Huckleberry Finn* was a *bad* book. American automobile makers did not do *badly* this year. After verbs that refer to any of the senses or after any other linking verb, use the adjective form: He looked *bad.* He felt *bad.* It seemed *bad.*

being as, being that   These awkward phrases add unnecessary words, thereby weakening your writing. Use *because* instead.

beside, besides   *Beside* is a preposition meaning "next to"; *besides* can be either a preposition meaning "except" or "other than" or an adverb meaning "as well": *Beside* the tower was a wall that ran the length of the city. *Besides* its industrial uses, laser technology has many other applications. Edison invented not only the lightbulb but the phonograph *besides.*

between, among   See **among, between.**

bring, take   *Bring* means "to transport from a farther place to a nearer place"; *take* means "to carry or convey from a nearer place to a farther place": *Bring* me a souvenir from your trip. *Take* this message to the general, and wait for a reply.

can, may   *Can* denotes ability; *may* indicates permission: If you *can* play, you *may* use my piano.

capital, capitol   *Capital* refers to a city that is an official seat of government; *capitol* refers to a building in which a legislature meets: Washington, DC, is the *capital* of the United States. When we were there, we visited the *Capitol* building.

center around This imprecise phrase is acceptable in speech and informal writing but not in college writing. Use *center on* instead.

cite, site *Cite* is a verb meaning "to quote as an authority or example"; *site* is a noun meaning "a place or setting"; it is also a shortened form of *Web site*: Jeff *cited* five sources in his research paper. The builder cleared the *site* for the new bank. Marisa uploaded her *site* to the Web.

climactic, climatic *Climactic* means "of or related to a climax"; *climatic* means "of or related to climate": The *climactic* moment of the movie occurred unexpectedly. If scientists are correct, the *climatic* conditions of Earth are changing.

coarse, course *Coarse* is an adjective meaning "inferior" or "having a rough, uneven texture"; *course* is a noun meaning "a route or path," "an area on which a sport is played," or "a unit of study": *Coarse* sandpaper is used to smooth the surface. The *course* of true love never runs smoothly. Last semester I had to drop a *course.*

complement, compliment *Complement* means "to complete or add to"; *compliment* means "to give praise": A double-blind study would *complement* their preliminary research. My instructor *complimented* me on my improvement.

conscious, conscience *Conscious* is an adjective meaning "having one's mental faculties awake"; *conscience* is a noun that means the moral sense of right and wrong: The patient will remain *conscious* during the procedure. His *conscience* would not allow him to lie.

continual, continuous *Continual* means "recurring at intervals"; *continuous* refers to an action that occurs without interruption: A pulsar is a star that emits a *continual* stream of electromagnetic radiation. (It emits radiation at regular intervals.) A small battery allows the watch to run *continuously* for five years. (It runs without stopping.)

could've, should've, would've The contractions *could've, should've,* and *would've* are often misspelled as the nonstandard constructions *could of, should of,* and *would of.* Use *could have, should have,* and *would have* in college writing.

council, counsel A *council* is "a body of people who serve in a legislative or advisory capacity"; *counsel* means "to offer advice or guidance": The city *council* argued about the proposed ban on smoking. The judge *counseled* the couple to settle their differences.

couple, couple of *Couple* means "a pair," but *couple of* is often used colloquially to mean "several" or "a few." In your college writing, specify "four points" or "two examples" rather than using "a couple of."

criterion, criteria *Criteria,* from the Greek, is the plural of *criterion,* meaning "standard for judgment": Of all the *criteria* for hiring graduating seniors, class rank is the most important *criterion.*

data *Data* is the plural of the Latin *datum,* meaning "fact." In everyday speech and writing, *data* is often used as the singular as well as the plural form. In college writing, use *data* only for the plural: The *data* discussed in this section *are* summarized in Appendix A.

different from, different than *Different than* is widely used in American speech. In college writing, use *different from.*

discreet, discrete *Discreet* means "careful or prudent"; *discrete* means "separate or individually distinct": Because Madame Bovary was not *discreet,* her reputation suffered. Atoms can be broken into hundreds of *discrete* particles.

disinterested, uninterested *Disinterested* means "objective" or "capable of making an impartial judgment"; *uninterested* means "indifferent or unconcerned": The American judicial system depends on *disinterested* jurors. Finding no treasure, Hernando de Soto was *uninterested* in going farther.

don't, doesn't *Don't* is the contraction of *do not; doesn't* is the contraction of *does not.* Do not confuse the two: My dog *doesn't* (not *don't*) like to walk in the rain. (Note that contractions are generally not acceptable in college writing.)

effect, affect See **affect, effect.**

e.g. *E.g.* is an abbreviation for the Latin *exempli gratia,* meaning "for example" or "for instance." In college writing, do not use *e.g.* Instead, use "for example" or "for instance."

emigrate from, immigrate to To *emigrate* is "to leave one's country and settle in another"; to *immigrate* is "to come to another country and reside there." The noun forms of these words are *emigrant* and *immigrant:* My greatgrandfather *emigrated from* Warsaw along with many other *emigrants* from Poland. Many people *immigrate* to the United States for economic reasons, but such *immigrants* still face great challenges.

enthused *Enthused,* a colloquial form of *enthusiastic,* should not be used in college writing.

etc. *Etc.,* the abbreviation of *et cetera,* means "and the rest." Do not use it in your college writing. Instead, use "and so on"—or, better yet, specify exactly what *etc.* stands for.

everyday, every day *Everyday* is an adjective that means "ordinary" or "commonplace"; *every day* means "occurring daily": In the Gettysburg Address, Lincoln used *everyday* language. She exercises almost *every day.*

everyone, every one *Everyone* is an indefinite pronoun meaning "every person"; *every one* means "every individual or thing in a particular group": *Everyone* seems happier in the spring. *Every one* of the packages had been opened.

except, accept See **accept, except.**

explicit, implicit *Explicit* means "expressed or stated directly"; *implicit* means "implied" or "expressed or stated indirectly": The director *explicitly* warned the actors to be on time for rehearsals. Her *implicit* message was that lateness would not be tolerated.

farther, further *Farther* designates distance; *further* designates degree: I have traveled *farther* from home than any of my relatives. Critics charge that welfare subsidies encourage *further* dependence.

fewer, less   Use *fewer* with nouns that can be counted: *fewer* books, *fewer* people, *fewer* dollars. Use *less* with quantities that cannot be counted: *less* pain, *less* power, *less* enthusiasm.

firstly (secondly, thirdly, . . .)   Archaic forms meaning "in the first . . . second . . . third place." Use *first, second, third* instead.

further, farther   See **farther, further.**

good, well   *Good* is an adjective, never an adverb: She is a *good* swimmer. *Well* can function as an adverb or as an adjective. As an adverb, it means "in a good manner": She swam *well* (not *good*) in the meet. *Well* is used as an adjective with verbs that denote a state of being or feeling. Here *well* can mean "in good health": I feel *well*.

got to   *Got to* is not acceptable in college writing. To indicate obligation, use *have to, has to,* or *must.*

hanged, hung   Both *hanged* and *hung* are past participles of *hang*. *Hanged* is used to refer to executions; *hung* is used to mean "suspended": Billy Budd was *hanged* for killing the master-at-arms. The stockings were *hung* by the chimney with care.

he, she   Traditionally *he* has been used in the generic sense to refer to both males and females. To acknowledge the equality of the sexes, however, avoid the generic *he*. Use plural pronouns whenever possible. **See 44f.**

hopefully   The adverb *hopefully,* meaning "in a hopeful manner," should modify a verb, an adjective, or another adverb. Do not use *hopefully* as a sentence modifier meaning "it is hoped." Rather than *"Hopefully,* scientists will soon discover a cure for AIDS," write *"I hope* scientists will soon discover a cure for AIDS."

i.e.   *I.e.* is an abbreviation for the Latin *id est,* meaning "that is." In college writing, do not use *i.e.* Instead, use its English equivalent.

if, whether   When asking indirect questions or expressing doubt, use *whether:* He asked *whether* (not *if*) the flight would be delayed. The flight attendant was not sure *whether* (not *if*) it would be delayed.

illusion, allusion   See **allusion, illusion.**

immigrate to, emigrate from   See **emigrate from, immigrate to.**

implicit, explicit   See **explicit, implicit.**

imply, infer   *Imply* means "to hint" or "to suggest"; *infer* means "to conclude from": Mark Antony *implied* that the conspirators had murdered Caesar. The crowd *inferred* his meaning and called for justice.

infer, imply   See **imply, infer.**

inside of, outside of   *Of* is unnecessary when *inside* and *outside* are used as prepositions. *Inside of* is colloquial in references to time: He waited *inside* (not *inside of*) the coffee shop. He could run a mile in *under* (not *inside of*) eight minutes.

irregardless, regardless *Irregardless* is a nonstandard version of *regardless*. Use *regardless* instead.

is when, is where These constructions are faulty when they appear in definitions: A playoff is (not *is when*) an additional game played to establish the winner of a tie.

its, it's *Its* is a possessive pronoun; *it's* is a contraction of *it is*: *It's* no secret that the bank is out to protect *its* assets.

kind of, sort of *Kind of* and *sort of* to mean "rather" or "somewhat" are colloquial and should not appear in college writing: It is well known that Napoleon was *rather* (not *kind of*) short.

lay, lie See **lie, lay.**

leave, let *Leave* means "to go away from" or "to *let* remain"; *let* means "to allow" or "to permit": *Let* (not *leave*) me give you a hand.

less, fewer See **fewer, less.**

let, leave See **leave, let.**

lie, lay *Lie* is an intransitive verb (one that does not take an object) meaning "to recline." Its principal forms are *lie, lay, lain, lying*: Each afternoon she would *lie* in the sun and listen to the surf. *As I Lay Dying* is a novel by William Faulkner. By 1871, Troy had *lain* undisturbed for two thousand years. The painting shows a nude *lying* on a couch.

    Lay is a transitive verb (one that takes an object) meaning "to put" or "to place." Its principal forms are *lay, laid, laid, laying*: The Federalist Papers *lay* the foundation for American conservatism. In October 1781, the British *laid* down their arms and surrendered. He had *laid* his money on the counter before leaving. We watched the stonemasons *laying* a wall.

like, as See **as, like.**

loose, lose *Loose* is an adjective meaning "not rigidly fastened or securely attached"; *lose* is a verb meaning "to misplace": The marble facing of the building became *loose* and fell to the sidewalk. After only two drinks, most people *lose* their ability to judge distance.

lots, lots of, a lot of These words are colloquial substitutes for *many, much,* or *a great deal of.* Avoid their use in college writing: The students had *many* (not *lots of* or *a lot of*) options for essay topics.

man Like the generic pronoun *he, man* has been used in English to denote members of both sexes. This usage is being replaced by *human beings, people,* or similar terms that do not specify gender. **See 44f.**

may, can See **can, may.**

may be, maybe *May be* is a verb phrase; *maybe* is an adverb meaning "perhaps": She *may be* the smartest student in the class. *Maybe* her experience has given her an advantage.

media, medium *Medium,* meaning "a means of conveying or broadcasting something," is singular; *media* is the plural form and requires a plural verb: The *media* have (not *has*) distorted the issue.

might have, might of *Might of* is a nonstandard spelling of the contraction of *might have (might've)*. Use *might have* in college writing.

number, amount See **amount, number.**

OK, O.K., okay All three spellings are acceptable, but this term should be avoided in college writing. Replace it with a more specific word or words: The lecture was *adequate* (not *okay*), if uninspiring.

outside of, inside of See **inside of, outside of.**

passed, past *Passed* is the past tense of the verb *pass; past* means "belonging to a former time" or "no longer current": The car must have been going eighty miles per hour when it *passed* us. In the envelope was a bill marked *past* due.

percent, percentage *Percent* indicates a part of a hundred when a specific number is referred to: "*10 percent* of his salary." *Percentage* is used when no specific number is referred to: "a *percentage* of next year's receipts." In technical and business writing, it is permissible to use the % sign after percentages you are comparing. Write out the word *percent* in college writing.

phenomenon, phenomena A *phenomenon* is a single observable fact or event. It can also refer to a rare or significant occurrence. *Phenomena* is the plural form and requires a plural verb: Many supposedly paranormal *phenomena* are easily explained.

plus As a preposition, *plus* means "in addition to." Avoid using *plus* as a substitute for *and*: Include the principal, *plus* the interest, in your calculations. Your quote was too high, and (not *plus*) it was also inaccurate.

precede, proceed *Precede* means "to go or come before"; *proceed* means "to go forward in an orderly way": Robert Frost's *North of Boston* was *preceded* by an earlier volume. In 1532, Francisco Pizarro landed at Tumbes and *proceeded* south.

principal, principle As a noun, *principal* means "a sum of money (minus interest) invested or lent" or "a person in the leading position"; as an adjective, it means "most important"; a *principle* is a noun meaning a rule of conduct or a basic truth: He wanted to reduce the *principal* of the loan. The *principal* of the high school is a talented administrator. Women are the *principal* wage earners in many American households. The Constitution embodies certain fundamental *principles.*

quote, quotation *Quote* is a verb. *Quotation* is a noun. In college writing, do not use *quote* as a shortened form of *quotation:* Scholars attribute these *quotations* (not *quotes*) to Shakespeare.

raise, rise *Raise* is a transitive verb, and *rise* is an intransitive verb—that is, *raise* takes an object, and *rise* does not: My grandparents *raised* a large family. The sun will *rise* at 6:12 this morning.

real, really *Real* means "genuine" or "authentic"; *really* means "actually." In your college writing, do not use *real* as an adjective meaning "very."

reason is that, reason is because *Reason* should be used with *that* and not with *because,* which is redundant: The *reason* he left is *that* (not *because*) you insulted him.

regardless, irregardless See **irregardless, regardless.**

respectably, respectfully, respectively *Respectably* means "worthy of respect"; *respectfully* means "giving honor or deference"; *respectively* means "in the order given": He skated quite *respectably* at his first Olympics. The seminar taught us to treat others *respectfully*. The first- and second-place winners were Tai and Kim, *respectively*.

rise, raise See **raise, rise.**

set, sit *Set* means "to put down" or "to lay." Its principal forms are *set* and *setting*: After rocking the baby to sleep, he *set* her down carefully in her crib. After *setting* her down, he took a nap.

> *Sit* means "to assume a sitting position." Its principal forms are *sit, sat,* and *sitting*: Many children *sit* in front of the television five to six hours a day. The dog *sat* by the fire. We were *sitting* in the airport when the flight was canceled.

shall, will *Will* has all but replaced *shall* to express all future action.

should of See **could've, should've, would've.**

since Do not use *since* for *because* if there is any chance of confusion. In the sentence "*Since* President Nixon traveled to China, trade between China and the United States has increased," *since* could mean either "from the time that" or "because." To be clear, use *because.*

sit, set See **set, sit.**

so Avoid using *so* as a vague intensifier meaning "very" or "extremely." Follow *so* with *that* and a clause that describes the result: She was *so* pleased with their work *that* she took them out to lunch.

sometime, sometimes, some time *Sometime* means "at some time in the future"; *sometimes* means "now and then"; *some time* means "a period of time": The president will address Congress *sometime* next week. All automobiles, no matter how reliable, *sometimes* need repairs. It has been *some time* since I read that book.

sort of, kind of See **kind of, sort of.**

stationary, stationery *Stationary* means "staying in one place"; *stationery* means "materials for writing" or "letter paper": The communications satellite appears to be *stationary* in the sky. The assistants supply departmental offices with *stationery.*

supposed to, used to *Supposed to* and *used to* are often misspelled. Both verbs require the final *d* to indicate past tense.

take, bring See **bring, take.**

than, then *Than* is a conjunction used to indicate a comparison; *then* is an adverb indicating time: The new shopping center is bigger *than* the old one. He did his research; *then,* he wrote a report.

that, which, who Use *that* or *which* when referring to a thing, use *who* when referring to a person: It was a speech *that* inspired many. The movie, *which* was a huge success, failed to impress her. Anyone *who* (not *that*) takes the course will benefit.

their, there, they're   *Their* is a possessive pronoun; *there* indicates place and is also used in the expressions *there is* and *there are*; *they're* is a contraction of *they are:* Watson and Crick did *their* DNA work at Cambridge University. I love Los Angeles, but I wouldn't want to live *there. There* is nothing we can do to resurrect an extinct species. When *they're* well treated, rabbits make excellent pets.

themselves, theirselves, theirself   *Theirselves* and *theirself* are nonstandard variants of *themselves.*

then, than   See **than, then.**

till, until, 'til   *Till* and *until* have the same meaning, and both are acceptable. *Until* is preferred in college writing. *'Til,* a contraction of *until,* should be avoided.

to, at   See **at, to.**

to, too, two   *To* is a preposition that indicates direction; *too* is an adverb that means "also" or "more than is needed"; *two* expresses the number 2: Last year we flew from New York *to* California. "Tippecanoe and Tyler, *too*" was William Henry Harrison's campaign slogan. The plot was *too* complicated for the average reader. Just north of *Two* Rivers, Wisconsin, is a petrified forest.

try to, try and   *Try and* is the colloquial equivalent of *try to:* He decided to *try to* (not *try and*) do better. In college writing, use *try to.*

-type   Deleting this empty suffix eliminates clutter and clarifies meaning. Found in the wreckage was an *incendiary* (not *incendiary-type*) device.

uninterested, disinterested   See **disinterested, uninterested.**

unique   Because *unique* means "the only one," not "remarkable" or "unusual," never use constructions like "the most unique" or "very unique."

until   See **till, until, 'til.**

used to   See **supposed to, used to.**

utilize   In most cases, replace *utilize* with *use* (*utilize* sounds pretentious).

wait for, wait on   To *wait for* means "to defer action until something occurs." To *wait on* means "to act as a waiter": I am *waiting for* (not *on*) dinner.

weather, whether   *Weather* is a noun meaning "the state of the atmosphere"; *whether* is a conjunction used to introduce an alternative: The *weather* will improve this weekend. It is doubtful *whether* we will be able to ski tomorrow.

well, good   See **good, well.**

were, we're   *Were* is a verb; *we're* is the contraction of *we are:* The Trojans *were* asleep when the Greeks attacked. We must act now if *we're* going to succeed.

whether, if   See **if, whether.**

which, who, that   See **that, which, who.**

who, whom   When a pronoun serves as the subject of its clause, use *who* or *whoever;* when it functions in a clause as an object, use *whom* or *whomever:* Sarah, *who* is studying ancient civilizations, would like to visit Greece. Sarah, *whom* I met in France, wants me to travel to Greece with her. To determine which to use at the beginning of a question, use a personal pronoun to answer the question: *Who* tried to call me? *He* called. (subject); *Whom* do you want for the job? I want *her.* (object)

who's, whose   *Who's* means "who is" or "who has"; *whose* indicates possession: *Who's* going to take calculus? *Who's* already left for the concert? The writer *whose* book was in the window was autographing copies.

will, shall   See **shall, will.**

would of   See **could've, should've, would've.**

your, you're   *Your* indicates possession; *you're* is the contraction of *you are:* You can improve *your* stamina by jogging two miles a day. *You're* certain to be the winner.

Index

Note: Blue type indicates definitions.

577

Writing in the Disciplines: An Overview

HUMANITIES

Disciplines	Assignments	Style and Format
Languages	Response essay	*Style*
Literature	Analysis essay	Specialized vocabulary
Philosophy	Annotated bibliography	Direct quotations from sources
History	Bibliographic essay	*Format*
Religion	Book or film review	Little use of internal headings
Art history		or visuals
Music		

SOCIAL SCIENCES

Disciplines	Assignments	Style and Format
Anthropology	Personal experience essay	*Style*
Psychology	Book review	Specialized vocabulary, including statistical terminology
Economics	Case study	
Business	Annotated bibliography	*Format*
Education	Literature review	Internal headings
Sociology	Proposal	Visuals (graphs, maps, flowcharts, photographs)
Political science		Numerical data (in tables)
Social work		
Criminal justice		
Linguistics		

NATURAL AND APPLIED SCIENCES

Disciplines	Assignments	Style and Format
Natural Sciences	Laboratory report	*Style*
Biology	Observation essay	Frequent use of passive voice
Chemistry	Literature survey	Few direct quotations
Physics	Abstract	*Format*
Astronomy	Biographical essay	Internal headings
Geology		Tables, graphs, and illustrations (exact formats vary)
Mathematics		
Applied Sciences		
Engineering		
Computer science		
Nursing		
Pharmacy		

Documentation	Research Methods and Sources	
English, languages, philosophy: **MLA**	Internet sources	See Ch. 21
History, art history: **Chicago**	Library sources (print and electronic)	
	Interviews	See Ch. 23
	Observations (museums, concerts)	
	Oral history	

Documentation	Research Methods and Sources	
APA	Internet sources	See Ch. 22
	Library sources (print and electronic)	
	Surveys	
	Observations (behavior of groups and individuals)	

Documentation	Research Methods and Sources	
Biological sciences: **CSE**	Internet sources	See Ch. 24
Other scientific disciplines use a variety of different documentation styles; **see 24d**	Library sources (print and electronic)	
	Observations	
	Experiments	
	Surveys